The JCT Standard Building Contract 2011

The JCT Standard Building Contract 2011

An explanation and guide for busy practitioners and students

David Chappell
BA(Hons Arch) MA(Arch) MA(Law) PhD RIBA

WILEY Blackwell

This edition first published 2014
© 2014 by David Chappell

Registered Office
John Wiley & Sons, Ltd, The Atrium, Southern Gate, Chichester, West Sussex, PO19 8SQ, United Kingdom.

Editorial Offices
9600 Garsington Road, Oxford, OX4 2DQ, United Kingdom.
The Atrium, Southern Gate, Chichester, West Sussex, PO19 8SQ, United Kingdom.

For details of our global editorial offices, for customer services and for information about how to apply for permission to reuse the copyright material in this book please see our website at www.wiley.com/wiley-blackwell.

Library of Congress Cataloging-in-Publication Data

Chappell, David (David M.)
The JCT standard building contract 2011 : (an explanation and guide for busy practitioners and students) / David Chappell.
    pages   cm
  Includes bibliographical references and index.
  ISBN 978-1-118-81975-3 (pbk.)
1. Construction contracts–Great Britain.   I. Joint Contracts Tribunal.   II. Title.
    KD1641.C487 2014
    343.4107′8624–dc23

                                             2013030499

A catalogue record for this book is available from the British Library.

Wiley also publishes its books in a variety of electronic formats. Some content that appears in print may not be available in electronic books.

Cover image: iStockphoto/A-Digit
Cover design by Steve Flemming, Workhaus Publishing Design and Advertising

Set in 10/12.5pt Minion by SPi Publisher Services, Pondicherry, India
Printed and bound in Malaysia by Vivar Printing Sdn Bhd

1   2014

To my wife
Margaret
1935 to 2012

Contents

Preface

It always seems to me that books about contracts are difficult to read, because they are littered with clause numbers and references to legal cases. Moreover, they make too much use of what I can only describe as legal words that may not be immediately comprehensible to many people. Therefore, it is a real chore to find exactly what one is seeking (and to understand it when found), even with the aid of a good subject index.

From the feedback I have received, what most architects, quantity surveyors, project managers, builders and yes, employers, are looking for is a book that sets out in plain words exactly what the contract requires in various circumstances. They do not want simply a repetition of the wording of the clauses nor a long exposition of the legal niceties. That is not to say there is not a place for detailed books on building contracts loaded with references to cases and full of legal argument – I have written some of them myself. But there is clearly a need for a book with a sensible down to earth approach to what the contract requires from the various participants.

In this volume I have tried to write a simple book about the JCT Standard Form of Contract 2011 which is a complex contract, but one in common use. By 'simple' I do not mean 'brief' or 'superficial' with poor grammar or full of jokes; but rather a book that is not full of legal phraseology with constant references to clause numbers and a book that does not assume any particular legal or contractual expertise on the part of the reader. But it does assume that the reader is a competent contractor or constructional professional. The text is not limited to words of one syllable.

I have used straightforward words, short paragraphs, many sub-headings and explained, often from first principles, many issues such as exactly what we mean by a contract, why there are extension of time clauses, why there is a rectification period and the limits on architects' powers. The book is divided into topics, because experience tells me that it is the most sensible way to deal with it. At the end of each chapter I have included a section dealing with some problems that have arisen in practice related to the subject matter of the chapter.

There are clause numbers in the margin next to the relevant text. For those who like to dig a little deeper, a list of relevant cases are in a section at the back and the reference numbers are also in the margin in a different typeface. Several tables are included, listing such things as architect's instructions, certificates to be issued and the powers and duties of architect, employer and contractor. There are also some flowcharts for those who like that kind of thing.

It is not difficult to write a complicated book about a complicated subject. The trick is to write a simple book about a complicated subject. This book has been one of the most difficult tasks I have attempted, but I believe that it was well worth doing. Just because this book is intended to be easy to read does not mean that things have been omitted. Hopefully, the book is just as comprehensive as any other book on this subject. Indeed I would want it to be more comprehensive than others.

One of the criticisms often made about a book like this is that is does not properly express what the contract says. That may well be true in an absolute sense. The only way to precisely express what the contract says is to reprint the contract in its entirety and nothing more. Any explanation will inevitably fall short in some way. Nevertheless, until the people responsible for drafting contracts find a way of drafting them in clear and simple English, users of the contract will seek simple explanations. Although it may be that certain parts of the contract are subject to various explanations, not all of them consistent, it is not helpful to busy people trying to administer or work under a contract to find that the advice is that it may be this or it may be that. In these situations, I have taken a view of the position.

In a book of this kind, which splits the content into topics, it is inevitable that some of the same things fall under different topics. For example, the issue of instructions naturally falls under the architect's duties, but also warrants a standalone chapter. Although there may be some repetition in these cases, I have tried to make such references complementary and cross-referenced the most important. The index is intended to signal all the places where information on a particular matter can be found.

Throughout the text, it has been assumed that the contractor and subcontractors are corporate bodies (e.g, limited companies) and they are each referred to as 'it'.

My thanks to Michael Cowlin LLB(Hons) DipOSH DipArb FCIArb Barrister (not practising) and Michael Dunn BSc(Hons) LLB LLM FRICS FCIArb who have given helpful feedback on various points.

I acknowledge a debt to John Parris, whose classic work on the JCT Standard Form of Building Contract it was my privilege to revise in 2002. He had a way with words that I cannot emulate but that made the most complex material eminently readable.

Finally, I acknowledge a lifetime of debt to my wife, Margaret, who died in April 2012 when I had just started this book. It is only the certainty that I will be reunited with her in the future that continues to fuel my enthusiasm for writing.

David Chappell
Wakefield

Abbreviations used in the text

ACA 3	The ACA Form of Building Agreement 2003
CC	Construction Confederation
CDP	Contractor's Designed Portion
CDM Regulations 2007	Construction (Design and Management) Regulations 2007
DB	Design and Build Contract 2011
GC/Works/1 (1998)	The General Conditions of Government Contracts for Building and Civil Engineering Works
IC	Intermediate Building Contract 2011
ICC	Infrastructure Conditions of Contract
ICD	Intermediate Building Contract 2011 with contractor's design
JCT	Joint Contracts Tribunal
MW	Minor Works Building Contract 2011
MWD	Minor Works Building Contract 2011 with contractor's design
NEC 3	Engineering and Construction Contract 2013
NFBTE	National Federation of Building Trades Employers
PPC2000	The ACA Standard form of Contract for Project Partnering 2008
RIBA	Royal Institute of British Architects
RICA	Royal Institution of Chartered Surveyors
SBC	Standard Building Contract 2011 with quantities
SMM	Standard Method of Measurement

Notes before reading

There are no references to contract clauses or legal cases in the text.

The relevant clause or schedule number is shown in the margin opposite the portion of text.

Reference numbers to legal cases and some other things are also in the margin. These notes can be found at the back of the book for those who really want them.

The idea is to present an unimpeded, easy to read explanation of the contract, but with the facility to easily locate the further information.

Clause and schedule numbers are in italic; reference numbers are in bold.

Part I   Preliminaries

1   Introduction

1.1   What is a contract?

Law

Everyone is subject to the law of the country in which they live. In general, the law is divided into two parts: criminal law and civil law. If we break the criminal law, we may find ourselves having an interview with the police. There are also Acts of Parliament that make doing things or failure to do other things a criminal offence. The Health and Safety at Work Act 1974 is an example of one such Act. Most people understand that very well.

The civil law governs the way we should behave to our neighbour. We all have rights and duties to each other. They are sometimes set out in Acts of Parliament and sometimes they are derived from the judgments of the courts. Law that is found in the judgments of the courts is usually referred to as the 'common law'. These are duties and rights that are there whether we like it or not.

Tort

In general 'tort' is a civil wrong for which the person suffering the wrong is entitled to take action through the courts for compensation. It is based on the duty that everyone owes to one another. There are many wrongs that most people will recognise and that will come under the headings of 'tort'. Such things as negligence, trespass, nuisance and defamation are concepts in general use; although not always properly understood.

Contract

As well as these legislative or common law rights and duties, two people may agree additional rights and duties to each other. For example, I may agree to

The JCT Standard Building Contract 2011, First Edition. David Chappell.
© 2014 by David Chappell. Published 2014 by John Wiley & Sons, Ltd.

buy a clock from a shop for £100. I have a right to receive a clock, but a duty to pay £100 for it to the shop. The shop has a right to the £100, but a duty to supply the clock. Where there are agreed rights and duties on both sides we call it a contract. Of course there are all kinds of other things that also might have to be agreed, such as the style, make and colour of the clock and the date on which I must pay. That is why even the simplest contracts can become quite complicated.

Breach of contract

We usually say that two people have 'entered into' a contract or that a contract has been 'executed' if documents have been signed. Contracts are legally binding, which means to say that usually once the contract is agreed, neither person can say: 'I've changed my mind now' without serious consequences. If one person does something that the contract does not allow or fails to do something that the contract requires, it is referred to as a 'breach' of contract.

For example, if I only pay £95 for the clock, or if the clock is supplied in a different colour or style, or if it does not work. These are all breaches of contract. It is not always appreciated that it would also be a breach of contract if I was supplied with a better clock worth £150 when we had agreed a particular clock for £100.

The person who is not in breach is usually referred to as the 'injured party' or the 'innocent party'. The injured party is entitled to receive payment from the person in breach to make up for the breach. That is called 'damages'. The amount of money to be paid is normally calculated to put the injured party back in the same position as if the breach had not occurred. Sometimes that is easy, for example, I could be ordered by a court to pay the additional £5 together with any other costs I had caused as a result of my failure to pay the full £100 for the clock. Sometimes it is not possible, but a court tries to do what it can to rectify the situation.

Repudiation

If the breach of contract is particularly serious, it may be what is called 'repudiation'. That is a breach that is so serious that it shows that one of the persons wants nothing more to do with the contract. Extreme examples would be if I refused to pay anything for the clock or the shop took my money but refused to provide any clock at all. In building terms, it might amount to a contractor walking off site, never to return, half-way through the project or the employer telling the contractor that he would not be paid any more money.

Faced with repudiation, the injured party has the choice of, either accepting the repudiation and seeking damages through the courts, or saying that the contract is still in place and carrying on with it (called 'affirmation'). The injured party is still entitled to seek damages even after affirmation. Obviously, there are many instances where it is just impossible to carry on as if nothing had happened; for example if the contractor walks off site.

Essentials of a contract

People sometimes get confused between a promise by one person to do something for another and a contract. In order for there to be a contract there must be three things:

- Agreement.
- An intention to create legal relations.
- Something given by both persons.

Agreement is usually demonstrated by showing that one person made an offer and another person accepted it. Using the clock example: if I offer £100 for the clock and the shopkeeper accepts, there is an agreement.

An intention to create legal relations is usually assumed in commercial dealings and it is for the person who says that there was no such intention to prove it. In a social context, people do not always intend to create legal relationships. If Tim says to Lucy that if she joins him at a restaurant that evening, he will buy her a meal, that is not a contract and the arrangement can be broken with impunity.

Something given by both persons is fairly straightforward. In the case of the purchase of the clock, I agree to give the shopkeeper £100 and the shopkeeper agrees to give me the clock. This can be expressed in various ways. For example, it can be said that the shopkeeper promises to give me the clock if I give the shopkeeper £100. In a construction contract, the contractor promises to construct the building and the employer promises to pay whatever is stated in the contract as the Contract Sum. In legal terms, it is usually referred to as 'consideration'. This consideration can take forms other than the ones just described. For example, one person may agree to pay another, if that second person agrees to stop doing something or not to do something he or she was about to do. The important thing is that both persons contribute something; not necessarily of apparent equal value.

When talking about contracts, it is customary to refer to the 'parties' to the contract. That is convenient when reference to 'persons' would not be appropriate – for example, where one or both parties are corporate bodies such as local authorities, universities or limited companies.

Two types of contract

There are two types of contract:

- Simple contracts.
- Deeds or specialty contracts.

Most contracts are simple contracts. If it is desired to make a contract in the form of a deed, it is necessary to observe a particular procedure. Before 1989, all deeds had to be made by fixing a seal to the document. That could be in wax, but more often it was simply a circular piece of red paper embossed with the name of the relevant party. Nowadays, the procedure is laid down by statute.

Essentially, the document must clearly state that it is a deed and the parties must sign in one of the prescribed ways. The alternative ways are usefully set out in JCT contracts on the attestation page.

A deed is a very serious form of contract. Its attributes are:

- There is no need for consideration. In other words, a promise that one party will do something for the other becomes legally binding.
- The limitation period is 12 years (see Chapter 4, Section 4.4 below).
- Statements in a deed are conclusive as to their truth as between the parties to the deed.

Therefore, a contract should not lightly be entered into as a deed.

1.2   Purpose of building contracts

Broadly, the purpose is to get a building erected. The contract sets out the rights and the duties of the parties: what each may do and what each must do. It also sets out the procedure for certain things. For example, how the contractor can have the time allowed for constructing the building extended, or how the architect can get an instruction carried out if the contractor is slow, or on what grounds either party may bring their duties under the contract to an end. In SBC, there will be an employer (who employs the contractor) and the contractor (who carries out the construction work). There is also a contractor administrator who is often, but not necessarily, an architect (and assumed to be so in this book) and who does the things allocated in the contract and a quantity surveyor who is principally concerned with valuing the work.

1.3   Types of construction contracts

Construction contracts can be analysed into three types relating to costs:

Fixed price contracts

This is where the contractor undertakes to do the specified work for a sum not adjustable in the price of goods or labour. This is the common situation when a contractor quotes for the installation of a shower or other minor building work. It is commonly thought that if a contractor submits what he terms an 'estimate', he will not be bound by the price. Indeed, if the final price is much higher, the contractor will often remark that what he originally gave was 'just an estimate'. That is certainly the colloquial meaning and the understanding in the industry generally. However, a contractor's estimate, depending on its terms, can amount to a firm offer so that acceptance by the employer will result in a binding contract. It is sometimes suggested that there is some custom that an estimate is not to be treated as an offer. There is no such custom. On the other hand, a 'quotation' is always an offer to do work for a specific sum that, on acceptance, becomes a binding contract.

1

Remeasurement contracts

This is where the price is based on quantities and there is an express right for the work to be remeasured after completion. The ICC contract is one such. SBC with approximate quantities is also a remeasurement contract as is the 'with quantities' version in practice.

Lump sum contracts

SBC is a lump sum contract in that a specific total figure is quoted, but it should be noted that the price is subject to alteration for:

- variations;
- fluctuations in price of goods and services;
- revaluation of prime or provisional sums;
- loss and/or expense.

John Parris memorably said that the only JCT contract that has ever been known to come out at the Contract Sum was that for the renovation of All Souls' Church in Langham Place, London and that may justly be regarded as a miracle of divine grace.

It is also possible to analyse building contracts by procurement method.

2

Traditional

In general, this is where the client commissions an independent architect who may have been the architect who produced designs and construction information, to administer the project during the construction period and deal with the final account. A contractor will have been chosen to carry out the project. If the building is other than small and straightforward, the architect will advise the client to appoint other consultants to deal with particular items, such as quantities, cost estimating, structural calculations and building services design. The contractor may have a minor degree of design responsibility.

The essentials of traditional procurement are that the architect is the independent adviser to the client responsible for the design. The contractor is only responsible for executing the work in accordance with the drawings and specifications produced by the architect and other professionals.

Project management

It has much in common with the traditional system. However, the architect may not be the leader of the team, The project manager, of course, can be an architect. Essentially, the project management system places most emphasis on planning and management. Therefore, a person, whether architect, engineer or surveyor, with the relevant project management skills is required. The project manager is likely to appear in one of two principal roles; either simply as the technical agent of the employer for the purposes of the project or as the professional with the authority to manage the project, including organising and co-ordinating all consultants. In either case, the project manager acts as a link between the client and the design team. Depending upon the particular kind of project management chosen, the contract administrator may be the project manager or the architect.

Design and build

This is a system that places responsibility for both design and construction in the hands of the contractor. There are variations in the name and there are subtle differences in meaning. *Design and build*, for example, refers to the basic system where a contractor carries out the two functions. *Design and construct* includes design and build and other types of construction such as purely engineering works. *Develop and construct* often describes a situation where a contractor takes a partially completed design and develops it into a fully detailed design. *Package deal* can be used to refer to either of these. In theory, the term suggests that the contractor is responsible for providing everything in one package and it is particularly apt when referring to an industrialised building. *Turnkey* contracting is a system in which the contractor really is responsible for everything, including furniture and pictures on the walls if required. The idea is that the employer simply turns the key and begins using the building – hence the name.

Unless the building is very simple, the contractor will seek an architect to carry out the design. From the client's point of view, an independent adviser is required to look after the client's interests before, during and after construction.

Design and manage

This is comparatively rare. Single-point responsibility rests with a professional who may be architect, engineer or surveyor. Besides being responsible for the design of the project, the professional also manages the project in the sense of managing the other professionals and also the construction process in the form of, probably, a number of sub-contractors and suppliers. In this situation, the architect must be careful to explain to the employer that if the employer requires independent professional advice, another architect must be appointed. This type of procurement is suitable where relatively small projects require very detailed control over every aspect of the design detailing.

Management contracting

In this system the contractor is selected at an early stage. It is not normally responsible for carrying out any of the construction work. The contractor simply has a management function for which a fee is paid. The construction work is divided into a number of packages with the contractor's advice and tenders for these individual packages are invited as appropriate to suit the programme. The works contractors are in contract with the management contractor and the employer pays only the works contracts' costs without the addition of any contractor's overheads or profit. In this respect the system has something in common with prime-cost contracting.

This is the system most often referred to as 'fast track'. The idea being that work begins on site as soon as sufficient information has been produced to enable the first works contractors to start. The architect and other consultants are then involved in a constant race against time to produce the remainder of the drawings in time for the succeeding works packages.

Construction management

This system calls upon the contractor to act simply in a management capacity for which a fee is paid. The design team is often appointed directly by the employer, but in some instances the contractor may appoint. In such cases, the system has some of the flavour of project management. The key difference between this system and management contracting is that the individual works contractors (they are usually termed 'trade contractors' under this system) are in contract with the employer.

Although details vary, the construction manager is usually responsible for managing not only the trade contractors, but also the other consultants. Some very large projects have been carried out using this system, which calls upon the same kind of skills from the design team as required under the management contract.

1.4   Characteristics of a standard form

Bespoke contracts

A bespoke contract is like a bespoke suit or a house designed for a specific family. Both are designed to match precisely the requirements of the purchaser.

In theory, it is much better to have every construction contract specially drafted to suit the detailed requirements of employers and/or contractors. In practice, such contracts would have their own particular disadvantages. They would each be much more expensive than a standard 'off the peg' contract. Instead of buying them for £40 and £50, it would cost several thousand pounds each time. Producing a bespoke contract would take time while requirements were thoroughly investigated and all the terms carefully drafted to ensure that all eventualities were covered.

Contractors may be loath to tender on the basis of an unfamiliar contract and if they tender they may submit an increased price to reflect the unknown contract. Architects will be unused to administering strange contracts and may well charge additional fees for doing so. Mistakes and wrong assumptions can be made as the parties begin to understand how each new contract works. Just as they all get used to it, the project will be complete and the next project will have a different bespoke contract. The situation would not be quite as bad as that of course, because every contract would have certain things in common. It is out of the common elements that the standard form emerges.

Standard forms

Standard forms of contract are relatively inexpensive. But the standardised versions of anything are based on a notion of a majority requirement. This is the main disadvantage of a standard form of contract. Acknowledging that one form will not suit every case, the JCT produces several different standard forms each one designed for a particular category such as Design and Build, Prime Cost and Traditional (see the list in Section 1.5 below). Even the 'Traditional' category has three distinct versions. Standard forms of contract are like standard suits, standard cars or standard housing. They are good enough across a broad spectrum of applications, but they are seldom entirely appropriate. The more complex the application the more unlikely it is that a standard solution will be right.

A big advantage with standard forms is that they are usually drafted by people with particular expertise in that particular field and the forms evolve over the years to suit changes in legislation and in line with decisions handed down by the courts. The result is, or should be, that the best parts of the forms are retained, mistakes are removed and omissions are rectified. Moreover, architects and contractors become used to them.

There is a danger that arises out of the number and variation of standard forms. Few if any architects and quantity surveyors can really get to grips with the differences. Architects and project managers commonly use forms with which they are familiar but that may not always be suitable for the procurement route and attendant circumstances. Too many architects always use the same standard form no matter what the circumstances. That may amount to professional negligence. It is possible to drive from Birmingham to Winchester in a tank, but to go by car is infinitely preferable. Therefore, the choice of the right standard form is important.

Hybrid

In order to avoid the substantial expense of having a form of contract especially drafted, but to overcome the problems inherent in a standard product that may be nearly but not quite suitable, employers sometimes have standard forms amended to suit their detailed requirements. That seems to be a sound idea in principle. However, the best advice is never to amend standard forms. That is principally because it is difficult to ensure that any amendment works correctly in the context of the form as a whole and there is a real danger that, say, the deletion of a clause is not carried through to delete all references to it and to amend anything else that depends upon that clause. Modern building contracts are complex documents with a multitude of interlocking provisions. Moreover, the person charged with administering the contract must be aware of the detailed effect of the amendments. Amendments are often necessary to 'customise' a standard form, but they should be carried out only by specialists who should clearly explain the effects of the amendments.

1.5   Commonly used contracts

A list of available JCT building contracts and sub-contracts at the time of writing is shown in Table 1.1.

The most commonly used JCT contracts are probably:

SBC – For use for larger Works that are designed for the employer and the contract is administered by an architect/contract administrator. The Works can be carried out in sections and there is provision for the contractor to design parts of the Works.

IC and ICD – For use for Works without complex services up to a value of about £450,000 where fairly detailed contract terms are required and that are designed for the employer and the contract is administered by an architect/contract administrator. The Works can be carried out in sections and, in ICD, there is provision for the contractor to design parts of the Works.

MW and MWD – For use for simple Works up to a value of about £200,000 where detailed contract terms are not required and that are designed for the employer and the contract is administered by an architect/contract administrator. In MWD, there is provision for the contractor to design parts of the Works.

DB – For use where the contractor is to design and build the project in accordance with the Employer's Requirements. The Works can be carried out in sections.

There are other contracts in use:

THE ACA FORM OF BUILDING AGREEMENT (ACA 3) – A relatively straightforward contract suitable for any size and value of project, basically a traditional contract with several options, some of which will effectively turn it into a design a build contract.

THE ACA STANDARD FORM OF CONTRACT FOR PROJECT PARTNERING (PPC2000) – An unusual contract in that it is multi-party and can be entered into by a mixture of client, contractor, consultants and certain sub-contractors. It is intended to be a partnering contract and it is recommended by Constructing Excellence as a means of encouraging collaborative working. It is endorsed by the Construction Industry Council. Although theoretically suitable for all sizes and values of project, its full benefits will only be experienced when used for projects over about £800,000.

THE GENERAL CONDITIONS OF GOVERNMENT CONTRACTS FOR BUILDING AND CIVIL ENGINEERING WORKS (GC/WORKS/1 (1998)) – Although originally drafted for government use, this contract has become quite popular for ordinary commercial projects. It is suitable for all kinds of major project work and there are several versions including design and build.

ENGINEERING AND CONSTRUCTION CONTRACT (NEC 3) – A contract that has become very popular for civil engineering work and it is used, and

Table 1.1   JCT Building contracts and sub-contracts (sub-contracts shown in italic).

Standard Building Contract (SBC)
   With Quantities (SBC/Q)
   With Approximate Quantities (SBC/AQ)
   Without Quantities (SBC/XQ)

Standard Building Sub-Contract with sub-contractor's design Agreement (SBCSub/D/A)
Standard Building Sub-Contract with sub-contractor's design Conditions (SBCSub/D/C)
Standard Building Sub-Contract Agreement (SBCSub/A)
Standard Building Sub-Contract Conditions (SBCSub/C)

Intermediate Building Contract (IC)
Intermediate Building Contract with contractor's design (ICD)

Intermediate Sub-Contract Agreement (ICSub/A)
Intermediate Sub-Contract Conditions (ICSub/C)
Intermediate Sub-Contract with sub-contractor's design Agreement (ICSub/D/A)
Intermediate Sub-Contract with sub-contractor's design Conditions (ICSub/D/C)
Intermediate Named Sub-Contract Tender & Agreement (ICSub/NAM)
Intermediate Named Sub-Contract Conditions (ICSub/NAM/C)
Intermediate Named Sub-Contractor/Employer Agreement (ICSub/NAM/E)

Minor Works Building Contract (MW)
Minor Works Building Contract with contractor's design (MWD)

Minor Works Sub-Contract with sub-contractor's design (MWSub/D)

Design and Build Contract (DB)

Design and Build Sub-Contract Agreement (DBSub/A)
Design and Build Sub-Contract Conditions (DBSub/C)

Major Project Construction Contract (MP)

Major Project Sub-Contract (MPSub)

Construction Management Trade Contract (CM/TC)
Construction Management Appointment (CM/A)
Management Building Contract (MC)

Management Works Contract Agreement (MCWC/A)
Management Works Contract Conditions (MCWC/C)
Management Works Contractor/Employer Agreement (MCWC/E)

Prime Cost Building Contract (PCC)
Measured Term Contract (MTC)
Framework Agreement (FA)

Constructing Excellence Contract (CE)
Constructing Excellence Project Team Agreement (CE/P)

Repair and Maintenance Contract Commercial (RM)

Pre-Construction Services Agreement (PCSA)

Building Contract for a Home Owner/Occupier (HOB)
Building Contract and Consultancy Agreement for a Home Owner/Occupier (HOC)

in some places strongly advocated, for building work. The philosophy of this form is intended to be different from that of the more common JCT and other contracts and, in wording, grammar, clause numbering and approach, it is very different from other contracts. It has been the subject of criticism by legal commentators and in court. The form is said to comply fully with the AEC (Achieving Excellence in Construction) principles. The title page records that the Office of Government Commerce (OGC) recommends the use of NEC 3 by public sector construction procurers on their construction projects. It has a number of options capable of turning it into different kinds of contract, e.g., target, management and cost reimbursable contracts.

1.6   Important background to SBC

3

The first standard form of building contract in the United Kingdom came into use towards the end of the nineteenth century. It had just nineteen clauses. After 1903 until 1977, it became known as 'the RIBA contract'. After that, it was called the 'JCT contract'. Despite the change, the judges took a long time to adjust and the law reports are full of references to 'the RIBA contract' for many years afterwards.

From 1903, the Standard Form of Building Contract was put together by a body consisting of representatives of the RIBA, the Construction Confederation (CC) as it is now called, and the Institute of Building (IOB), as it then was. In 1931, the IOB withdrew, so that henceforth, the body was a 'Joint' one consisting of the RIBA and the National Federation of Building Trades Employers (NFBTE), now the CC. In 1952, the Royal Institution of Chartered Surveyors (RICS) became involved and by the year 1963, the Joint Contracts Tribunal consisted of representatives of ten bodies in the construction industry. Bodies representing sub-contractors eventually joined. The Standard Form was substantially rewritten in 1939, 1963 and 1980. Following a great many published amendments, it was revised in 1998 and again substantially revised in 2005. The current version (2011) was amended principally to take account of changes

4

in legislation.

1.7   SBC and variants

SBC is available in 3 versions:

- Standard Building Contract With Quantities 2011 (SBC/Q).
- Standard Building Contract With Approximate Quantities 2011 (SBC/AQ).
- Standard Building Contract Without Quantities 2011 (SBC/XQ).

SBC/Q is the version that will be considered in this book.

SBC/AQ is used where approximate quantities are to be provided that are subject to remeasurement. The reason for using this version may be because there is insufficient time to produce the detailed drawings necessary for the preparation of accurate bills of quantities or it may be that the nature of the project means that quantities cannot be known with accuracy until the construction work is in progress. Obviously, there can be no Contract Sum and the final cost cannot be known until the Works are complete or nearly so.

SBC/XQ is used where it is thought that the nature of the Works does not warrant quantities and, therefore, drawings together with a specification or work schedules have been provided. Effectively, the contractor is being asked to prepare its own quantities from the information provided. Whether contractors are prepared to submit a price on that basis rather depends on the overall value of the Works and whether any contractor is short of work.

All of these versions are suitable for use by private and local authority employers.

2 Basic matters

2.1 Works

SBC uses the words 'Works' with a capital 'W' to mean the total of all the work, goods and materials that the contractor agrees to provide and it includes all variations.

2.2 Drawings

5

It is important to understand what the contract means when it refers to drawings. In this context, a drawing is a visual representation of a building or a part of a building to a particular scale. The contract also refers to 'details' that are usually taken to mean a large scale drawing of a relatively small part of the building. Where 'details' plural is mentioned what it usually intended is an in-depth description rather than a drawing. For example, details of sanitary fittings may best be conveyed by means of a schedule and specification.

Types of drawings

Drawings can be categorised in different ways. So far as SBC is concerned, there are two specific kinds of drawings:

third recital
eleventh recital

2.11

2.12, 3.14

2.9.4 and 2.9.5

2.40

- Drawings that are part of the contract documents, such as the contract drawings or the drawings produced by the contractor and that form part of the Contractor's Proposals.
- Drawings that are provided by the architect during the progress of the work in accordance with the information release schedule or simply as part of further drawings and information that the contractor requires to carry out the Works or as part of instructions requiring variations. In this category are the additional drawings that the contractor must provide as reasonably necessary to explain or amplify the Contractor's Proposals and the as-built drawings that the contractor must supply before practical completion to show the CPD work if any.

The JCT Standard Building Contract 2011, First Edition. David Chappell.
© 2014 by David Chappell. Published 2014 by John Wiley & Sons, Ltd.

Copyright

Copyright in the architect's drawings (and in specifications, schedules and the like) is owned by the architect. What that means is that although someone else may actually have or even own the drawings, they cannot copy or reproduce what is on them without the architect's permission. The law concerning copyright is quite complex and it is a mixture of legislation and decisions of the courts. If the architect and client have entered into terms of engagement as they should, the terms will usually state that the client has a licence to use the drawings when the architect's fees are paid. If they have not entered into a proper formal agreement, the law will usually imply a term (see Chapter 4, Section 4.3) that the client has the right to reproduce the architect's drawings in the form of a building when the client has paid a reasonable fee. Like many terms that are implied, it is not always easy to say what a reasonable fee might be.

2.41   The contract specifically states that copyright in drawings and other documents supplied by the contractor will remain in the contractor's ownership (the usual term is 'vested' to mean that the contractor owns the right). But the contractor grants a licence to the employer to copy and use the documents for any purpose including the main purpose of reproducing them in relation to the Works. The only exclusion is that the employer may not reproduce the designs in order to carry out any extension to the finished building. That is a standard exclusion in copyright clauses to prevent someone using the documents for purposes that go beyond what is necessary for the Works in question.

There is a proviso that all sums due and payable to the contractor must have been paid. Subject to that, the licence is said to be 'irrevocable' – it cannot be withdrawn under any circumstances. It is said to be 'royalty-free' – which is just a way of saying that the contractor cannot expect any payment other than what it receives under the contract terms. It is said to be 'non-exclusive' – which is the normal position. If the contractor was to grant an exclusive licence it would prevent anyone (including the contractor) from using the documents again for another purpose. The grant of a non-exclusive licence makes clear that the contractor still retains its rights over the documents.

2.3   Specification

A specification is a document that describes in detail, together with the drawings, how a building is to be constructed: quality of workmanship and materials, the way in which the elements fit together and where they occur throughout the building. It may or may not contain quantities. However, where bills of quantities are used (as in SBC/Q) the specification will not contain quantities and it will form part of the bills of quantities. Under SBC/Q, which is being considered here, the specification is not referred to as a separate contract document from the bills of quantities. Where there are no bills of quantities, the specification is an important document.

2.4   Schedules

Architects commonly make use of schedules to a greater or lesser extent as a useful means of describing the work and materials in a building. Common schedules are ironmongery, sanitary fittings, doors, windows and colour schedules. Obviously, almost anything can be scheduled. SBC notably refers to a schedule of defects to be produced by the architect at the end of the rectification period. Work schedules may be part of the contract documents under SBC/XQ and also under the Intermediate and Minor Works Contracts, but they are not part of the contract documents under SBC/Q. Work schedules are usually lists of all the work and materials needed to construct the Works. The list may use very broad descriptions or it may be very precisely detailed. The bills of quantities remove the need for work schedules.

2.38.1

2.5   Bills of quantities

The use of bills of quantities is a peculiarly British practice. Bills were described in the Simon Report of 1944, 'The Placing and Management of Building Contracts' as 'putting into words every obligation or service that will be required in carrying out the building project'. That is still a serviceable definition.

Where bills of quantities are used, before inviting tenders, it is necessary for the architect to prepare the drawings and other information in sufficient detail to enable a quantity surveyor to measure from them the actual amounts to be executed, sub-divided into various trades. This bill of quantities normally starts with what are termed the 'preliminaries', which are items that relate to the project as a whole, for example, the provision of site accommodation. The preliminaries are followed by the itemised bills.

In tendering

Contractors are invited to tender on the basis of the bills of quantities and to insert the total price they require. Subsequently, before the tender can be accepted, the prospective contractor must break its total price down into a rate and price for each item of the work. In reality, the contractor will have arrived at its total price by pricing the individual parts of the bills of quantities and then adding up all the items.

In theory, bills of quantities remove the necessity for each tenderer to work out for itself the quantities of material and labour required. The system should ensure that each contractor tenders on exactly the same basis. The risk of several contractors, each effectively tendering on different, perhaps wrongly measured, amounts of work is removed. In practice it does not work quite in that way.

First, the architect's drawings are rarely in sufficient detail to enable a bill of quantities to be prepared with total accuracy. Often, the quantity surveyor will be left to guess what the architect may be intending and to measure something to cover the situation. The result is that any further detailed information in the form of drawings, schedules and the like will be treated under the contract as architect's instructions requiring variations that may well lead to additional costs to the employer. It is probably sensible to have a clause in the bills of quantities to the following effect:

> 'Where and to the extent that materials, goods and workmanship are not fully specified they are to be suitable for the purpose of the Works stated in or reasonably to be inferred from the contract documents and they are to be in accordance with good building practice, including the relevant provisions of current British standard documents.'

7

Secondly, the art of evaluating from drawings the exact amount of materials and work required varies from the difficult, as in the case of an air-conditioned computer room, to the impossible, as in the case of excavations.

In valuation

The bills of quantities also provide a way in which the inevitable variations are to be valued and to enable a fair valuation of work done to be made for the purposes of interim payment certificates. Theory and practice seldom coincide. At one time it was common for contractors to make sure that, in pricing, items in the bills of quantities scheduled for early construction carried most of the value of the Works. The practice was known as 'front loading'. The idea was to transfer as much of the employer's money to the contractor as soon as possible. This could result in later items being executed at a loss and desperate efforts being made to fabricate claims.

The opposite approach in times of high inflation was to 'back load' the tender in order to get the advantage of the fluctuations clause, particularly if the contractor could afford to buy in materials early.

A contractor may gamble by putting a high rate on an item of which there is a small quantity or a low rate on items of which there is a large quantity, hoping that the quantities will increase or decrease, respectively. The former will net him additional profit while the latter may secure him the contract. The practice

8

has been dubbed part of the contractor's commercial strategy.

The general view in the industry is that contractors will load their tenders when quantities are not used and uneconomic prices will be quoted. That may not be necessarily so.

2.6   The Standard Method of Measurement

In order that there might be some standardisation in the way in which bills of quantities were prepared, the RICS and what was then the NFBTE (now the CC) prepared what is termed the 'Standard Method of Measurement' usually abbreviated to SMM.

2.13.1

The contract bills are to have been prepared in accordance with SMM. The quality and the quantity of the work that is included in the Contract Sum

4.1

is what is included in the contract bills. Therefore, it is extremely important that the bills of quantities accurately represent the work to be done and the materials to be used. It has already been stated that it is virtually impossible to accurately reduce every part of building operations into words, so there will be ambiguities and gaps in any bills of quantities. Therefore, the position under SBC is that the contractor is likely to be entitled to some additional payment on this basis. It is sometimes argued that the contractor must have included for things that everybody must have understood are to be done but that happen to be omitted from the quantities. However, it is likely that, for that argument to have any chance of success, terms must be included to the effect that the contractor should supply everything needed for the Works according to the true intent of the drawings, specification and quantities whether or not particularly described. It is difficult to see how a term like that can be reconciled with the contract that sets up the bills of quantities as being the benchmark for the amount of work included.

2.7   Privity of contract and the Third Party Act

Privity of contract is the name for an old principle that only the parties to a contract can exercise rights under that contract. For example, a contract between A and B might say that A will do work for B and that B will pay A £500. It might also say that in addition B will pay C £100. If A did the work, A could demand the £500 from B, but C until comparatively recently could not legally demand the £100 because C was not a party to the contract. Conversely, a person who is not a party to a contract cannot have obligations imposed by the contract. Therefore, in the previous example, if the contract had said that C must pay A £100, C could not be made to do so even though C knew that the term had been included. All that appears to be eminently sensible and in accordance with common sense. However, it was thought that a strict application of the privity principle could lead to injustice in certain cases and Parliament decided to change the law dramatically.

The Contracts (Rights of Third Parties) Act 1999

The Contracts (Rights of Third Parties) Act 1999 came into force on 11 May 2000 and it applies throughout the UK. It interferes with the principle of privity of contract by giving the entitlement to third parties, who are not parties to the contract in question, to enforce certain rights under the contract. In order to apply:

- The contract must give the third party a right.
- The terms must confer a benefit (unless it is clear that the parties did not intend a benefit to be conferred).
- The third party must be identified in the contract. That can be by name, by class or by description. (It should be noted that the third party may not have existed at the time the contract was entered into, e.g., a newly formed limited company).

Such a right may only be enforced in accordance with the terms of the contract and the party against whom the third party seeks to enforce the terms may use any defences and remedies available under the contract and may raise any set-off or counterclaim. Therefore, the position of C today in our earlier example is that if B had agreed to pay C £100, C can legally demand it, but if a term has been included to require C to pay £100 to A, A cannot legally enforce it. The parties can bring the contract to an end or vary the contract in order to remove the right, but not if:

- the third party has communicated its agreement to the term; *and* the parties know that the third party has relied on the term; *or*
- It was reasonably foreseeable that the third party would rely on the term and it has relied on it.

To overcome that, the Act allows parties to include a term in the contract by which they agree to bring the contract to an end or vary it without the consent of the third party or setting out circumstances for the third party's consent. Most usefully, parties to a contract may expressly exclude third party rights under that contract. That seems to be the simplest approach and it is the approach favoured by the Joint Contracts Tribunal that has inserted that kind of excluding provision in SBC. So, the position under SBC is almost the same as before the Act came into force. 'Almost', because use is made of the Act to give third party rights instead of warranties from the contractor.

Architect not a party

It must be borne in mind that, although SBC makes frequent references to what the architect may or must do, the architect is not a party to that contract. Therefore, these references do not create a contractual obligation on the architect to do any of those things. The architect's obligation to act stems from the terms of engagement with the employer that usually require the architect to administer the contract. The contractor, however, has no such contractual link. Therefore, it cannot bring an action against the architect for breach of contract for failure to do that which SBC stipulated the architect should do. Neither can the contractor make the architect take part in any arbitration arising out of SBC despite there being an arbitration agreement in both SBC and the architect's terms of engagement. That is not to say, however, that the contractor cannot bring a legal action against the architect outside the contract.

12

2.8 Third party rights and collateral warranties

Strictly speaking a collateral warranty is a contract that runs alongside another contract and is subsidiary to it. Such documents have proliferated in recent years and it is common for contractors, domestic sub-contractors and suppliers and all the consultants to be required to execute a collateral warranty in favour of the building owner, the funder providing the money for the project and/or any number of prospective tenants. It used to be the view that such an agreement was not very important because it merely stated in contractual terms the duties that everyone knew the architect owed to a third party under the law of tort, specifically negligence. That view is no longer tenable, because duties in negligence have been held to be quite limited.

13

Before looking at some of the provisions commonly encountered in forms of warranty, or duty of care agreements (as they are often called when used in relation to consultants), it should be understood why they are so important to the building owner.

Applying this principle to the architect's conditions of engagement, if something goes wrong with the building that is clearly a design fault, only the client can take action against the architect for breach of the conditions of engagement. For example, if an architect designs a house for the client, the house is sold on to a third party and a design defect then becomes apparent, the third party cannot take action against the architect under the conditions of engagement between the architect and client. At one time, the third party would have been able to overcome this kind of problem by suing in the tort of negligence if there was no contractual relationship.

The purpose of a duty of care agreement is to create a contractual relationship between the architect and third parties who otherwise would be unlikely to have any remedy if design defects became apparent after completion. At the time of writing, there is a standard form of warranty (CoWa/F) in favour of funders and (CoWa/P&T) in favour of purchasers or tenants. There are also a great many other forms of warranty in circulation, some of which have been especially drafted by solicitors with a greater or lesser experience of the architectural profession and the construction industry generally.

7E

7C, 7D

SBC makes reference to various warranties that a sub-contractor can give if so stated in the contract particulars. They are SCWa/P&T (for purchasers and tenants), SCWa/F (for funders) and SCWa/E (for the employer). The contract particulars can also require the contractor to give warranties to purchasers and tenants (CWa/P&T) and to funders (CWa/F).

Schedule 5

Importantly, the Third Party Rights Act provides an alternative for the contractor. By including a set of terms, usually found in a warranty, in the contract, the purchasers, tenants and funders can be given third party rights to enforce those terms against the contractor. Whether that is overall easier than getting the contractor to sign a warranty is a matter of opinion. The important thing is that the power exists to do it.

2.9 Base Date

This is a date from which certain things are to be measured. In contracts issued before 1987, the same date used to be referred to as the 'date of tender'. The problem was in setting the date. Very often, the date stipulated for the return of tenders (i.e. the date of tender) had to be extended due to a difficulty with the tendering process. In such cases, the date of tender as stated in what was then known as the

'Appendix' and now as the 'Contract Particulars' was very often a date earlier than the actual date of tender. Therefore, it was wrong to call it the 'date of tender'.

The current expression 'base date' much more accurately expresses what was intended. For example, the base date is mentioned in clause 2.29.13 when referring to the exercise by the UK Government of any statutory power. It specifically refers to a power exercised after the base date.

2.10 Common problems

Defective product in the specification

There are four ways in which a specified product may be said to be defective:

- The architect may have specified the wrong product.
- The specification may be too broad, permitting the contractor to provide a satisfactory or an unsatisfactory product.
- The product may be correctly specified but the product supplied does not match the specification.
- The product may be specified to be in accordance with an approved sample that turns out to be defective.

Wrong product

If the wrong product has been specified, that is to say a product that will not perform in the way required, the contractor is not normally responsible for the failure. The contractor would only be responsible if the unsuitability of the product was so obvious that no contractor acting reasonably would have ordered it without first checking with the architect. Whether the contractor has a duty to warn the architect is discussed in Chapter 6, Section 6.13.

If the architect had carried out all sensible checks on the product, including writing to the manufacturer and obtaining its specific assurance that the product was suitable for the purpose proposed, it is likely that the manufacturer may be liable. However, that would be a matter to be sorted out between architect, employer and manufacturer. The contractor would be entitled to a variation instruction for a suitable product.

If the architect had failed to properly check whether the product was suitable and had simply relied on the manufacturer's technical literature or, worse, relied on a chat with the sales representative, the architect would be liable to the employer for any additional costs caused by the defective product. These costs could be considerable if the product was used extensively and already built into the construction before the problem was discovered.

Specification too broad

It sometimes happens that the architect fails to include all the necessary criteria in a specification. A simple example of this would be if the architect specified a ready-mixed concrete, but gave no details of the mix required. In most cases, the contractor would no doubt simply order a mix that was suitable for the situation in which the concrete was to be used. For example: mass concrete in foundations, exposed concrete in walls, concrete for reinforced concrete work and so on. Or the architect might specify locks for doors but fail to say whether they were deadlocks or mortice locks or the type of bolt. In these cases, the contractor is not responsible for choosing the correct type of concrete or lock or whatever the product may be, from among the range of possibilities. In the first example, the contractor could supply concrete of any mix. The responsibility would lie with the architect.

14

Product does not comply with the specification

This is fairly and squarely the contractor's responsibility. However, if the specified product is unobtainable, the contractor is entitled to report the matter to the architect who must then instruct an alternative product and that may result in an increase in cost for the employer.

2.3.1

Approved sample

Specifications sometimes require the contractor to supply a product in accordance with a sample to be approved by the architect. This often happens in the case of stone or brick or timber that is to be exposed. Because the contractor has no way of knowing what the architect may approve, this kind of specification is not often priced at tender stage, but is usually the subject of a provisional sum. The architect may approve a sample that, unknown to the architect, and possibly to the supplier, has hidden defects. It will not avail the supplier to later say that the architect-approved sample was defective and therefore the architect must accept defective products; because the architect was approving what was apparent. Therefore, if the architect approves, bricks, stone or timber that has hidden flaws, it will be the sample without the flaws that will be the approved sample.

15

The contractor or sub-contractor does not provide a warranty when requested

This is a common problem. Where construction professionals are required to provide warranties, commercial clients often try to insist on a clause in the architect's appointment that gives the client power of attorney (the legal right to do certain things on behalf of the professional) for the professional so as to enable the client to complete the warranty on the professionals behalf. Needless to say, there are serious dangers for any professional who agrees to this kind of clause.

So far as the contractor is concerned, the contract states that the contractor may be required to provide a warranty in the form stated in the contract within 14 days of the employer writing to the contractor requiring the warranty (called a 'notice'). In the case of a sub-contractor, the contractor has 21 days from

7C and 7D

receipt of the employer's notice. That is on the assumption that the warranties concerned are listed in the contract particulars.

If the contractor does not comply within the time period in the contract (14 or 21 days), it is in breach of contract. The employer would be entitled to take action through adjudication or either arbitration or legal proceedings (depending on which is chosen in the contract) to recover any damages. The problem is that neither the employer nor any prospective beneficiary of the warranty would suffer any loss until a situation arose that permitted a claim to be made on the warranty. That is when the absence of the warranty could cause real and possible substantial losses. Therefore, the important thing is to have the warranty in place within the contract timescale.

Sometimes, the employer will ask for a clause to be inserted in the contract to say that if the employer requires a warranty, no further certificates will be issued until the warranty is delivered. Quite apart from the difficulty of wording such a clause so that it does not hopelessly complicate the already complicated payment provisions, that kind of clause would be thrown out by an adjudicator, arbitrator or judge, because it is a penalty that is unenforceable (see Chapter 15, Section 15.1).

16

It is possible that an application could be made to a judge for what is known as a 'mandatory injunction' or 'specific performance'. That is an order of the court for someone to do something. Injunctions and orders for specific performance are not readily given if damages are an appropriate remedy, but this might be an suitable situation. Usually, the threat of seeking an injunction is sufficient to cause the necessary warranties to be produced.

3 About the contract documents

3.1 What constitutes the contract?

What SBC says

1.1

There are still a great many people who think that when reference is made to the 'contract' the reference is to the printed form SBC properly filled in and signed by the parties. Actually, the contract usually consists of a bundle of documents that are referred to in SBC as the 'Contract Documents'. The contract documents consist of the contract drawings, the bills of quantities and the printed form. If the contractor is to design a portion of the Works (the Contractor's Designed Portion or CDP), the documents will also include the Employer's Requirements, the Contractor's Proposals and the CDP Analysis.

Incorporating other documents

In addition, other documents may be made part of the contract by what is termed 'incorporation'. To do that, it is necessary to clearly state in the printed form that these other documents are to be incorporated in the contract. A good example of incorporation of other documents is in the third recital that leaves space for the contract drawings to be listed but, if there is insufficient space to list them, they may be listed on a separate sheet that must be clearly identified in the space and attached to the back of the printed form. It is a good idea and avoids any doubt if the sheet is signed and dated by the parties, although the form does not mention that. Similar provisions for incorporating other documents are to be found in various places in the recitals and in the contract particulars.

It is unfortunately common for document-happy employers and their advisors to try to incorporate all kinds of other documents besides those specifically mentioned in SBC. For example, if there has been correspondence between employer and contractor after tender stage, it might be thought useful to include it. Generally, the inclusion of extraneous pieces of correspondence as part of the contract only serves to confuse the issues if a dispute arises and may even be a cause of the dispute as the parties form radically different ideas of what they said, or intended to say, in the correspondence. If the contents of

The JCT Standard Building Contract 2011, First Edition. David Chappell.
© 2014 by David Chappell. Published 2014 by John Wiley & Sons, Ltd.

letters are judged to be so important, it is better to have what was said formally agreed and the contract documents amended accordingly.

Occasionally, an attempt will be made to incorporate the whole of a contract simply by reference to it in a letter, e.g., 'on the JCT Standard Contract terms and conditions'. That cannot work, because it overlooks the fact that there are many blanks in the printed form (such as the recitals and the contract particulars) that must be filled in before the contract makes any sense.

Incorporating terms by reference is a dangerous practice. It ignores the fact that not only may there be earlier versions still existent but there may be different editions of a contract so that it is impossible to say with certainty which amendment applies. The result is that since the parties are rarely in agreement regarding which contract is referred to, there is in many cases no contract and the one who has done work will simply be entitled to a *quantum meruit* (see Chapter 4, Section 4.6).

3.2   What are articles and recitals?

The structure of SBC

The first page is titled 'Articles of Agreement' and contains the essential information about the parties to the contract. The title actually refers to the whole of the first part of SBC up to and including the attestation pages. The next two pages are the 'Recitals' or introductory statement saying what the contract is about. Following the recitals comes three pages entitled 'Articles' that sets out the basic agreement. Then comes the 'Contract Particulars' that are to be filled in as appropriate depending on the particular project details. At the end of the contract particulars is found the attestation pages for the parties to sign the contract as a simple contract or as a deed.

The body of SBC is taken up by what JCT terms 'The Conditions'. These are the clauses that say how the contract is to be conducted. At the end of the conditions there are a set of schedules that contain further material referred to in the clauses.

Recitals

The recitals normally explain the background to the contract and set out what the parties intend to do and perhaps what they have already done. They are not usually essential to the contract and they cannot override the rest of the contract if it is clear. However, it is permissible to look at the recitals to assist in getting at the true meaning if other parts of the contract are ambiguous. SBC uses the recitals to convey specific information such as the list of drawings and the definition of the Works.

17

Articles

The articles are the formal opening parts of a contract that set out the essential elements that are agreed and made subject to the rest of the contract terms. For example, the articles include the names and addresses of the parties and the professionals involved with the contract and sets out the Contract Sum to be paid by the employer and what is to be done by the contractor.

3.3 How to complete the contract form

It cannot be stressed too much that the form must be completed carefully. Although it may not very much appeal, it is a job for the architect or other person who will actually administer the contract with the advice and assistance of the quantity surveyor where appropriate. It is not a task for the quantity surveyor alone, still less for the employer's solicitor who may or may not have a full understanding of SBC but who will certainly not have experience in administering a building contract in progress.

It should be noted that although the bills of quantities state in the preliminaries section how the contract form is to be completed, most of that information must be provided by the architect to the quantity surveyor. That means that the architect is effectively completing SBC when providing that information. Theoretically, when an acceptable tender is received, the architect simply copies the information in the bills of quantities into the contract form. Realistically, the process of accepting a tender may not be straightforward, certain things may be changed and the transfer of information from bills of quantities to the contract form may be subject to adjustment.

First page

Conveniently, the part of the contract requiring completion is at the beginning of the document and extends to and includes the attestation. Before and while completing the contract, it is essential to read the relevant clauses with great care to see that in filling in the blanks and deleting, the results are exactly what is intended. The document is complicated and the architect should never 'take a stab' at an entry. If there is any doubt, the advice of a contract expert should be obtained. This may entail rather more than referring to the quantity surveyor.

On the first page the date of the agreement should be left blank until the last party signs. The date must be the date on which the last party signs even if that is when the Works are very far advanced or even completed. Obviously, every effort must be made to have the contract signed before work starts on site. It becomes more difficult afterwards.

1.7

The names and addresses of the parties should be entered in the contract particulars. These will be the addresses to which communications will be sent. If either party is a company, a company number must be inserted. It is the only sure means of identification; companies sometimes change their names.

Recitals

The first recital is important, because it gives a description of the Works and the location. The description must be entered carefully but not in too great detail, because there must be scope for the architect to issue instructions requiring variations without altering the character and scope of the Works. The second recital confirms that the contractor has supplied the employer with one priced copy of the contract bills initialled or signed by the parties and there are no insertions or deletions required. Reference to the priced schedule of activities

4.16.1.1

must be deleted if the contractor is not to provide one.

The third recital requires the contract drawing numbers to be entered. If there is insufficient space, the reference to a clearly identifiable list of numbers of all contract drawings must be inserted. The list must be firmly attached to the contract, signed and dated by the parties. It is essential that the contract drawings are exactly the same as the tender drawings. Any post-tender amendments should be shown by means of an addendum bill attached to the contract. No entries are required in the fourth recital that merely refers to the contract particulars. The fifth recital must be deleted if the contractor has not been pro-

see 2.11

vided with an information release schedule. The sixth recital must be deleted if the Works are not divided into sections. No entries are required in the seventh and eighth recitals that merely refer to the contract particulars.

The ninth to twelfth Recitals inclusive only apply if there is to be a contractor's designed portion (CDP). If not, for the sake of clarity it is a good idea to delete them. If there is to be a CDP, these recitals must be retained and the ninth recital must be completed to unambiguously state the work that the contractor is to design. If the space is insufficient, reference must be made to a separate sheet firmly attached to the contract, signed and dated by the parties. Recitals ten, eleven and twelve are descriptive and do not require insertions.

Articles

Article 1 simply sets out the contractor's obligation in brief and requires no insertions. The Contract Sum (excluding VAT) must be inserted in article 2 in words and figures. The Contract Sum is always this figure. If the contract states that amounts are to be added to, or deducted from it, the figure becomes the adjusted Contract Sum. The name and address of the architect must be inserted in article 3. That is usually the name of the firm. The alternative description, 'Contract Administrator' is used here and throughout the contract where the

18

person is not entitled to use the description 'Architect'. If the architect ceases to act as contract administrator for any reason, the employer must appoint a

3.5

replacement within 21 days. The name and address of the quantity surveyor must be inserted in article 4. If the quantity surveyor ceases to act for any rea-

3.5

son, the employer must appoint a replacement within 21 days.

If the CDM Regulations apply, article 5 states that the architect will act as the CDM co-ordinator, unless the name of another person is entered as CDM co-ordinator. Article 6 states that the contractor will be the principal contractor for the purposes of the CDM Regulations and the SWMP Regulations unless another person is inserted. If the Regulations do not apply, strike out articles 5 and 6.

Article 7 does not require any insertions or deletions. It merely states the right of either party to refer any dispute to adjudication. If the employer is a residential occupier, article 7 may be deleted, but not otherwise. The adjudicator can be named in the contract particulars, agreed between the parties or nominated by one of the nominating bodies listed. Articles 8 and 9 refer to the right of the parties to refer disputes to arbitration or legal proceedings, respectively. The choice is to be made in the contract particulars. Some people delete the article not required, but that is not important. What is important is that the choice is correctly indicated in the contract particulars.

In February 2012, the JCT introduced the Named Specialist Update. This is a downloadable provision to allow specialist sub-contractors to be named and it was probably introduced to fill the gap that was left after the nominated sub-contract provisions were omitted when the SBC was issued in 2005. If it is intended to be used, the best way to incorporate it is to follow the guidance at the end of the update.

Contract particulars

Part 1

It is important that the contract particulars are completed so as to correspond precisely with the information given to the contractor at tender stage. If any changes were agreed for example, in the date of possession, the changed information must be faithfully recorded. The words 'to be agreed' or sometimes 'TBA' should be avoided. The best chance of agreement is always before, not after, the contract is signed. In some instances, leaving the entry blank will trigger a default position that may not be what is required. Most of the entries are self-evident, but special care should be taken with the following:

fourth recital and 4.7; **19**
- Whether the employer is a 'contractor' for the purposes of the Construction Industry Scheme. Generally, an employer will not be a contractor in this sense, but to make sure it is best to check with the legislation.
- Note the default position that if no deletions are made against a paragraph, that paragraph is to apply. Confusingly, if the Named Specialist Update has been incorporated and neither of the first two options has been selected, paragraph 7 does not apply.

eighth recital
- It should be noted that a deletion must be made to show whether arbitration is or is not to apply. If no deletion is made, arbitration will not apply (article 8).
- Enter the date by which the Works should be completed or a method of calculating the date for completion, e.g. '15 weeks from the Date of Possession'. If Sections are to be used, the previous entry must be deleted and dates inserted for each section. If one section is dependent on the completion of another, the date of the dependent section should be indicated by reference to the date of practical completion of the primary section, e.g. '5 days after practical completion of section 2'. The date for completion can then be indicated in relation to the date of possession, e.g., '10 weeks from

1.1
the Date of Possession of this section'.
- When entering the rate of liquidated damages, the period concerned, e.g. 'per day' or 'per week' must be stated. The phrase 'per week or part thereof'

must not be used. It does not, as commonly thought, mean that the damages are to be calculated pro-rata for part of a week. It means that the same damages are applicable for just one day as for a whole week; which is probably not enforceable. If the word 'Nil' is entered for the rate, no liquidated

20

2.32.2

damages will be recoverable. If the rate is left blank the position is uncertain. It may be that no damages can be recovered.

■ It should be noted that it is the *due date* of interim payments that is to be inserted, not the dates of the certificates themselves, which was the position

4.9.1

under SBC05.

6.4.1.2, 6.5.1,   ■ Decisions about levels of insurance and the like should be the subject of

6.7, 6.10, 6.12,   discussion between the employer and an insurance expert such as an

6.14 and 6.17   insurance broker. Few architects have any degree of expertise in insurance

21   matters and should refrain from advising the employer.

■ The employer may want to be able to assign the right to bring an action

7.2   against the contractor by a future purchaser or tenant. The default position is that the employer will have the right.

■ The periods of suspension referred to in various termination provisions

8.9.2, 8.11.1.1   must be entered. The default position is that the periods will each be

to 8.11.1.5   2 months.

■ An adjudicator can be named in the contract particulars. Whether or not that is done, the chosen nominating body must be indicated by deleting the

9.2.1   rest.

■ If arbitration has been chosen instead of legal proceedings, one of the bodies must be chosen to appoint the Arbitrator by deleting the rest. The default appointer is the President or a Vice-President of the Royal Institute of British Architects.

Part 2

This part must be completed carefully if third party rights or warranties from the contractor, or the sub-contractors, are to be provided. It is quite complex (see Chapter 2, Section 2.8).

■ Section (A) should be filled in with the names, class or description of the purchasers and/or tenants who are to be given rights. Identify the part of the Works to be let. It is important to state whether rights are to be con-

7C 7A   ferred as third party rights or as a collateral warranty. Third party rights is the default position.

■ Section (B) is to be filled in whether rights are to be conferred as third party rights or by collateral warranty. Clause numbers refer to both warranty

Schedule 5,   CWa/P&T or third party rights.

part 1   ■ Section (C) is to be filled in with the names, class or description of the funder who is to be given rights. The default position is that funder rights are not required from the contractor.

■ Section (D) is to be filled in whether third party rights or collateral warranty

Schedule 5,   is involved. Clause numbers refer to both warranty CWa/F or third party

part 2   rights. The default position is third party rights. Details of collateral warranties required from sub-contractors must be inserted in section (E) stating which warranty is required: SCWa/P&T – Purchaser / tenant; SCWa/F – Funder; SCWa/E – Employer. If a sub-contractor has been given design responsibility, the level of professional indemnity insurance must be stated.

Attestation

There are three attestation pages preceded by a page of mercifully brief notes. The attestation pages are simply the pages on which the parties to the contract sign to signify their agreement to the contract terms. 'Attestation' means the witnessing of an act or an event. When the parties attest, they are said to 'execute' the contract. There are three pages, because there are two options and four ways in which to carry out the second option. The first option is to execute the contract under hand (referred to as a 'simple' contract). The second option is to execute the contract as a deed (referred to as a 'specialty' contract. The differences are set out in Chapter 1, Section 1.1). The notes are very clear.

The conditions

It may be appropriate to amend certain of the clauses in this section:

- *Clause 1.1* Amend the definition of Public Holiday if a different definition is applicable.
- *Clause 1.11* Amend the clause if the law of England is not required.
- *Clause 6.8* If it is not possible for insurance to be taken out against all risks, the employer should consult an insurance broker or other expert for advice before the contract is completed.

3.4   Priority of documents

It is important to understand the relative importance of the various contract documents. This is crucial when there is a dispute and it is necessary to discover what was agreed. In various places, the contract refers to work and materials being (or perhaps not being) in accordance with the contract. That means in accordance with the contract documents as a whole. Unfortunately, it is common for parts of documents to be in conflict with other documents. That is particularly the case when they have been assembled in a hurry, perhaps after a long and difficult negotiation following tender stage.

1.3   The most important document is the printed form containing the articles, recitals, contract particulars and the conditions. If there is a conflict between this document and any other document, the printed form takes precedence. For example, if the bills of quantities state that the employer will have 21 days instead of 14 days from the due date in which to pay, that will not be effective unless the change has actually been made in the clause in the printed form.

It is not permissible to simply pick out a clause in isolation in order to prove a point. Unless they are in conflict, all the parts of the printed form must be

22   read together, because some clauses may qualify others. For example, the
            contractor's obligation to complete the Works by the date for completion must
            be read with the clause that requires the architect to give an extension of time
            in certain circumstances.

Work included

            Another related question concerns what work has been included in the Contract
            Sum. Is it the work shown on the contract drawings or is it the work measured
            in the bills of quantities? The answer is that it is the work measured in the bills

4.1   of quantities and, if relevant, in the CDP documents. Under this contract, the
            employer guarantees to the contractor that the bills of quantities and the
            Employer's Requirements in the CDP documents are accurate. If not, they are to

2.14   be corrected and the contractor will have the Contract Sum adjusted accordingly.

3.5   Errors, discrepancies and divergences

            The contract has quite a lot to say about this. It covers errors in the contract
            bills and the Employer's Requirements, discrepancies in or between any of the
            documents and divergences from statutory requirements.

Errors in the contract bills

            The bills of quantities must have been prepared in accordance with the SMM,
            unless they specifically state that something has been measured in a different

2.13.1   way. Therefore, an unspecified departure from the SMM amounts to an error.
            Other errors are if there is an error in description or in quantity or if items are

2.14.1   missing. If there is an error, it must be corrected. This kind of correction is to
            be treated as a variation. That should mean that there is no need for the archi-
            tect to issue an instruction about it. The quantity surveyor is to simply pick up
            the error and correct it in any valuation.

            Obviously, in order to deal with them, the quantity surveyor must be aware of
            errors and the contractor has a duty to give notice to the architect immediately it

2.15.1   becomes aware of any such error. Where the correction of an error results in an
            additional payment to the contractor, no doubt the contractor may be relied upon
            to go through the bills of quantities with a fine tooth comb. If the error is in the
            contractor's favour, there will be a temptation for the contractor not to notify the
            architect. Usually, the quantity surveyor will check the quantities as the valuations of
            work progress. What the contractor's obligation to notify means is discussed below.

Errors and discrepancies in the Employer's Requirements

            Under this contract, the contractor is not responsible for anything in the
            Employer's Requirements. In particular, it is not responsible for checking to see

2.13.2 ; **23**   that any design contained in the Employer's Requirements is 'adequate'. Very often Employer's Requirements include very substantial design of the project leaving the contractor with little more than to detail elements of construction. What this means is that the contractor is entitled to assume that the design will work and to proceed accordingly.

24

It is doubtful that the contractor is entitled to ignore a design error that is, or becomes, obvious. Indeed, it may well be that the contractor has already dealt with some design flaws in the Employer's Requirements when preparing the Contractor's Proposals. However, if any inadequacy in the Employer's Requirements comes to light that is not dealt with in the Contractor's Proposals, it must be corrected just as if it was an error in the bills of quantities. The major difference is that the correction of a design error on the part of the employer could well involve quite significant variation and cost, whereas an error in bills of quantities is often simply a matter of adding or subtracting quantities, although it could also of course be more complex than that.

People often get confused between an error in a document and a discrepancy. Errors in bills of quantities have been described earlier in this section. Although it might be said that all discrepancies are errors, it is obviously not the case that all errors are discrepancies. Where the contract refers to errors, the reference does not include discrepancies if, as here, discrepancies are dealt with separately.

If there is a discrepancy, rather than an error, in the Employer's Requirements and any properly instructed variation to them, the first thing is to examine the Contractor's Proposals. If the Contractor's Proposals deal with the matter and they are not at variance with statutory requirements, they are to be followed. For example, if the Employer's Requirements state that a conference room must be able to accommodate 60 people, but elsewhere require the accommodation to be for 100 people, that is a clear discrepancy. If the Contractor's proposals allow for 80 people, that is what the Contract Sum is deemed to include. If the employer wishes the accommodation to be for 60 or 100 people, the architect

3.14.3

must issue a variation instruction accordingly and the contractor is entitled to be paid for it in the usual way.

The word 'deemed' is often used where things are to be treated in a certain way although that is not quite correct, such as in this instance where the Contract Sum is deemed to include for 80 people even if it is possible to ascertain that it includes for more or less. Strictly, to deem something means to concede that it is not true but to treat it as being true. This word will be encountered several times.

25

If the Contractor's Proposals do not address the discrepancy, the contractor must amend its Proposals to address the issue. The architect, obviously after consulting the employer, has to decide whether to accept the amendment or to instruct a different method of addressing the discrepancy for which the con-

2.16.2

tractor is entitled to payment.

Discrepancies in general

If there is any discrepancy between the contract drawings, the bills, architect's instructions, further issued drawings and the CDP documents of which the contractor becomes aware, it must immediately notify the architect who must

2.15   issue instructions. With its notice, the contractor must include details of the discrepancy. Presumably this is to prevent the contractor simply stating that there is a discrepancy between drawing ABC and the bills of quantities and leaving the architect to look for it. Even without the express requirement for details, a contractor who behaved in that way could scarcely be said to have properly notified the architect.

Discrepancies in the Contractor's Proposals or the CDP Analysis

The Contractor's Proposals and the CDP Analysis will have been prepared by the contractor. Therefore, discrepancies in or between them are the contractor's responsibility to remedy. However, it is not for the contractor to remedy them in any way it sees fit. Because it may affect other parts of the Works, the contractor must first send to the employer a statement giving details of what it proposes in order to correct the discrepancy. The architect's duty to issue an instruction does not commence in this instance until the architect receives the contractor's statement. The contractor is obliged to comply with the architect's instruction and the employer will not have to pay any extra (described in the contract as being no 'addition to the Contract Sum') so long as the architect's instructions are solely addressed to the removal of the discrepancy. The architect does not have to accept the contractor's statement for correction of the discrepancy. The discrepancy may be complicated and the architect may give an instruction to correct the discrepancy in some other appropriate way. But if the architect's instructions go beyond what is necessary to correct the discrepancy, the employer will be responsible for paying for the additional work and/

2.16.1   or materials.

Divergences from statutory requirements

2.1   The obligation of the contractor is to comply with statutory requirements. The obligation would be there even if not specifically set out in the contract. The position about what the contract calls 'divergences' from statutory requirements is complicated by the possibility that the contractor has been given some design work to carry out.

Both architect and contractor have an obligation to notify each other if either is aware of a divergence between the contract drawings, the bills, architect's instructions, further issued drawings and the CDP documents and statutory requirements. If the CDP documents are involved, the contractor must addi-

2.17.1   tionally tell the architect how the divergence is to be removed. So it may be that it is the architect who finds the divergence between CDP documents and statutory requirements and notifies the contractor. It is then for the contractor to set out the solution to the problem.

The architect has 7 days to issue an instruction from becoming aware of the divergence or, in the case of a divergence involving the CDP, receiving the con-

2.17.2   tractor's solution. Obviously, every change has a cost. Usually, most of the project will have been designed by the architect and a divergence from statutory requirements will mean that the architect's instruction will vary the work to be carried out or the materials to be supplied. Although no doubt the architect will try to make the variation no more expensive than the original contract work, that may be difficult to achieve and the contractor will be entitled to payment of any additional cost.

If CDP work is involved

However, where the divergence concerns CDP work, it is the contractor's responsibility to see that the work and materials are compliant with statutory regulations. Therefore if they do not comply, the contractor is liable for the cost of amending the CDP documents to make them comply. The contract does not actually say that the architect must accept the contractor's solution even if, looked at objectively, it is adequate. The architect may prefer a different solution. The contract simply says that the contractor must comply with the architect's instruction at no cost to the employer.

Simply reading the contract, it appears that there is no limit to the content of the instruction issued by the architect and with which the contractor must comply at its own cost. In practice, it would be implied that the architect could not instruct a solution that cost the contractor substantially more to carry out than the contractor's own solution. For example, if the contractor's solution radically altered the appearance of the building, the architect would be entitled to issue an instruction that preserved the original appearance. Having said that, the precise circumstances would dictate the extent to which the contractor could be expected to spend additional money complying with the architect's instruction. The architect cannot simply take the opportunity to improve the building.

The only circumstance in which the contractor would not be liable for the cost is if the divergence results from a change in the statutory requirements themselves after the base date. In that case, the instruction will be treated as a normal instruction requiring a variation.

2.17.2.1

When a contractor is not liable for non-compliance

There is a somewhat misleading provision in the contract, although it is valuable to the contractor. It states that if:

- the contractor notifies the architect of any divergence of which it becomes aware, and
- if the contractor has carried out the Works in accordance with the contract documents and any architects instructions,

it will not be liable to the employer for any non-compliance with statutory requirements.

2.17.3

This does not apply to CDP work or to instructions varying CDP work. The provision is valuable to the contractor, because if it is required to rectify work that is non-compliant, it should be able to recover its costs from the employer.

The kind of situation envisaged is if the contractor notifies the architect of a divergence, but the architect instructs the contractor to carry on without change. Another situation would be if the contractor is not aware of the divergence but simply gets on with constructing the Works and it is later discovered that there is a divergence.

The provision is misleading, because the contractor's obligation to comply with statutory requirements prevails over any contractual provision. The contractor will still be liable for compliance so far as the local authority is concerned. The contractual provision stops short of indemnifying the contractor against non-compliance (see Chapter 12, Section 12.3 for an explanation of 'indemnity' and 'indemnify'). So if the local authority chose to take action against the contractor directly (probably unlikely), the contractor cannot rely on this provision of the contract to protect it.

3.6 Custody and copies

The contract documents must remain in the custody of the employer. The contractor must be allowed to inspect them at all reasonable times, but this stipulation appears to be redundant in the light of the fact that the architect must provide the contractor with a copy of the documents certified on behalf of the employer. It is essential that the copy is the same as the original. Very often, two sets of documents are prepared and all are signed by both parties, but contrary to the belief of some contractors it is not strictly necessary. The employer should check that the copy is the same as the original and sign the certificate, since that is the employer's responsibility. The certificate is usually inscribed on each document, including the drawings. Some architects favour a very elaborate pseudo-legal turn of phrase, but it is sufficient to state, 'I certify that this is a true copy of the contract document'.

The architect has a duty to supply the contractor with two copies (uncertified) of each of the contract documents and unpriced bills of quantities. These are for general use in the contractor's office and on site. The contractor must keep on site copies of all the contract documents and other issued information together with the master programme so that the architect or the architect's representative can see them.

The contract requires the architect to provide the contractor with further drawings and details, but they are not contract documents. They are intended merely to amplify the information contained in the contract documents. The drawings must be accurate and any revisions must be clearly identified. The obligation of the architect is to supply only such drawings and details as are reasonably necessary to enable the contractor to carry out and complete the Works in accordance with the conditions: i.e. among other things, to complete by the stipulated completion date or any extended date. It used to be thought that the architect was not entitled to delay provision of the details simply because it appeared unlikely that the contractor would be ready for them before the date for completion. That is not the situation now (see Chapter 5, Section 5.10).

2.8.1

2.8.2

2.8.3

*2.9, 2.11
and 2.12*
26

But it should be remembered that the contractor has grounds for extension of time or loss and/or expense if the architect delays the contractor (see Chapter 14, Section 14.3 and Chapter 16, Section 16.7).

3.7   Limits to use

None of the contract documents (or other documents such as additional drawings, details, schedules and architect's instructions) may be used by the contractor for any purpose other than the contract. The employer, the architect, and the quantity surveyor are prohibited from using any of the contractor's rates or prices in the contract documents, the Contract Sum analysis or the schedule of rates for any purpose other than the contract. None of the contrac-

2.8.4   tor's rates or prices must be divulged to third parties.

The prohibition against the use of documents by the contractor simply states expressly what is understood from the general law with regard to the architect's copyright.

The prohibition against divulging the contractor's rates is designed to protect the contractor's most precious possession – the ability to tender competitively and thus secure work. To divulge the rates to a competitor is probably one of the most harmful things that could be done to any contractor. In practice, it is extremely difficult for the contractor to ensure that such prices are not used. For example, the quantity surveyor my use them to help estimate the cost of some other current job.

There is no requirement for the contractor to return any drawings or details at the end of the contract. There is nothing to prevent the architect from asking for them in order to be sure that they will not be used for any other purpose and a clause can be incorporated in the preliminaries to the bills of quantities to that effect. The architect cannot require the contractor to return the certified copy of the contract documents, which will be needed for the contractor's own records. Realistically, the drawings and details issued to the contractor for use on site will usually be good for nothing but throwing away at the end of the project. Even then, they should be destroyed and not just simply put with waste paper.

3.8   Reckoning days

If something must be done within a certain number of days from a particular date, the period begins to be counted on the day after that date. Therefore, if something is to be done within 7 days from the 12th of a month, day one is the 13th and the last day for doing that action will be the 19th of that month. Days that are public holidays are excluded. Public holidays are defined in the con-

1.1   tract as 'Christmas Day, Good Friday or a day that under the Banking and Financial Dealings Act 1971 is a bank holiday'. If different public holidays apply, the definition should be amended to suit if necessary. It should be noted that Saturdays and Sundays are included in the calculation so that, in the example above, if the 12th is a Thursday, the last day of the 7 days will be the following Thursday if there are no public holidays in between.

The contract says nothing about what time on any particular day is the latest that the action can be considered done on that day. Commonsense ought to prevail and suggests that close of business should be the latest time. Unfortunately 'close of business' is not the same everywhere. Generally, one might say that close of business is 5.30 pm, but some businesses close at 5.00 pm and some stay open much later. The Civil Procedure Rules stipulate the latest times in connection with various communications, mostly connected with litigation. With the exception of a claim form (formerly known as a writ) the deemed time of service for a personal delivery, a fax or an e-mail if delivered, faxed or transmitted on a business day before 4.30 pm is on that day. If not sent on a business day or sent after 4.30 pm, deemed time of service is on the next business day. However, the Civil Procedure Rules are not binding unless litigation is in progress or envisaged.

3.9   Certificates, notices and other communications

Giving of notice simply means informing someone of something. Usually the 'notice' is in the form of a letter but, depending on what the parties to the contract agree, it might be acceptable to give notice by fax or e-mail, but not by text.

1.7

27

It must be in writing. A fax or e-mail is capable of being easily converted to a tangible document with writing or printing on it. That is not currently the case with texts.

It has been established by the courts that a requirement that the contractor notifies the architect if it becomes aware of a discrepancy does not impose an obligation on the contractor to actively search for discrepancies, but only to notify them if it becomes aware in the ordinary course of carrying out of the

28

Works.

The contract has quite a big clause dealing with the issue of notices and other

1.7

communications. It sets out the requirements for the giving or service of notices or other documents. The most important point is that all such communications that are specifically mentioned in the contract must be in writing. In an emergency, notice may be given orally, but it must be confirmed in writing as soon as reasonably practicable, which means as soon as, in practice, the person can

1.7.5

confirm it.

Specific notices

Certain notices (e.g. notices of default before termination and notices of termination) are to be served by means of delivery by hand, recorded signed for or

1.7.4

special delivery. In all other cases, service is to be by whatever method has been agreed. That kind of agreement should not be a casual thing. It is good practice to set out the acceptable methods in the preliminaries to the bills of quantities or, at least, to have the parties come to a formal agreement as soon as possible when it is known which tenderer has been successful. If nothing is agreed, any effective means may be used to send the communication to the address given in the contract particulars or to any notified address. If no address is available, service can be achieved by addressing the document to the last known principal business address or if the addressee is a body corporate, to that body's registered office or its principal office provided it is delivered by hand or prepaid

1.7.3   and sent by post.

Certificates

Certificates of all kinds must be issued to the employer with a copy to the contractor that must be sent at the same time. Putting a first class stamp on the employer's copy and a second class stamp for the contractor would be contrary to this requirement. In practice, certificates should always be sent by special delivery post for guaranteed delivery on a certain day.

3.10 Applicable law

1.12   The law applicable to the contract is to be the law of England even though the nationality, residence or domicile of any of the parties may be elsewhere. Where a different system of law is required, this clause must be amended. Therefore, if the Works are being carried out in Northern Ireland, the parties will wish the applicable law to be the law of Northern Ireland. Curiously, the applicable law of the three bonds in Schedule 6 of the contract has been stated to be the law of England and Wales since they were first introduced and there is no specific note to amend. However, parties who amend the law of the contract will doubtless, for consistency, wish to amend the applicable law of the bonds also. Although it may be argued that there is currently no real difference between the two jurisdictions, that situation may well change.

3.11 Common problems

If the architect refuses an instruction to resolve a discrepancy

Take a simple discrepancy between aluminium and brass door furniture. It says brass on the drawings but aluminium is in the bills of quantities. Some architects have a deep-seated fear of issuing instructions. It is common in this situation for an architect to argue that the drawings are what the contractor must follow and that he should have priced for brass, therefore, there is no need to issue an instruction. However, the contract is clear that the quality and quantity of work included in the Contract Sum (i.e. what the contractor has priced) is

4.1   what is in the bills of quantities. Therefore, the contract requires the architect to issue an instruction and failure to issue it is a breach of obligation on the part

2.15   of the architect. In that case, the contractor must follow the drawing and

2.14   correcting the error in description in the bills is to be treated as a variation.

If the discrepancy is that aluminium is in the bills but both aluminium and brass are noted on different drawings, the contractor must give notice to the architect who must issue an instruction. Failure to issue an instruction in these circumstances would entitle the contractor to delay ordering the ironmongery and, after completing all other work, to cease work. There would obviously be consequences in the form of extension of time and possible loss and/or expense for the contractor.

It is rare, but not unknown for a discrepancy to occur in the bills. But if brass and aluminium are both measured and if the drawings are silent on the subject, the architect must instruct which is required and omit the other. That will result in an omission of the value of the unwanted set of ironmongery.

Replacing the contract administrator with another of a different discipline

3.5.1

The contract says that if the contract administrator ceases to act for some reason, the employer must appoint another contract administrator as soon as reasonably practicable but certainly within 21 days. The contract simply refers to a 'replacement'. It sometimes occurs that an architect resigns and the employer appoints a building surveyor as a replacement. Or the contract administrator may be a quantity surveyor whom the employer replaces by an architect. Supposing the employer appoints a person who is unqualified or even attempts to appoint him or herself. The contract does not specifically say that an architect must be replaced by another architect or a surveyor by another surveyor or even by a suitably qualified person. Nevertheless, the contractor may feel uncomfortable and it is entitled to object.

A cogent argument against the employer being able to appoint a replacement contract administrator of a different discipline is that, as the name suggests, the contract administrator is the key figure in the administration of the contract. When pricing the job, the contractor will have taken the identity and discipline of the contract administrator into account. Although, when replacing, the employer cannot preserve the identity of the original contract administrator, there is no real difficulty in ensuring that the discipline and experience of the replacement is similar to the original. Therefore if the original appointment was an architect, the replacement should also be an architect. If the original was a building surveyor, the replacement should be the same.

If the original appointment was an architect, an additional point to consider is that throughout the contract the term(s) 'Architect/Contract Administrator' is used. The reason is that only a properly registered person may call them-

29

selves an 'architect'. It can be argued that if the original contract administrator was an architect, the term 'Architect/Contractor Administrator' is to be read as 'Architect'. Therefore, the appointment of a contract administrator who is not an architect is unlawful.

30

An employer who self-appoints to replace a contract administrator is behaving unlawfully. The contract administrator provides the contractor with a layer of protection. The employer cannot instruct the contract administrator to issue or withhold a certificate. The person appointed is not only acting as an agent with limited authority for the employer, but also as a decision maker. It is obviously quite wrong for the employer to suddenly take over that role. It is a different matter if the employer has indicated that he or she will act as contract administrator from the beginning so that the contractor can tender with that in mind. In that case the contractor has entered into the contract with its eyes open. An employer who does take on the role from the beginning must be aware that his or her actions will be closely scrutinised and that certificates issued will not have the same status as if issued by an independent contract administrator.

4

Related matters

4.1   The Housing Grants, Construction and Regeneration Act 1996 as amended

Background

Although this is one of the most significant pieces of legislation in recent years so far as construction contracts are concerned, it is quite startling how many members of the industry have no, or only an imperfect, grasp of its provisions. The Act was significantly amended by Part 8 of the Local Democracy, Economic Development and Construction Act 2009 that came into force on 1 October 2011.

Part II of the Act as amended is the important part so far as construction contracts are concerned. Nothing replaces a careful study of the Act, but what follows is a general survey of the principal provisions of Part II. Part II deals with construction contracts and every architect should have a copy. It is only a few pages long. Included in the definition of construction contracts is an agreement 'to do architectural, design, or surveying work, or … to provide advice on building, engineering, interior or exterior decoration or on the laying out of landscape in relation to construction operations'.

'Construction operations' are defined in some detail. Broadly they are the construction, alteration, repair, etc. of buildings, structures, roadworks, docks and harbours, powers lines, sewers and the like. They also include installation of fittings such as heating, electrical or air conditioning, external or internal cleaning carried out as part of construction and site clearance, tunnelling, foundations and other preparatory work and painting or decorating. Excluded are such things as drilling for natural gas, mineral extraction, manufacture of certain components, construction or demolition of plant where the primary activity is nuclear processing, effluent treatment or chemicals, construction of artistic works, sign writing and other peripheral installations. More importantly, it does not bite where one of the parties intends to take residence in the subject of the construction operations.

The provisions of the Act used to apply only to 'agreements in writing', but that has been removed by the 2009 Act and oral contracts are now caught by

The JCT Standard Building Contract 2011, First Edition. David Chappell.
© 2014 by David Chappell. Published 2014 by John Wiley & Sons, Ltd.

the Act. The Act requires that all construction contracts must include certain provisions. They are:

- *Adjudication*   Either party must have the right to refer disputes to adjudication with the object of obtaining a decision within 28 days of referral. 'Referral' is both the name of the claim document and the name used for giving the claim to the adjudicator and the other party. A party may give notice of intention to refer at any time and the referral must take place within 7 days. The 28-day deadline may be extended by up to 14 days if the referring party wishes or indefinitely if both parties agree. The adjudicator may take the initiative in finding out the facts and the law. In other words, the adjudicator does not have to wait until one party raises a point, but can ask for evidence. The adjudicator's decision is binding until the dispute is decided by litigation, arbitration or by agreement. The parties may agree to accept the adjudicator's decision as final. The adjudicator is not to be liable for acts or omissions unless there has been bad faith. The adjudicator has power to correct a decision to remove clerical and typing errors. Provisions dealing with the allocation of costs between the parties must be made after the notice of adjudication has been given. These provisions must be inserted in the contract in writing. Therefore, even if the contract is otherwise oral, this part must be written.
- *Stage payments*   A party is entitled to stage payments unless the duration of the project is less than 45 days. The parties are free to agree the intervals between payments and the amounts of such payments.
- *Date for payment*   Every contract must contain the means of working out the amount due and the date on which it is due and must provide a final date for payment. This must not depend on the contractor's performance on another contract. There is a strict notice regime to establish the amount that is to be paid.
- *Set-off*   Payment may not be withheld, nor money set-off unless notice has been given to pay less than the notified sum particularising the amount to be paid and the basis of calculation. The notice must be given no later than the prescribed period before the final date for payment.
- *Suspension of performance of obligations*   If the amount properly due has not been paid by the final date for payment and no effective notice withholding payment has been given, a party has the right, after giving a 7-day written notice, to suspend performance of obligations under the contract until payment has been made.
- *Pay when paid*   Except in cases of insolvency, a clause making payment dependent upon receipt of money from a third party is void. This is intended to outlaw the so-called 'pay-when-paid clause', but it may not be sufficient to do so. It does not take effect if the third party is insolvent.

If that a construction contract does not include these provisions, the Scheme for Construction Contracts (England and Wales) Regulations 1998 as amended by the Scheme for Construction Contracts (England and Wales) Regulations 1998 (Amendment) (England) Regulations 2011 comes into effect just as if the clauses contained in the Scheme were written into the contract. Most standard form construction contracts and all the RIBA terms of engagement comply with the Act and, therefore, the Scheme is not relevant where such terms are used.

4.2   Entire contracts

In a situation where the second mate of a ship had contracted to sail from Jamaica to Liverpool for the sum of thirty guineas, he served for only seven weeks on the voyage, but just before the ship docked at Liverpool, he died. A court held that his widow was entitled to nothing since he had not completely
34   carried out what he had undertaken to do. From this comes the principle of an entire contract where one party's obligations have to be entirely fulfilled before it is entitled to any payment at all. Strictly, under contracts where a contractor undertakes to do work for a fixed sum, nothing is due until the whole of the
35   work has been completed.

In the 1880s, a builder undertook to build a house, but abandoned the project half-way through. A court held that he was entitled to nothing for the work
36   he had done. If the roles had been reversed so that it was the employer who had refused to let the contractor complete, the contractor would have had the option of charging for the work on a *quantum meruit* (see Section 4.6) basis or of claiming damages that would have included all the profit it would have made on the job.

That harsh rule has been softened so far as construction work is concerned
37, 38   by two ideas: 'divisible contracts' and 'substantial completion'.

Divisible contracts simply means that, although on the face of it there may appear to be only one contract, in reality it can relate to distinct operations, such as completion of the foundations, work below ground level and so on. Substantial completion refers to completion even though there were minor defects and/or some minor work still to be done. JCT contracts use the term 'Practical Completion' and the meaning is explained later (see Chapter 21, Section 21.1).

In construction contracts, a contractor who stops work part way through a building contract is entitled to be paid the value of the work done up to the stopping point less the extra costs of completing the building as a result of the stoppage.

Conferring a benefit

Contractors frequently believe that even if they do not comply exactly with the contract, they are entitled to be paid if they confer some benefit on the employer. They fall into the same error as did a shipyard that did repairs to a ship under a lump sum contract in the late nineteenth century. There, the shipyard did not comply with the contract specifications, but instead did work that was more expensive and used better materials. It was held that they could recover

39   nothing. English contract law is based upon what the parties promise, not on benefit given or received. The idea that someone is entitled to some payment for providing something other than was agreed is applicable only where the other party has an option to accept or reject. A judge in an old case said 'If a man, unsolicited, cleans my shoes, what can I do but put them on?'

Of course, it is possible for any contract to be varied with the consent of the other party or for any departure from the specification to be ratified subsequently; but in the absence of either, a contractor who provides something other than what was agreed is entitled to nothing even though the contractor may have expended considerable sums and enriched the owner.

4.3   Express and implied terms

It is important to understand the difference between express and implied terms. An express term is printed or written in the contract or a term that the parties have agreed orally at the time they made the contract. Before considering in detail the express contractual obligations in SBC, it is necessary to consider whether there are any terms that the law will write into the contract.

Implied terms

A term of a contract that the parties to that contract did not expressly agree either in writing or orally and that is not inconsistent with the other express terms and that the law holds is part of the bargain and is binding on the parties as if it were expressly incorporated into the contract is called an implied term. Terms may be implied in various ways:

- By Statute, e.g.; under the Supply of Goods and Services Act 1982 and the Sale of Goods Act 1979. In appropriate circumstances important terms as to fitness, quality, price and the like may be implied into a contract.
- At common law where, for example, unless there is any exclusion or express term to the contrary, certain warranties will be implied warranties; e.g., that a contractor will supply good and proper materials and will provide completed work that is constructed in a good and workmanlike manner.
- A term will be implied where necessary to make the contract work.
- If the contract as it stands is perfectly workable but if the parties obviously intended something to be included, but it was not made an express term, then a term to that obvious effect will be implied. In deciding whether or not such a term should be implied the question will be whether it can be said confidently that if at the time the contract was being negotiated someone had said to the parties, 'What will happen in such and such a case?' They would have replied: 'Of course, so and so will happen; we did not trouble to say that; it is too clear.'
- Unless the express terms of the contract stipulate something different, a term will be implied if the courts have already laid down that in particular types of agreement certain terms will automatically be implied. Therefore,

under SBC there will be an implied term that the employer, and the architect on the employer's behalf, will do all that is necessary to enable the contractor to carry out the work and that the Architect will provide the contractor with accurate drawings and information.

- By custom and usage, e.g.; if it has invariably been the longstanding practice in a particular trade, profession or business, then unless the parties have expressly stated to the contrary they will be presumed to have contracted with the intention of operating the agreement according to that custom.
- If the parties have consistently, regularly and invariably entered into previous agreements on certain terms and conditions then it may be taken that in future dealings of the same kind, unless expressly provided to the contrary, they are conducting their business on similar terms to those used in their previous course of dealings.

There are important and often ignored limits to when terms will be implied. A term will not, for example, be implied merely because a court thinks it would be reasonable to insert it into the contract. Even where one or other of the situations referred to above may arise, terms will generally be implied only if it is not in conflict with or inconsistent with an express term and it must be based on the presumed intention of the parties.

Implied terms that were written into the Sale of Goods Act 1893 were those that existed in common law before the law relating to the sale of goods was codified into statute. So far as dwellings are concerned, their construction is subject to the provisions of the Defective Premises Act 1972. This statute probably imposes greater obligations on developers, contractors, sub-contractors, architects or engineers than are contained in SBC. Section 1(1) states:

> 'Any person taking on work for or in connection with the provision of a dwelling ... owes a duty to see that the work that he takes on is done in a workmanlike manner, with proper materials ... and so as to be fit for the purpose required ...'

Apart from legislation, the courts have progressively implied in all building contracts terms that 'the builder will do his work in a good and workmanlike manner; that he will supply good and proper materials; and that it will be reasonably fit for the purpose required.'

40

4.4   Limitation periods

The law recognises that there has to be a limit on the length of time after the event that someone can bring an action through the courts for redress. The Limitation Act 1980 specifies a limitation of six years for actions based on simple contract. That is to say that if one party commits a breach of contract, the other party has six years from the date of the breach in which to issue a claim form (what used to be known as a 'writ').

The right to sue

One thing that is not always understood is that the Limitation Act does not extinguish the right to sue: it merely limits the period within which any particular claimant must commence the action if the claimant is not to be barred by lapse of time, often referred to as being 'time barred' or 'statute barred'. Therefore, the claimant can sue even twenty years after the breach of contract. It is up to the defendant to raise the limitation point in the defence. If the point is not raised, the claimant can carry on with the legal action.

In the case of a breach of contract the right to sue begins when the breach of contract takes place, whether the claimant knows of it or not. Under a building contract, a court has held that a contractor has two separate obligations. The first is to carry out the work in accordance with the contract during the course of the contract. If the contractor is in breach of this obligation it means that the employer can sue as a breach occurs. The second obligation is to complete the Works in accordance with the contract. A distinct breach of contract does

41   not occur in that respect until practical completion has been certified. Therefore, in the case of a long contract where the breach of contract occurs in the early stages, it is not fatal if no action is taken in the first instance. Time will not start to run under the second obligation until practical completion.

Length of period

A contract entered into as a deed has a twelve-year limitation period. A simple contract just signed by the parties has a six-year limitation period. Generally speaking, therefore, a contractor can be sure that six years after it has completed any particular work no legal action can be successfully brought against the contractor for breach of contract unless the contract is executed as a deed when the period will be twelve years.

It is clear, therefore, that there are advantages for every employer to require the main contractor to enter into a contract as a deed. If the contractor does so, it should ensure that every sub-contractor, whether named or domestic, does the same.

Exceptions to the rule

There are two exceptions to the limitation position:

42   ■ The Limitation Act 1980 provides that time will not start to run if the claimant's right of action has been concealed by the fraud of the defendant Normally, in law 'fraud' involves moral obliquity, a deliberate intention to cheat. However, the courts have tended to interpret this fairly widely to include cases where they believed it would have been inequitable to allow the defendant to rely on the statutory defence provided by Parliament. Where a contractor has committed a breach of contract of which it was

43   unaware, it may still be able to rely on the limitation defence.

■   If the contractor has given indemnities to the employer under the insurance
clauses of the contract, the limitation period may consequently be effectively
extended.

4.5   Letters of intent

Absence of a signed contract

For some reason, which is not always very clear, many projects commence on
site before the building contract has been signed (strictly one should say 'has
been executed'). It may be that the architect or quantity surveyor has not finished filling in and assembling all the parts of the contract documents, it may
be that there are still things that have not been agreed, or it may be that one or
other of the parties has just not got around to signing. It is always dangerous to
start work on site before the contract is signed, but to do so before everything
is agreed is suicidal for both parties. Usually, there really is no excuse for the
failure to execute the contract before commencement. In the absence of a
signed contract, the employer will often send or more likely ask the architect to
send to the contractor what is known as a 'letter of intent'.

What is a letter of intent?

The idea of a letter of intent in its simplest form is that the employer is writing
to the contractor to say that the tender (perhaps after negotiation) seems satisfactory and that the employer intends to accept it, but that for one reason or
another it cannot be accepted yet and that if the contractor starts work, the
employer will see that it is paid at the rates in the bills of quantities until the
contract is signed. It may then go on to say that the amount of work the contractor can carry out in this way is limited to £X and that the employer can stop
the work at any time. Crucially, the letter should make clear that it is not to be
considered as accepting the contractor's tender nor is it forming a binding
building contract.

It is quite extraordinary the number of cases in which contractors start work
on the basis of a 'letter of intent'. The dangers are:

■   Instead of being a letter of intent, the letter may actually be an acceptance
of the contractor's tender and a binding contract is formed before the
employer, and possibly the contractor, is ready.
■   It may be a letter of intent, but may itself contain complicated provisions
that amount to the parties entering into a contract under the letter of intent
that is disadvantageous to one or the other. Some letters of intent are many
pages long – which misses the point of a letter of intent that should be a
short and simple document.
■   It may be a straightforward simple letter of intent. That itself is a problem,
because the employer or the contractor will probably be able to simply walk
away from the work if they are not happy and that could be very awkward

for the other. Neither would be in breach of contract if the letter does not bind them to continue working.

If the letter of intent is a contract

There may be rare occasions when a letter of intent may be what is strictly a unilateral contract, but which the courts seem to describe as 'if' contracts. An 'if' contract, as the name suggests, is one where I say to a person 'if you wash my car, I will give you £10'. If the person washes my car, there is a contract binding me to pay £10.

A letter of intent may be a continuing offer: 'if you start this work, we will pay you suitable remuneration.' This creates no obligation on the other party to do the work and if it does it, there are no express or implied warranties as to its quality. Damages can never be awarded for breach of contract of a unilateral contract, because there is no obligation on the person to whom the promise is made.

Starting work on the basis of a letter of intent or terms incorporated by reference are, therefore, recipes for litigation. It is far better for an employer and a contractor at an early stage to enter into a formal agreement in the current JCT or other form accepted by both parties.

44

4.6   Quantum meruit

The words '*quantum meruit*' are often encountered in connection with construction work. They literally mean 'as much as is deserved'. They are often used instead of *quantum valebat*, which means 'as much as something is worth'. It is rare for a distinction to be drawn between the expressions. The words are used in four different situations:

- If work is done under a contract that has no terms stating the amount to be paid. That would never be the case under a standard form contract such as SBC provided all the necessary parts have been completed. It sometimes occurs if a contract has been formed just by exchange of correspondence.
- If there is an agreement simply to pay a reasonable sum.
- If work is carried out under what was assumed to be a valid contract, but that turns out to be void and, therefore, inapplicable.
- If work is carried out by one party at the request of another, e.g., following a letter of intent.

A court will not order a *quantum meruit* to be paid if the contract clearly provides for payments of a specified amount or where, as in JCT contracts, there is a mechanism in the contract to determine the amount. An architect cannot certify anything other than what the JCT contract authorises. Therefore, unless the employer specifically authorises it, the architect cannot certify *quantum meruit* payments. The payment on a *quantum meruit* basis is not to be taken to mean that payment will be calculated on a 'cost plus' basis with an allowance for profit, but rather on the basis of a fair commercial rate.

45

4.7   Limited companies

Types

The phrase 'limited company' really means 'limited liability company'. There are two types of limited company:

- A private limited company.
- A public limited company.

An important difference between them is that members of the public can buy and sell shares in a public limited company. In general, a private limited company may only offer shares to existing shareholders unless all shareholders agree to offer them to some other person. They are not traded on the stock exchange. A company is governed by the Companies Act 2006 that replaces most of the Companies Acts 1985 and 1989. It comes into existence only after registration by the Registrar of Companies. From that time, it can act only in accordance with the Acts. If the company carries out transactions before registration, they may be treated as the transactions of a partnership.

Important points

A private limited company can be tailor-made by a solicitor quite inexpensively. It is even cheaper to buy a company 'off the shelf'. Such companies are ready formed. All the paper work is complete and they generally have a code name. After purchase it is a relatively simple matter to change the name.

The liability of the members (shareholders) is limited to the nominal value of the share holding. What that means is that if the company is faced with a debt that is greater than the company's assets, the company can be wound up and the shareholders lose their shares but they have no further liability. However, the Insolvency Act 1986 provides severe penalties for directors who continue to trade whilst insolvent. The court has power to order them to contribute to the company's debts out of personal assets. There are other measures the court may order against culpable directors for example that after insolvency liquidation, a former director may not be involved in the formation of a company with a similar name for a period of five years.

Position on insolvency

A key point is that when the shareholders form a company, they are creating a separate legal entity like another person: different from directors and shareholders. Contracts are made with the company, not with its directors or shareholders. Although a director may incur personal liability by making incautious statements, the situations where a director becomes personally liable to the other party to a contract with the limited company are quite rare. Therefore, if either party to a contract is a limited company, it is important to try and establish that the company is financially stable. Whereas if an individual or partnership (excluding limited liability partnerships that in many ways are akin to limited companies) is unable to pay its debts, the persons concerned can be pursued for their personal wealth, a company is quite different. If a company cannot pay its debts, it may be wound up and then the directors and shareholders can walk away with their personal wealth intact unless they have made themselves personally liable for some of the debt by giving a personal guarantee to a bank.

Danger points

There are some people who form companies for a particular project in the knowledge that they can liquidate it (i.e. wind it up) if the financial pressures become too great. On the face of it, there is nothing illegal about that, although in certain cases it could become fraud, but obviously anyone dealing with such a company must take care. Architects must always be careful not to over-certify, but this is especially important if the contractor is a limited company with limited assets. Modern JCT contracts always contain provision for the company registration number to be inserted after the name. That is to enable a company to be readily identified. A company can be created and can change its name with ease, but it cannot change its number.

Before it became common to insert company registration numbers in a contract, the author encountered a situation where a contractor operated two companies with the same shareholders and directors. The headed paper was identical except for the company name and the registration number (in small print at the bottom of the sheet). One company was asset rich, the other had no assets. The asset-rich company was involved in negotiations to secure a building contract and it was successful on the basis of its long and impressive track record. Some months after the contract was signed, it was discovered that the two companies had swapped names prior to signing and the contract was actually signed by the company without assets.

4.8 Bonds

A bond is a special kind of agreement that is usually executed as a deed. The person giving the bond is usually called the surety and is often a bank or insurance company. The surety agrees to be answerable to a third party for the debt or the default of another party. In this context, the third party is normally the employer and the party on whose behalf the surety is giving the bond is usually the contractor. The employer is usually referred to as the beneficiary. Since the bond is a guarantee, it must be in writing. Sometimes, and increasingly nowadays, a bond will state that it remains in force no matter what changes may be made to the building contract between the employer and the contractor. Without such provisions, changes to the building contract after the date of the bond may discharge the surety from its liability under the bond unless the changes are made with the surety's agreement.

Types of bond

There are various types of bond, but in general their purpose is to guarantee payment of a stipulated sum as compensation for non-performance of some contractual obligation. The contract makes provision for three different kinds of bonds and includes sample documents:

- Advance payment bond.
- Off-site materials and goods bond.
- Retention bond.

Each of these bonds are mentioned in later chapters. Another type is the performance bond.

Performance bond

The one, very common, bond not mentioned in the contract is the performance bond. A performance bond is a bond in which a surety indemnifies the employer against the contractor's failure to perform the contract. Performance bonds are usually for 10% of the Contract Sum and the employer pays the premium as part of the tendered price. The wording of bonds is relatively standard, but there are some differences and some specially drafted versions that can lead to difficulties in interpretation.

On demand or on default

Bonds are theoretically of two types: 'on demand' or 'on default'. The most common are 'on demand' bonds. They are favoured by banks called upon to provide bonds. That is because, on receiving a demand that complies with the criteria set out in the bond, the surety is entitled to pay without the necessity of carrying out any kind of investigation. In other words, it does not have to decide whether the demand is valid. The surety will not be too concerned as it will have ensured that it had security from the contractor for such an eventuality and will therefore not be out of pocket.

In contrast, 'on default' bonds (sometimes called 'conditional' bonds) require the beneficiary (the party in whose favour the bond is made – usually the employer) to prove to the satisfaction of the surety that a default, within the bond's criteria, has occurred. This can become an expensive exercise for the surety that is placed in the position of having to make a judgment when a judgment of the court on the same issue may be issued at a later date.

Bonds are often written in archaic language that makes them difficult to understand even for lawyers. In trying to decide whether a bond is on demand or on default, a court will look at the whole document and not just at a few words. They will look at its commercial purpose. There is a presumption that a bond provided by a bank will be on demand. On the other hand, the fact that the bond includes the word 'on demand' is not conclusive.

46, 47
48

Parent company guarantee

This is a special kind of bond given, as the name suggests, by a holding or parent company in respect of the company being guaranteed. Although one of the dangers with doing business with a limited company is that it may liquidate, leaving creditors high and dry, this is not as likely when a guarantee is being provided by a company that itself holds the fate of several other companies in its hands. The board of directors may be prepared to let a subsidiary company liquidate if its is struggling against worsening debts, but they are unlikely to let the holding company go.

This kind of bond may also be on demand or on default and whether it is one or the other is often decided in the courts.

49

4.9   Common problems

Providing a bond before start on site

Where a performance bond is required, there is usually something in the bills of quantities that requires the contractor to provide it before starting on site. Often, a contractor will not provide it immediately, but will do so some weeks later. Occasionally, the bond is not provided at all and there may be serious consequences if the bonded money is needed to complete the Works after the contractor has defaulted. It is not lawful to withhold certificates until the bond has been produced. One way to get over the problem is to make the contractor's possession of the site dependent upon first having produced the bond. Obviously, there has to be wording inserted in the extension of time, loss and/ or expense and termination provisions to prevent the contractor gaining some advantage by withholding the bond. In practice, many employers are not prepared to wait until a bond is produced before allowing the contractor onto the site. Once the contractor is on site, there is very little that the architect can do to make the contractor produce the bond. An architect who raises and records the matter at each site meeting and writes letters to the contractor demanding the bond and chases the contractor at every opportunity, is unlikely to be found negligent.

50

The importance of contractors and architects understanding legislation

It is quite amazing that many architect seem to have a very limited knowledge of the Housing Grants, Construction and Regeneration Act 1996 (as amended), commonly known as the 'Construction Act'. It is amazing because sizeable chunks of building contracts and terms of engagement are based on the Act. Moreover, the relevant part of the Act is only about 7 or 8 pages long and easily obtainable on the web. Many architects still choose to enter into terms of engagement by sending their own letter to the client setting out their terms. Very often, these terms are not only insufficient to satisfy the Code of Conduct of both the RIBA and the ARB, but are also insufficient to comply with the Act. The result is that the relevant terms of the Scheme for Construction Contracts in (England and Wales) Regulations 1998 (as amended) will take effect. Needless to say, even fewer architects and other professionals have read, or even heard of, the Scheme.

These gaps in knowledge usually come to the fore when a dispute arises and the architect, perhaps relying on his or her own letter of engagement, asserts something only to be informed that the relevant legislation overturns that particular something in the letter. This is usually a very expensive stage to discover this kind of thing.

In many instances, lack of knowledge of legislation, for example the Building Regulations, will be indicative of professional negligence. A few years ago, an architect enquired what the CDM Regulations were as she thought she ought to have a 'rough idea' of them.

Legislation, such as the Unfair Terms in Consumer Contracts Regulations 1999 or the Late Payment of Commercial Debts (Interest) Act 1998, are very important and every architect should have read them and know the general thrust of them. In some cases a detailed knowledge is important. Legislation is often difficult to read. It is not fun. It often seems to be drafted as obscurely as humanly possible. Masses of cases go through the courts endeavouring to explain just what various bits of legislation mean. But often, it is possible to get summaries or reviews of the Acts and Regulations and all the construction professions should make sure that they are up to date.

Part II   Participants

5   The architect's powers and duties

5.1   What the architect can do or must do

There is a myth prevalent among architects and contractors that the architect has what might best be termed 'general powers' under SBC to do whatever, in the architect's professional wisdom, it is appropriate to do. That is quite simply wrong. The contract sets out in detail what the architect has the power to do and also what the architect has an obligation to do. The architect can do nothing that is not set out in the contract. In addition, it is not very well understood by contractors and, it must be said, by architects, that the architect has little room for the exercise of discretion under SBC. As one judge memorably said of the architect's discretion: 'It is circumscribed almost to the point of extinction'. An architect recently said that although the contract stated that certificates should be at monthly intervals, he had issued a further certificate after two weeks, because he deemed it reasonable to do so. Clearly, that architect was guilty of professional negligence and breach of his obligations to his client. Yet the myth remains that the architect can ignore the terms of the contract and act as sole arbiter in such matters. The architect's powers and duties are set out in Tables 5.1 and 5.2, respectively.

The duties laid on an architect under SBC serve two purposes: they limit the architect's authority in relation to the contractor and they limit the area in which the architect is acting as authorised agent of the employer. The architect is simply the administrator of the contract with no power to modify or supplement the terms of the contract as agreed between the parties.

3.5.1   If either architect or quantity surveyor ceases to act for any reason, the employer must nominate a replacement within 21 days. The language is depressingly convoluted, but effectively the contractor has 7 days from receiving notice of the nomination in which to object. The reason for the objection must be capable of being thought sufficient by an adjudicator, arbitrator or

51

The JCT Standard Building Contract 2011, First Edition. David Chappell.
© 2014 by David Chappell. Published 2014 by John Wiley & Sons, Ltd.

3.5.2

judge as appropriate. There is an additional proviso in the case of a replacement architect. A replacement architect is not entitled to disregard or overrule any certificate, opinion, decision, approval or instruction given by the former architect. The proviso clearly cannot mean that certificates or instructions given by the former architect cannot be changed – even if wrong. The proviso is there so that if it is necessary for the successor architect to make changes, they will be treated as variations and the contractor will be entitled to payment accordingly. For example, if the former architect had given instructions for the construction of a detail that, in the opinion of the new architect, would lead to trouble, the new architect could issue further instructions correcting the matter and the contractor would be paid for the rectification work.

5.2   Specific requirements under the JCT contract

The duties laid on an architect under SBC serve two purposes: they set out the architect's authority in relation to the contractor and they limit the ways in which the architect is acting as authorised agent of the employer.

The contract administrator need not be an architect, although traditionally architects have been identified as taking that role. During the contract period, the architect has a great many powers and duties. Key powers and duties are:

- The issue of drawings, information.
- The inspection of work and its certification for payment.
- The issue of instructions in regard to variations, postponement and defective work.
- The certification of practical completion.
- Inspection and listing of defects appearing with the rectification period.
- Certification that the contractor has made good the defects.
- The issue of the final certificate stating the amount due to the contractor or to the employer.

5.3   Powers

The architect's powers are the things that the contract says the architect 'may' do – meaning that the architect can choose whether or not to do something. They are list in table 5.1.

5.4   The architect's design role under SBC

The designer of a building has the same liabilities as any other person – the designer may have liabilities in contract or in tort (see Chapter 1, Section 1.1 for a brief description of tort).

Table 5.1   Powers of the architect under SBC.

Clause	Power	Comment
2.3.4	may request contractor to provide reasonable proof that materials or goods comply with contract kinds and standards.	
2.10	instruct that errors arising from contractor's inaccurate setting out be not amended.	a deduction is to be made from the Contract Sum.
2.16.2	agree amendment when discrepancy found in Employer's Requirements.	if Contractor's Proposals do not deal with it.
2.24	consent to the removal of unfixed goods or materials.	consent must not be unreasonably delayed or withheld.
2.28.4	reduce extension to take account of omissions.	after the first extension is given.
2.38.2	issue instructions for defects to be made good.	not after the issue of the schedule of defects or 14 days after the expiry of the rectification period.
2.38	instruct that defects are not to be made good.	if employer consents.
3.1	authorise any person to have right of access to workshops and premises.	at all reasonable times.
3.7	give consent in writing to sub-contract work or, if relevant CDP design.	consent must not be unreasonably delayed or withheld.
3.11	issue notice to contractor to comply with instructions.	contractor has 7 days to comply or employer may employ and pay others and an appropriate deduction is to be made from the Contract Sum.
3.12	confirm instructions in writing.	instructions other than in writing are to be of no immediate effect until confirmed in writing by either architect or contractor.
3.14	issue instructions to vary the Works or restrictions or, for CDP work, to vary the Employer's Requirements.	architect may sanction unauthorised variations.
3.15	issue instructions to postpone work.	
3.17	issue instructions on testing or inspection of work or materials.	the cost is to be added to the Contract Sum unless the work is found to be not in accordance with the contract.

(continued)

Table 5.1   *(Cont'd)*

Clause	Power	Comment
3.18.1	issue instructions requiring removal of defective work and materials from the site.	note: not to rectify the work.
3.18.2	allow defective work to remain,	after consultation with contractor and the agreement of employer.
3.18.3	issue instructions for variations necessary after a clause 3.18.1 instruction.	after consultation with contractor.
3.18.4	issue instructions for further tests or opening up following discovery of non-compliance.	after consulting the code of practice in Schedule 4.
3.19	issue instructions as reasonably necessary.	if work is not carried out in a proper and workmanlike manner, or is not in accordance with the construction phase plan and after consultation with contractor.
3.21	issue instructions requiring the exclusion of any person from the site.	must not be issued unreasonably or vexatiously.
4.12.5	give a pay less notice on behalf of the employer.	not later than 5 days before the final date for payment.
5.3.1	in an instruction for a variation, request contractor to provide a quotation.	contractor has 7 days to object to the procedure.
5.3.2	give a further instruction that the variation is to be carried out and valued by valuation.	if contractor objects.
6.12.3	request contractor to produce evidence of CDP professional indemnity insurance.	the request must be reasonable.
8.4.1	give notice to contractor specifying one or more of 5 possible defaults	if contractor does not rectify the default within 14 days, employer may give notice of termination of contractor's employment.
Schedule 1, para 1	agree to vary contractor's obligation to submit 2 copies of its design documents.	if the means and format are not stated in the Employer's Requirements.

Reasonable skill and care

An architect, an engineer or any other professional designer must exercise
reasonable skill and care. A designer, unless also providing the end product,
is not required to guarantee the result. The standard of skill and care of a
professional person was laid down over fifty years ago

52
53

54

> 'it is sufficient if he exercises the ordinary skill of an ordinary competent man exercising that particular art.'

An architect will be considered to be acting correctly if acting with the kind of skill an average architect would display. In order to decide such issues, the court listens to expert evidence from other designers on the matter in question. It is not always sufficient for a designer to be able to maintain that he or she simply did the same as other designers were doing if it can be shown that generally

55

accepted practice is not correct. The fact that the vast majority of architects acted in a particular way is irrelevant if it can be demonstrated that it was unreasona-

56

ble, illogical or irresponsible for the particular architect to act in that way

On the other hand, the standards to be applied to a professional person will be the standard at the time the professional acted and not the standards com-

57

monly practised at some time after the act. Therefore, an architect whose design proves to be defective, is entitled to say that, at the time the design was done, no other architect knew of the fact that caused the problem. This is usually referred to as the 'state of the art' defence.

Another factor is that a particular architect will be judged on the basis of the skills that architect professes to have. Therefore, if an architect says that he or she has special expertise in the design of museum buildings, a failure in that design will be compared to the performance of other architects who have that special expertise, whether or not the original architect does in fact have such expertise. This is something that must be remembered when architects are talking to clients and possibly exaggerating their experience and capabilities in order to secure a commission.

The designer's responsibility does not always end when the design is completed and handed to the builder. If the architect is engaged to administer the contract as under SBC, there is a continuing responsibility to review the design

58

and revise it if any problems become apparent at least up to practical completion of the Works. This duty probably ends after the designer's initial involvement ends so that the designer is not burdened with the responsibility of

59

reviewing designs for an infinite period of time.

The terms of a contract between an architect and the client will usually include a term that the architect will use reasonable skill and care in the execution of duties under the contract. Such a term will usually be express, but if not express, it will be implied because anyone holding him or herself out as an architect warrants by implication the possession of the necessary ability and skill.

Whether an architect is liable if a client misuses the design depends on whether the kind of misuse is reasonably foreseeable. If it is reasonably foreseeable, the architect will be expected to have taken that into account in the design.

60

If not reasonably foreseeable, the architect will not be liable for the misuse.

New methods or materials

Some architects pride themselves on being the first to try out new methods of construction or materials. This is a dangerous path to follow and such architects will be just as liable for design failures as in the case of a failure while using well-tried methods and materials. The architect is not entitled to blame a general lack of knowledge. That is not to say that new methods or materials should never be used. If that was the case, we would all still be living in caves. But special care is needed before new techniques are put into operation. Architects wishing to try out new things must get the express (preferably written) agreement of their clients. Clients should be put completely in the picture and acquainted with all the known advantages and disadvantages before agreeing. Moreover, the architect is under a continuing duty to check that the method or materials work in practice.

61

62

Fitness for purpose

The law will require a professional person, such as an architect or an engineer, to exercise reasonable skill in care in the performance of his or her duties. This standard is also required of the designer by the Supply of Goods and Services Act 1982 in respect of any contract for the supply of design services. But this statutory duty can be displaced by the imposition of a stricter duty in a contract.

The stricter duty is normally what is known as 'fitness for purpose'. That a duty may be stated in a contract in those words, or words to the same effect, or it will usually be implied if the contract is on the basis of work and materials unless it is clear that the employer is not relying on the contractor.

63

If an employer relies on a contractor to provide an entire building and there is no independent designer involved, a term of reasonable fitness for purpose will be implied irrespective of any negligence or fault or whether the unfitness results from the quality of work or materials or from defects in the design.

64

Where a JCT traditional standard form is being used, such as SBC, the contractor will have no design liability at all unless expressly stated to be part of the contractor's designed portion (CDP). In SBC, it is made clear that in carrying out the design of the CDP, the contractor's responsibility is reasonable skill and care.

65

2.19.1

Employee's liability

So far as a client is concerned, a firm of architects is responsible for the actions of its employees carried out in the course of employment. But an architect employee who produces a negligent design is liable to the firm of architects. The fact that, in practice, professionals in employment do not carry personal professional indemnity insurance will probably ensure that it is not worthwhile for the firm to sue them. However, the employee may become exposed if he or she carries out negligent design for which the firm is sued. The firm's PI insurers will be expected to pay out any successful claim, but having done so the insurers are entitled to exercise the right of subrogation; that is to stand in the shoes of the firm and sue the person responsible for the negligence. Professional employees will want to be assured that there is a waiver of the insurer's subrogation rights for their benefit in their firm's policy.

66

Specified items and sub-contractors

Architects often ask the question whether they are responsible for the design of everything they specify, such as roof trusses or door handles or standard windows frames. The answer is broadly: Yes. The architect is responsible for the whole of the design of a building unless the client has given express consent to part of the design being assigned or transferred to another party such as a consultant or a sub-contractor.

67

Some architects think that *design* refers only to what is drawn. That is certainly what a lay person probably thinks; an architect should know better. When the architect specifies something, he or she must use reasonable skill and care to see that the specified thing acts as it is intended to do. That is the case whether the architect is specifying fill material under a concrete floor or a special door closer. It is the architect's job to be satisfied with the specified item. That is why an architect will visit a factory to see window assemblies being tested against water penetration and why samples are requested so that the architect can carefully inspect them to be sure that principles of design have been respected

68

To what extent is the architect entitled to rely on manufacturer's literature? Not to any great extent unfortunately. If the architect specifies the item in reliance on the manufacturer's assurances, it may amount to a warranty on the

69

manufacturer's part. It is better for the architect to carefully set out the conditions under which the particular manufactured item will be used and then to ask the manufacturer to confirm that the item will be entirely appropriate for use under those conditions.

For something like the design of roof trusses or foundation piling the architect will usually wish to transfer the design liability. With the client's consent, it can be transferred to a consultant, the contractor or to a sub-contractor. All the main JCT contracts (SBC, ICD and MWD) contain provision for part of the design work to be transferred to the contractor and included as Contractors Designed Portion (CDP). If it is to be transferred to a sub-contractor, there may be difficulties. That is because the sub-contractor will be liable to the contractor for the design, but the contractor may not be liable to the employer for the sub-contractor's design. In those circumstances it is most important that a warranty is signed by the sub-contractor in favour of the employer. Without a direct warranty, the employer would have no remedy. There must be a clear clause in the main contract that requires such a warranty from the sub-contractor. Fortunately, SBC includes provision for such warranties in the

7

contract particulars. An architect who obtains the client's agreement to transferring design responsibility to a sub-contractor will not be liable if the design is defective, but could become liable for negligent advice if the architect failed to ensure that the relevant warranties were completed.

Design responsibility cannot be transferred to the contractor or sub-contractor by simply sticking something in the bills of quantities or in an architect's instruction. That is because nothing in the bills of quantities can override or

1.3

modify what is in the printed form. To transfer it to the contractor, it must be included as part of the Contractor's Designed Portion (Ninth Recital).

To transfer it to the sub-contractor, involves indicating that the domestic sub-contractor carries out part of the Works. In SBC, the only provision for that involves the insertion of a list of sub-contractors in the bills of quantities. The work must be measured or otherwise described in the bills and obviously a warranty must be required and noted in the contract particulars.

3.8

3.7 and 3.9

Design and workmanship

There is undoubtedly a blurred line between design and workmanship that is often difficult to draw. Architects do not usually or even often design the whole of a building. There is usually a point at which they stop designing and effectively leave it to the particular tradesperson. Even if the architect remembers to draw sections through every portion of the Works, such things as the details of screws, timber to timber joints, packings and glued surfaces will seldom be specified. The architect will assume, probably correctly, that the particular operative concerned will know the kind of fixings, sizes, materials and spacing required. This is often referred to as 'second-order design'. Architects vary in the amount of second-order design they leave to the contractor and it is very difficult in some instances to decide what is the difference between this level of design and workmanship. If it can be shown that the amount and degree of second-order design that a particular architect left to the operative was customary and similar to what the average architect designing that kind of building would have left, it is possible that defects in that second-order design would be considered failures in workmanship rather than the architect's design failures.

70

Consultant's errors

It has already been said that an architect wishing to transfer design responsibility to a consultant, say for structural steelwork, would need the express consent of the client. Whether or not the architect retains any liability at all for errors in the consultant's design is sometimes a concern. For example, what responsibility does the architect have for ensuring that the pipe runs designed by the heating and mechanical engineer do not conflict with parts of the building such as columns and beams and other services? The architect acting as the lead designer would normally be responsible for such co-ordination. A more difficult problem is caused by a consultant who makes a design error that has significant consequences but that is not a matter of co-ordination.

An architect will normally carry no legal responsibility for the work to be done by a consultant that is beyond the capability of an ordinarily competent architect. So far as the work allotted to the consultant is concerned, the architect's legal responsibility will normally be confined to directing and co-ordinating the consultant's work as a whole. However, this is subject to one important qualification. If any danger or problem arises in connection with the work allotted to the consultant of which an ordinarily competent architect reasonably ought to be aware and reasonably could be expected to warn the client despite the employment of the consultant, and despite what the expert says

71   or does about it, it is the duty of the architect to warn the client. In such a contingency the architect is not entitled to rely blindly on the consultant, on matters that must or should have been apparent to the architect.

5.5   The architect as agent for the employer

What is agency?

72   It is said that an architect certifying under the contract is exercising professional judgment independently of the employer and not as agent for the employer. But what exactly do we mean by acting 'as agent'? We are all familiar with travel agents and estate agents and agents for insurance companies. In each case the agent is only exercising the agency in a limited way in respect of selling travel arrangements, property or insurance respectively. An agent is one who does something on behalf of someone else.

Usually, the agent will be trying to form a contract on behalf of the person who is employing the agent. That person is referred to as the 'principal'. Thus, an estate agent will be trying to set up a contract for the sale of a property, usually on behalf of the vendor. The vendor is the principal. But an agent may be authorised to do other things for the principal. When the agent enters into a contract on behalf of a principal, the contract is formed between the principal and the other party. The agent is not a party to the contract. That state of affairs assumes that the agent has revealed the identity of the principal to the other party. If the agent has concealed the identity of the principal, the contract may well be formed between the agent and the other party.

Usual duties of an agent

The duties of an agent in broad terms are:

- To act for the principal in the particular area for which the agent has been appointed. The agent may be liable to the principal for failure to act at the appropriate time.
- To obey the principal's lawful and reasonable instructions.
- To reveal any conflict of interest to the principal.
- To keep proper accounts.
- To act personally. In other words, not to delegate to another person. That duty does not normally apply if the principal appoints a firm as agents so far as delegation within the company is concerned unless the engagement specified a particular person to act as agent.

Difficult situations

An architect must be careful not to give the contractor the impression that he or she is acting as the employer's agent. This misapprehension on the part of the contractor may arise in various circumstances. For example, if the architect purports to accept the contractor's tender on behalf of the employer. The contractor may well be justified in assuming that the architect has authority from the employer to do that. If, for some reason, the architect has no such authority, the architect may find that he or she has incurred personal liability. Another situation is if the architect issues instructions to the contractor that the contract does not empower. If the contractor acts on the instruction, the architect may again incur personal liability although the contractor would be guilty of carrying out an instruction that it could see was not empowered by the contract.

The position is somewhat complicated. The golden rule for architects is never to appear to act on behalf of the employer. If there is something that the contract states must be done by the employer, make sure that it is the employer who does it.

There are some instances where the architect may be regarded solely as the agent of the employer as a result of the employer's actions as where an architect is employed by a local council or large commercial organisation and the employer dictates and controls the architect's actions in certain situations. It is not unknown for a local authority to refuse to allow its employed architects to issue final certificates until the council's audit department have satisfied themselves about every particular in a final account prepared by the quantity surveyor. Similar pressure is sometimes brought on independent consultants to await the results of an audit before certifying. Such councils may make themselves liable, at least in the case of employed architects. Interfering with the proper exercise of the duty of a truly independent consultant raises still further issues. In such cases, the independent consultant must ask for clear instructions. If the instructions are that the certificate must await the results of the audit, it probably amounts to a serious breach of contract on the part of the employer that the consultant has little choice but to accept and step down.

Disputes sometimes arise because an architect has given an instruction to the contractor to vary the work under the contract, but the architect has omitted to obtain the employer's consent. But the contractor does not have to worry whether or not the architect actually has the consent of the employer for any instructions issued within the terms of SBC; the law will prevent the employer, so far as the contractor is concerned, from denying that such variations were made with the employer's consent.

5.6   No power to direct contractor

The contractor has the right and it is its task to carry out its building operations in accordance with its own views. Unless the contract specifically states otherwise, the architect has no power to tell a contractor how to do the work or in what sequence. Many architects believe that they have the power to direct a contractor how or when it is to do the work. That is clearly a wrong view. Obviously, an architect who sees that the contractor has done something that

76

77

will result in injury to property or individuals, has an obligation to warn the contractor, but no more than that. The architect is not required nor entitled to supervise the contractor's working methods, unless the contract requires the contractor to adopt certain methods or timing.

5.1.2

3.14

An example of an express contract provision to enable the architect to intrude into what would normally be the exclusive province of the contractor is found in SBC. One of the possible variations that an architect may instruct is the imposition, addition or omission, or the alteration of any obligations or restrictions already imposed in the bills of quantities, by the employer. The types of obligations and restrictions are listed as access or use of specific parts of the site, limitation of working space or hours and the carrying out or the completion of the work in any particular order. It is probably because this kind of variation is a variation to the terms of the contract, rather than a variation of work, that the contract refers to imposition or changes by the employer. Nevertheless, it is clear that the architect is given power to instruct this type of variation under SBC.

3.10.1

It is probably because of the intrusion into matters usually reserved to the contractor that the contractor is entitled to object to an instruction issued under this clause. If wishing to object, the contractor must make reasonable written objection. What is a reasonable objection can be referred to adjudication by the contractor or the employer if the architect will not accept it. It is easy to see how the question could cause problems. Is it a reasonable objection that the contractor would not make as much money as it would have made without the restriction being imposed, even when payment for the variation is taken into account?

5.7   Issue of certificates

78

An architect's certificate is the formal expression of the architect's professional opinion. It is the most important type of document that the architect issues. Once issued, it cannot be withdrawn except in the case of arithmetical and similar factual errors when it may be corrected. Obviously, either the employer or the contractor may refer the question of whether an architect's certificate has been properly issued to one of the dispute resolution procedures. The contract lists the following certificates that the architect must issue:

2.31   ■ Non-completion certificate.
2.30.1   ■ Practical completion certificate.
2.30.2   ■ Section completion certificate.
2.39   ■ Certificate of making good.
4.10.1   ■ Interim certificate.
4.15.1   ■ Final certificate.
8.7.4   ■ Certificate following employer's termination of the contractor's
            employment.
Schedule 3,
Option A.4.4 ■ Certificates releasing insurance money.

Non-completion certificate

This is the certificate that the architect must issue if the contractor fails to complete the Works by the date for completion in the contract or by any extended date. The architect has no discretion; the certificate must be issued. Although there is no time limit set, it is good practice to issue the certificate promptly after the contractor's failure. Although it is common to do so, the architect must not delay the issue simply because there is a fear that the contractor may take it as an indication that liquidated damages will be recovered. (For the detailed procedure see Chapter 15, Section 15.2.)

Practical completion certificate

Although the contract seems to suggest that the architect has quite a lot of discretion when issuing the certificate of practical completion, that is not so. The contract refers to the architect issuing it when 'in his opinion' it is achieved. However, the architect's opinion must be exercised in accordance with what courts have said about the matter. The architect may issue the certificate when:

79

- the Works are nearly complete except for minor things still to be done and there are no defects visible or that the architect knows about, and
- when the contractor has provided any design drawings in connection with CDP work as specified in the contract documents showing the work as-built, and
- when the contractor has provided information for the health and safety file as the CDM Co-ordinator reasonably requires.

The certificate must be issued as soon as the architect can reasonably do so after ascertaining that all the criteria are met. Once the criteria are satisfied, the architect may not withhold the certificate. The certificate of practical completion must not be issued just because the employer instructs the architect to do so or because the employer has decided to re-take possession of the property. To issue a certificate other than strictly in accordance with the contract is probably a negligent action for which the architect would be liable. (For more information see Chapter 21, Section 21.2.)

Section completion certificate

This is identical to the certificate of practical completion except that it refers to the practical completion of a section. Otherwise, the criteria for issue are the same as if the architect was issuing a certificate of practical completion for the Works.

Certificate of making good

This is also subject to misunderstandings. Many architects refuse to issue this certificate until all current defects have been made good. In fact, what the contract says is that the architect must issue this certificate when all the defects notified to the contractor during the rectification period and in the schedule sent to the contractor during the 14 days after the end of the period have been made good. Those are the only defects to which the certificate refers. Defects discovered and notified to the contractor after the schedule of defects has been sent to the contractor are not covered by the certificate of making good. (For more details see Chapter 22, Section 22.6.)

Interim certificate

80

This certifies the payment to be made to the contractor. The architect may request a valuation from the quantity surveyor before issuing the certificate, but is not obliged to certify the amount in the valuation. It is essential that the architect issues the certificate no later than 5 days after the due date stated in the contract particulars. Certificates issued after that time are invalid. (For details of procedures relating to interim certificates see Chapter 19, Section 19.4.)

Final certificate

This certificate must be issued in accordance with a strict time schedule. Failure to do so will prevent the architect from issuing a valid final certificate with serious consequences for the employer. An architect who has issued a final certificate has no further powers or duties under the contract. The final certificate marks the final act. (For further information about the final certificate see Chapter 19, Section 19.6.)

Certificate following employer's termination of the contractor's employment

After the employer has terminated the contractor's employment, the employer is entitled to get in another contractor to complete the Works. After completion and the making good of defects, an account must be drawn up to reflect the various elements of cost incurred by the employer and money paid to the contractor. The account can be set out in an architect's certificate. This is a certificate that may or may not be issued. As an alternative, the contract permits the employer to put the information in a statement. If the architect is to issue the account as a certificate, it is not a certificate such as those normally issued by the architect during the contract period. It is simply a piece of paper signed by the architect bearing the words 'I certify ....'. The architect is simply certifying to both employer and contractor that the account is a proper representation of the financial position at that point. (For further details see Chapter 23, Section 23.8.)

Certificates releasing insurance money

If the contractor is to insure new building Works, it must also authorise the insurers to pay all the insurance money to the employer. If there is any loss or damage to the Works caused by one of the insured risks, the contractor must notify the architect. After any necessary inspections by the insurers, the restoration work proceeds and the architect must issue certificates for payment of all the insurance money (but no more than that) in instalments on the dates on which interim certificates are to be issued. If the restoration work is not too extensive, it may be that it will be carried out at the same time as normal construction work is proceeding. In that case, it is likely that interim certificates as well as certificates releasing insurance money may be issued on the same day. This kind of certificate will not be on any standard format such as used for interim certificates, but rather be an 'I certify....' kind of certificate that the architect will produce. It could even be in the form of a letter so long as it certifies the amount of money to be paid to the contractor in respect of the insurance money. (For more details see Chapter 12, Section 12.9.)

5.8   The issue of instructions

The instruction procedure is set out in a flowchart in Figure 5.1. The contract states that the contractor must comply with all instructions issued by the archi-

3.10

tect. But there are four important conditions attached to that:

81

- The contractor need only comply if the instruction is specifically empowered by the contract. Following that, it might be expected that the clause would go on to list all the empowered instructions as other contracts do. Not so, the architect and the contractor are left to read through over a hundred pages of the document in order to locate the information. The empowered instructions are listed in Table 17.1.
- If the instruction requires a variation of obligations or restrictions concerning access to the site, working space or hours, or carrying out the work in a particular order, the contractor need not comply if it notifies the

3.10.1

architect of a reasonable objection.
- If the architect's instruction requires the contractor to provide a variation quotation, the contractor need not comply until the architect has issued a

3.10.2

confirmed acceptance or the contractor has notified his disagreement with the procedure within 7 days of receipt of the instruction and the architect

5.3.2

has issued another instruction.
- If part of the Works is CPD and the contractor notifies the architect within 7 days of receiving the instruction that, in its opinion, compliance would have a harmful effect on the effectiveness of the design of the CDP or the contractor's duty to comply with regulations 11, 12 and

3.10.3

18 of the CDM Regulations 2007. If the architect wishes the contractor to comply in the face of its objections, the architect must issue another instruction. Directions issued to the contractor for integration of the CDP work with the Works as a whole are included with instructions. Indeed, it is difficult to see how a direction of the architect differs from

2.2.2

an instruction.

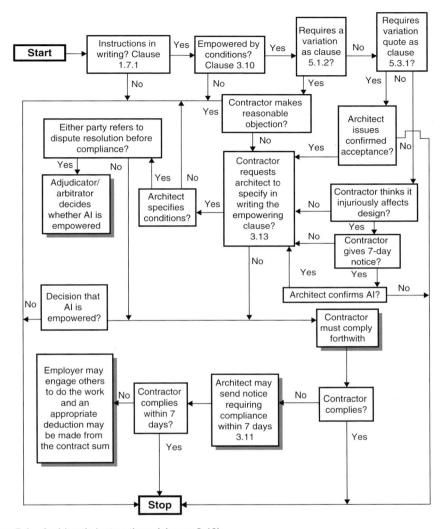

Figure 5.1 Architect's instructions (clause 3.10).

Confirmation of instructions

1.7.1 All instructions issued by the architect must be in writing. But there are elaborate provisions to cover the situation where the architect only gives oral instructions. The contractor must confirm them within seven days and if within a further seven days from receipt of the confirmation notice the architect has not dissented from them, the instructions will be effective not, surprisingly, from the date of the original oral instruction, but from the date that is seven days

3.12.1 from the date on which the architect received the contractor's notice.

The contractor is not obliged to confirm in writing if the architect issues

3.12.2 a written confirmation within seven days. The problem is that that if the contractor waits to see if the architect will confirm in writing within the seven days allotted, the contractor will miss its own opportunity to confirm. A sensible contractor will not wait, but will confirm all oral instructions from architects promptly. Most contractors seem to have a standard form that they call, erroneously, a CVI (confirmation of verbal instruction). 'Verbal' simply means 'relating to words'; it should not be used to mean 'word of mouth' as many in the construction industry appear to believe. An 'oral' instruction is one given by mouth i.e. spoken. Where the architect confirms, the instruction is effective from the date of confirmation.

The contract goes on to provide that if neither architect nor contractor confirms in writing, but the contractor nevertheless complies with the instruction, the architect may (but is not obliged to) confirm the instruction in writing at any time up to the issue of the final certificate (after which of course the architect can do nothing). Oddly, the instruction is then stated to

3.12.3   be effective from the date of the original oral instruction. Therefore, the position would be that the later the architect decides to confirm, the earlier the effective date of the instruction. The architect also has the right to 'sanction in writing' a variation carried out by the contractor even if not

3.14.4   instructed by the architect. So if the contractor carries out work that is not in accordance with the contract, the architect may effectively bring the work within the contract by using the sanction and then it is to be valued in the normal way.

The effective date

What is the significance of the date on which the instruction becomes effective? Simply that the date is when the contractor becomes obliged to comply with it. If both architect and contractor fail to confirm an oral instruction and, therefore, the contractor, quite correctly, does not comply but the architect confirms the instruction much later, the instruction is deemed to have taken effect on the date it was orally issued. Theoretically, this leaves the contractor open to accusations of breach of its obligation to comply with an instruction. It is difficult to imagine the circumstances in which an architect would be inclined to criticise the contractor on that basis.

Right to payment

If the contractor has neither an instruction in writing before it does the work, nor a confirmation by itself or the architect, it has no right to payment under the terms of the contract. In spite of this, contractors commonly carry out architect's oral instructions without waiting for written confirmation. They say, often with good reason, that if they waited for confirmation of the instruction before complying, the project would be seriously delayed. There never was any excuse for oral instructions. There is always some means by which the architect can record the instruction. Even if the instruction is given over the telephone, the architect can easily fax or e-mail written confirmation within minutes. In certain

82

circumstances, the employer may be considered to have waived or dispensed with the requirement for instructions to be in writing if instructions are routinely given orally. In such circumstances, the employer may not be able to refuse payment.

Failure to comply

8.4.1.3

3.11

If the contractor fails to comply with an architect's instruction, the architect has some very effective powers. If the instruction is in relation to the removal of defective work from site, the architect may, subject to certain provisos, serve a notice of default leading to termination of the contractor's employment if the default is not rectified. Otherwise, the architect may issue a notice requiring the contractor to comply with the instruction within seven days. If the contractor does not comply, the employer may engage another contractor to carry out the work necessary to comply with the instruction. All additional costs that the employer incurs in connection with employing the other contractor are the contractor's liability and may be deducted from the Contract Sum. Many contractors and architects do not appreciate the wide nature of such costs. They will include the costs of obtaining competitive prices from other contractors together with any consultants' fees. The obvious intention is that the employer should not suffer any financial loss due to the contractor's non-compliance. It is worth stressing that the costs deductible from the Contract Sum are 'additional' costs. In other words, they are the costs over and above the costs that would have had to be paid to the contractor for carrying out the instruction if it had complied.

83

If the contractor refuses access to the other contractor, it is likely that the employer can obtain an injunction from a court to compel the contractor to give access.

Instruction after practical completion

2.38

3.18

3.11

3.14

84

A question that arises from time to time is whether the architect has power to issue an instruction after the date of practical completion. Clearly the architect is entitled to issue certain instructions; for example, instructions requiring the contractor to make good defects appearing during the rectification period and instructions to remove defective work from site, allowing such work to remain and associated instructions. There appears to be no reason in principle why the architect cannot also issue a notice to the contractor to comply with an instruction with all that implies. The architect cannot issue an instruction requiring a variation, because the issue of the certificate of practical completion signifies, among other things, the end of the physical work.

Instructions after the date for completion

A related question is whether the architect is entitled to give an instruction requiring a variation after the date of completion in the contract when the contractor is in culpable delay, i.e. when the contractor has run over time and

85

is not entitled to any extension of the contract period. The answer to that question is that the architect can issue that kind of instruction. A key difference between variation instructions issued after practical completion or after the date for completion is that in the first instance, the contractor has left the site and would have to return to site possibly with plant and equipment to carry out the instruction, half the retention will have been released. In the second instance, the contractor is still on site and can easily do the work with the plant and equipment on the site already. The certificate due after practical completion has not been issued and effectively full retention is kept on the value of the instructed variation.

5.9   Instructions in detail

All the instructions that the architect is empowered to issue are listed in Table 17.1 and described in Chapter 17.

5.10   Issue of information

2.8.2

86

One of the architect's principal functions is to design the building and then to give the contractor enough information to construct it. The design may be a work of genius, but if the architect does not produce and issue the relevant drawings and other information, it may as well remain in the architect's head. As a matter of course, the architect must provide the contractor with two copies of each of the contract drawings and the unpriced bills of quantities. This has to be done immediately after execution of the contract. That is to say, with all reasonable speed. The proportion of building contracts actually signed before work begins on site must be quite small and strict adherence to this requirement would often see the contractor without these crucial documents, sometimes until after the project was complete. That would be a nonsense and, if the contract is not signed, everyone tends to carry on as if it was, albeit not a wise thing to do.

2.9.1.1

As soon as possible after execution of the contract, the architect must provide the contractor with two copies of 'descriptive schedules or other similar documents' that are necessary for the carrying out of the Works as well as preconstruction information needed under regulation 10 of the CDM Regulations 2007. The term 'descriptive schedule' is not defined and it is by no means easy to understand what is meant by 'other similar documents'. One may surmise that a descriptive schedule is something like an ironmongery, lintel or door schedule. The only documents similar to those are other schedules. On the reasonable, but perhaps unjustified, basis that the draftsman would not have included the add-on phrase if he had not considered it necessary, 'other similar documents' must add something; precisely what is unclear.

2.9.3

The documents issued are purely explanatory of the contract documents and must not impose further or indeed different obligations on the contractor (this prohibition also extends to the master programme).

The information release schedule

The contract allows for the provision of an information release schedule if the architect thinks it is a good idea. It must not be confused with an information request schedule that is produced by most contractors on securing a contract and whose purpose is to tell the architect when the contractor needs, or at any rate wants: various drawings and other information. In contrast, an information release schedule tells the contractor when it will receive information.

2.11

If there is an information release schedule, the architect must provide the information listed in the schedule at the times stated. There are just two exceptions:

- If the contractor, by act or default, prevents the issue.
- If the employer and the contractor agree to alter the time for release. The agreement must not be delayed or withheld unreasonably. It may be that the architect wishes to delay the issue of a drawing and wants the contractor to agree, or that the contractor wants the architect to agree to issue some information earlier than stated. Presumably the employer is mentioned, because the architect has no power to alter the information release schedule. In practice, it will be the architect who discusses the matter with the contractor and then drafts a letter for the employer to sign. It is likely that the withholding of agreement in either circumstance could usually be justified as reasonable, depending on the precise circumstances.

87

The information release schedule is not really a good idea. The contractor is entitled to construct the Works in any way it wishes provided only that it complies with the completion date and any sectional completion dates specified in the contract. The wording of the contract is such as to make clear that the schedule has been provided at the time the contract is executed. That makes perfect sense. If the employer intends to provide the schedule, it is obvious that the contractor must be told when tenders are invited. Moreover, if the tenders are to be accurate, it is essential that each tenderer is provided with a copy of the schedule, because the contractor will need to know when it can expect the construction information so that it can plan the progress of the Works. Although the contract is silent on the point, it seems that the schedule must be prepared by the architect. That means that the architect must prepare it without knowing how the contractor wishes to plan its work or whether it will find it more efficient or economical to start from north or south or even, at the time the schedule is prepared, who will be the contractor. So, where a schedule is to be used, the contractor will be deprived of its right to organise the work as it chooses. It will be tied to working to suit the delivery of information programmed by an architect whose expertise rarely includes organising work on site.

An alternative is for the tenderers to be told that an information release schedule will be issued after it has been agreed between the architect and the successful contractor. A problem with that approach is the difficulty of reaching agreement and at the very time when, if the contractor is to be able to make a prompt start, the appropriate drawings should be available. Anecdotal evidence suggests that in practice the provision of an information release schedule is something of a rarity.

Other information

2.12

If there is no information release schedule or if it is not entirely comprehensive, other information must be released in accordance with certain rules. Even if a schedule is provided, it will never be comprehensive. The architect must do two things:

- provide the contractor, from time to time as necessary, with two copies of the further drawings or details that are reasonably necessary to explain or amplify the contract drawings that have already been provided; *and*
- issue instructions to enable the contractor to carry out and complete the Works in accordance with the contract.

2.12.1

The timing of the provision of the drawings and details is to be as reasonably necessary. If this was not qualified by the remainder of the clause, it would suggest that the architect is obliged to keep up with the contractor's progress.

One of the terms of the contract is the date for completion. Therefore, if this was not also qualified by the remainder of the clause, the architect's obligation would be to issue instructions in time to enable the contractor to complete by the date for completion.

The obligations so far as the timing is concerned are set out. For this purpose and for simplicity, reference to both drawings and instructions will be to 'information'. There are two situations:

- *The architect must supply information to match the progress of the Works.* That means that if the contractor is proceeding regularly and diligently with the Works, the architect must provide information to suit that progress. But if the contractor is falling behind its programme and it is not going to finish by the completion date, the architect is entitled to adjust the supply of information accordingly provided the contractor receives the information when it is 'reasonably necessary' for him to do so. This clause allows the architect to issue information, even after the completion date has passed when the contractor could not possibly use it to complete on time, provided the architect can say that it was issued to suit the contractor's actual progress on site. For the architect to take advantage of this power would be very ill-advised. If the contractor is late and if the architect does adjust the supply of information to match the contractor's progress, there is the real risk that at a subsequent date, the contractor may contend that the cause of its delay was the architect's failure to supply information to enable the contractor to complete by the completion date. It is notoriously difficult in those circumstances to dispute the contractor's version of events, particularly in adjudication that by its very nature is a short, sharp process. To avoid that danger, architects should always endeavour to supply information at such times as will enable the contractor to complete by the date for completion even if realistically the contractor has no hope of achieving it.

88; *2.12.2*

■ *The architect need not provide information to suit the contractor's progress* if, in the architect's opinion, the Works are likely to reach practical completion before the completion date. In those circumstances, the architect's obligation is simply to provide the information so that the contractor can achieve the completion date.

2.9.1.1

The big question is how the architect is supposed to know when the contractor needs to receive any particular information. In practice, the contractor will furnish its own schedules of information required and there is a powerful argument that the contractor is entitled to virtually all the information when the contract is executed. If the contractor knows, but has reasonable grounds for believing that the architect does not know, when the contractor should receive further information, the contractor must inform the architect. There are two qualifications:

■ The contractor need only advise the architect to the extent that it is 'reasonably practicable'. It is not clear what that means. There is no requirement that the contractor must write to the architect, although it is always wise to put such matters in writing. Apparently it is sufficient if the contractor merely telephones the architect, asks for the information at a site meeting or just mentions it as the architect is carrying out a site inspection. It is difficult to envisage a situation when it will not be 'reasonably practicable' for the contractor to tell the architect that it needs some information.

■ The contractor must do so in sufficient time before it needs the information so that the architect is able to provide the information at the right time.

In practice, the problem would be that by the time the contractor realised that the architect was not going to provide the information, the latest time for receipt of the information would either be gone or so close that the architect would have no chance to meet the deadline. Contractors will no doubt continue to issue lists of all the information required and the latest dates required at the beginning of the project – a kind of 'information please release schedule'.

5.11 Duties under the contract

The architect's specific duties under the contract are set out in Table 5.2.

Table 5.2 Duties of the architect under SBC.

Clause	Duty	Comment
1.7.1	Issue instructions and all other communications in writing.	All communications referred to in the contract.
1.8	Issue certificates to employer and to contractor at the same time.	Refers to all certificates, not simply financial ones.
2.2.2	Issue directions regarding integration of CDP with the design of the Works.	Contractor has the right to object.
2.8.2.1	Provide certified copy of contract documents to contractor.	Originals in the custody of employer must be available for inspection by contractor at reasonable times.
2.8.2.2 and 2.8.2.3	Provide two further copies of contract drawings and unpriced bills	Copies of drawings, unpriced bills and CDP documents must be kept on site by contractor.
2.9.1.1	Provide descriptive schedules or other such documents to contractor.	Together with pre-construction information for CDM Regulation 10.
2.10	Determine levels and provide accurately dimensioned drawings for setting out the Works.	Contractor responsible for setting out.
2.11	Ensure that information is released to contractor at times scheduled on the information release schedule (where applicable).	Unless prevented by contractor's act or default. Employer and contractor may agree to vary the times.
2.12	Provide further drawings or details to contractor.	As reasonably necessary to explain and amplify contract drawings.
2.15 and 2.16	Issue instructions to contractor if discrepancies in or divergence between documents is reported.	Contractor must notify if it becomes aware.
2.17.1	Notify divergence between statutory requirements and information provided.	Contractor has similar duty.
2.17.2	Issue instructions to contractor if divergence between statutory requirements and information provided, is notified.	Within 7 days of becoming aware or 14 days of receipt of contractor's proposed amendment.
2.28	Give a fair and reasonable extension of time or notify contractor that no extension is to be given.	If contractor gives written notice.
2.28.5	Review extensions of time and fix completion date later or earlier or confirm previous extension.	Not later than 12 weeks after practical completion.

Table 5.2 (Cont'd)

Clause	Duty	Comment
2.30.1	Issue a practical completion certificate for the Works.	In addition to any certificates issued previously for section completion. This certificate also signifies sufficient compliance with the requirement to provide health and safety file information and, where CDP is involved, the as-built information.
2.30.2	Issue a section completion certificate for each section.	This certificate also signifies sufficient compliance of each section with the requirement to provide health and safety file information and, where CDP is involved, the as-built information.
2.31	Issue a non-completion certificate of the Works or section.	A further certificate must be issued if architect issues a further extension of time.
2.33	Issue a written notice confirming partial possession of any part of the Works by employer.	If employer takes possession of part of the Works with contractor's consent.
2.35	Issue a certificate of making good in respect of the part taken into partial possession.	When all defects notified in respect of the part have been made good.
2.38.1	Prepare a schedule of defects at the end of the rectification period and issue it to contractor not later than 14 days after expiry of the period.	Contractor must make good the defects within a reasonable time.
2.39	Issue a certificate of making good in respect of the Works.	When all defects notified have been made good.
3.13	Specify in writing the clause that empowers the issuing of particular instructions	If requested to do so by contractor. The instruction will be deemed given under the clause stated by architect.
3.16	Issue instructions about provisional sums.	Only if in the bills of quantities or in the employer's requirements.
3.20	Give reasons for dissatisfaction within a reasonable time of the execution of unsatisfactory work.	If the work is to be to the reasonable satisfaction of architect.
3.22.2	Issue instructions if antiquities are found.	May require the examination or removal of objects by third party (such as an archaeologist).

(continued)

Table 5.2 *(Cont'd)*

Clause	Duty	Comment
4.5.2.1	Unless already ascertained, ascertain loss and/or expense or instruct quantity surveyor to do so.	As part of the final account.
4.5.2	Send to contractor a copy of the final account.	Within 3 months of receipt of all necessary documents from contractor.
4.10.1	Issue interim certificate no later than 5 days after the due date.	Stated sum due and basis of calculation.
4.14	Deal with applications for costs and expenses following suspension.	If contractor correctly suspends its performance because employer has failed to pay money due.
4.15.1	Issue the final certificate within 2 months of sending the final account to contractor, or from the end of the rectification period, or from the issue of the certificate of making good.	If architect fails to issue within this period, power to issue it ceases.
4.18.2	Prepare or instruct quantity surveyor to prepare a statement of the amount of retention deducted.	Prior to issue date of each interim certificate.
4.19.1	Where there is a retention bond, prepare or instruct quantity surveyor to prepare a statement of the amount of retention that would have been deducted.	Prior to issue date of each interim certificate.
4.23	Ascertain, or instruct quantity surveyor to ascertain, loss and expense because regular progress of the Works or part thereof has been materially affected by deferment or one of the relevant matters.	If the contractor makes application within a reasonable time and provides further information and details of the loss and/or expense as requested.
6.5	Where requested, instruct contractor to take out a joint names policy for the amount of indemnity in the contract particulars. See that policies and receipts are deposited with employer before work starts on site and that employer is advised to obtain specialist insurance advice about the adequacy of such policies. Check continuity of cover at appropriate intervals.	Against employer's liability.

Table 5.2   *(Cont'd)*

Clause	Duty	Comment
8.7.4	Issue a certificate setting out an account of termination costs if employer does not send a statement to that effect.	After completion of the Works and making good of defects.
6.16.2	Issue any necessary instructions to the extent that remedial measures require a variation.	Following breach of the joint fire code.
Schedule 1, para 2	Return copy of contractor's design document marked 'A', 'B' or 'C' with comments as appropriate.	After submission by contractor.
Schedule 1, para 7	Confirm or withdraw a comment on contractor's design documents.	Within 7 days of receipt of contractor's notice.
Schedule 2, para 1.1	Provide information reasonably required by contractor.	If contractor reasonably consider information not sufficient.
Schedule 2, para 2.1	Invite contractor's proposals.	If acceleration required.
Schedule 2, para 4	Confirm acceptance by employer of variation or acceleration quotation.	If employer wishes to accept.
Schedule 2, para 5.1	Give instructions on variation.	If employer does not accept Schedule 2 quotation.

5.12   General duties

3.6

It is entirely the contractor's responsibility to carry out and complete the Works in accordance with the contract. That is no more than the position under the general law. The following are common factors on which contractors may try to rely to excuse their own shortcomings. However, these factors will not affect the contractor's obligation in any way:

- The architect's obligations to the employer.
- The employer's appointment of a clerk of works.
- Inspection visits to the Works or any workshop by the architect or the clerk of works.
- Inclusion of the value of work, materials or goods in a certificate.
- Issue of the certificates of practical completion, section completion or completion of making good defects.

The architect has general duties by virtue of the terms of engagement between architect and client (employer under SBC) such as the duty to inspect the progress of the Works. Although SBC contains clauses that imply that the architect

3.17 to 3.20 will be inspecting the Works, for example, the power to instruct the contractor to remove defective work from site and carrying out testing, SBC does not expressly state that the architect must inspect.

Inspections

It has long been a principle that the architect's inspections on site are carried out for the benefit of the employer and the contractor cannot draw any conclusions from them. Certainly, the architect owes no duty to the contractor **89** to find defects. Having said that, the contract says that if any materials, goods or workmanship are to be to the satisfaction of the architect and the architect is not satisfied, the architect must 'give reasons for dissatisfaction' within a rea-*3.20* sonable time after it is carried out. This seems to make the architect responsible for taking positive steps to find defects. The architect cannot, as hitherto, merely act as a bystander. It has been held by a court that all materials and **90** workmanship are matters on which the architect should be satisfied.

Reasonable time

The question of what constitutes a 'reasonable time' in which the architect must act is always difficult to answer. It will depend upon circumstances. It is suggested that the architect will comply with this requirement if the dissatisfaction is expressed before the contractor is ready to move to the next stage in the construction. Therefore, if the defect is several bad courses of brickwork, the contractor must be informed before it places further courses on top. However, architects do not usually visit site on a daily basis, therefore, the architect's obligation must be further qualified with reference to the architect's first visit after the defective work is executed by which time, a metre height of brickwork could have been added. There will be some instances where a reasonable time will stretch almost to practical completion, for example, the laying of a concrete screed that is not due to receive any floor covering until the project is virtually complete. There will of course be some instances where the architect will have no obligation, because the contractor has covered up the defective work before the architect has had the opportunity to inspect it.

If it is established that the architect did not notify the contractor within a reasonable time, it is a breach of the architect's obligations under the contract. There is no contractual machinery available to deal with it. It may be that the employer can be held to be liable and the contractor may be able to recover whatever losses it has suffered as a result. Thus, the employer may be put in the strange position of having to pay the contractor to dismantle and re-build part of the structure in order to get at the defective item, because the architect has failed to spot the contractor's own breach of contract. Of course, the contractor would be liable for the correction of the original defect. In this respect, the contract imposes a duty on the architect that goes against the normal and sen-**91** sible position as established by the courts. That particular clause should be deleted.

5.13   Does the architect have any duty to the contractor?

This is an extremely complex question. In a nutshell, the answer is a strong 'maybe'. Essentially, the important thing is whether the contractor was relying on the architect and whether the architect knew it. For example, the contractor relies on the architect to certify in accordance with the contract whether the certificate is financial or in connection with something else. The architect must know that the contractor is relying on him or her to certify properly. Any contractor thinking of bringing a claim against the architect personally or any architect on the receiving end of such a claim should seek proper legal advice.

92

5.14   Common problems

The contractor says that it does not have enough information to build

This is a very common situation. Sometimes it is that the contractor demands all the information at the very beginning of the contract period, or sometimes it demands further drawings during the progress of the Works and the architect believes that the contractor has all the drawings necessary to build.

If the contractor wants every scrap of information before work commences, it is usually a sign that the contractor is not ready to start and looking for excuses to delay. The contract is quite clear that, if there is an information release schedule (unlikely), the architect must release the information in accordance with that schedule, but not in advance of it. If there is no schedule, the architect must release information as necessary to enable the contractor to complete the Works in accordance with the contract. Neither system envisages the provision of all information before the contractor starts work and the contractor is not entitled to it.

2.11

2.12

Often, a contractor will request further details of some part of the building. Usually, this is a perfectly reasonable request and, provided the contractor has not waited until the last minute to notify the architect, it is a request that the architect should be happy to receive. It shows that the contractor is conscientious in wanting to achieve a good result. More difficult are the requests that are made for details that the architect believes are perfectly clear from the drawings as issued.

At the extreme, a contractor once asked the architect to provide a section through the skirting board at the base of each of the four walls in a room. It availed the architect nothing to say that they were all the same. More demands of a broadly similar nature ensued and the whole matter ended in adjudication that, unsurprisingly, the contractor lost. A contractor is not entitled to have a section through every conceivable part of a building, but only sufficient to enable it to construct the building correctly. In each case, it is a matter of fact whether or not the contractor actually needs all the requested information.

Extreme demands are usually because relationships have broken down. Some architects are unreasonably parsimonious in providing information and that too can cause difficulties. The usual problem in those cases is that the contractor ploughs on with what it assumes to be required, only to find that it is wrong and is in breach of contract. The answer is for each request by the contractor to be carefully examined. If there is doubt as to its necessity, the architect should speak to the contractor (better than e-mail or text) to see why it needs something that appears to be superfluous. The answer will usually be that the contractor has missed the information that is provided on other documents or the architect has not understood the request properly. Unless there are underlying bad relations, one must proceed on the assumption that all parties are attempting, albeit for their own reasons, to get the job done as quickly and correctly as possible.

Defects appearing after the rectification period but before the certificate of making good has been issued

A question that frequently arises concerns defects that are only apparent after the contractor has been provided with a schedule of defects at the end of the rectification period. Can the architect issue the certificate of making good or must it be delayed until after the fresh defects have been rectified? The answer to that is very straightforward. The certificate of making good only certifies the making good of the defects that have been notified to the contractor during or *2.39* at the end of the rectification period. Therefore, it must be issued when these defects have been made good irrespective of any other defects that have subsequently come to light.

There is usually a second part to this question. What if the new defect is very serious and the issue of the certificate will signal release the second half of the retention? That also is straightforward. When the architect issues an interim certificate to release the second half of the retention, the employer is entitled to issue a pay less notice by which the amount payable can be reduced based on a *4.13* calculation of the estimated cost of the defect.

The employer giving instructions to the contractor for extra work

It frequently occurs that the employer goes on site and gives direct instructions to the person-in-charge. This is particularly common if it is the employer's own house. Often, the first time the architect hears about it is when the contractor includes the work in a claim for payment to the quantity surveyor and the quantity surveyor asks the architect if it has been instructed. The position is that there is no provision in the contract for the employer to give direct instructions to the contractor. This is wrong on so many levels:

- it is not authorised;
- the employer should seek the architect advice on all proposed changes;
- the architect may go on site and condemn the work as being in breach of contract because it is not what is on the contract documents;
- it suggests the employer has no faith in the architect;
- if done frequently, it completely confuses any forecasting of the final account;

- it may effectively sanction defective work;
- it may give rise to serious constructional problems; and
- only the architect may give instructions.

On hearing of the instruction, the architect should discuss the matter with the employer and point out the difficulties and emphasise that it should never occur again. There are two options:

- Since it is not a valid instruction under the contract, the employer simply pays the contractor directly for it on receipt of its invoice. That is the strictly correct position and the architect and quantity surveyor have no involvement at all.
- The architect issues an instruction sanctioning the contractor's action in carrying out the employer's instruction. The architect has power to do this under the terms of the contract. Obviously, the architect must only adopt this latter course if completely satisfied that there are no difficult consequences to the Works.

3.14.4

The employer may tell the contractor that it cannot have any extensions of time

This amounts to interference in the architect's duties. Clearly it is wrong and if it is an attempt to countermand an extension already given or about to be given by the architect, it probably amounts to a repudiation of the architect's terms of engagement. It is worth noting (and pointing out to the employer) that interference or obstruction in the issue of any certificate is something for which the contractor can commence termination proceedings. This applies to any certificate and not just interim certificates for payment.

93

8.9.1.2

Although the giving of an extension of time by the architect is not referred to as a 'certificate' by the contract, it is often referred as such by the courts. It is quite possible that a contractor could use that argument to serve a default notice on the employer.

94

6 The contractor's powers and duties

6.1 What the contractor can do or must do

The contractor's powers and duties are set out in Tables 6.1 and 6.2, respectively.

6.2 Person-in-charge

3.2

The contractor must constantly keep a competent person-in-charge on the Works. That is a rather quaint way of putting it. Why not say 'on the site'. The reason is probably that the site may be fairly large and the Works to be constructed may be relatively small in size. Therefore, in those circumstances, it is important that the person-in-charge is in among the work being carried out rather than just somewhere in the general vicinity. There is no requirement, as in some forms of contract, that this person should be named by the contractor or agreed by the architect. The expression 'foreman-in-charge' that was used at one time has been changed to what the JCT describe as 'the more neutral phrase'. Presumably this is to allow for the unusual circumstance in which the person-in-charge may be a woman. Some contracts use the term 'site manager' or 'site agent', which is probably better.

The word 'constantly' is not to be taken literally. A better view is that the person-in-charge must be constantly on the Works during any period when work is in progress.

Instructions given by the architect or directions given by the clerk of works are treated as having been given to the contractor. This is particularly important where the architect hands written instructions to the person-in-charge on site and does not confirm them to the contractor's head office.

6.3 Access to the Works and premises

3.1

The architect and any representatives of the architect must have access to the Works at all reasonable times. The inclusion of the architect's representatives is simply to ensure that the architect named in the contract may nominate others

The JCT Standard Building Contract 2011, First Edition. David Chappell.
© 2014 by David Chappell. Published 2014 by John Wiley & Sons, Ltd.

Table 6.1 Contractor's powers.

Clause	Power	Precondition/comment
2.6.1	Consent to employer using or occupying the site or Works before the issue of practical completion certificate.	If insurers confirm that insurance will not be prejudiced.
2.7.2	Consent to carrying out of such work.	Where employer requests and contract documents do not so provide. Consent must not be unreasonably delayed or withheld.
2.11	Agree with employer to vary time for release of information from the information release schedule.	
2.25	Consent to employer taking possession of part of the Works before practical completion or section completion certificate has been issued.	Consent must not be unreasonably delayed or withheld.
3.5.1	Object to a replacement architect.	Must be for reasons that will be considered sufficient by a person under the dispute resolution procedure.
3.8.1	Select any person from the list of sub-contractors.	At the contractor's sole discretion.
3.8.2	Add additional persons to the list.	With the consent of employer.
3.8.2	Consent to employer adding additional persons to the list.	
3.8.3.1	Agree to add additional persons to the list.	Agreement not to be unreasonably delayed or withheld.
3.10.1	Notify a reasonable objection.	If the instruction requires a variation to obligations or restrictions imposed by employer.
3.10.3	Form an opinion that an instruction has a bad effect on the design of the CDP.	
3.13	Request architect to specify in writing the empowering clause for an instruction.	Architect must comply as soon as it is reasonable to do so.

(continued)

Table 6.1   *(Cont'd)*

Clause	Power	Precondition/comment
4.11.1	Submit an interim application to quantity surveyor, setting out contractor's view of amount due.	Not later than 7 days before the due date. Will become an interim payment notice if certificate not issued in time.
4.11.2.2	Give an interim payment notice.	At any time after 5 days after the due date if contractor has not made an interim application.
4.14.1	Suspend performance of obligations.	If the contractor has given 7 days written notice of intention after the employer has failed to pay in full the amount on a certificate by the final date for payment.
4.17	Make written application to the architect within a reasonable time.	If it becomes apparent that regular progress is being materially affected by one or more of the relevant matters or due to deferment of possession of the site by the employer.
4.15.6.1	Give a final payment notice to employer with copy to architect stating its opinion of the final amount payment due to it.	At any time after the 2-month period within which architect must issue the final certificate.
4.18.3	Request employer to place retention in a separate bank account.	Must be designated so as to identify the amount held by employer on trust.
4.23	May apply for loss and/or expense.	If incurred due to deferment of possession or the relevant matters.
5.2	Agree with employer the amount of a variation instruction or instruction on the expenditure of a provisional sum.	
8.9	Serve a notice on employer by special delivery, recorded signed for or delivery by hand specifying the default or suspension event.	If the employer: Does not pay by the final date for payment an amount properly due to the contractor on any interim or final certificate; *or* Interferes with or obstructs the issue of any certificate; *or*

Table 6.1 *(Cont'd)*

Clause	Power	Precondition/comment
		Fails to comply with the assignment provisions; *or* Fails to comply in accordance with the contract with the CDM Regulations; *or* The carrying out of the whole or substantially the whole of the uncompleted Works is suspended for a continuous period as stated in the contract particulars by reason of ■ Architect's instructions regarding discrepancies, variations postponement ■ Any impediment or default of the employer, architect, quantity surveyor or employer's persons unless caused by contractor's or contractor's persons' negligence or default.
8.9.3	Terminate its employment within 21 days of expiry of the 14-day period.	If default or suspension event has not ceased within 14 days.
8.9.4	Terminate its employment.	Within a reasonable time after repetition if employer repeats a default or suspension event for which contractor for any reason has not already terminated.
8.10.1	Terminate its employment.	If employer is insolvent.
8.11.1	Give 7 days notice of termination.	If the carrying out of the whole or substantially the whole of the Works is suspended for a period stated in the contract particulars by reason of *force majeure* or architect's instructions regarding discrepancies, variations or postponement resulting from statutory undertaker's negligence or default or loss or damage due to specified perils or civil commotion or threat of terrorism or exercise by UK government of statutory powers

(continued)

Table 6.1 *(Cont'd)*

Clause	Power	Precondition/comment
9.1	Give further notice of termination.	If suspension has not ceased within the 7-day period.
	Agree to resolve a dispute by mediation.	
9.3	By written notice jointly with employer to arbitrator state that they wish the arbitration to be conducted in accordance with any amendments to the JCT 2011 CIMAR.	
9.4.3	Give a further arbitration notice to employer referring to any other dispute.	After arbitrator has been appointed. Rule 3.3 applies.
Schedule 3 para B.2.1.1	Reasonably require employer to produce documentary evidence of insurance.	
Schedule 3 para B.2.1.2	Take out joint names insurance.	If employer defaults.
Schedule 3 para B.2.2	Reasonably require employer to produce a copy of the cover certificate relating to terrorism cover.	
Schedule 3 para C.3.1.1	Reasonably require employer to produce documentary evidence of insurance.	Unless employer is a local authority.
Schedule 3 para C.3.1.2	Take out joint names insurance.	Unless employer is a local authority. If employer defaults.
Schedule 3 para C.3.2	Reasonably require employer to produce a copy of the cover certificate relating to terrorism cover.	Where employer is a local authority.
Schedule 3 para C.4.4	Terminate contractor's employment within 28 days of loss or damage.	If just and equitable.
Schedule 3 para C.4.4.1	Invoke the dispute resolution procedures.	Within 7 days of receiving a termination notice.

Table 6.2 Contractor's duties.

Clause	Duty	Precondition/comment
2.1	Carry out and complete the Works in a proper and workmanlike manner and in accordance with the contract documents, construction phase plan and statutory requirements.	
2.2.1	Complete the design for CDP.	To include selection of specifications and materials, goods and workmanship so far as not in Employer's Requirements or Contractor's Proposals.
2.2.2	Comply with architect's integration directions.	Subject to the right to object if contractor considers that the directions badly affect the design of the CDP work.
2.3.1	Not to substitute materials or goods.	Without the architect's consent.
2.3.4	Provide proof that materials and goods comply with contract documents.	If the architect so requests.
2.3.5	Take reasonable steps to encourage contractor's persons to be registered under CSCS.	
2.4	Thereupon begin construction, regularly and diligently proceed and complete on or before the relevant completion date.	After being given possession and subject to extension of time provisions.
2.6	Notify insurers (Options A, B or C) and obtain confirmation that insurance will not be prejudiced. Notify employer of additional premium and provide premium receipt to employer on request.	If employer with contractor's consent wishes to occupy or use the site or the Works.
2.7.1	Permit execution of work not forming part of the contract to be carried out by employer or person directly engaged concurrent with the contract Works.	If contract documents so provide.
2.8.3	Keep available to architect on site all drawings, details and other construction information.	At all reasonable times.
2.8.4	Use contract documents and any further documents issued under the contract only for the purposes of the contract.	

(continued)

Table 6.2   (Cont'd)

Clause	Duty	Precondition/comment
2.9.1.2	Provide architect with master programme.	Containing particulars as required in the contract documents.
2.9.2	Provide amendment to the master programme.	Within 14 days of an extension of time or pre-agreed adjustment.
2.9.4	Provide architect with contractor's design documents and calculations to explain or amplify the Contractor's Proposals and all levels and setting out dimensions.	In relation to the CDP Works and without charge.
2.9.5	Not to commence any work until the submission procedure has been complied with.	In relation to CDP Works.
2.10	Be responsible for setting out.	Contractor must amend any errors arising from inaccurate setting out at no cost to employer.
2.12.3	Advise the architect sufficiently in advance that drawings are needed.	If the contractor has reason to believe that the architect is not aware of the time by which the contractor needs the drawings.
2.15	Immediately give written notice to the architect with details.	If contractor finds departure, error, omission or inconsistency in or between documents.
2.16.1	As soon as practicable make written proposals for necessary amendments. Comply with architect's instructions.	If there is a discrepancy in or between CDP documents other than Employer's Requirements.
2.16.2	Give the architect written notice of proposed amendment for dealing with the discrepancy.	Where the discrepancy is in the Employer's Requirements and the Contractor's Proposals do not deal with it.
2.17.1	Immediately give notice to architect specifying the divergence.	If contractor finds any divergence between statutory requirements contract documents, further information and instructions.
2.15.2	Comply with architect's instructions without cost to employer.	Unless after base date there is change in statutory requirements requiring an alteration in the CDP.
2.18.1	Supply such limited materials as are reasonably necessary to secure immediate compliance with statutory requirements.	In an emergency where it is necessary to act before receiving an architect's instruction.
2.18.2	Forthwith inform architect of such emergency compliance.	

Table 6.2   (*Cont'd*)

Clause	Duty	Precondition/comment
2.21	Pay all fees and charges. Indemnify employer.	Legally recoverable. Amount to be added to the Contract Sum unless they are to be included or relate solely to CDP.
2.22	Indemnify employer against all claims or proceedings.	If contractor infringes patent rights.
2.27.1	Notify architect in writing forthwith of any cause of delay and identify relevant events.	If it becomes reasonably apparent that progress of the Works is being or is likely to be delayed. The duty covers all causes of delay and is not confined to the relevant events.
2.27.2	Give particulars of effects.	In respect of each relevant event, in the notice or as soon as possible afterwards.
2.27.3	Forthwith notify architect of any change in the particulars. Supply further information.	If architect so requires.
2.28.6	Constantly use best endeavours to prevent delay and do all reasonably required to architect's satisfaction. Provide such information required by architect as reasonably necessary.	Contractor is not expected to spend large sums of money or there would be no need for an extension of time clause.
2.32	Pay or allow to employer liquidated damages at the rate specified in the contract particulars.	If the Works are not completed by the specified or extended completion date; *and* If architect has issued a certificate of non-completion; *and* If employer has informed contractor in writing before the date of the final certificate that payment may be required or a deduction made; *and* If employer has required liquidated damages in writing not later than 5 days before the final date for payment.
2.38	Make good any defects, shrinkages or other faults at no cost to employer.	If the defects, etc., appear and are notified to contractor by architect not later than 14 days after expiry of the rectification period; *and* If they are due to materials or workmanship not in accordance with the contract; *and* Architect has not instructed otherwise.

(*continued*)

Table 6.2 *(Cont'd)*

Clause	Duty	Precondition/comment
2.40	Supply for retention and use of the employer such CDP documents and related information as may be specified or employer may reasonably require showing the CDP as built.	Before practical completion without further charge to employer.
3.1	Secure as far as possible right of access to workshops and premises of sub-contractor.	For architect or authorised representatives. Access may be subject to restrictions.
3.2	Ensure that there is a person in charge on the site.	At all times.
3.7.1	Not to sub-contract any part of the Works without prior consent of architect.	Consent not to be unreasonably delayed or withheld.
3.7.2	Not to sub-contract the design of the CDP without prior consent of architect.	Consent not to be unreasonably delayed or withheld.
3.9	Engage sub-contractors using the relevant version of the JCT Standard Building Sub-Contract. Not to consent to removal of materials from site without prior consent of architect.	If appropriate. If delivered to site by sub-contractor. Consent not to be unreasonably delayed or withheld.
3.10	Forthwith comply with architect's instructions	If architect is empowered to issue them. Contractor need not comply with an instruction: ■ requiring variations to restrictions if reasonable written objections given; or ■ requiring variation quotation until confirmed acceptance; or ■ if it badly affects the design of the CDP unless confirmed by architect.
3.10.3	Specify in writing injurious effect of direction or instruction	If direction or instruction in the contractor's opinion will injuriously affect efficacy of the design of CDP.
3.12.1	Confirm instruction in writing within 7 days.	If architect issues instruction not in writing.
3.22.1.1	Use best endeavours not to disturb any fossil or other antiquity. Cease work.	If continuance would endanger object or impede excavation or removal.
3.22.1.2	Take all steps to preserve object in exact position and condition.	

Table 6.2 (*Cont'd*)

Clause	Duty	Precondition/comment
3.22.1.3	Inform architect or clerk of works of discovery and location.	
3.23	Duly comply with the CDM Regulations.	In relation to the Works.
3.23.2.1	Ensure that the construction phase plan is received by employer before construction work commences.	If contractor is the principal contractor.
	Notify employer.	If contractor amends the plan.
3.23.2.2	Ensure that welfare facilities are provided from start to finish of construction.	To comply with Schedule 2 of the CDM Regulations.
3.23.3	Promptly notify principal contractor of the identity of each sub-contractor.	If contractor is not the principal contractor.
3.23.4	Promptly provide and ensure any sub-contractor provides information reasonably required for the health and safety file.	At the written request of CDM Co-ordinator.
3.24	Comply at no cost with all requirements.	If a successor principal contractor is appointed.
4.5.1	Not later than 6 months after practical completion send to architect all documents reasonably required for the purposes of the adjustment of the Contract Sum.	Or to quantity surveyor if architect so instructs.
4.23.1	Make application as soon as it has become or should reasonably have become apparent to contractor that regular progress has been or is likely to be affected.	This is a pre-condition to consideration by the architect.
4.23.2	Submit to the architect on request information to reasonably enable the architect to form an opinion.	This is a pre-condition to consideration by the architect.
4.23.3	Submit to architect or quantity surveyor such information as is reasonably necessary to enable an ascertainment of direct loss and/or expense to be made.	This is a pre-condition to consideration by the architect.
6.1	Indemnify employer against any expense, liability, loss claim or proceedings whatsoever in respect of personal injury or death of any person.	The claim must arise out of, or in the course of, or be caused by, the carrying out of the Works except to the extent due to any act or neglect of employer or any of employer's persons.

(*continued*)

Table 6.2   (Cont'd)

Clause	Duty	Precondition/comment
6.2	Similarly indemnify employer against property damage	If the claim arises out of, or in the cause of, or is caused by reason of the carrying out of the Works *and* to the extent due to any negligence, omission or default of the contractor or contractor's persons.
6.4.1	Maintain insurance for claims for injury or death of persons or damage to property for such amounts of indemnity as are specified in the contract particulars and in compliance with all relevant legislation.	
6.4.2	Send documentary evidence of insurance to the architect for inspection by employer.	As and when reasonably required by employer.
6.5.1	Take out insurance in joint names in respect of any expense, liability, loss, claim or proceedings incurred by the employer for injury or damage caused by collapse, subsidence, heave, vibration, etc. by reason of carrying out the Works.	If the contract particulars so state and if architect so instructs.
6.5.2	Send to architect for deposit with employer, the policy and premium receipts.	Insurers to be approved by employer.
6.9.1	Ensure that joint names policy *either*: — provides for recognition of each sub-contractor as an insured; *or* — includes a waiver of subrogation in regard to such sub-contractors.	Where insurance option A applies. In respect of loss or damage by specified perils to the Works or section. Continues to practical completion or termination if earlier.
6.10.1	Take out and maintain such terrorism cover as specified in contract particulars.	If insurance option A applies and to the extent that the joint names policy excludes terrorism damage unless otherwise agreed.
6.11.1	Inform employer.	If insurers named in joint names policy notify contractor that terrorism cover will no longer be available.
6.11.4.1	With due diligence restore damaged work, replace or repair materials, dispose of debris and proceed with carrying out the Works	If work or materials suffer loss or damage due to terrorism and employer has not given notice of termination

Table 6.2   (*Cont'd*)

Clause	Duty	Precondition/comment
6.12	As soon as it reasonably can do after the contract has been entered into, take out professional indemnity insurance as stated in contract particulars.	Where there is a CDP.
	Maintain insurance until end of period stated in contract particulars from practical completion.	If available at commercially reasonable rates.
	Produce evidence that insurance is taken out and being maintained.	When reasonably requested by employer.
6.13	Immediately give notice to employer so that they can discuss ways of protecting their interests.	If insurance ceases to be available at commercially reasonable rates.
6.15	Ensure compliance with Joint Fire Code of all contractor's persons.	
6.16.1	Send copies of notice to employer and architect.	If breach of Joint Fire Code occurs and insurers notify contractor of remedial measures required.
6.16.1.1	Ensure the remedial measures are carried out by the specified date.	If the measures relate to contractor's obligation to carry out and complete the Works.
6.16.1.2	Supply limited materials and execute limited work as reasonably necessary. Inform the architect of the emergency and steps taken.	In the case of emergency compliance with remedial measures. As soon as it reasonably can do so.
7C	Enter into a collateral warranty in form CWa/P&T with purchaser or tenant.	Within 14 days of employer notifying the names and interests of such persons who are already identified in contract particulars.
7D	Enter into a collateral warranty in form CWa/F with funder.	Within 14 days of employer notifying the names and interests of such person who is already identified in contract particulars.
7E	Comply with requirements regarding the obtaining of warranties from sub-contractors to purchasers, tenants, funder or employer in form SCWa/P&T or SCWa/F or SCWa/E.	Within 21 days of employer giving notice identifying such persons who are already named in contract particulars.
8.5.2	Immediately inform employer in writing.	If contractor makes any proposal, gives notice of meeting or becomes subject of proceedings, etc., relating to insolvency matters.

(*continued*)

Table 6.2 (Cont'd)

Clause	Duty	Precondition/comment
8.12.2.1	Remove temporary buildings, plant, etc. from site.	If contractor's employment is terminated for employer defaults, employer insolvency, neutral events, cessation of terrorism cover or insured damage.
8.12.2.2	Provide employer with copies of as-built drawings.	If there is a CDP and without charge to employer.
8.12.3	Prepare an account. At employer's choice either: — prepare and submit an account or — not later than 2 months after termination provide all documents for employer to do so.	As soon as reasonably practicable following termination by contractor under 8.9 or 8.10. If terminated under 8.11 or 6.11.2.2 or under Schedule 3 paragraph C.4.4.
9.4.1	Serve on employer a written notice.	If contractor wishes a dispute to be resolved by arbitration.
Schedule 1 para 1	Submit each contractor design document to architect.	By means and in format in the Employer's Requirements and in enough time to allow architect's comments to be incorporated. If not in Employer's Requirements, contractor must send two copies.
Schedule 1 para 5	Carry out CDP Works in strict accordance with document.	If returned by architect marked A.
	Carry out CDP Works in accordance with document incorporating architect's comments.	If returned by architect marked B.
	Take account of architect's comments and resubmit or notify architect under paragraph 7.	If returned by architect marked C.
Schedule 1 para 7	Notify architect of disagreement within 7 days and that compliance with comment would constitute a variation.	If contractor thinks submitted documents are in accordance with the contract.
	Amend and resubmit the document.	If architect confirms the comment.
Schedule 3 para A.1	Take out and maintain insurance for new buildings.	In joint names for all risks.
Schedule 3 para A.2	Send the para A.1 policy to architect.	For deposit with employer.
Schedule 3 para A.4.1	Give written notice of extent nature and location	As soon as it reasonably can do so if loss or damage affects the work or site materials.
Schedule 3 para A.4.3	Restore damaged work, replace or repair materials, remove debris and complete the Works.	After any insurance inspection, with due diligence.

Table 6.2   (Cont'd)

Clause	Duty	Precondition/comment
Schedule 3 para A.4.4	Authorise insurers to pay insurance monies to employer.	For contractor and all sub-contractors.
Schedule 3 para B.3.4	Authorise insurers to pay insurance monies to employer.	For contractor and all sub-contractors.
Schedule 3 para C.1	Authorise insurers to pay insurance monies to employer.	For contractor and all sub-contractors.
Schedule 3 para C.4.1	Give written notice of extent, nature and location.	As soon as it reasonably can do so if loss or damage affects the work or site materials.
Schedule 3 para C.4.3	Authorise insurers to pay insurance monies to employer.	For contractor and all sub-contractors.
Schedule 3 para C.4.5.1	Restore damaged work, replace or repair materials, remove debris and complete the Works.	After any insurance inspection, with due diligence.

to carry out the task of visiting the site. The architect named in the contract may be the name of a firm or the chief architect of an organisation. It is prudent, however, for the architect to formally nominate representatives in writing to the contractor, so that they are not barred access. In addition, of course, it is ordinary courtesy to do so. There is no express provision that entitles the contractor to object to such nomination. The contractor could make a reasonable objection and if the architect ignored it, the contractor would have to decide whether the issue was important enough to seek an adjudicator's opinion.

Access must be allowed to workshops and other places where work is being prepared for the contract. If any of the workshops or places belong to domestic sub-contractors (but strangely not suppliers), the contractor must include a term in the sub-contract to achieve a similar right of access for architect and representatives. The contract uses the phrase 'so far as possible'. It is not clear why the contractor should not readily and successfully step down the requirement to sub-contractors. Indeed, it is already done in sub-contracts SBCSub/C and SBCSub/D/C. The contractor has a further obligation to do 'all things reasonably necessary' to make the right effective. This is probably wide enough to require the contractor to institute proceedings against a sub-contractor if the architect or the architect's representatives are refused admission to sub-contractor's premises.

The contractor or any sub-contractor may impose reasonable restrictions that are necessary to protect their proprietary rights. These rights are patent rights, design rights and trade secrets.

Others on the site

2.7

The draftsmen of SBC apparently take the view that the contractor is not merely a licensee on the employer's premises but is in possession of them, because they create an obligation to permit the execution of work not forming part of the contract. That is if the contract bills have provided the information about the work that is necessary to enable the contractor to execute the Works in accordance with the contract. It is suggested that the information to be provided must be detailed enough so that the contractor knows precisely what is intended to be carried out by others and exactly how the work fits with work the contractor must carry out.

2.7.2

Where the contract bills do not provide that information, it appears that the contractor is entitled to refuse consent to other persons entering the site to execute work. If the employer requires some work to be done by others, the contractor may not unreasonably delay or withhold his consent.

6.4   Carrying out the Works

The contract requires the contractor to:

■ carry out and complete the Works in a proper and workmanlike manner; and
■ in compliance with the contract documents; and
■ in compliance with the construction phase plan; and
2.1
■ other statutory requirements.

2.30

This is a basic obligation that nicely encapsulates the contractor's duties. It is not qualified in any way. It is clear from the rest of the contract that the contractor must bring the Works to a state where they are practically completed so that the architect can issue a certificate. This assumes, of course, that everything proceeds according to plan and that there are no unexpected events (such as weeks of ice and frost). It may be too simplistic to say that the remainder of the contract is simply dealing with how to put that into effect, but that is generally the case.

The contract documents

The contract documents are key to the finished product. It is the architect's responsibility to ensure that the work is comprehensively described in drawings and in words. The bills of quantities that form part of the contract documents are only to show the amounts of work, goods and materials. The architect is responsible for the specification and preliminaries parts of the bills although it is common, but bad, practice to let the quantity surveyor deal with both by taking what is available from notes on the drawings. In preparing drawings and specifications, the architect must bear in mind that generalisations are impossible to enforce. The contract documents must contain all the requirements that the employer wishes to impose, and the use of vague phrases such as 'best of its kind' or 'in accordance with good practice' should be avoided in favour of precisely specifying what is required.

The work

The contractor must complete all the work shown in the contract documents. This obligation comes to an end only when the architect issues the final certificate. The certificate of practical completion marks a staging point when the Works must be complete except for minor things left to be done and there must be no visible or known defects at that point. From then on, the contractor must rectify defects that have become apparent during a limited time (the specified rectification period).

Workmanlike manner

The contractor is expected to show a reasonable degree of competence and to employ skilled tradesmen and others, although the architect has no power to direct how the work should be carried out. The contractor is required to carry out all work in a 'proper and workmanlike manner'. There is clearly a difference between 'workmanship' and carrying out work 'in a workmanlike manner'. This requirement is not concerned with the permanent Works, but with the way in which the finished product is achieved. To take a simple example: an aluminium set of sliding patio doors is obviously material or goods, its final position, whether it is truly horizontal and vertical, absence of twist, its relationship with a weather bar beneath and vertical damp proof courses at either side, the correct alignment with the lintel above and the anodised finish are all matters of workmanship. However, the act of lifting and manoeuvring the doors into position and setting the unit on the base may or may not be accomplished in a workmanlike manner. In addition to the strictly constructional aspects of the task, there are questions of safety in handling for the operatives engaged on the task and for any person or property that might be injured or damaged during the process. Of course, if a process is not carried out in a workmanlike manner, it is probable that the finished work will not be

95   satisfactory either.

Progress

Once given possession of the site, the contractor must begin and proceed regularly and diligently with the Works and complete them on or before the specified completion date, as extended. Failure to proceed regularly and diligently is one of the grounds that entitle the employer to terminate the

8.4.1.2   contractor's employment under the contract. It is a question of fact whether the contractor is going ahead regularly and diligently and this must be judged by the standards to be expected of the average competent and experienced contractor. 'Regularly and diligently' means that the contractor must work continuously, efficiently and industriously with physical resources appropriate to the Works so as to progress the Works steadily towards completion substantially in accordance with the contractual requirements about time, sequence and quality of work. In deciding whether the contractor is working as required, the architect must consider such things as: the number of men on site compared to the number of men required; the amount of plant and equipment in use; the work to be done; the time available for completion of the work; the actual progress being made; whether the work is of the standards required by the contract and factors outside the contractor's control (which may not all be relevant events) that hinder progress. It has been said that the failure to proceed regularly and diligently is 'like the elephant, far easier to recognise than to describe.'

96

6.5   Levels and setting out

The architect must decide upon levels and provide the contractor with accurately dimensioned drawings showing the information necessary to enable the contractor to set out the Works. The contractor is entitled to rely on the accuracy of the setting out information, subject to any implied obligation to warn the employer if he becomes aware of a serious error. The obligation on the architect is to provide 'accurately dimensioned drawings'. This probably means that if the contractor sets out wrongly as a result of inaccurate information provided by the architect and there is a legal action for trespass from a disgruntled neighbour, the employer will be unable to pass liability to the contractor.

97

The contractor has an obligation to set out accurately and if the setting out is inaccurate, it must rectify the setting out at its own cost. If the discovery is made at a late stage, rectification may involve the expenditure of many thousands of pounds on the part of the contractor. The law is perfectly clear. In such a case, the employer is entitled to be put in the same position, so far as money can do it, as if the contractor had set out correctly. This strict view is apt to be modified in practice if the benefit gained by the employer is substantially outweighed by the cost of rectification. In any event, it is open to the architect, if the employer consents, to instruct the contractor not to amend the error. If the contractor is instructed not to amend the error, an 'appropriate deduction' is to be made to the Contract Sum. How the deduction is to be calculated is a matter of conjecture. It will clearly depend on the effect of the error and perhaps any continuing expense to the employer, e.g., the increased cost of heating and lighting a larger than expected building.

98

99

6.6   Workmanship and materials

Materials and goods and workmanship must be of the kind and standards described in the contract documents. That is just an elaboration on the contractor's obligation to comply with the contract documents. Obviously, so far as CDP work is concerned, the materials, goods and workmanship must be of the standards in the Employer's Requirements or if not described in the Employer's Requirements, they must be as described in the Contractor's Proposals.

2.3.1 and
2.3.2

Procurable materials

There is a little 'get out' phrase for the contractor. It need only provide the goods and materials if they are procurable. That is, if the contractor can get them. The contractor is afforded a valuable protection if materials or goods are truly unobtainable. Taken literally, the contractor is protected even if the materials or goods were not procurable when the contract was signed. A straightforward reading of the contract results in the harsh conclusion, so far as the employer is concerned, that if the items are not procurable for any reason, the contractor has no obligation to provide them. It would then become necessary for the architect to issue an architect's instruction requiring as a variation the provision of a substitute material. The variation is to be valued in the usual way. This conclusion has the effect of removing from the contractor any obligation to check that specified goods and materials are procurable before tendering. In order to moderate this harsh view and return to a sensible view, it may be necessary to substitute some such words as 'except in so far as they become not procurable after the Base Date'. There is of course no protection for a contractor who finds it more difficult or expensive to provide what is specified. In that case the goods are procurable; they are just more expensive.

Architect's satisfaction

2.3.3

If the approval of workmanship or materials is a matter for the architect's opinion, then the quality and standard must be to the architect's reasonable satisfaction. That has the potential to lead to many disputes and it is best to avoid that phraseology if possible in favour of very precise specification. Moreover, the things left to the architect's satisfaction will be deemed to his or her satisfaction when the final certificate is issued (see Chapter 19, Section 19.7).

If not described

2.3.3

If the goods or materials or workmanship are not described and not stated as being to the architect's approval or satisfaction, the standard must be 'appropriate to the Works'. This strongly suggests that if nothing is properly specified, the contractor has the task of deciding what is appropriate (but see the discussion in Section 6.14 of common problems). In principle, everyone knows what is intended by 'appropriate to the Works'. If the project is a prestigious hotel, it will be expected that the standards will be higher than for a block of flats intended for cheap rental. The problem arises, not in the extremes, but in the intermediate kinds of buildings. There will be grave differences of opinion about the appropriate standards in an office block depending on the company concerned, whether it is to be leased and its intended life. The phrase is obviously intended as a fail-safe in case some part of the specification is inadvertently omitted.

2.24 and 2.25
4.17

Other contractual references to materials and goods are concerned solely with the transfer of ownership in materials and goods and payment for off-site materials and goods (see Chapter 19, Section 19.8).

6.7 Contractor's master programme and other documents

Many architects believe that the contractor is obliged to provide them with a master programme and, moreover to update the programme on request. This is a misconception. The misconception goes further to the extent that an architect may think that a contractor has an obligation to comply with its own programme. All that may make very good sense, but the reality is quite different.

2.9.1.2   The contractor must provide the architect with a copy of its master programme. But nothing in the contract obliges the contractor to have a master programme. Therefore, if it does not have one, it can have no obligation to provide it.

Although it is probably unlikely that the contractor will not have a programme on even the smallest project, it may be worthwhile amending the clause to oblige the contractor to produce a master programme showing its intentions. There is nothing to prevent the architect including in the specification or the preliminaries to the contract bills, more details of the kind of programme

1.3   required. That kind of requirement does not fall foul of the priority clause, because it does not attempt to 'override or modify' what is in the contract, but merely to add to it. Among other things, it is useful if the contract bills require the programme to be in network or precedence diagram form as well as a bar chart, fully resourced and indicating all the logic links. The use of such a programme when analysing such matters as extensions of time has been approved

100   by the court.

Approval or comments on programme

The contract neither requires nor empowers the architect to make any comment about the contractor's programme, much less to approve it. If the architect, on receipt of the programme, notices anything that causes concern, it makes sense to convey this concern to the contractor, but it cannot be done in the form of an instruction. It is best done as a question, e.g.: 'Are you sure that you have allowed sufficient time/labour/plant to complete the foundations within four weeks?' Even if the architect does approve the contractor's programme, it is doubtful whether it has any significance unless the programme shows an early comple-

101   tion date. An architect who does approve the programme, is probably doing no more than signifying in a broad way that if the contractor carries out the work in accordance with the programme, the architect will be satisfied with the progress. Approval does not transfer responsibility for the contents of the programme to the architect. Whether or not it is correctly calculated taking all resources into account is always a matter for the contractor.

Compliance with programme

There is no contractual provision that obliges a contractor to comply with the programme it has submitted. In practice, it would be very perverse of a contractor to proceed to execute the Works in a completely difference sequence as well as being highly unlikely, but it can do so if it wishes. It follows, therefore, that individual dates in a programme have no binding effect. The contract is not a contract document, although it may perhaps be termed a 'contractual document', being generated by a term in the contract. It would be possible, although rarely advisable, to make the programme a contract document. The result would be that every deviation potentially would be a breach of contract on the part of the author of the deviation.

102

Updating the programme

The architect has no power to require the contractor to provide an updated programme just when the architect feels an updated programme would be a good idea. The only times the contractor must update its programme is if the architect has given an extension of time or there has been a pre-agreed adjust-
Schedule 2 ment of the date for completion by means of a variation quotation. The contractor has 14 days in which to supply its updated programme from the architect's decision in either case.

There will be many instances when an architect will want the contractor to provide an up-dated programme although the architect has neither given an extension of time nor confirmed acceptance of a variation quotation. A common example is when a contractor's progress is seriously delayed due to his own fault. The answer is to amend the clause to allow the architect to require the contractor to provide an updated programme upon the architect's reasonable request. In practice, the provision of update after update does not seem to expedite the completion date. It is actually quite useful for the architect to have only the contractor's original programme, because it enables the architect to precisely compare what the contractor said it would achieve with what it actually achieved.

Early completion

It is also quite common for a contractor to produce a programme that shows that it intends to complete the Works before the date for completion stated in the appendix. There is nothing to prevent it doing so, because the contract requires the contractor to complete the Works 'on or before' the completion
2.4 date. However, the architect is not obliged to provide information at the right
2.1.2 ; 103 times to enable the contractor to complete early. The submission of a programme showing early completion may be taken into account by the architect when considering whether an extension of time is due in any particular circumstance. For example, a contractor whose programme states that it will complete the Works two weeks early will have a difficult job persuading the architect to give a week extension of time for late information, because presumably it will simply mean that the contractor will finish one, instead of two, weeks early.

The contractor must keep on site a copy of the contract drawings, a copy of the unpriced bill of quantities, a copy of descriptive schedules 'or similar documents', a copy of its master programme (if it has one) and a copy of further
2.8.3 drawings.

Mandatory notices

The contract provides that the contractor must give to the employer or to the architect various notices. The mandatory notices are listed in Table 6.3

Table 6.3   Mandatory notices from the contractor.

Clause	Notice
2.6.1	To insurers if employer wishes to use or occupy part of the Works and does not notify the insurers.
2.6.2	Notify the employer of the amount of any additional premium.
2.12.3	Requesting information from architect, if contractor is aware and has reasonable grounds to believe that architect is not aware that information is required by a specific time.
2.15	Immediately in writing to architect, upon discovery of any discrepancies in or between the drawings, the bills of quantities, architect's instructions and further architect's drawings and CDP documents.
2.16.1	To architect if contractor finds any discrepancies in or between the CDP documents other than Employer's Requirements.
2.16.2	To architect of proposed amendment if the discrepancy is in the Employer's Requirements and the Contractor's Proposals do not address it.
2.17	To architect if contractor finds any divergence between statutory requirements and the drawings, the bills of quantities, architect's instructions and further architect's drawings and CDP documents.
2.18.2	To architect if emergency and contractor has taken steps to deal with it.
2.27.1	To architect forthwith if and whenever it becomes reasonably apparent that the progress of the Works is likely to be delayed stating material circumstances, the cause and identifying any relevant events.
2.27.2	To architect as soon as possible after a notice, identifying a relevant event, give separate particulars of the effects of the delay and the estimated effect on completion date of every identified relevant event.
2.27.3	As reasonably necessary or requested by architect to update previous information about delay.
3.10.3	To architect if in contractor's opinion compliance with an integration direction or any instruction will badly affect the design of the CDP.
3.22.1	Inform architect or clerk of works on discovery of a fossil.
3.23.3	Promptly notify principal contractor of each sub-contractor appointment if contractor is not principal contractor.
4.14.1	To employer if contractor intends to suspend performance of work following employer's failure to pay.
4.15.4	To employer if contractor intends to pay less than the sum in the final certificate.

Table 6.3 (Cont'd)

Clause	Notice
6.11.1	To employer if notified by insurers that terrorism cover will cease.
6.13	To employer if professional indemnity cover ceases to be available at commercially reasonable rates.
8.5.2	To employer if contractor becomes insolvent.
9.4.1	To employer if contractor wishes to refer a dispute to arbitration.
Schedule 1 para 7	To architect if contractor disagrees with architect's comment and believes that the design document is in accordance with the contract.
Schedule 2 para 1.1	To architect if contractor reasonably considers information is insufficient.
Schedule 3 para A.4.1	Forthwith, to architect and to employer, notice of the extent, nature and location of damage caused by any of the all risks to the work executed or site materials.
Schedule 3 para B.3.1	Forthwith, to architect and to employer, notice of the extent, nature and location of damage caused by any of the all risks to the work executed or site materials.
Schedule 3 para 4.1	Forthwith, to architect and to employer, notice of the extent, nature and location of damage caused by any of the all risks to existing structure, contents, the work executed or site materials.
Schedule 7 para A.4.1	To architect of occurrence of events in paragraphs A.1.2, A.1.6, A.2.2 and A.3.2.
Schedule 7 para B.5.1	To architect of occurrence of events in paragraphs B.1.2, B.1.6, B.2.2, B.2.5, B.3.2 and B.4.2.

6.8   Statutory obligations

2.1

The contractor is obliged to comply with all statutory obligations. It is also obliged to give immediate notice to the architect in writing if it discovers any divergence between the contract documents, contract bills, drawings, CDP documents (where used) and architect's instructions and statutory obligations

2.17.1

that include, of course, the Building Regulations.

This seems to cover, among other things, the situation where the contractor finds out that, because of soil conditions, the designed foundations will not comply with the Building Regulations. The contract states that if the contractor complies with its obligation to notify the architect if it discovers a divergence and otherwise the contractor constructs the Works in accordance with the contract documents and any further drawings and architect's instructions, it will not be liable to the employer if the Works do not comply with statutory requirements as a result. In short, the contract purports to exonerate the con-

2.17.3

tractor from any liability to the employer if it builds the architect's design.

It is likely that this provision may not always be effective to achieve its intended purpose if the employer can be described as a 'consumer'.

104   The provision is clearly caught by legislation. This applies to construction contracts. The primary liability, both criminally and civil for breach of the Building Regulations, rests with the contractor, and it will be liable to the employer if it fails to comply with the Regulations. The contractor may have recourse for an indemnity for its loss from the architect. Quite apart from legal considerations, this must be common sense. Whatever the contractor's liability to the employer may be, it is still obliged to build in accordance with statutory requirements and the local authority may still take account directly against the contractor in these circumstances.

6.9   Antiquities

Antiquities are elaborated in the contract to include fossils, antiquities and other objects of interest or value found on the site or during excavations.
3.22.1   They are assumed under the contract to be the property of the employer. That of course may not be the last word on the topic or even the true position, but the contractor is entitled to take the statement at face value. The important point is that antiquities do not belong to the contractor. The contractor's duties are clearly set out. As soon as it finds anything falling under the description of 'antiquities', it must use best endeavours not to move the object and, if possible must work around it. If not practicable to do
3.1.1   so, the contractor must stop work. The contractor must do everything necessary to keep the antiquity in exactly the position and condition in which it
3.22.1.2   was discovered. Much depends on the skill and experience of the particular operative or the person-in-charge. Antiquities in the form of broken pieces of pottery may never be identified. The architect or the clerk of work must
3.22.1.3   be informed of the discovery and its position on site. Neither employer nor contractor likes to find antiquities of any major importance, because the site could be brought to a standstill while archaeologists painstakingly check the find. Anecdotal evidence suggests that the odd Roman coin or small artefact is swiftly pocketed and work proceeds.

On being notified of a discovery, the architect must issue instructions about it. If the find appears at all major, the architect must take advice before giving instructions. The contractor must permit the excavation and removal of the
3.22.2   object by third parties such as archaeologists and specialist contractors.
2.29.4   The contractor is entitled to an extension of time and it may make a claim for
4.24.3   loss and/or expense, assuming of course that the Works have been delayed or loss and/or expense has been suffered.

6.10   Drawings, details and information

If there is an information release schedule provided as stated in the fifth recital, the architect must provide the information stipulated at the times stipulated. The architect is excused from doing so if prevented by some act or

2.11   default of the contractor or of any contractor's person. It is difficult to envisage what such an act of prevention could encompass, because the architect should be in a position to issue all information without any input from the contractor. The employer and the contractor may agree to vary the time of issue of the information.

Anecdotal evidence suggests that the provision of an information release schedule is not common. The principle of the provision of such a schedule contains a fundamental flaw. It is well established that the contractor is entitled to organise the work in whatever way it chooses and to decide, within reason-

105   able limits, when information and details should be provided.

Not only must the contractor know at the time of tender that an information release schedule is to be provided, it must actually be provided so that the contractor can plan its work on the basis of information to be received. Clearly, this involves the architect being able to guess the way in which each separate tenderer intends to tackle the project. It also circumscribes the contractor's right to organise the work in its own way.

The alternative, an agreed schedule between architect and contractor shortly after the contract has been let, assumes a level and speed of agreement that experience teaches is unlikely.

If no information release schedule

If the information release schedule is not provided, the architect must provide the contractor from time to time with further drawings, details and information enabling it to carry out and complete the Works by the date for comple-

2.12.1   tion. But the contractor is also under contractual duty to make a request for particular details or instructions if it knows when it needs the information and it has reasonable grounds for thinking that the architect does not know when

2.12.3   the information is required. The contractor is only obliged to advise the architect to the extent that it is reasonably practicable to do so. There is no express requirement for the contractor to notify the architect in writing, but in practice the prudent contractor will continue the customary practice of notifying the architect in good time of all information required and it will do it in writing if for no other reason than that there will then be a record of the notification.

Factors to be borne in mind include the state the Works have reached and whether the contractor can act on the information; the nature of the instruction or information; any other of the contractor's activities that may depend on the supply of information (e.g. pre-ordering of materials); and the time it may

106   reasonably take for the architect to prepare the information. If a contractor's progress is slow, the architect is to have 'regard' to the progress that effectively

2.12.2   means that the architect may issue information to suit the slow progress. In practice, it may be difficult later to establish whether the information was issued in response to the slow progress or whether the slow progress is a result of late information. The prudent approach is for the architect to issue the information in such time as will allow the contractor to complete by the completion date irrespective of actual progress.

6.11   Compliance with architect's instructions

3.10

The contractor is obliged to obey all instructions given by the architect that are within the architect' powers under the contract.

Empowering clause

3.13

An important point about instructions is that the contractor is entitled to request from the architect in writing details of the clause of the contract under which the instructions are given. The architect must answer the request by specifying a clause and the contractor can choose whether or not to dispute it. If it chooses to dispute it, the matter can be resolved by adjudication or whichever of the alternative dispute resolution procedures, arbitration or legal proceedings, are stipulated in the contract. If the contractor chooses not to dispute the specified clause, the architect is deemed to have properly issued the instruction under the clause for all the purposes of the contract. This means that the contractor will not be able to subsequently claim that the architect's instruction was not validly given. In view of the clear power to challenge given by the contract, the result is probably the same if the architect does not specify the empowering clause and the contractor does not exercise its right to request the information.

A very important consideration is sometimes overlooked. The contractor must not comply with instructions that the architect is not empowered to issue and if it does so, it is in breach of contract and certainly not entitled to payment. If the contractor does not query the clause specified by the architect and, therefore, the architect is deemed to have properly issued it for all the purposes of the contract, one of the purposes is to enable the instruction to be valued if appropriate. This is an important safeguard for the contractor even if the architect specifies the wrong clause.

Objections

3.10.1

The contractor also has the right to object to certain instructions. These are instructions that amount to variations dealing with the imposition or alteration of obligations or restrictions in respect of access to, or use of, any part of the site, limitation of working space or hours and the execution of the work in a particular order.

The contractor is not confined to objecting, it may refuse to carry out such variations to the extent that the objection is reasonable and made in writing. If the contractor's objection is directed only at part of the variation, it must comply with the other part. How exactly, that will be achieved will depend on circumstances, but it is likely to throw up problems. If there is dispute about whether the objection is reasonable, either party may refer the matter to adjudication. One sympathises with an adjudicator in this situation since there are no guidelines to follow.

If the instruction relates to the CDP and if the contractor believes that compliance will adversely affect the effectiveness of the design including

3.10.3

the contractor's obligations to comply with regulations 11, 12 and 18 of the CDM Regulations, the contractor has 7 days in which to write to the architect with details. Once this has been done, the contractor is not obliged to comply with the instruction unless the architect confirms it.

Failure to comply

3.11

If the contractor fails to comply with an instruction, the architect may issue a written notice to the contractor requiring compliance. If the contractor has not complied within 7 days after receipt of the notice, the employer may engage other persons to do whatever is necessary to carry out the instruction. It is probably good practice, although not essential, for the architect to issue a further notice to the contractor at the end of the 7-day period, setting out what the employer intends to do and pointing out that any last minute attention to the instruction on the part of the contractor will not alter the contractor's liability to the employer for any irrecoverable costs.

Wherever practicable, the employer should invite 3 other persons to tender for the work in order to mitigate the loss and to counter any future contentions from the contractor that the work was needlessly expensive. The contractor is liable for all additional costs incurred '*in connection*' with the employment of others and the amount must be deducted from the Contract Sum. Use of the italicised phrase broadens the scope of such costs to include all additional money the employer must expend over what would have had to be paid to the original contractor. Clearly, extra architect's and quantity surveyor's fees necessarily incurred are recoverable as part of the total additional costs.

107

It has been suggested that if the architect and employer fail to take prompt action on the contractor's failure to comply, the employer may be taken to have waived any rights to take action subsequently. That seems unlikely.

6.12   Suspension of performance

4.14

If the employer fails to pay the contractor any sums properly due to it under the terms of the contract, the contractor is entitled to give a 7-day notice to the employer with a copy to the architect of its intention to suspend performance of all its obligations. The contractor must state the ground for suspension that, presumably, will be failure to pay. It is probable that the contractor must spell out in reasonable detail the circumstances of the failure; for example, specifying the date and number of the relevant architect's certificate. It may be worth noting that if the project is a 'construction contract' under the relevant legislation the contractor can give notice of suspension under the Act and there is no need to copy in the architect.

108

The suspension of performance of its obligations includes of course the obligation to insure the Works. The consequences for the employer of a valid notice of suspension will be very serious unless the employer pays any outstanding money immediately. The suspension continues until the amount is paid in full including any VAT.

2.29.6   Assuming that the employer does eventually pay the amount owed, the contractor will be entitled to an appropriate extension of time and to apply to the architect for all costs and expenses reasonably incurred as a result of the suspension.

6.13   Does the contractor have a duty to warn of design defects?

Without express provision to the contrary, for example by use of the CDP, the contractor has no liability for design. Its obligation is simply to carry out and complete the Works in accordance with the contract documents, the construction phase plan and other statutory requirements. Does that mean that it is entitled to blindly build what the drawings and specifications set out, even if there are obvious errors? Most architects and sound commonsense would say not, but the position is not entirely clear. There has been a multitude of cases through the courts, some of them conflicting.

109   Probably the contractor's duty to warn only arises if the design is seriously defective. A contractor who did not warn an architect who had made an error in an eaves detail would be unlikely to have any liability. The key point seems to be whether the employer is entitled to rely and does rely upon the contractor. Where it can be shown that the employer does rely, even partly, on the contractor, there will be a duty to warn of serious defects. It will be rare for the contractor to have a duty to warn the architect, because the architect seldom, if ever, relies or should rely on the contractor. In the context of SBC, the duty is extremely limited, because the employer will usually be relying on the architect and not the contractor. The contractor is certainly not charged with checking the architect's work.

6.14   Common problems

The contractor asks for an instruction about whether something is 'appropriate to the Works'

If goods, materials or workmanship are not described or for the architect's satisfaction, they are to be 'appropriate to the Works'. Is that the contractor's decision? If it is not to be to the architect's satisfaction, presumably the architect cannot refuse something as being inappropriate to the Works. These are difficult questions for which the contract does not provide any ready answers. Obviously, there is always the possibility of reference to adjudication to obtain a (fairly) quick answer, but that can be quite expensive and there must first be a dispute.

Except in the case of CDP work, the contractor has no design responsibility under SBC. If the contractor decides that the goods, materials or workmanship in question are appropriate to the Works, it is clear that it is exercising a design function. The answer is for the contractor to request an instruction from the architect clarifying the specification. However, by the time the contractor is able to do this, it must have already submitted its tender within which it must have allowed something for the item. In making that financial allowance, the contractor has to make a decision about the appropriate standard. If the architect eventually, in response to the contractor's request, instructs something of a higher standard than what the contractor has allowed, either the architect must allow that as a variation or must argue that the standard instructed, rather than the standard for which the contractor has allowed, is appropriate to the Works. If there is no agreement and sufficient money is at stake, adjudication is indicated.

If the contractor demands that the architect checks the setting out

Sometimes a contractor will ask the architect to check its setting out, particularly if it is difficult, such as very close to a boundary with adjacent property. The contract is clear that it is the architect's duty to provide the necessary measurements and levels (except in the case of CDP work), but that it is the contractor's duty to set out the building from this information. The contractor cannot require the architect to check the setting out.

2.10

Having said that, the architect will often want to check the setting out, on behalf of the employer, because it is so fundamental. A serious mistake in setting out may mean that the whole building must be demolished. The architect should not approve the contractor's setting out and if the contractor tries to confirm the architect's approval, the architect would be wise to deny it in writing. Even though the architect has checked, the responsibility for accuracy still remains with the contractor under the contract.

7 The employer's powers and duties

7.1 What the employer can or must do

Many would say that the employer's chief duty is to pay the contractor. Looked at in the simplest way, that is exactly true. The contractor must construct and the employer must pay for it. It is worth remembering that, whatever else the contract may lay down as an employer duty, payment is the chief duty. However, SBC, like life, is not simple and it sets out a raft of powers and duties for the employer. It is part of the architect's job to advise the employer about these powers and duties, particularly because most employers are only involved as employers in building work once or twice in a lifetime.

7.2 Express and implied powers and duties

Like those of the contractor, some of the employer's powers and duties arise from the express provisions of SBC itself. These are set out in Tables 7.1 and 7.2.

Others are imposed by the general law in the form of implied terms. These are provisions that the law writes into every building contract and apply so far as they are not excluded or modified by the express terms of the contract itself. In practice, there are two important implied terms that are not affected by the contractual provisions. These two terms are like two sides of the same coin.

To co-operate and not to hinder

Under the general law, it is an implied term in every building contract that the employer will do all that it is reasonably necessary to bring about completion of the contract. Hand in hand with that is the implied term that the employer will not act so as to prevent the contractor from completing in the time and in the manner set out in the agreement. Breach of either of these implied terms is not specifically dealt with under the contract, but a breach that results in loss to the contractor will entitle the contractor to make a claim for damages at common law if it wishes to do so.

110

111

The JCT Standard Building Contract 2011, First Edition. David Chappell.
© 2014 by David Chappell. Published 2014 by John Wiley & Sons, Ltd.

Table 7.1   Employer's powers.

Clause	Power	Precondition/comment
2.5	Defer the giving of possession of the site or part.	For a period not exceeding 6 weeks or the period in the contract particulars.
2.6	Use or occupy the site or Works.	With the contractor's written consent before practical completion.
2.7	Require work not forming part of the contract to be carried out by the employer or employer's persons.	If contract documents provide necessary information, the contractor must permit it. If contract documents do not provide information, contractor's consent is required, not to be unreasonably delayed or withheld.
2.10	Consent that errors in setting out are not to be amended.	An appropriate deduction is to be made from the Contract Sum.
2.11	Agree with the contractor to vary time of issue of information.	In the information release schedule.
2.32.1	Give written notice to the contractor requiring payment of liquidated damages or that they will be withheld in respect of the period between completion date and practical completion.	Not later than 5 days before the final date for payment of the final certificate provided that: ■ architect has issued certificate of non-completion; and ■ employer has notified contractor before the date of the final certificate that employer may deduct liquidated damages or require their payment.
2.33	Take possession of part of the Works.	If the employer so wishes and the contractor has given consent.
2.38	Consent that defects are not to be made good.	An appropriate deduction is to be made to the Contract Sum.
2.40	Reasonably require CDP documents or other information relating to the CDP as-built.	Does not affect the contractor's obligations regarding the health and safety file.
2.41.2	Copy and use the CDP documents and reproduce any designs in them.	For any purpose relating to the Works except as a design for any extension of the Works.
3.3	Appoint an employer's representative.	By notice to contractor to carry out all employer's functions under the contract except those stated in the notice.
3.4	Appoint a clerk of works.	To act as inspector under the direction of the architect.

(continued)

Table 7.1   (*Cont'd*)

Clause	Power	Precondition/comment
3.11	Employ and pay other persons to execute any necessary work in connection with an instruction.	If the contractor has not complied with an instruction within 7 days of receiving a written notice.
3.18.2	Agree that defective work or materials may remain.	An appropriate deduction is to be made to the Contract Sum.
4.8	Approve a surety.	If an advance payment is to be made to contractor and the contract particulars require a bond.
4.17.4	Approve a surety.	If there are uniquely identified listed items for which a bond is required from contractor.
4.18	Have recourse to retention.	For payment of any amount to which the employer is entitled under the contract provisions
4.18.3	Receive interest on the retention money.	Need not account for the interest to contractor or any sub-contractor.
4.19.2	Approve a surety.	For the retention bond, if stated to apply.
4.20	Deduct retention.	As stated in the contract particulars.
5.1.2	Impose or alter obligations or restrictions.	In regard to access to or use of site, limitations of space or hours and order of work.
5.2.1	Agree amount of variation or method of valuation.	Except where a confirmed acceptance of a variation quotation has been issued.
6.4.2	Require the contractor to send documentary evidence of insurance to the architect.	Must be exercised reasonably.
	Require that relevant policies are sent to the architect.	At any time (but not unreasonably or vexatiously).
6.4.3	Insure and deduct premium amounts from monies due to the contractor or recover them as a debt.	If the contractor fails to insure against personal injury or death or injury to property.
6.5.2	Approve insurers.	For insurance of employer's liability.
6.10.4	Instruct contractor not to renew terrorism cover.	If option A applies, employer is a local authority and there is an increase in premium rate.
6.11.3	Instruct contractor to obtain alternative or additional terrorism cover.	If option A applies and employer instructs work to continue. Addition cost is to be added to the Contract Sum.

Table 7.1   (*Cont'd*)

Clause	Power	Precondition/comment
6.16.2	Employ and pay others to carry out the remedial work.	If contractor has not begun to carry out remedial measures within 7 days of receipt of insurer's notice about remedial measures.
7.2	Grant or assign the right to bring proceedings to enforce any term of the contract made for employer's benefit.	If this clause is stated to apply in the contract particulars.
7B.1	By notice to contractor, confer funder rights on the funder.	If this clause is stated to apply in part 2 of the contract particulars and the funder is identified in the notice.
7B.2	Agree with contractor to amend, vary or waive any term of this contract and to settle any dispute arising in connection with the contract.	Without the funder's consent unless funder has given notice under paragraph 5 or 6.4 of part 2 of Schedule 5.
7C	In a notice to contractor identify purchaser or tenant and interest in the Works and require contractor to enter into a warranty.	Warranty must be executed within 14 days of receipt of notice using form CWa/P&T.
7D	In a notice to contractor identify funder and require contractor to enter into a warranty.	Warranty must be executed within 14 days of receipt of notice using form CWa/F.
7E	In a notice to contractor identify sub-contractor and require sub-contractor to enter into a warranty with the purchaser, tenant, funder or employer.	If the contract particulars so provide. Warranty must be executed within 21 days of receipt of notice using forms SCWa/P&T, SCWa/F or SCWa/E.
8.4.2	Terminate contractor's employment by written notice served by recorded, signed for or special delivery or delivery by hand.	If contractor has not ceased a specified default within 14 days of receiving a default notice.
8.4.3	By written notice terminate contractor's employment.	Upon or within a reasonable time of contractor repeating a default.
8.5.1	At any time by notice terminate contractor's employment.	If contractor is insolvent.
8.5.3.3	Take reasonable measures to ensure that the site, Works and materials are protected.	After insolvency.
8.6	By written notice, terminate contractor's employment.	If contractor commits a corrupt act.

(*continued*)

Table 7.1   *(Cont'd)*

Clause	Power	Precondition/comment
8.7.1	Employ and pay others to carry out the Works. Take possession of the site and use all temporary building, etc.	If contractor's employment terminated for contractor's default, contractor's insolvency or corruptionunder.
8.11.1	Give 7 days notice of termination.	If the carrying out of the whole or substantially the whole of the Works is suspended for a period stated in the contract particulars by reason of *force majeure* or architect's instructions regarding discrepancies, variations or postponement resulting from statutory undertaker's negligence or default or loss or damage due to specified perils or civil commotion or threat of terrorism or exercise by UK government of statutory powers.
	Give further notice of termination.	If suspension has not ceased within the 7-day period.
9.1	Agree to resolve a dispute by mediation.	
9.3	By written notice jointly with contractor to the arbitrator state that they wish the arbitration to be conducted in accordance with any amendments to the JCT 2011 CIMAR.	
9.4.3	Give a further arbitration notice to the contractor referring to any other dispute.	After the arbitrator has been appointed. Rule 3.3 applies.
Schedule 2 para 2.1	Investigate possibility of achieving practical completion before the completion date.	If so, architect is to invite contractor's proposals.
Schedule 2 para 2.2	Seek revised proposals.	On or before receipt of quotation.
Schedule 2 para 3.3	Agree to increase or reduce any period in regard to a quotation.	Confirmation must be notified to contractor by or on employer's behalf.
Schedule 3 para A.1	Approve insurers.	In regard to insurance against all risks for new buildings by contractor.
Schedule 3 para A.2	Take out insurance.	If contractor fails to insure against all risks for new buildings.
Schedule 3 para A.3	Inspect the policy and premium receipts for all risks insurance in joint names.	At all reasonable times.

Table 7.1 *(Cont'd)*

Clause	Power	Precondition/comment
Schedule 3 para A.4.5	Retain amount properly incurred in respect of professional fees.	From monies paid by insurers.
Schedule 3 para C.4.4	Terminate contractor's employment within 28 days of loss or damage.	If just and equitable.
Schedule 3 para C.4.4.1	Invoke the dispute resolution procedures.	Within 7 days of receiving a termination notice.
Schedule 8 para 5.3	Inform contractor.	If employer considers that any performance indicators will not be met.

If the employer, either personally or acting through the agency of the architect or that of anyone else for whom the employer is responsible in law, hinders or prevents the contractor from completing by the completion date, the employer is in breach of contract and that conduct may also prevent liquidated damages from being recovered by the employer if any delay results. The extension of time clause is in the contract to deal with that and other kinds of delay.

The duty may be put in different ways, but the position may be summarised as follows:

> The employer and employer's persons must do everything necessary to enable the contractor to carry out and complete the Works and they must not in any way hinder or prevent the contractor from carrying out and completing the Works, in accordance with the contract.

The scope of these implied obligations is very broad. For example, the employer must not attempt to tell the architect how to exercise discretion, nor must the employer attempt to give direct orders to the contractor. The architect's independent role under the contract is so important that the architect is entitled to terminate his or her engagement if the employer interferes with the giving of extensions of time under the contract. Similarly, the employer must see that the site is available for the contractor and that access to it is not prevented by employer's persons.

Some potential acts of hindrance or prevention by the employer are covered by express clauses in the contract, but there are a number of grey areas.

112
113

7.3   General powers

Although the contract is between the employer and the contractor – who are the only parties to it - an analysis of the contract clauses shows that the employer has few express rights of any substance.

The employer's most important right is, of course, to receive the completed Works by the completion date, properly completed in accordance with the contract documents. Other rights are important as the contract proceeds. Some of the more important rights are set out below and the employer's powers and duties are set out in Tables 7.1 and 7.2, respectively.

Table 7.2 Employer's duties.

Clause	Duty	Precondition/comment
2.6	Notify the insurers under insurance option A, B or C and get confirmation that such use or occupation will not prejudice insurance.	If employer wishes to use or occupy part of the Works and before contractor gives consent. Contractor may notify instead of employer. Contractor's consent must not be unreasonably delayed or withheld.
2.8.1	Be custodian of the contract documents.	Must be available for inspection by contractor at all reasonable times.
2.8.3	Not to divulge or use any of the contractor's rates or prices.	Except for the purposes of the contract.
2.32.3	Pay or repay any amounts deducted or recovered in respect of liquidated damages.	If liquidated damages have been recovered, an extension of time has been given and the non-completion certificate has been cancelled or a later completion date is stated in a confirmed acceptance of a variation quotation.
3.5.1	Nominate a replacement architect or quantity surveyor.	If architect or quantity surveyor ceases to hold the post. Must be done within 14 days of cessation.
	Nominate an acceptable replacement.	Except where employer is a local authority and the replacement is an official, if contractor for sufficient reason objects.
3.23.1	Ensure that the CDM co-ordinator carries out duties. Ensure that the principal contractor carries out duties.	If contractor is not the principal contractor.
3.24	Immediately notify contractor of the name and address of new appointee.	If employer replaces the CDM co-ordinator or the principal contractor.
4.8	Pay the advanced payment on the specified date.	If the contract particulars so specify.
4.12.2	Pay the sum stated as due in the interim certificate.	Subject to any pay less notice
4.12.3	Pay the sum stated as due in an interim payment notice.	If no interim certificate has been issued and subject to any pay less notice.
4.12.5	Issue a pay less notice.	No later than 5 days before the final date for payment if employer intends to pay less than the amount on the interim certificate or the interim payment notice.

Table 7.2   (Cont'd)

Clause	Duty	Precondition/comment
4.12.6	Pay contractor simple interest.	If employer fails to pay the amount due by the final date for payment.
4.15.3	Pay any balance stated as due to contractor within 28 days of the issue of the final certificate.	If no final payment notice or pay less notice is issued.
4.15.4	Issue a pay less notice.	Not later than 5 days before the final date for payment of the final certificate.
4.15.6.1	Pay the sum stated as due in a final payment notice.	If no final certificate issued and subject to any pay less notice.
4.15.6.3	Issue a pay less notice.	Not later than 5 days before the final date for payment of the final payment notice.
4.15.7	Pay contractor simple interest.	If employer fails to pay the amount due by the final date for payment.
6.9.1	Ensure that joint names policy *either*: ■ provides for recognition of each sub-contractor as an insured; *or* ■ includes a waiver of subrogation in regard to such sub-contractors.	Where insurance option B or C applies. In respect of loss or damage by specified perils to the Works or section. Continues to practical completion or termination if earlier.
6.10.1	Take out and maintain an extension to the joint names policy for terrorism cover.	As specified in the contract particulars if insurance option B or C applies if the policy excludes terrorism cover.
6.11.1	Inform contractor.	If insurers named in joint names policy notify employer that terrorism cover will no longer be available.
6.11.2	Give written notice to the contractor *either* ■ the Works must be carried out; *or* ■ contractor's employment will terminate on the date stated in the notice	If employer receives notification from insurers or contractor that terrorism cover will cease.
6.15	Ensure compliance with Joint Fire Code of all employer's persons.	
6.16.1	Send copies of notice to contractor and architect.	If breach of Joint Fire Code occurs and insurers notify employer of remedial measures required.

(continued)

Table 7.2   *(Cont'd)*

Clause	Duty	Precondition/comment
8.8.1	Forthwith send notice to contractor.	If, within 6 months from termination, employer decides not to complete the Works.
	Send a statement to the contractor setting out the total value of work properly executed and any other amounts due to the contractor under the contract and the aggregate amount of expenses and direct loss and/or damage caused to the employer.	Within a reasonable time of such notification or, if no notice is given but the employer does not begin work during the 6-month period.
8.10.2	Immediately notify contractor.	If employer becomes insolvent.
8.12.5	Pay the contractor the amount properly due.	Must be done within 28 days of submission by the contractor, after taking account of amounts previously paid, but without deducting retention.
9.4.1	Serve on contractor a notice.	If employer wishes a dispute to be resolved by arbitration.
Schedule 3 para A.4.4	Pay insurance monies to contractor by instalments under architect's certificates.	Less only amounts in respect of professional fees.
Schedule 3 para B.2.1.1	Produce documentary evidence showing that joint names policy has been taken out and is being maintained.	When reasonably required by contractor if employer is not a local authority.
Schedule 3 para B.2.2	Produce copy of cover certificate regarding terrorism cover.	If employer is a local authority as and when reasonably required by contractor.
Schedule 3 para C.1	Take out and maintain joint names policy for existing structures.	
Schedule 3 para C.2	Take out and maintain joint names policy for all risks for the Works.	
Schedule 3 para C.3.1.1	Produce documentary evidence of insurance and receipts for premium payments.	As and when reasonably required by contractor if employer is not a local authority.
Schedule 3 para C.3.2	Produce copy of cover certificate regarding terrorism cover.	Where employer is a local authority as and when reasonably required by contractor.
Schedule 8 para 5.1	Monitor and assess contractor's performance.	By reference to any performance indicators in the contract documents.
Schedule 8 para 6	Promptly notify contractor of anything that seems likely to give rise to dispute or difference.	To avoid or speedily resolve disputes or differences.

Deferment of possession of the site

2.5

114

2.4

The contract gives a right that the employer would not otherwise have, namely the right to defer giving possession of the site or, if the Works are in sections, any section to the contractor for a period up to six weeks (the contract particulars must be completed to state that this provision is to apply). This is an important right because, under the general law, failure to give the contractor sufficient possession to enable the Works to progress is a serious breach of contract. Possession of the site means possession of the whole of the site.

This power can be useful when dealing with renovation works, although the normal intention must be that it is to be exercised only if it is essential to do so. When the parties have signed the contract, the contractor will understandably assume that it will have possession of the whole site on the date of possession stated in the contract. Without the right in the contract to defer possession, there would be no power to defer or postpone giving possession. It would be necessary for the employer and the contractor to reach a separate agreement. Deferring possession is not without consequences and the contractor may be entitled to an extension of time and loss and/or expense depending on the precise circumstances.

Deduction/repayment of liquidated damages

2.32

If the contractor is late in completing the Works and if it is not entitled to any extension of time, the employer is entitled to recover liquidated damages at the rate specified in the contract particulars. This is usually done by deduction from sums due to the contractor under interim certificates or the final certificate. Alternatively, the employer can recover them as a debt.

Preconditions

There are three preconditions to deduction or recovery. Payment of liquidated damages does not follow on automatically from late completion. The mere fact of late completion is not sufficient. The preconditions are:

2.31

- The architect must have given a certificate to the employer and the contractor that the contractor has failed to complete by the contract completion date (or of course by any extended date).

2.32.1.2

- The employer must give notice to the contractor, not later than the date of the final certificate stating that payment of liquidated damages may be required or may be withheld. The reference to the final certificate may be misleading. It simply means that that is the last occasion on which the notice may be issued. In practice, of course, it is usually issued much earlier – in fact as soon as it is clear that the employer has become entitled to liquidated damages.
- The contract states that no later than 5 days before the final date for payment of the final certificate the employer must notify the contractor of the intention to recover or deduct. Again, the reference to the final certificate is

misleading. Again, it simply indicates the last date it can be issued. Obviously, it can be issued as soon as the architect issues the non-completion notice. The employer's notice must state that for the period between the completion date and the date of practical completion, the contractor is required to pay liquidated damages at the rate stated in the contract particulars or at a lesser rate stated in the notice or that the employer will withhold or deduct liquidated damages at the rate in the contract particulars or at a lesser rated stated in the notice from any sums due to the contractor. If the employer intends to deduct the liquidated damages from an interim certificate or the final certificate, a pay less notice must be issued in the usual way no later

4.12.5 or 4.15.4   than 5 days before the final date for payment to indicate the fact.

Obviously, it is important to know what the contract says, but it is even more important to understand what it means in practice. The bullet points above can be summarised in a number of easily digestible points. The employer can recover liquidated damages once the following has happened:

2.31
- The architect has issued a non-completion certificate.
- The employer has written to the contractor saying that liquidated damages may be required to be paid or may be withheld from a certificate. The notice must be given, at the latest, 5 days before the final date for payment

2.32.1.2   of the final certificate, but can be given earlier.
- The employer has written to the contractor either saying that it must pay liquidated damages and stating calculation – weeks × rate, or that the dam-

2.32.2   ages will be deducted from the next certificate. The notice must be given, at latest, 5 days before the final date for payment of the final certificate, but can

4.13   be given earlier. In the case of deduction, a pay less notice also must be issued.

Failure to give notices

If an employer fails to give the right notices, liquidated damages cannot be recovered. Moreover, the employer cannot then revert to claiming ordinary damages for breach of contract, because the damages inserted in the contract particulars are instead of the employer's rights under the general law to claim for breach of contract. Another point that the employer should bear in mind is that the amount of liquidated damages in the contract particulars is everything that the employer can recover for late completion. It must include extra profes-sional fees, storage of furniture, cost of leasing other premises; absolutely eve-

115   rything resulting from a late completion.

Extension of time

If the architect makes a further extension of time after some liquidated damages have been deducted by the employer, there are two immediate consequences:

2.32.3
- The employer must repay any liquidated damages that have been deducted up to the newly fixed completion date.

2.31
- The already issued non-completion certificate is cancelled.

Only the employer can recover damages

The architect has nothing to do with the deduction or enforcement of liquidated damages. The architect's duty is to issue financial certificates at the correct times and in the correct amounts. It is entirely a matter for the employer whether or not to deduct liquidated damages. The architect should advise the employer of the options open and, the employer wishes to deduct, how that should be achieved in the form of notices.

Employment of direct contractors

2.7 The employer has the right to carry out or have carried out by others work that is not part of the contract. The contractor must allow this work to be carried out while the contract Works are in progress in two circumstances:

- If reference is made to the work in the contract documents.
- If there is no such reference, the employer can still have the work carried out if the contractor consents. It must not unreasonably withhold consent.

This is an important right that the employer would not have under the general law, because the contractor is entitled to exclusive possession of the site during the time the contract is being carried out. The limitations of the provision must be noted. It applies only to work that does not form part of the contract. For example, it cannot be used to take work away from the contractor to give to another contractor to carry out. That would be a breach of contract on the

116 employer's part.

The fundamental principle is that a clause of this sort cannot in general be used to omit contract work to give to others, because the contractor has agreed to do a certain quantity of work and has a right to do it. A provision allowing the employer to carry out what is sometimes known as 'direct work' does enable the employer to carry out that work while the contract is in progress. For example, the employer can use its own direct works department or bring in others to do the work.

The words 'not forming part of this Contract' mean exactly what they say. It is not work that the employer can require the contractor to do (except by means of an instruction of the architect). There are implications in terms of time and cost. It can readily be understood that in cases where the employer does bring in others to do work, it is likely that the contractor will suffer delay and perhaps

2.7.1 disruption as a result. The fact that the work is described in the contract or that

2.7.2 the contractor has consented will not change that position. Inevitably there will be a cost implication and the employer may well find that the contractor is entitled to an extension of time and loss and/or expense as a result.

Obviously, where the architect has issued a compliance instruction and the contractor has not complied within 7 days, the employer is entitled to bring another contractor on site to carry out the instruction on which the contractor

3.11 has defaulted. That situation is not 'work not forming part of this Contract' because it clearly does form part of the contract having being instructed (although the contractor has not carried it out) by the architect.

The use of direct contractors by the employer is not something to be encouraged. It often leads to disputes and confusion on site. It is far better, under SBC to allow the contractor to carry out all of the work that the employer wishes to be done. In that way, the contractor is liable for organising the work and for its satisfactory execution within the contract period.

Rights to insure in default

Chapter 12 deals with the complicated insurance clauses. The employer has various rights relating to insurance.

6.4.3 and
Schedule 3
Option A.2

Importantly, the employer has the right to insure or maintain policies in force if the contractor fails to do so and the employer can recover the cost out of any money due or to become due to the contractor or can recover the money as a debt.

Schedule 3
Option C.4.4

The employer can exercise the power to terminate the contractor's employment if it is just and equitable so to do. This is intended to cover the situation where the employer has insured, there is some loss or damage to the existing structure and as a result, there is no real point in proceeding with the Works. The classic situation is if an extension is planned to an existing building and if the existing building is burned to the ground. Realistically, one cannot extend something that has ceased to exist and, if building something is still a possibility, it is more likely to be the rebuilding of the property to incorporate the additional accommodation that the extension would have provided. In either case, the immediate continuation of the contract would be pointless.

The employer's other contractual rights, including general rights to terminate, are summarised in Table 7.1, where they are described as 'powers'. They are discussed in the appropriate chapters.

7.4   General duties

The essential thing about a duty is that it must be carried out. It is not at the option of the employer. Breach of a duty imposed by the contract will make the employer liable in damages to the contractor for any foreseeable loss that the contractor can prove.

It is not every breach of a contractual duty that will entitle the contractor to treat the contract as being at an end: only breach of a term that goes to the root or basis of the contract will do that, for example, permanently stopping the contractor from entering the site or refusing to pay the contractor in accordance with the contract terms. That is called 'repudiation' (see Chapter 1, Section 1.1). But a breach of any contractual duty will always, in theory, entitle the contractor to at least nominal damages, although in many cases loss may be difficult for the contractor to quantify and, therefore, to claim. Some of the employer's more important duties are set out below.

Payment

From the contractor's point of view, the most fundamental duty of the employer is to make payment in accordance with the terms of the contract. However, while steady payment of certificates is essential from the contractor's

117

point of view, the general law does not usually regard failure to pay, or to pay on time, as a major breach of contract unless repeated failure by the employer to pay the amounts certified by the architect was involved. Once the architect has issued an interim certificate, payment must be made by the final date for payment.

Pay less notice

4.12.5 and
4.15.4

SBC is quite specific about payment (see Chapter 19). If the employer feels justified in paying less than the amount certified by the architect or claimed in an interim payment notice by the contractor, whichever determines the amount to be paid in any particular instance, the employer must submit a pay less notice to the contractor no later than 5 days before the final date for payment setting out the basis of the calculation.

Suspension of work

4.14
8.9.1
4.12.6 and
4.15.7

If the employer fails to carry out the notice procedure correctly before paying less than certified or claimed, the contractor is entitled to exercise a contractual right to suspend work until payment in full is made or to serve a default notice before terminating its employment. In addition, the employer is liable to pay interest on amounts not paid in time. These procedures are set out in detail in Chapter 23, Section 23.17.

Retention

4.18.3

118

The employer has certain rights in the retention percentage, but also obligations. The retention monies are a trust fund, except where the employer is a local authority.

Since the retention money is trust money, it is not the employer's property. The employer must, if the contractor makes a request, set the percentage withheld aside in a separate bank account. The employer must set the money aside in a separate bank account even if the contractor does not actually request it. This is an obligation under the general law.

Other duties

The employer's other duties are summarised in Table 7.2 and are commented on as necessary in appropriate chapters.

7.5   Common problems

The rate of liquidated damages in the contract particulars may have been left blank

If for some reason the liquidated damages rate is left blank, it is likely that liquidated damages do not apply and the employer can then recover general damages by way of adjudication, arbitration or litigation, subject to proof of actual loss. However, if a £Nil figure is inserted as the rate, liquidated damages will apply, but at the rate of £Nil per week.

The employer tells the contractor that liquidated damages will not be deducted

In that case, the employer may not be able to change its mind later. Once someone has said that they will not exercise a contractual right, they can be held to it. It is called being 'estopped' or prevented. In general, it will only apply if the person to whom the statement is given (in this case the contractor) then does something that means to say that it will be out of pocket if the first person went back on the statement. For example, if the contractor, reassured that liquidated damages would not be deducted for delay, did not in turn deduct damages from sub-contractors who had contributed to the delay.

119

The contractor claims interest on repaid liquidated damages

Sometimes some or all of the damages deducted have to be repaid, for example if the architect gives the contractor a further extension of time. Undoubtedly, contractors will argue that any damages repaid should attract interest. There are no grounds for the claim. The contract already allows for interest on late payment. If it had been thought appropriate to add interest to repaid damages, there is no reason why it could not have been included in the contract. The contractor may say that the damages are because the deduction was in breach of contract. That cannot be so, because if the contract permits the employer to deduct damages, the deduction of the damages cannot be in breach of the contract. The position is that, at the time the damages were deducted, they were perfectly valid. Subsequently, when an extension of time was given, the damages became not deductible and they were then repaid.

Payment by cheque

Payment by cheque is probably good payment, although some contractors have been known to argue to the contrary under other forms of contract. Strictly speaking a cheque is accepted as conditional payment until such time as the cheque is honoured. If the cheque is dishonoured, interest runs on the original certified amount without interruption until it is paid.

8 Consultants

8.1 General points

article 4
article 3
3.3

The contract only makes reference to one consultant: the quantity surveyor. Even the architect is not mentioned other than in the role of contract administrator who might actually be an engineer or a building surveyor. Reference is made briefly to the employer's representative.

Engagement

It is good practice, and now the general rule, that all consultants are employed directly by the employer. That very conveniently separates the responsibilities so that each consultant is responsible directly to the employer for the proper performance of its services. However, sometimes the architect is asked to take on all consultants as sub-consultants so that the employer need only deal with one person: the architect.

Engagement through the architect

Obviously, there are serious implications for the architect in employing the consultants as sub-consultants. For example, each consultant may wish to contract on its own terms of engagement, whereas, to ensure that responsibilities are properly stepped up and down, the architect will want them all to contract on terms that are compatible with the architect's own terms of engagement. Another problem is that if there is a fault in, say, the structural design that leads to more expense for the employer, the employer, having no direct contract with the structural engineer, has no option but to take legal action against the architect. In turn, the architect must then take action against the structural engineer or, if the action is through the courts, the architect may be able to 'join in' the engineer into the proceedings. None of this will assist the architect if the structural engineer's professional indemnity insurers will not, for some reason, pay out. Where consultants are engaged through the architect, the architect must ensure that the giving of a warranty to the employer is part of the consultant's terms of engagement.

The JCT Standard Building Contract 2011, First Edition. David Chappell.
© 2014 by David Chappell. Published 2014 by John Wiley & Sons, Ltd.

Access

3.1
Other than the architect, no consultant has any right of access to the Works. In order for a consultant to be allowed onto the Works, the architect must notify the contractor that the consultant is authorised to have access to the site and all relevant workshops. Ideally, a consultant should never visit site without the architect in attendance. It is during visits to site that many consultants give instructions to the person-in-charge often without any written record. This may lead to serious disputes if the contractor complies with the instruction without confirming it and there are significant costs for the employer or if the instruction leads to a defect in the work.

Instructions

3.10
Under no circumstances may any consultant give instructions directly to the contractor. Only the architect may give instructions. This means that a consultant must not orally instruct the person-in-charge (or worse still the sub-contractor actually doing the work) and must not send written instructions to the contractor. The practice that consultants sometimes adopt, of writing to the contractor with a copy to the architect, is not acceptable. Each consultant must be informed, in writing, that if an instruction is thought desirable, the consultant must send it in draft to the architect who will issue it as an architect's instruction. Before doing so, the architect must be satisfied that it is necessary and what the cost implications may be.

8.2 Quantity surveyors

Quantity surveyors are specifically mentioned by name in the contract. Moreover, the quantity surveyor is given specific powers and duties in the contract. Most of these powers and duties relate to valuation of work carried out and the finalisation of what is commonly referred to as the 'final account'.

Replacement

In a similar way to the architect, if the quantity surveyor is unable to continue to act under the contract, the employer must nominate a replacement as soon as reasonably practicable and certainly within 21 days. Except where the employer is a local authority and the replacement is an employee, the contractor has the right to object to the nomination within 7 days. If the employer accepts the objection or if it is considered sufficient under the dispute resolution procedure, the employer must renominate.

Bills of quantities

One of the key tasks will be to prepare the bills of quantities. They must be prepared in accordance with the Standard Method of Measurement (SMM) unless, in respect of some particular items, the bills state that they have been

4.1

2.14.1

1.1

measured in some other way. The bills are a key document. The employer effectively guarantees to the contractor that they accurately represent the work to be done. If there are any errors in the bills or any omissions, misdescriptions or the like, they are to be corrected and the correction is to be treated as a variation. In other words, the Contract Sum covers the work and materials in the bills and nothing more. If more or different things are required, the Contract Sum must be adjusted by a variation. Obviously, by the time the contract is signed, the bills of quantities will have been prepared and will form part of the contract documents.

Interim valuations

4.10.2

It is generally accepted that in projects where the Contract Sum is substantial, in other words most projects using SBC, the quantity surveyor will prepare a valuation before the architect issues a certificate. However, it is clear from the contract that it is only when the architect considers a valuation to be necessary that the quantity surveyor is empowered to act unless the fluctuation Option C (formula adjustment) applies when a valuation must be made before each certificate. The valuation must be carried out no more than 7 days before the due date of an interim payment. That is to avoid a situation where a valuation is done, say, 14 days before the due date and by the time it is paid, 14 days after the due date, the contractor has incurred substantial additional costs. The idea is to provide the contractor with a reasonable cash flow.

The contractor may send an application for payment stating the sum it believes is due and attaching a calculation no later than 7 days before the due date. The quantity surveyor is not required to respond directly to the contractor (as was the case in the previous edition of this contract (SBC05), but no doubt the contractor's calculations will be taken into account in the subsequent valuation.

120

Many if not all quantity surveyors are in the habit of sending a copy of their interim valuations to the contractor. This is thoroughly bad practice. The reason is that the valuation is prepared for the benefit of the architect who may not agree with parts of the valuation and may wish to discuss it with the quantity surveyor. For example, it may only be on receipt of the valuation that the architect realises that he or she has failed to notify the quantity surveyor of a significant defect that has subsequently been valued as properly executed work. The architect may have other issues. Many contractors take the quantity surveyor's valuation as being the definitive statement of the amount the employer must pay. In fact, at any rate in the first instance, it is the architect's interim certificate that states the sum due and the architect is entitled to certify something other than what is in the quantity surveyor's valuation. It is misleading even to send a copy to the employer if the architect eventually certifies a different sum. For these reasons, the quantity surveyor should be instructed not to send the valuation to anyone other than the architect.

8.3   Employer's representative/project manager

3.3

The contract allows the employer to appoint what it calls an 'Employer's Representative'. In order to do that, the employer must write to the contractor to tell him:

- the name of the person appointed;
- that the representative will do everything that the contract requires the employer to do except the things specifically listed by the employer;
- the date from which the representative will start to act.

The employer can terminate the appointment, so far as the contractor is concerned, by simply writing again to the contractor to tell it so. Obviously, whether appointing or terminating, one would hope that the employer would first discuss the intention with the architect.

The contract suggests that, if a representative is appointed, it should not be either the architect or the quantity surveyor, because that could lead to confusion. That seems perfectly sensible advice.

Project manager

Sometimes an employer will appoint a project manager. This is a spectacularly vague term. It has a capable ring about it, but the question is what does (or perhaps should) a project manager actually do? Project managers grew in popularity over the last twenty years, but enthusiasm for their appointment seems to be on the wane at present. There are two types of project managers:

First type

This type of project manager performs all the functions of a contract administrator in regard to the building contract and, indeed, must be named as contract administrator in the contract. This person alone may issue instructions and certificates. In such circumstances, it is essential that the appointment documents of the other construction professionals reflect the situation. For example, the project manager is thought of as responsible for co-ordinating their roles, but cannot do so without authority and unless the terms of engagement of the other professionals acknowledge the project manager's authority. If the project manager's function is to manage the project as the name suggests, this type of project manager is closest to that role. However, it is comparatively rare to find a project manager in this position. This is the role traditionally taken by architects.

Second type

This type of project manager acts as the client's representative and it is the most usual type of project manager. They are usually appointed in addition to the normal phalanx of professionals. Generally project managers act as agent for the client with the power to do, in relation to the project, everything the client could do. They will interview and appoint consultants and carry out the briefing exercise having first been briefed by the client. The advantage is that there is a skilled professional look-ing after the client's interests and being paid to watch the other professionals. The disadvantage of course is that it is rather sad if the employer has to appoint a pro-fessional simply to make sure that all the other professionals are acting in a profes-sional way. One might enquire if there was yet another professional watching the project manager? However, that is an entirely different topic. It is this kind of pro-ject manager to which the contract appears to refer as 'Employer's Representative.

3.3

It is important to understand that the project manager or employer's repre-sentative has no powers under the building contract other than those that the employer has. The project manager has no power to issue certificates nor to recommend payment. Indeed, any interference by the project manager in the running of the contract will be interpreted as interference by the employer with significant adverse consequences. For example, interference by the employer in the issue of a certificate is grounds for the contractor to terminate

8.9.1.2

its employment. This kind of project manager has no more right than the employer to enter site, to attend site meetings and certainly not to give instruc-tions to the contractor. This means that, if a contractor takes instructions from a project manager, the quantity surveyor has no power to value the work done. The project manager has no status on site or even to enter the site during the progress of the Works. The project manager has no authority to organise, run or chair site meetings and his or her presence should be by invitation only.

8.4   Structural engineers, mechanical engineers and others

There is a vast array of possible consultants who may be engaged on a construc-tion contract. There are acoustic engineers, drainage engineers, swimming pool consultants, interior decorators and so on. None of them are mentioned in the contract. It does not even use the generic 'consultants'. None of them have powers or duties under the contract and their responsibilities depend on their individual terms of engagement. At the beginning of this chapter, something was said about access and the issuing of instructions. Their position can be summed up very simply: other than the architect/contract administrator, the quantity surveyor and the employer's representative (if appointed), no consultant may enter the site or communicate with any other consultant or the contractor without the express authority of the architect.

8.5   Common problems

The mechanical consultant goes on site without the architect's authority and issues instructions directly to the operative on site who carries out the instruction that proves to be wrong

The consultant should not issue instructions except through the architect. All instructions issued on site should be issued to the person-in-charge. The contractor's operatives should not take instructions from anyone other than the person-in-charge. In this case, the operative probably worked for the mechanical sub-contractor. While on site, the sub-contractor should only take instructions from the person-in-charge. So this is wrong in every respect, but sadly very common in practice.

Looked at strictly, this is an instruction that was issued by someone unauthorised to issue it and received by someone unauthorised to receive it. It was not an instruction under the contract and not to be valued. Therefore, the contractor cannot claim payment under the contract, nor directly from the employer who probably knows nothing about it. Moreover, the work carried out was in breach of contract, because it was different from what was in the contract documents or properly instructed. Therefore, the architect can instruct the contractor to put the situation back to before the instruction was issued. The contractor cannot claim against the consultant personally because the contractor should know not to take direct instructions from anyone but the architect and the consultant could not, in any case, issue instructions about something that was not his or her property.

The project manager insists on counter signing certificates and chairing meetings

Unless the project manager is acting as contract administrator, he or she has no authority to sign certificates or chair site meetings or do any of the dozens of things that the architect would normally do in administering the contract. If the project manager tries to insist on interfering, the architect should inform the employer immediately, because interference in certificates by the employer (whom the project manager is representing) is a ground for the contractor to commence termination.

8.9.1.2

The architect should also explain to the employer that the project manager must not interfere with the architect in carrying out the contract administration duties. If that interference prevents the architect from carrying out the relevant duties effectively, the architect may be entitled to accept the employer's conduct as a repudiation.

9 The clerk of works

9.1 Method of appointment

3.4

121

A clerk of works must always be appointed where constant or frequent inspection is required. The clerk of works should be appointed by the employer. Sometimes, an architectural practice will have a permanent clerk of works on its staff and will use him or her as the clerk of works. That is not a good idea so far as the architect is concerned. Suppose there is a problem with inspection of the Works and the architect is found to be negligent and sued by the employer. The damages payable by the architect may be reduced to reflect any contributory negligence by the clerk of works if the clerk of works is engaged by the employer. That is because, as employer of the clerk of works, the employer is liable for the clerk of works' actions. It is called 'vicarious liability'. All employers are liable for the actions of their employees while carrying out their employment duties. It is obvious that if the architect employs a clerk of works, there will be no reduction in liability, because the architect will be liable and liable for the clerk of works.

9.2 Duties

The contract emphasises that the clerk of works only duty is to inspect. The clerk of works is certainly not the architect's agent even though, in practice, architects often use the clerk of works to carry out many tasks such as checking dimensions on site. The clerk of works is stated to be under the 'direction', and often stated to be the 'eyes' and 'ears', of the architect. So far as the contract is concerned, the only directions the architect may give must refer to the materials and operations that require inspection and the quality and standards that are specified.

The contractor must give all reasonable facilities to enable the clerk of works to inspect. For example, that means that the clerk of works must be allowed access to the Works via scaffolding, but it does not mean that the contractor is required to erect scaffolding especially for the clerk of works.

The JCT Standard Building Contract 2011, First Edition. David Chappell.
© 2014 by David Chappell. Published 2014 by John Wiley & Sons, Ltd.

The contract does not empower the issue of directions by the clerk of works. But it seems to tolerate them. It simply says that if a direction is given, it is of no effect unless:

- the direction is given in regard to something that the architect is also empowered to issue an instruction; and
- the architect confirms the direction within two working days.

If confirmed, the clerk of works' direction becomes an architect's instruction effective from the date of confirmation. It is difficult to see why the provision regarding directions is included at all. At present, it is common for clerks of works virtually to run many jobs in the sense of answering questions from the contractor and even instructing variations. Many contracts would grind to a halt if that situation was not tolerated. But a good outcome is never an excuse for a bad practice and any contractor who acts on the basis of a clerk of work's direction is in breach of contract. It should be noted that the contract states that the contractor is wholly responsible for carrying out and completing the Works in accordance with the contract whether or not a clerk of works is appointed.

3.6

9.3 Snagging lists

Many clerks of works issue 'snagging lists', especially in the period before practical completion. They usually go much further than the usual list of defects that a clerk of works will hand to the contractor on a daily basis. There is, of course, no reference to 'snagging lists' in the contract although there is reference to a 'schedule of defects' in connection with the rectification period. 'Snagging' seems to be used to describe a more informal kind of list. The contents still amount to breaches of contract on the part of the contractor. Clearly, clerks of works are trying to be helpful and their efforts are generally appreciated by contractors. Care should be taken, however, that the clerk of works is not simply doing the job that should be done by the contractor's person-in-charge. A big problem with snagging lists is that a contractor given such a list often assumes that the list is comprehensive and that if all the 'snags' are dealt with, the Works will be finished. The clerk of works seldom intends that to be the case and, even if that was the case, those intentions would be irrelevant. Merely complying with a clerk of work's snagging list can never take the place of compliance with the contract.

9.4 Defacing materials

Some clerks of works insist on marking, with indelible crayon or even the point of a chisel, materials and goods that they consider not to be in accordance with the contract. There is no justification for that. Goods that are not in accordance with the contract are not accepted by the employer and, therefore, those goods remain the property of the contractor. As such, the employer or even the clerk of works personally could be liable for defacement. One might expect the contractor to issue a strong letter to employer and architect requiring the practice to cease. It is probable that, after a warning, the contractor is entitled to charge the employer for that kind of damage.

9.5   Common problems

Some employers, particularly local authorities, employ large numbers of specialist clerks of works. Is the contractor obliged to allow all of them to wander around the site causing confusion?

3.4

The contract allows the appointment of a clerk of works. The contractor must afford the clerk of works every reasonable facility to inspect the Works. It seems clear that the contract envisages a single clerk of works. If the project is very large and complex, it is probable that the term 'clerk of works' could be interpreted to mean a group of clerks of works on the basis that it would be unreasonable to expect a singled clerk of works to inspect a substantial development. Reference to the architect or the quantity surveyor may actually mean a firm employing numbers of people. The architect is entitled to authorise people to have access to the Works and those people could be specialist clerks of works.

However, none of the people authorised by the architect is entitled to issue directions to the contractor; only the clerk of works may do that. The position seems to be that unless the project is substantial, only one clerk of works is authorised. If more or specialised clerks of works are required, the architect must authorise their access and they may not deal directly with the contractor but only through the clerk of works or the architect.

The clerk of works orders the contractor to stop work

3.15

Occasionally a clerk of works will order the contractor to stop work, but more often it will be a threat. The contract says that the clerk of works can issue directions about anything for which the architect may issue instructions and the architect can issue instructions to postpone the Works or any part of them. However, no clerk of work's direction has any validity unless confirmed in writing by the architect within 2 working days. It is difficult to imagine an architect confirming a clerk of work's direction to stop work, because to do so would entitle the contractor to an extension of time and possibly loss and/or expense. Postponement is something that the architect would instruct only after serious consideration with the employer and for something that could not be dealt with in any other way. For example, the architect would not postpone work because the contractor's work had defects.

Therefore, in the ordinary course of things, the clerk of work's threat to stop work would be an empty threat. A direction from the clerk of works that work should actually stop would not be immediately effective and not effective at all unless the architect confirmed it within 2 working days. The chances of the architect confirming a postponement of work by the clerk of works are probably little to none.

10 Sub-contractors and suppliers

10.1 General

Assignment and sub-contracting are often confused or perhaps, more accurately, not understood. Before considering the contract provisions in detail, it is important to understand the difference between these terms. They are significantly different.

Assignment

This is the transfer of the *benefit* of an obligation that A owes to B into a benefit from A to C. This might be an obligation to pay money, construct a building or any other contractual duty. However, it is important to understand that the nature and content of the obligation cannot be changed by the assignment. Therefore, if A is obliged to provide B with tiles for his roof, the benefit to B is the tiles. A cannot be obliged to provide C, after assignment, with a different kind of tile even if the tiles that A was obliged to provide to B are not suitable for C. This is why contracts for personal service, such as chauffeur, cook or gardener are not assignable. C may have entirely different tastes in cars, food and gardens to B. A different kind of assignment is when the *obligation* that A owes to B is assigned so that the obligation is owed by C (instead of A) to B. This kind of assignment can only be properly done by novation (see below).

Sub-contracting

Sub-contracting is when A has an obligation to B and A delegates the carrying out of the obligation to C. This is frequently done in construction contracts. Importantly, sub-contracting does not remove A's obligation to B. If C fails to carry out the obligation, it is up to A to sort out the problem. Under this system, A is liable for performance to B and C is liable for the same performance to A. C is not liable to B for any failure to perform. In a construction contract, the contractor may be obliged to install some electrical work and the contractor may sub-contract the electrical work to an electrician. If the electrical work is poor or late or does not get finished, the electrician will be liable to the

The JCT Standard Building Contract 2011, First Edition. David Chappell.
© 2014 by David Chappell. Published 2014 by John Wiley & Sons, Ltd.

contractor and the contractor will be liable to the employer, but the electrician will not be liable to the employer.

Novation

Although not mentioned in SBC, novation is related to assignment and should be clearly understood. It is a process by which a contract between A and B is changed into a contract between C and B. It can only be carried out if A, B and C all agree. The importance of this is that it is the only way in which A can rid himself of his obligation to B. Even if the benefit of a contract is assigned by B to C, A still remains liable. A true novation, removes all rights and obligations between A and B and transfers them between C and B. A has no further rights against, or duties to, B and B has no further rights against, or duties to, A. C assumes the rights and duties in respect of B and B assumes the rights and duties, formerly owed in respect of A, to C. A proper novation will provide that the rights and duties between C and B are as if C had been in the place of A from the beginning of the contract. Parties entering into novation agreements should be wary of agreements that do not include all these provisions or that attempt to leave some residual obligations between A and B. Those are not true novation agreements.

122

10.2 Assignment

Neither the employer nor the contractor is entitled to assign the contract without the written consent of the other. It has already been seen that the law does not allow the assignment of the obligation to do something except by novation. Therefore, this can only refer to assignment of the benefit of a contract, i.e. the right to receive something. For example, the employer might wish to sell the building before the final certificate is issued or the contractor may wish to assign the right to receive payment in return for a cash advance from a funder. Consent has to be given by the other party in each case. A party may refuse consent on grounds that might be considered unreasonable. This can pose real problems and if the employer wishes to assign the benefit of the contract (i.e. sell or otherwise transfer the property to another) before practical completion, an amendment to the clause is advisable.

7.1

The contract deals with the situation where the employer sells the freehold or the leasehold interest in the premises comprising the Works to a third party, or where the employer grants a leasehold interest in the premises. It will only apply if it is stated to apply in the contract particulars. In any of these instances, the employer may assign to that third party the right to bring proceedings in the employer's name and to enforce any of the terms of the contract. The employer does not have the right to sell the premises before receiving them from the contractor at practical completion. However, once the employer has received the building and disposed of it by sale or lease, it enables the purchaser to act as if the purchaser was the employer so far as the benefits of the contract

7.2

are concerned. For example, the obligation to pay the contractor remains with the employer, but the purchaser can enforce the rectification period provisions.

There is a proviso that the third party cannot dispute any agreement that is legally enforceable and that is entered into between the employer and the contractor before the assignment. Therefore, if the employer and the contractor have entered into an agreement under which the contractor is not obliged to make good certain defects and no monetary deduction is to be made, it is binding on the purchaser of the premises.

10.3   Sub-contracting

3.7.1

The contractor must not sub-let without the architect's consent. The architect must not unreasonably delay or withhold consent, but there is no requirement that the contractor must inform the architect of the names of sub-contractors. It is merely consent to the fact of sub-contracting that is required. Nevertheless, it is probably reasonable for the architect to refuse to give consent until the name and perhaps other details of the prospective sub-contractor were made known. If the architect does give consent, the contractor's obligations to carry out and complete the Works in accordance with the contract documents, the construction phase plan and statutory requirements are not affected by

2.1

sub-contracting part of the Works. In practice, the architect will normally give consent if the contractor provides evidence that the proposed sub-contractor is capable of doing the work in accordance with the contract and the contractor's programme.

Insolvency issues

If the contractor has become insolvent when a defect is found in a sub-contractor's work, the employer has no effective contractual remedy against the

123

sub-contractor and little hope of a tortious remedy. This may pose difficulties at that late stage. To overcome such problems, the architect may make the provision of an acceptable warranty to the employer on the part of all sub-contractors a precondition to the giving of any consent to sub-letting. A better solution is for the architect to insert that stipulation, accompanied by an example of the warranty required, in the specification or bills of quantities so that contractors are aware of the requirement at tender stage. SBC has provision for

124

standard warranties from sub-contractors to be listed in part 2 of the contract

7E

particulars. The provision of a warranty from the sub-contractor to the employer creates a contractual relationship and enables the employer to exercise rights against the sub-contractor (depending on the precise terms of the warranty) in the event of the contractor's insolvency.

In some instances of contractor insolvency or imminent insolvency, sub-contractors approach the employer with requests to be paid directly instead of through the contractor. Employers should refuse these requests. The contractor has contracted to carry out the whole of the Works including some parts that are sub-let. Therefore, if the sub-let work is done, the contractor is entitled to payment for it. The fact that the employer has already paid the sub-contractor directly makes no difference. There is no clause in the contract that entitles the employer to deduct from the contractor money that has been paid directly to the sub-contractor. As far as the contract is concerned, any deduction of that kind would simply amount to a breach of contract.

Sub-contract terms

3.9; **125** The contract states that 'where considered appropriate' the relevant JCT sub-contract should be used for sub-letting. The contract does not state whose opinion is intended and it leaves the contractor plenty of scope to decide to use an entirely different sub-contract; perhaps of its own making. However, the contractor is required to make sure that every sub-contract has some specific terms. They are quite important, because they affect the contractor's work and ultimately the employer's entitlements. They can be summarised as follows:

- The employment of the sub-contractor terminates immediately termination of the contractor's employment takes place.
- Unfixed materials and goods delivered to the Works or adjacent to the Works must not be removed without the architect's consent.
- Ownership of materials and goods is to be automatically transferred to the employer after the value has been included in an interim certificate for which payment has been made.
- If the contractor has paid for materials and goods before certification, ownership passes to the contractor.
- The sub-contractor must grant right of access for the architect to its workshops where work is being prepared.
- Contractor and sub-contractor undertake to comply with the CDM Regulations.
- The contractor must pay simple interest at the rate in the contract particulars for unpaid sums.
- The sub-contractor will provide the collateral warranties stipulated in the contract particulars.
- The operation of this clause is not to affect ownership in off-site materials passing to the contractor.

The architect should try to ensure that these provisions are included in sub-contracts and it seems reasonable that the architect should refuse to consent to sub-contracting unless evidence of the inclusion is produced. However, the contract does not place any specific duty on the architect to check. Although the JCT standard sub-contracts contain these provisions, many contractors habitually sub-contract using their own terms that not only do not contain such provisions, but also do not create a satisfactory 'back to back' sub-contractual arrangement. A 'back to back' sub-contract is one that passes liabilities down to the sub-contractor and up to the contractor.

Retention of title

Even if all these provisions are included, they are ineffective to safeguard the employer from the perils of what is known as 'retention of title'. It is a complex topic, but essentially it amounts to this: a sub-contractor cannot pass ownership of material to the contractor if the sub-contractor does not itself own it. If the sub-contractor has bought the goods itself on terms that the supplier retains ownership until payment is made, title (i.e. ownership) in the material cannot pass to the subcontractor until payment is made. Therefore, although the terms of SBC my protect the employer against problems with the contractor failing to own material and the sub-contractor may afford similar protection to the contractor and through it to the employer, there is no protection against claims by the supplier to the sub-contractor. Building contract chains are so long that it is virtually impossible to check down to the ultimate supplier that ownership has passed unimpeded up to the contractor. Failure of the contractor to comply with the obligation to insert these terms into a sub-contract is a ground for termination by the employer, although it may be a disproportionate remedy in most circumstances.

8.4.1.4

10.4 Listed sub-contractors

The contract provides for the listing of a selection of sub-contractors. It is a way of limiting the contractor's choice of sub-contractors for certain work. That is the theory although, in practice, that may not be the result, as can be seen below. The contractor may choose any one of the sub-contractors listed for a particular part of the work. The resultant sub-contractor is just an ordinary or a domestic sub-contractor. That is a sub-contractor for which the contractor is solely responsible. In order to list sub-contractors, the following requirements must be observed:

3.8

- The bills of quantities must specify certain work as required to be carried out by persons selected by the contractor from a list in or attached to the bills of quantities.

3.8.1

- There must be no less than three persons on the list that can be increased by names added by the employer and/or the contractor with each other's consent at any time until the sub-contract is signed. But consent cannot be unreasonably delayed or withheld and this of course means that it will be difficult for the employer to block any names submitted by the contractor unless they are obviously unsuitable. The effect of this is that the main purpose of the list, to allow the employer to restrict the choice to certain sub-contractors well known and probably trusted by the employer is defeated, because the contractor can add any sub-contractors of its own choice provided the employer is not able to say convincingly that they are unsuitable in some way.

3.8.2

- If the number on the list falls below three, the employer and the contractor must agree the addition of further names or the contractor may carry out the work. In doing so, the contractor may, if it wishes, sub-let to any sub-contractor in the usual way with the architect's consent.

3.8.3

3.7

Importantly, once the contractor has entered into a sub-contract with someone on the list, the architect has no involvement in sub-contract extensions of time, financial claims or termination of the sub-contractor's employment.

10.5   Named specialists

It may be, because the editions of SBC since 2005 omitted the use of nominated sub-contractors, that it has been thought necessary to allow for something now referred to as 'named specialists'. Although the nomination procedure in JCT 98 and early contracts was full of problems, there is no doubt that many architects made use of it. Whatever the reason, if it is desired to name certain specialists, a series of standard clauses must be incorporated into the contract

Schedule 8, (see Chapter 3, Section 3.1 for details of incorporation) and various amend-
paragraph 7 ments made to the rest of the contract.

The way the named specialist provisions work is this: the specialist may be named in the contract together with the work to be carried out, or a provisional sum may be inserted in the bills of quantities and the architect may issue an instruction to expend the provisional sum naming the specialist and identify-
paragraph 7.1 ing the work. The first option is called 'Pre-Named Specialist Work' and the second option is inevitably called 'Post-Named Specialist Work'. The contract particulars have an extra entry that has to be completed to show which kind of named specialist is included.

The contractor must enter into a contract with the specialist as soon as 'reasonably practicable', which means that the cost of complying in terms of money, time and effort must not be excessive compared to the benefit to be obtained
paragraph 7.2 from complying within any particular period of time. If the contractor cannot
126 enter into a contract as required, it must notify the architect of the reason and the architect must give instructions to the contractor that either:

- remove the reason preventing the contract; or
- name another specialist who can do the work; or
- direct the contractor to do the work itself or choose its own specialist sub-contractor approved by the architect; or
paragraph 7.3 - omit the work altogether.

Specialists who are named in architect's instructions are dealt with slightly differently. The contractor has the right to raise a reasonable objection within 7 days of receiving the instruction. The objection must be in writing to the architect and the architect then has a further 7 days in which to issue an instruction naming another specialist, directing the contractor to do the work itself or
paragraph 7.4 through its sub-contractor or omitting the work altogether.

If the contractor becomes entitled to terminate the employment of the specialist or to give default notice or to treat the specialists' conduct as repudiation (repudiation is explained in Chapter 1, Section 1.1), the contractor, before doing anything, must notify the architect and consult the architect and also the employer if asked to do so. The contractor must wait 14 days after having given that notification before giving notice of termination or of repudiation unless the specialist has become insolvent. In that case, the matter is out of the contractor's control. The contractor must send the architect copies of all the notices that it sends to the specialist under the sub-contract.

If matters progress and the contractor does terminate the employment of the specialist or treats the sub-contract as repudiated, the architect must issue instructions to the contractor naming another specialist, directing the contractor to do the work itself or through its sub-contractor or omitting the work
paragraph 7.6   altogether.

The standard clauses end by stating that the contractor's responsibility for carrying out and completing the Works is not affected by the architect naming
paragraph 7.7   a specialist or by anything the architect is entitled to do by the standard clauses.

10.6   Common problems

The sub-contractor sends the architect shop drawings for approval

It is a time-honoured custom for the contractor to forward shop drawings to the architect. If they form part of the CDP, the contract lays down specific
Schedule 1   rules for dealing with them. Often they are just the sub-contractor's interpretation of the architect's drawings, perhaps to a larger scale and sometimes with changes to fit in with the sub-contractor's patent systems. In this case, the architect will usually want to check through them to make sure that the sub-contractor has properly interpreted the architect's drawings. The contract does not refer to the architect approving drawings. If there is reference to 'approval', it must be in the preliminaries to the bills of quantities. The architect should check and see that no reference to 'approval' is in the preliminaries before they are sent out for tender.

When the architect checks the shop drawings, it is appropriate either, to say that there are no comments or, that there are comments and list them. Even if the architect were to approve drawings, it is by no means certain that the approval would have the effect of transferring responsibility from the sub-contractor to the architect if the sub-contractor had made an error that was not on
127   the architect's original drawings.

The sub-contractor says it is going to remove its fittings from site because the contractor has not paid

The contract says that the contractor must include in any sub-contract that site materials become the employer's property if their value has been included in a certificate and paid by the employer. The problem is that the employer does not know whether the contractor has included that in any particular sub-contract. If so, then the sub-contractor is quite simply in breach of its sub-contract if it attempts to remove any site materials. If there is nothing in the sub-contract, the contractor is in breach and the employer can claim from the contractor the value of any site materials removed. The contractor may be in liquidation, in which case, it will be very difficult to refuse a claim from the sub-contractor for the materials even though the employer may have secured the site. If the materials have been incorporated into the Works, they are owned by the employer and the sub-contractor would be acting unlawfully in removing them.

128

The employer wishes to pay the sub-contractor directly and deduct the money from payments to the contractor

The simple answer is that the employer cannot do that or, rather, that there is no provision in the contract to allow that to happen. Employers do pay sub-contractors directly and then they deduct the amount from monies certified to the contractor. This is often done after a direct request from the sub-contractor to the employer saying that the contractor is not paying. Of course, the contractor may have a very good reason for not paying: defective work, failure to turn up on site and so on. If the sub-contractor believes it is entitled to be paid, it can very easily seek adjudication on the point. Whether or not the sub-contractor chooses to do this is a matter for the sub-contractor and it is no concern of the employer.

The contractor has entered into a contract to carry out the whole of the Works. Some of the Works will be sub-contracted, but under the terms of the contract, the architect must certify, and the employer must pay to the contractor, the value of all the work carried out. If the employer tries to deduct money from a certificate, even with a pay less notice, it can be challenged by the contractor on the basis that direct payment of the same amount is not a good ground for deducting it from the contractor. Because there is nothing in the contract that allows that kind of deduction, the employer will, sooner or later, have to pay it to the contractor. Therefore, the employer will pay for the same work twice. The contractor does not have to prove that it has paid the sub-contractor; only that the work has been properly carried out.

4.16.1.1

A sub-contractor has been specified by name in the bills of quantities and the sub-contractor has now gone into liquidation half-way through its work

The first thing to note is that, although architects often specify by reference to a sub-contractor by name, there is nothing in the unamended contract that permits that to be done. Therefore, when an architect refers to roof tiling to be carried out by Acme Roof Tiling Specialists Limited, it is simply wrong. The contract makes provision for the contractor to pick a sub-contractor and to ask the architect to consent to the sub-contracting. Alternatively, the architect can insert the names of at least three sub-contractors in the bills of quantities so that the contractor can pick one of them or the Named Specialist Update can be incorporated into the contract that allows the architect to name a specialist. Despite this, architects still name sub-contractors without using the Named Specialist Update.

In that case, the contractor could always refuse to tender or submit a tender that confirms its right to choose its own sub-contractor and risk being disqualified. However, generally contractors will simply go to that sub-contractor for a price to include in the main contract tender. Usually, there is no problem and the sub-contractor performs, the contractor knows it is responsible for the sub-contractor and if the sub-contract price goes up, the contractor has to deal with it.

The problem arises if the sub-contractor goes into liquidation or simply walks off the project refusing to return. The architect may think, and often does think, that it is up to the contractor to find a replacement. Some architects try to insist on the contractor absorbing any extra costs on the misplaced idea that the contractor is liable for the named sub-contractor as for any other sub-contractor. That is quite wrong. If the architect decides to make the use of a particular sub-contractor part of the contract requirements, the contractor who tenders on that basis is obliged to use that sub-contractor. The contractor cannot use any other sub-contractor even if the original named sub-contractor ceases to trade, because to use a different sub-contractor would be a breach of the contract obligation that required the use of the sub-contractor now in liquidation. The architect cannot issue an instruction to use another sub-contractor, because the architect has no power to issue an instruction of that kind. It is not a variation of work or materials or the alteration or modification of design and it does not fall into any of the other permitted instructions.

If the architect refuses to do anything, strictly speaking, the contract will be frustrated, because there is no fault on either side yet the contractor finds it impossible to comply with the requirement to use a particular sub-contractor. However, the employer, as a party to the contract, can agree with the contractor (the other party) that another sub-contractor is to be used. In those circumstances, the contractor can claim from the employer any additional cost of the new sub-contractor. In practice, the architect will usually issue an instruction to change the sub-contractor, the contractor will simply comply and the quantity surveyor will treat it as a variation and value it accordingly.

11 Statutory authorities

11.1 Work not forming part of the contract

2.7

129

The employer has the right to engage persons other than the contractor to carry out work on the site. But the employer is not entitled to deduct work from the contractor so as to give it to another contractor to do. That is very important. If the employer did that it would be a breach of contract for which the contractor would be entitled to claim damages from the employer.

There are two situations in which the employer may engage other persons:

2.7.1

■ If the bills of quantities provide the contractor with very full information so that the contractor knows which part of the work is to be carried out by others so it can properly carry out its own work required under the contract. In such an instance, the contractor must permit the specific work.

2.7.2

■ If the bills of quantities do not provide the full information noted above. In that case, the employer may still employ other persons to do work not included in the contract provided that the contractor gives its consent. The contractor must not unreasonably delay or withhold its consent.

2.29.7
4.24.5

It is worth remembering that delays caused by persons engaged by the employer may result in entitlement to an extension of time for the contractor or the payment of direct loss and/or expense. The delays may be caused by the separately engaged persons failing to carry out the work, carrying it out slowly or even carrying it out properly. For the employer to engage other contractors is like signing a blank cheque.

Persons engaged by the employer in this way are persons for whom the employer is responsible and not sub-contractors.

11.2 Statutory authorities in contract

The gas, electricity and water suppliers and other bodies regulated by statute including local authorities, may be involved either in performance of their statutory obligations or as contractors. An important point to note is that

The JCT Standard Building Contract 2011, First Edition. David Chappell.
© 2014 by David Chappell. Published 2014 by John Wiley & Sons, Ltd.

while they are performing their statutory obligations, they do not enter into
130   contracts. The obligation of a statutory undertaker, if any, depends on statute
and not upon contract.

Although they may not be liable for damages for breach of contract, that
does not exonerate them in tort, e.g., for negligence.

Therefore, SBC draws a distinction between statutory undertakers performing their statutory duties and those situations where they act as contractors or
sub-contractors. The contract states that the sub-contract provisions of the
contract do not apply to statutory undertakers carrying out part of the Works
and they are not sub-contractors as referred to under the contract. Obviously,
if a statutory undertaker were to be engaged to carry out part of the contract
under a sub-contract, it would be a sub-contractor. The statutory undertaker
providing the electricity service to a property is carrying out a statutory duty; a
statutory undertaker carrying out electrical wiring to the inside of a property
will be acting as a sub-contractor.

Every person or firm must comply with requirements laid down by statute.
A contractor's duty to comply with statutory requirements will prevail over any
131   express contractual obligation.

Statutory requirements

The meaning of 'statutory requirements' is helpfully defined as being requirements of any statute, statutory instrument, regulation, rule or order made
under any statute or directive that affects the Works or performance of any
obligations under this Contract and any regulation or by-law of any local
1.1   authority or any statutory undertaker' relative to the Works. Statutory instru-
ments are usually made by a Secretary of State and the most important, from
the contractor's point of view, will probably be the Building Regulations 2010
and the Construction (Design and Management) Regulations 2007, usually
referred to as the CDM Regulations.

The contractor must comply with all statutory requirements and give all
2.1   notices that may be required by them. The contractor is also responsible
2.21   for paying all fees and charges legally demandable in respect of the Works.
If the fees are stated as provisional sums, they must be dealt with accordingly. Otherwise, the contractor is entitled to have the amount of the fees
added to the Contract Sum unless they are already provided for in the contract.

Indemnity

Not only must the contractor pay the charges as already noted, but it agrees to
indemnify the employer against liability in respect of such charges. What that
means is that, if the contractor fails to pay as legally required, the contractor
assumes liability on behalf of the employer. Such liability might well extend to
undoing work already done, delays or fines. This is an onerous provision that

might easily be overlooked. Its purpose is to keep the employer safe from damage or loss. Although indemnity clauses tend to be interpreted against the person relying on them, it is not thought that this will give the contractor much comfort here. In addition, the time during which the contractor remains liable (the limitation period already explained) under an indemnity clause does not begin to run until the liability of the employer has been established, usually by a court.

The position if the architect or the contractor finds a divergence between the contract documents and statutory requirements has already been considered in Chapter 3, Section 3.5.

Building control officer's directions

Contractors are not entitled to carry out instructions from anyone other than the architect. It is not unknown for a building control officer to visit a site and to direct the contractor that work does not comply with the Building Regulations. However tempting it may be for the contractor simply to comply with the direction, particularly if it seems that there is no possible alternative, the contractor must do nothing until it has referred the matter immediately to the architect and received an instruction. The only exception to this is in the case of an emergency. If the matter really is urgent, the contractor may carry out the necessary work immediately provided that it notifies the architect, as soon as it reasonably can do so, of the steps it is taking, and supplies only sufficient materials and carries out just enough work to ensure compliance. The contractor is then entitled to payment for what it has done just as though *2.18* the architect had issued an instruction.

11.3   The CDM Regulations 2007

Breach of the *Construction (Design and Management) Regulations 2007* will be a criminal offence, but a breach of the Regulations will not usually give rise to civil liability. Thus, one person cannot normally sue another for breach of the Regulations. That is why compliance with the Regulations is made a contractual duty so that breach of the Regulations is also a breach of contract. This is likely to cause problems for the employer.

CDM co-ordinator

Article 5 assumes that the architect will be the CDM co-ordinator. In practice, many architects do not act as CDM co-ordinators and the word 'or' is inserted to enable the user to insert an alternative name. Article 5 is not sufficient to act as a contract between the architect and the employer for the purpose of carrying out the function of CDM co-ordinator and a separate contract for these services should be entered into.

Principal contractor

Article 6 defines the principal contractor as the contractor. Again the word 'or' is inserted to allow another person to be specified as the principal contractor. In practice it is rare for someone other than the contractor to be the principal contractor. Both the employer and the contractor undertake to comply with the CDM Regulations.

3.23

The employer must 'ensure' that the CDM co-ordinator will carry out all his or her duties and that, if the principal contractor is not the contractor, it will carry out its duties in accordance with the Regulations. This is little short of a guarantee whether the employer realises it or not. There are also provisions that if the contractor is the principal contractor, it will prepare the construction phase plan and notify amendments to the plan to the employer, CDM co-ordinator and the architect and see that welfare facilities are in place from the beginning to the end of the construction phase.

3.23.1

2.38.2

If the contractor is not the principal contractor, it must promptly notify the principal contractor when any sub-contractor is appointed.

2.38.3

If the CDM co-ordinator asks, the contractor must promptly provide information for the preparation of the health and safety file. The request must be reasonable and if the contractor (unusually) is not the principal contractor, it must provide it to the principal contractor rather than to the CDM co-ordinator. The contractor must also 'ensure' that the sub-contractors provide the similar information.

2.38.4

2.29.7, 4.24.5

Compliance or non-compliance by the employer with the CDM Regulations is a 'relevant event' and a 'relevant matter'. What this means is that the employer must ensure that the CDM co-ordinator and the principal contractor (if it is not the contractor) perform correctly and if they do not, or even if they do, any resultant delay or disruption will give entitlement to extension of time and loss and/or expense. This may well be a most fruitful source of claims for contractors. Every instruction potentially carries a health and safety implication that should be addressed under the Regulations. The Regulations impose substantial duties on the CDM co-ordinator. Most of them are to be found in Regulations 20 and 21. Some of these duties must be carried out before work is commenced on site that may present difficulties where the contractor is not appointed until comparatively late in the process. If necessary actions delay the issue of an instruction or, once issued, they delay its execution, the contractor may be able to claim.

There may be rare occasions when the Regulations do not fully apply to the Works as described in the contract. If the situation changes due to the issue of an instruction or some other cause, the employer may be faced with substantial delay as appointments of CDM co-ordinator and principal contractor are made and appropriate duties are carried out under the full Regulations.

It is certain that the key factor will be for employers, CDM co-ordinators and principal contractors to structure their administrative procedures very carefully if they are to avoid becoming in breach of their contractual obligations in regard to the CDM Regulations.

11.4   Common problems

The electricity supplier failed to install the service at the right time

This is a difficult problem. Usually, the provision of electrical and other mains will be included in the bills of quantities to be provided by the statutory undertaker responsible. The contractor may have discussions with the provider and will issue an order for the incoming main. However, the undertaker will not enter into a contract because the obligation to install the main derives from legislation. It is a statutory duty. Therefore, it is important to make sure that the contractor sends in the order to the statutory undertaker allowing plenty of time for the work to be done. There is no point in the contractor sending the order before it is ready to receive the main. That will simply delay matters. Promptly sending the order is the answer, but a system of chasing up must be adopted by the contractor and the architect must in turn regularly pursue the contractor to see that it is done. The contract allows for an extension of time to be given to the contractor for delay on the part of a statutory undertaker in carrying out its statutory duties.

2.29.8

The contractor damages a main underground electricity cable

Main cables are supposed to be protected and the contractor should have been provided with a site plan showing its position. Generally, the contractor will be liable to the statutory undertaker for any damage done to a main cable and the cost of repair. It is conceivable that the statutory undertaker may be responsible for its own repair if the contractor can show that the cable was not in the position shown on the drawing or that it was not at the correct depth below ground level (before the contractor cleared anything from the site). The employer could be liable to the contractor if the drawing showing the position of the cable was supplied to the contractor by the architect. Obviously, in those circumstances, the employer ought to be able to recover the cost from the statutory undertaker assuming that it supplied the drawing in the first place.

Part III   Work in Progress

12   Insurance

12.1   Why insurance?

The insurance required by the contract is for the same purpose that anyone requires insurance. It is to provide money to restore a situation or to provide compensation if restoration is not practicable.

Insurance advice

The employer will often expect the architect or other contract administer to give advice about the insurance clauses and the whole business of obtaining insurance; which can be difficult at times. It is unlikely that the architect or any other construction profession has the necessary skill or experience to competently advise the employer. Obviously, the architect can show the employer the insurance clauses and can say what the options mean. However, if there is any difficulty or any situation in which the employer requires some advice on what the wording means in detail or what should be done if insurance is not available, the architect should advise the employer to seek the advice of its insurance broker. An architect would not dream of giving advice regarding complex mechanical systems or a structural frame. Insurance is just another specialism for which the employer must seek specialist advice. It is good practice for the architect, as a matter of course, to advise the employer to seek insurance advice well before tenders are invited.

12.2   Types of insurance in the contract

Under this contract, insurance is to cover the contractor's liabilities and to provide for various occurrences that may result in damage to the Works or to existing property. Details of the insurances are set out in this chapter.

The JCT Standard Building Contract 2011, First Edition. David Chappell.
© 2014 by David Chappell. Published 2014 by John Wiley & Sons, Ltd.

12.3   What is an indemnity?

What does it mean when the contractor gives an indemnity or indemnifies the employer? It means that the contractor agrees to make good all loss suffered by the employer in certain circumstances that the indemnity will set out. At its most basic, If Emma says to a builder, 'I understand you are building a house for my friend Lucy. I will pay whatever it costs', Emma is indemnifying Lucy against the cost of the house. Joe and Tim may have agreed to share the costs of building a joint garage, but Joe may not be able to afford more than a certain sum, say £4,000. Tim may agree to indemnify Joe against any costs of the garage over £8,000 (£4,000 each). Therefore, if the total cost of the garage eventually comes to £9.500, Tim must pay the builder £5,500 (his own £4,000 plus the £1,500 extra). Joe just pays the £4,000.

When an architect (let us call him Jim) takes over a project on which another architect has been engaged (let us call her Jane), Jane may say that Jim has no licence to use the original drawings. That is essentially a dispute between Jane and the client. However, Jim may rightly have concerns that use of the original drawings may result in Jane suing him for infringement of copyright. In those circumstances, the client will often offer to indemnify Jim against any legal proceedings brought by Jane. That means that if Jane successfully sues Jim for infringement of copyright, the client will pay all the damages and costs a court may award against Jim.

Contractor's indemnity

1.1

There are two important definitions: 'Contractor's Persons' and 'Employer's Persons'. In the case of the contractor, they include employees, agents, sub-contractors and anyone on site at the contractor's behest. In the case of the employer, they include the architect, quantity surveyor, clerk of works, any others engaged by the employer and statutory undertakers.

The contractor assumes liability for, and indemnifies the employer against, any liability arising out of the carrying out of the Works in respect of the following:

6.1
- Personal injury or death of any person, unless and to the extent due to act or neglect of the employer or of the employer's persons.

6.2
- Injury or damage to any kind of property arising from the Works if and to the extent that it is due to the negligence, breach of statutory duty, omission, or default of the contractor or of any of the contractor's persons.

That takes careful reading to understand, but the actual wording in the contract is worse.

Schedule 3, paragraph C.1

The contractor's liability is limited with regard to property damage, compared to its liability for personal injury or death, because the contractor must be at fault for the indemnity to be operative. The contractor has no liability under this clause for any loss or damage that the employer has to insure for existing buildings. Therefore, where work is being carried out to existing premises the contractor will not be liable for damage to the existing premises or their contents, because they will already be insured by the employer.

The employer is responsible for the injury or death of any person only insofar as the injury or death was caused by the employer's or the employer's person's act or neglect. The employer is responsible for all loss or damage to property except to the extent it is caused by the contractor's or contractor's person's default. In practice, if any claim does arise, it is likely to be the employer who will be sued. In turn, the employer will join the contractor as a third party in any action and claim an indemnity under the contract.

Exclusion from the indemnities

6.3   The Works and site materials are excluded from these indemnities.

12.4   Injury to persons and property

6.4.1
The contractor must take out insurance (unless its existing insurances are adequate) to cover its liabilities to indemnify the employer against injury to persons and property. The fact that the contractor has taken out or maintains the appropriate insurance cover does not affect its liabilities. If, for some reason, the insurance company refused to pay in the case of an incident, the contractor would be obliged to find the money itself. The insurance is simply a way of trying to make sure that money is available. Even if the contractor failed to get insurance, it would still be liable.

Amount of cover

The insurance cover must be for a sum not less than whatever is stated in the contract particulars to the contract for any one occurrence or series of occurrences arising out of one event. The insurance against claims for personal injury or death of an employee or apprentice of the contractor must comply with all relevant legislation.

Right to inspect insurance

6.4.2
The employer has the right to inspect documentary evidence that the contractor is maintaining proper insurance cover, and in particular to inspect policies and premium receipts. They are to be sent to the architect for inspection by the employer. The employer must not exercise this right unreasonably or vexatiously. It would be reasonable to request the documents at the beginning of the contract and at the time of any required premium renewal.

It has already been said that is wise for the employer to retain the service of an insurance broker in connection with all the insurance provisions of the contract and it is for the employer to appoint a person on the architect's advice. The broker should inspect the relevant documents and confirm in writing that they comply with the contract requirements. On no account should the architect

132

simply send the policy to the employer without comment. That could lead to the architect becoming liable for any shortcomings in the documents.

Failure to insure

6.4.3
4.12.5 or
4.15.4

If the contractor fails to insure, the employer has the right to take out the appropriate insurance and to deduct the amount of any premium from monies due to the contractor or to recover it as a debt. In the case of deduction, the employer must give the relevant pay less notice. These are the notices relevant to interim certificates. In view of the importance of the insurance it seems unlikely, to say the least, that the employer will need to use the notice relevant to the final certificate. If the employer has to do so, there is something seriously wrong with the contract administration. It is essential that the employer exercises the right, and such is the importance of maintaining continuous insurance cover, the architect should lose no time in advising the employer if it is discovered that the contractor has defaulted. It cannot be over-emphasised that the cover should be effected through and on the advice of the employer's broker.

12.5   Things that are the liability of the employer

6.5.1

It sometimes happens that damage is caused to neighbouring property by the carrying out of the Works when there is no negligence or default by any party. In that case, the contractor would have no liability for the damage. For example, take the situation where a contractor is instructed to carry out piling work to a city centre site surrounded by other, possibly old buildings. The contractor may use proper skill and care in carrying out the piling work, but there may still be cracking of the adjacent structures. The contractor would have no liability to the employer or to the adjacent owner, but the employer would be liable. The contract provides for insurance to be taken out against this eventuality. It is operative only if it is stated in the contract particulars that the insurance may be required. The contractor, if instructed by the architect, must maintain the insurance in the joint names of the employer and the contractor. The amount of cover must be specified in the contract particulars and it should not expire until the end of the rectification period. Realistically, because the contractor will be rectifying work after that date, the insurance ought to extend until the contractor completes making good of defects.

Type of liability

The liability envisaged by the contract covers damage to any property (other than the Works and site materials) caused by collapse, subsidence, heave, vibration, weakening or removal of support, or lowering of ground water resulting from the Works. Not covered is damage:

- for which the contractor is liable;
- due to errors or omissions in the architect's design;

- reasonably foreseen to be inevitable;
- that is the responsibility of the employer to insure;
- due to nuclear risk, or sonic booms;
- arising from war, hostilities, civil war, etc.;
- caused directly or indirectly by pollution unless occurring suddenly as a result of an unexpected incident;
- to the Works and site materials unless they or parts of them are the subject of a certificate of practical completion; or
- that results in the employer paying damages for breach of contract.

The contractor must obtain the employer's approval of the insurers proposed, but not, apparently, to the amount of the premium. One method of sorting this out is for the employer to place the matter in the hands of the broker. The broker's advice will be needed in any event. If the employer later indicates to the contractor that approval will be forthcoming for the insurer recommended by the broker, the contractor will probably be delighted to place the insurance with whomsoever the employer wishes.

6.5.2   The contractor must deposit the policy and premium receipts with the employer. The amounts paid by the contractor in premiums under this clause are to be added to the Contract Sum. Since the employer, or certainly the architect, knows what insurance is needed and with which insurer it is desired to place the cover, there may be something to be said for amending this clause to make the employer responsible for insuring under this clause.

12.6   Insurance terms

Joint names

6.8   A joint names insurance policy is one in which two or more people are named as insured. In the case of SBC, it is a policy in which the employer and contractor are named as insured. The key thing is that the insurers have no rights against either employer or contractor. This is very important. The usual position is that, if a claim is made by the insured person against the insurance company the insurance company, after paying out, may stand in the shoes of the insured person (called 'subrogation') and claim against whoever was actually responsible for the loss. If the insurance is in joint names, the insurer cannot claim against the contractor even if it is responsible for the damage.

Excepted risks

6.6 ; 133   The contractor is not liable to indemnify the employer or to insure against damage to the Works, the site, or any property against damage due to nuclear perils and the like.

All risks or specified perils insurance

6.8

2.29.10

There are two very important definitions in the contract: 'all risks insurance' and 'specified perils'. The key point about 'all risks insurance' is that it must provide cover against 'any physical loss or damage to work executed and Site Materials'. Cover is not limited to 'specified perils' (see below). It includes other risks such as impact, subsidence, theft and vandalism. The distinction between the two types of risk has to be carefully noted because the contract very often limits the risks to 'specified perils', for example when an extension of time is being considered.

'Specified perils' are fire, lightning, explosion, storm, tempest, flood, escape of water from any water tank, apparatus or pipes, earthquake, aircraft and other aerial devices or articles dropped from them, riot and civil commotion, excluding any loss or damage caused by ionising radiations or contamination by radioactivity from any nuclear fuel or from any nuclear waste from the combustion of nuclear fuel, radioactive toxic explosive or other hazardous properties of any explosive nuclear assembly or nuclear component of them, pressure waves caused by aircraft or other aerial devices travelling at sonic or supersonic speeds.

Although the architect and contractor should be aware of these definitions and what they mean in general terms. Detailed advice on them is a matter for the employer's insurance broker.

12.7   Insurance of the Works: alternatives

6.7

Schedule 3

Insurance must be obtained to cover damage to the Works, unfixed materials and, if appropriate, existing structures and contents. There are three standard options. The applicable insurance option must be stated in the contract particulars. The options are:

- Option A – As far as new buildings are concerned, this is the most usual provision. The contractor is required to take out all risks insurance for the Works.
- Option B – This deals with the situation if the employer wishes to take out insurance for the new building Works: quite rare.
- Option C – This deals with the insurance of Works in or extensions to existing buildings. The employer is required to insure the existing structure and contents and the new Works.

One or other of these options must apply, as stated in the contract particulars.

Only one option will apply. Therefore, two options do not apply. So, if the contractor is to insure a new building, option B and C do not apply. If, rarely, the employer is to insure a new building, options A and C do not apply. Options A and B do not apply if the employer is to insure existing structures and the Works to them. These options bear examining in more detail. Each one requires insurance to be taken out in joint names.

12.8   A new building where the contractor is required to insure

Schedule 3, Option A covers this situation. The contractor must take out and maintain a
Option A joint names policy for all risks insurance. The list of risks is extensive and some
of the risks may not be able to be covered. The matter should be agreed at
tender stage with the assistance of the employer's broker and appropriate
amendments made to the clause. The insurance must cover:

- The full reinstatement value of the Works; and
- The cost of any professional fees expressed as a percentage. These are the
  fees payable if reinstatement is required after damage to the Works. The
  percentage must be inserted in the contract particulars by the employer.
  Failure to make the insertion would probably result in the cost of professional fees being borne by the employer.

Full reinstatement value

Care must be taken in regard to full reinstatement value. It should be remembered that the Works will increase in value as the contract progresses. The sum
insured must reflect the actual cost of reinstatement of the Works and any lost
or damaged site materials, which will include the cost of removing debris.
It should be noted that all risks insurance does not cover what is referred to

134   as 'consequential loss' (see Chapter 16, Section 16.1). An example of this would
be where the employer suffered loss because of the increased costs of carrying
out work not completed at the time of the damage.

The policy

The policy must be maintained up to and including practical completion of the
Works or the date of termination of the contractor's employment (whether or
not the validity is contested) whichever is the earlier. The joint names policy is
to be taken out with insurers approved by the employer. The policy, premium
receipts and any relevant endorsements must be sent to the architect who must
deposit them with the employer. Contractors usually have general insurance to
cover the risk of damage to the Works. This type of insurance is acceptable
under the terms of the contract if the policy provides all risks cover for no less
than full reinstatement value and the appropriate percentage of professional
fees and it is in joint names and the contractor can send documentary evidence
that the insurance is in force.

If the contractor defaults

Schedule 3, If the contractor defaults in taking out or in maintaining the insurance, the
paragraph A.2 employer is entitled to take out the insurance. In that situation, the employer may
deduct the amounts of any premiums from the sums otherwise due to the contractor (e.g. certified amounts) or they may be recovered as a debt. It is unlikely that
any employer will take the latter course when the former is so readily available.

Loss or damage

Schedule 3,
paragraph
A.4.1

If loss or damage occurs due to one of the risks covered by the policy, the contractor is obliged to notify the architect and the employer. The contractor must do this as soon as the loss or damage is discovered.

Payment of the contractor

Schedule 3,
paragraph
A.4.4

The contractor and the subcontractors must authorise the insurers to pay the insurance monies to the employer who must pay all the money received, less only professional fees, to the contractor in instalments under the architect's certificates. These certificates will not be the normal interim payment certificates, but rather special certificates that the architect must issue just for the amount the insurer pays out. The architect can issue these certificates in the form of a letter, provided that the letter is headed 'Certificate' or that it contains the words 'I certify'. The contractor can only recover the actual insured sum. If it proves to be insufficient, it has to bear the excess.

The occurrence of loss or damage is to be disregarded in calculating amounts payable to the contractor under the contract. The way that works is that, if the architect issues a certificate that includes work that is later damaged, later certificates are not to show any reduction for the damaged work. The damaged work must be treated, for certification purposes, as if it was undamaged. Thus, the architect may have to certify, as work properly done, work that has been destroyed by one of the insured risks.

Although at first sight that may seem odd, it is perfectly fair. If the contract did not require the damaged work to be included in payment certificates, the contractor could be in the position of doing work twice for which it is only paid once: by the insurance company.

12.9 A new building where the employer insures

Schedule 3,
Option B

This is not very common, but where the employer wishes to insure, option B deals with the situation. It is similar to option A. The employer must take out insurance in joint names for the full reinstatement value of the Works together with an appropriate percentage for professional fees. The contractor must give notice as before if there is any loss or damage.

Important difference

A very important difference to the position under option A is that the restoration and repair work is to be treated as a variation. The result of this is that, although the employer is entitled to be paid the full amount of any insurance money by the insurers, the employer must stand any further expense; for example any excess figure. The contractor, on the other hand, receives the full cost of repair under architect's certificates as noted above under 'Payment of the contractor' in Section 12.9. Of course, the contractor must also be paid in interim certificates for work that has been damaged.

12.10   Alterations or extensions to an existing building

Schedule 3,   Option C treats loss or damage to existing structures and contents and loss or
Option C   damage to the Works carried out to the structures or as extensions quite separately. If an existing building is involved, even if it is to be demolished except for the front elevation this is the only insurance option available. The employer must take out and maintain insurance.

Existing structures and contents

Schedule 3,   Existing structures and contents owned by the employer or for which the
paragraph C.1   employer is responsible must be insured in joint names. The risks to be covered are specified perils. If the Works consist of an extension to an existing property and if part of the extension is taken into the employer's possession (i.e. partial possession), that part will form part of the existing structures for insurance purposes from the date it is taken into possession.

The Works

Schedule 3,   The position of loss or damage to the Works under this option is similar to the
paragraph C.2   position under option B against all risks. Insurance must be in joint names.

If the employer defaults

Schedule 3,   Except where the employer is a local authority, the contractor is entitled to
paragraph   demand proof that the insurances have been taken out and maintained. If the
C.3.1.2   employer defaults, the contractor may take out the appropriate insurance itself and the amount it pays is to be added to the Contract Sum. The contractor has an important extra power. It has right of entry to the existing property as may be required to make a survey and inventory of the existing structures and contents.

Loss or damage

Schedule 3,   The contractor must notify the employer and the architect in writing upon dis-
paragraph   covering loss or damage to the existing structure or contents or to the Works.
C.4.1   There is provision for either party to terminate the contractor's employment if there is significant damage to existing structures (see Chapter 23, Section 23.9). If neither party terminates the contractor's employment the contractor must proceed to carry out appropriate restoration work after the insurers have carried out any inspection they may require.

Payment of the contractor

Schedule 3, The contractor must authorise payment of insurance money directly to the
paragraphs employer. In common with option B, if the insurance payment is insufficient to
C.4.2 and C.4.3 cover the cost of restoration, the employer must stand the amount of shortfall.
The contractor, on the other hand, receives the full cost of repair under architect's certificates as noted above under 'Payment of the contractor' in Section
12.9. The occurrence of loss or damage is to be disregarded in calculating
amounts payable to the contractor under the contract. The way that works is
that, if the architect issues a certificate that includes work that is later damaged,
later certificates are not to show any reduction for the damaged work. The
damaged work must be treated, for certification purposes, as if it was undamaged. Thus, the architect may have to certify, as work properly done, work that
has been destroyed by one of the insured risks.

12.11   Benefits for sub-contractors

6.9 The joint names policies required from the contractor under option A or from
the employer under option B and option C (new Works only) must provide
either for recognition of each subcontractor as an insured party or it must
include a waiver (i.e. the insurer agrees not to enforce the right) of the insurer's
rights of subrogation against any sub-contractor in respect of loss or damage by
6.9.1 any of the specified perils. This is a very useful provision for sub-contractors
who, if responsible for the loss, may otherwise face a claim from the insurers.
Joint names policies taken out by the employer or the contractor in the case of
default by the other must also comply with this.

12.12   The Joint Fire Code

6.14 to 6.17 In the definitions the 'Joint Fire Code' is said to be the 'Joint Code of Practice
1.1 on the Protection from Fire of Construction Sites and Buildings Undergoing
Renovation published by the Construction Confederation and the Fire
Protection Association, current at the Base Date'. The code states that non-
compliance could result in insurance ceasing to be available.

   If the insurer of the Works requires compliance with the code, the contract
particulars entry should be completed to make that clear. Special requirements
apply if the insurer categorises the Works as a 'Large Project' and the contract
particulars must be completed appropriately.

   Both employer and contractor and anyone employed by them or anyone on
the Works must comply with the code.

   If there is a breach of the code and the insurer specifies remedial measures in
a notice, the contractor must ensure the measures are carried out by the date
specified and, if the measures require a variation, they must be carried out in
accordance with any architect's instructions. If the measures do not require an

architect's instruction and if the contractor does not begin the remedial measures in seven days from receipt of the notice, or fails to proceed regularly and diligently, the employer may employ and pay others to do the work. In that
6.16   case an appropriate deduction is to be made from the Contract Sum.

If the code is amended after the base date any additional costs are to be borne by either the employer or contractor, depending on which is noted in the contract particulars. If the employer is to bear the cost, it must be added to the
6.17   Contract Sum.

12.13   Terrorism cover

There are complicated provisions that apply if the joint names policy excludes terrorism cover. In that case, it is important that the employer seeks the advice of the insurance broker. If the insurers notify either party that terrorism cover will cease from a specified date, either the employer or the contractor, as appropriate, must notify the other. The employer has two options. The employer may either require that the Works continue to be carried out or specify that the contractor's employment will terminate on a date after the
6.11.4   date of the insurer's notification (see Chapter 23, Sections 23.7 and 23.15), but before the date of cessation of cover. The employer's notice must be in writing. If the decision is not to terminate and damage is suffered as a result of terrorism, the resulting remedial work must be carried out by the contractor, but it
6.11.5   is treated as a variation.

12.14   Common problems

The contractor fails to insure or to maintain the insurance for employer's liability and the employer wants to take out the insurance

In regard to this kind of insurance, the contract does not say that the employer can take it out if the contractor fails to do so as it does for other kinds of insurance. The answer lies in the way in which the contractor is to take out the insurance. It may do so only if the architect gives an instruction. Therefore, if the contractor fails to insure, it is a failure to comply with an instruction.
3.11   The architect must issue a notice requiring compliance within 7 days. If the contractor still does not comply, the employer may do what is necessary to give effect to that instruction. In other words, the employer may take out the insurance.

The contract goes on to say that an appropriate deduction must be made from the Contract Sum. The insurance provision states that the cost to the contractor of taking out the insurance must be added to the Contract Sum. If the contractor fails to insure, nothing will be added, therefore, nothing need be deducted unless the employer has incurred some additional expense of some kind due to the contractor's failure. The cost to the employer of the insurance is not additional expenditure because the employer would have paid for it if the contractor had complied with the architect's instruction.

The employer cannot obtain insurance in joint names

If the employer has to insure the existing property and the Works under option C, there may sometimes be a difficulty because an insurer is not prepared to insure in joint names. The architect should then advise the employer to seek the assistance of an insurance broker to arrange insurance that complies with the requirements of option C. If it proves impossible to obtain that insurance, it may be necessary to amend option C to allow for insurance of the Works by the contractor in joint names and the insurance of the existing property by the employer in own name only. Needless to say, this must be done with the agreement of the contractor and under advice from the employer's insurance broker. A solicitor may need to be engaged by the employer to draft a suitable clause acceptable to both parties.

It is never good for insurance to be split between two different insurers because of the difficulties that may arise in the event of a claim.

13 Possession of the site

13.1 General

3.1

To be in possession of something is the next best thing to owning it. If the owner of a DVD lends it to a friend, the friend has a better claim to the DVD than anyone else except the true owner. The contractor who is in possession of a site can, in general terms, exclude everyone from the site except the owner. In practice, there are exceptions to this general rule, which are laid down by the building contract and by various statutory regulations dealing with statutory inspections. There is a specific term in SBC allowing access to the Works at all reasonable times for the architect and any person authorised by the architect. This will usually mean other people from the architect's practice, consultants and the clerk of works. It is suggested that authorisation implies that the architect will give written notice to the contractor listing the relevant persons.

Licence to occupy the site

8.7.1

As a general principle, one can say that a contractor carrying out building Works is said to have a licence from the employer to occupy the site of the Works for the length of time necessary to complete the Works. The owner has no power to revoke that licence during the contract except as laid down in the contract itself. For example, possession may be brought to an end if the contractor's employment or the contract itself is lawfully brought to an end. Therefore, even if there was no specific term in the contract giving the contractor possession of the site, a term would be implied that the contractor must have possession in sufficient time to allow it to complete by the contract completion date. The contractor normally gives up possession of the site at practical completion or on termination of its employment. The contractor has a restricted licence to enter the site after practical completion for the purposes of remedying defects.

The JCT Standard Building Contract 2011, First Edition. David Chappell.
© 2014 by David Chappell. Published 2014 by John Wiley & Sons, Ltd.

13.2   Date of possession

The date (or dates if sections are used) for possession is to be entered in the contract particulars. That is the date on which, possession must be given to the contractor and, subject to any extension of time that may be awarded, the contractor must proceed regularly and diligently with the Works and complete them on or before the date for completion in the contract particulars (the phrase 'regularly and diligently' is explained in Chapter 6, Section 6.4).

Under the general law, if the employer fails to give possession on the due date, it is normally a serious breach of contract. By 'possession of the site is meant possession of the whole site and not just a part, unless of course sections are being used. The contractor would have a claim for damages at common law, and the time for completion would become 'at large'. That is to say, the contractor's obligation would be to complete the Works within a reasonable time.

Although failure to give possession on the date for completion is a serious breach of contract, SBC provides for the giving of an extension of time and loss and/or expense for a range of things under the general heading of 'impediment, prevention or default, whether by act or omission'. These catch-all clauses will clearly include a failure to give possession by the completion date. They remove the need for a contractor to try and recover damages at common law for the breach if the failure to give possession extends beyond any deferment by the employer. Of course, despite the existence of such clauses, the contractor always has the option to try to recover damages instead of or as well as using the contractual route, subject only to the proviso that there must be no double recovery.

The problem is partially overcome in SBC because the employer is permitted to defer giving possession for a time that must not exceed a period to be inserted in the contract particulars. From the employer's point of view the clause should always be included for protection. The contract recommends that the period of deferment should not exceed six weeks. The period is somewhat arbitrary because, at the time of tender or of signing the contract, the employer intends to give possession on the date stated in the contract particulars, otherwise the contract should not be signed with that date included. If it was known at the time of signing that the date was going to be deferred, the date in the contract could be adjusted accordingly by agreement.

The six-week deferment period suggested in the contract is probably intended to take care of some minor hitch in giving possession. If possession is delayed it is usually delayed for a relatively short time (because demolition contractors have not finished their work, or because planning or building-regulation permission is delayed, or for some other similar cause). Otherwise, the delay is caused by some major problem that lasts for a considerable period and in those circumstances it would be unfair to rely on a clause permitting deferment. The best-laid plans can go wrong, so although the architect may, in consultation with the employer, decide to insert a period shorter than six weeks, an insertion should not be omitted altogether.

135

136

2.29.7
4.24.5

2.5

A longer period could be inserted, but a long period would almost certainly result in increased tender prices. Whatever period is put in the contract, the employer cannot defer possession with impunity. The contractor would be entitled, at the very least, to an extension of the contract date for completion and possibly to loss and/or expense.

There is no prescribed form of notice for deferment, but it must come from the employer. The architect can, and probably would normally, draft a suitable letter, which need not give any reason.

3.15

The power to defer possession must not be confused with the power to order postponement of the work to be executed under the provisions of the contract. If there is postponement, the contractor has possession of the site, but the architect has suspended work. The contractor may decide to use some or all of the time the work is suspended to carry out work specifically connected with its occupation of the site (for example, repairing or improving site office accommodation, sorting materials, attending to security, etc.).

13.3   Common problems

A peaceful demonstration blocks the access to the site

The employer must give the contractor access to the site, but only in so far as the employer has control over the access. Therefore, if there is a peaceful demonstration on the public highway that is blocking access, the employer is not responsible.

The contractor inadvertently builds over the boundary line onto land belonging to someone else

2.10

The contract permits the architect to allow errors in setting out to remain uncorrected and for an appropriate deduction to be made to the Contract Sum. Sometimes, if the trespass is not substantial, it may be possible for the property owners to come to an agreement whereby the trespasser pays a lump sum to the injured party and that lump sum can be deducted from the Contract Sum. Much will depend on the cost of demolition and rebuilding compared to the compensatory sum.

Otherwise, the contractor is in breach of contract and must correct the setting out by demolition and rebuilding.

If the employer cannot give possession of section 2 until section 1 is completed, but the completion of section 1 is delayed beyond the date of possession of section 2

2.5

This situation is not unusual. The contractor is entitled to possession of each section on the date for possession in the contract. The employer can defer possession of course, but only for a period of up to 6 weeks. Therefore, even if completion of section 1 is delayed entirely due to the contractor, it is still entitled to possession of section 2 on the due date. The sections are treated separately. The way to get around this particular problem is as follows: if one section is linked to another as indicated above, the dates for possession and completion of section 1 should be stated in the contract particulars. The dates for possession of section 2 should be expressed by stating that the date for possession of section 2 is X days after the date of practical completion of section 1. The date for completion of section 2 is X months after its date of possession. In that way, the period for section 2 is a fixed period subject to movement in its entirety depending on the date of practical completion of section 1.

14 Extension of time

14.1 Basics

The reasons for the inclusion of clauses in the contract dealing with extensions of time are not sufficiently understood by many architects and contractors. Suppose, say, Mr Green gets a price from a contractor for laying some paving stones in his garden. The contractor wants £100 for laying the stones and they both agree that the contractor will start the following Monday and finish by the end of the week on Friday afternoon. Suppose that, by Wednesday, Mr Green has decided that he wants more paving stones laying and he agrees a price with the contractor for a further £50. What is the position if, on Friday, the contractor informs Mr Green that there is no chance that the whole of the work will be finished until the following Tuesday at the earliest? Can Mr Green give the contractor an extension of time to a date that Mr Green thinks is fair and reasonable? Is the contractor obliged to complete by the date originally agreed? Can the contractor simply complete within a reasonable time; whatever that may be?

Reasonable time

There is no doubt that in the circumstances outlined, the contractor is entitled to complete within a reasonable time. That is because Mr Green, by asking the contractor to carry out more work, has prevented the contractor from finishing by the originally agreed time of Friday afternoon. Therefore, the contractor's obligation to finish by Friday afternoon is ended. There is no date for completion. Mr Green has no power to give an extension of time; reasonable or otherwise. In common parlance time is 'at large'. The only person who can decide what a reasonable would be in the circumstances is a judge because neither adjudication nor arbitration is applicable (see Chapter 24). Obviously, bearing in mind the sums concerned, involving a judge is unlikely to be cost effective.

The JCT Standard Building Contract 2011, First Edition. David Chappell.
© 2014 by David Chappell. Published 2014 by John Wiley & Sons, Ltd.

Why extensions of time?

It is to avoid time becoming at large that extension of time clauses are included in building contracts. They give the architect power to extend time for delays that are the result of actions or inactions on the part of the employer or the architect as well as for a selection of other reasons for which neither employer nor contractor are responsible. The proper exercise of this power by the architect should prevent time becoming at large. This is important because where, as in this contract, there are provisions for the employer to recover liquidated damages if the contractor does not complete the Works by the completion date, **137** they cannot be recovered unless there is a definite date for completion. In that case, the employer would be obliged to try to recover unliquidated damages by suing the contractor for breach of contract and then trying to prove the amount **138** lost. An architect who fails to give an extension of time that is properly due to the contractor may be held to be negligent.

14.2   Extension of time

2.26 to 2.29

The date for completion is stated in the contract particulars. The contract devotes two and a half pages to extensions of time. It sets out the procedure; that is what the contractor and the architect must do and when they must do it and it sets out the grounds on which the contractor is entitled to an extension of time. These grounds are referred to as 'Relevant Events'. Flowcharts showing the contractor's and architect's duties are in Figures 14.1 and 14.2, respectively.

Extension of time and loss and/or expense

The only purpose of the two and a half pages is to provide the way in which the contract date for completion can be extended to a new date. It is really important to understand that. The fact that the architect gives an extension of time by fixing a new date for completion does not automatically entitle the contractor to claim any money. Sometimes the contractor will call its claim for money 'additional preliminaries'. Sometimes, it will give the correct name: 'loss and/or expense'. Whatever it is called, the contractor is not entitled to any extra money **139** just because there is an extension of time. The fallacy that a contractor who gets an extension of time is entitled to some money as a result has arisen because some of the grounds for an extension of time are the same as grounds for loss and/or expense. It is not unknown for some quantity surveyors to automatically include 'additional preliminaries' in a valuation after an extension of time has been given, often without any application for the money by the contractor. That practice is quite simply wrong and may be negligent. The payment of loss and/or expense to the contractor can only arise after the contractor has applied for it properly strictly in accordance with the contract and after the architect has judged the application to be valid. More about the way in which a contractor can claim loss and/or expense will be presented later (see Chapter 16).

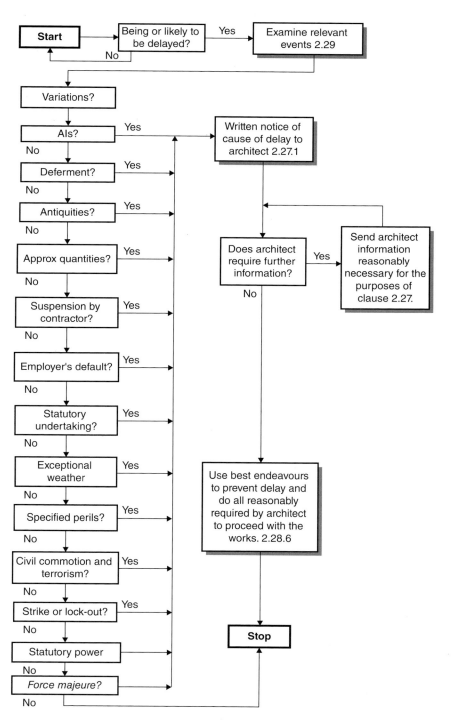

Figure 14.1 Contractor's duties if there is a delay (clause 2.27).

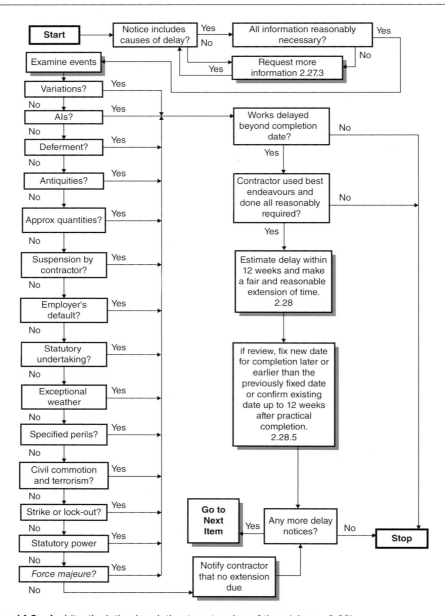

Figure 14.2   Architect's duties in relation to extension of time (clause 2.28).

14.3   Grounds

2.29.1 to 2.29.7   The contract lists the grounds (relevant events) on the basis of which the archi-
inclusive   tect is required to revise the date of completion by the contractor. They can be
divided into two groups:

2.29.8 to
2.29.14   ■ those that are the responsibility of the employer or the architect;
inclusive   ■ those that are the fault of neither party.

These are the grounds for extending time:

Grounds that are the responsibility of the employer

2.29.1   ### Variations

This ground includes anything that the contract says is to be treated as requiring a variation. Departures from the stipulated method of preparation of the contract bills, errors or omissions in the bills and inadequacies in design in the Employer's

2.14.3 and   Requirements (if used) and the correction of discrepancies in the Employer's
2.16.2   Requirements are to be treated as variations. Architect's instructions requiring a
3.14   variation and are obviously covered.

2.29.2   ### Architect's instructions

The instructions referred to are:

2.15   ■ To deal with discrepancies in drawings, contract bills, etc.
3.15   ■ To postpone any work to be executed under the contract.
■ To expend provisional sums (except provisional sums for defined work, because the contractor has been given sufficient information to enable it to make an appropriate allowance in planning its work at
3.16   tender stage).
5.3.2   ■ To deal with a variation quotation.
3.17   ■ For inspections and tests.
3.18.4   ■ For opening up after discovery of defective work.

2.29.3   ### Deferment of possession of site:

Failure by the employer to give possession of the site by the date of possession is quite common. The employer can defer giving the contractor possession of the site for a period of up to six weeks, unless a shorter period was stipulated in the contract particulars. It is important to emphasise that the employer only has this power if it is expressly stated in the contract particulars. The deferment is stated to be 6 weeks or whatever shorter period is stipulated by the employer. In view of the often unpredictable nature of demolition, site clearance works and tenants, to say nothing of unlawful squatters, it seems risky to reduce this period. Where the employer does defer the giving of possession, obviously there will be an entitlement to an extension of time. Deferment is a positive activity and the employer should make it clear that it is being exercised by giving written notice although the contract does not specifically say so. It should be noted that the extension can only be given where the employer has actually exercised the right to defer. This relevant event probably does not apply if the employer, without formally deferring possession by giving a written notice, has simply failed to give possession on the due date.

2.29.4   ### *Antiquities*

3.22.1   This concerns the action to be taken by the contractor on finding antiquities
3.22.2   and in carrying out the architect's instructions following a find. Actions include
using best endeavours not to disturb the find, ceasing work if appropriate, taking necessary steps to preserve the object and its location and informing the
architect of its discovery and whereabouts.

2.29.5   ### *Approximate quantity not a reasonably accurate forecast*

This ground is on the perfectly reasonable basis that a contractor will plan its
work using, among other things, the quantities in the bills of quantities. Where
such quantities are described as 'approximate', it is because the architect and/or
the quantity surveyor either does not know, or has not quite decided upon, the
amount required. All the contractor can do is to use the approximate quantities
as if they gave a reasonably accurate forecast of the quantities required. If they
give a significantly lower forecast, it will presumably need additional time to
carry out the work.

The question is: what is a reasonable forecast? The answer is likely to depend
to a large extent upon the nature of the materials measured in the contract bills
and the likely effect of a difference in quantity, because changes in quantity will
invariably lead to changes in the amount of work required. It will be an unusual
situation if the contractor is entitled to an extension of time because the actual
quantities are less than the forecast. If a thousand metre run of plain wall panelling approximately are measured for walls, it may be not important if a further
five metres have to be erected at the same time. However, an increase of five
metres on twenty metres of complicated panelling is significant.

2.29.6   ### *Suspension by the contractor of performance of its obligations*

140   This ground is included to comply with statute that entitles a contractor to
suspend performance of its obligations on 7 days written notice if the employer
does not pay a sum due in full by the final date for payment.

The relevant event is more generous than the Act that apparently provides
that if a party suspends performance for 6 days, the effective extension to the
period for completing the work is to be 6 days. This ignores any time the contractor may need to get ready to recommence. The relevant event, read with the
contractor's contractual right to suspend clearly requires the architect to consider all the delay including remobilisation and not just the actual period of
suspension.

2.29.7   ### *Impediment, prevention or default by the employer*

This is obviously intended as a catch all clause to avoid any possibility of
time becoming at large due to an act of prevention or the like on the
part of the employer for which there was no relevant event. It excludes any

part of any act or omission of the employer that was caused or contributed to by the default of the contractor, its servants, agents or sub-contractors. To impede is to retard or hinder. To prevent is to hinder or stop. A default certainly covers a breach of contract, but it may go further than that in some circumstances. The introduction of this relevant event gave the JCT the opportunity to reduce the number of relevant events, because many are now covered by this one.

It will be useful to list the former relevant events that the introduction of this one replaces, because they are likely to be the most common reasons why a contractor will cite this relevant event. They are:

Late instructions and drawings

There are two parts to this former relevant event. The first part is if an information release schedule is used and the architect fails to issue information in accordance with it.

2.11

The second part of the relevant event refers to the failure of the architect to provide information. This deals with the situation if an information release schedule has not been provided or if there is information required that is not listed on the schedule. Assessing delays under this ground is less easy than when considering the architect's failure to comply with the information release schedule, because there are no dates to act as benchmarks on which information should have been provided. It is rather a matter of judgment by the architect who must decide when the information should have been provided and whether or not it was done (see Chapter 5, Section 5.10).

2.12

Work not forming part of the contract

Work not forming part of the contract has been discussed in Chapter 11, Section 11.1. There are two separate situations. The first situation is if the employer engages others to carry out part of the Works and the contract bills contain information to enable the contractor to understand the extent and nature of the work concerned. The work could be anything, but in practice it is usually more convenient if such work is easy to identify and preferably separate from other work. The contractor must permit the employer to carry out the work.

2.7.1

The second situation is if the employer engages others to carry out part of the Works and the contract bills do not contain information to enable the contractor to understand the extent and nature of the work concerned. In that instance, the employer may only arrange for the work to be done after obtaining the contractor's consent. The employment of two contractors on the same site has a great deal of potential for causing delay to the Works as a whole. The delay is arguably less likely where the main contractor knows at time of tender exactly what another contractor will be called upon to carry out. That is because the contractor will be deemed to have taken account of the likely effect on the Works. Obviously, if the other contractor

2.7.2

does not work to the contractor's programme, there is still much scope for delay. However, where the main contractor has not been pre-warned about the size and scope of the work to be carried out by directly employed labour, there is considerable scope for claiming that the directly employed contractor caused delay.

Provision of materials by the employer

Unlike the execution of work by others, there is no contractual term that entitles the employer to provide materials or goods. Nevertheless, it is common, particularly in the case of large houses, for the employer to decide to provide certain goods and also common for the supply to be delayed. Invariably the supply will be initiated by the employer, possibly in the belief that a source of supply has been located that will result in a financial saving.

The contractor may be entitled to an extension of time if the goods are supplied late or if they differ in an important respect from what the contractor could reasonably have expected from the description and delay is caused to progress.

Failure to give ingress or egress

It is likely that claims for lack of ingress or egress are now possible on a broad basis. The employer has an implied obligation to afford the contractor reasonable access to the site on which the project is to be carried out. Obstructions within the site boundaries are the employer's responsibility but not obstructions in the highway outside the site; unless of course caused by the employer. If the access is via a right of way, it is the employer's duty to ensure that the right of way does not cease for any reason. However, it is the contractor's responsibility to inspect the means of access and to ensure that they are adequate for the contractor's requirements in carrying out the Works.

3.23

Compliance or non-compliance with CDM Regulations

The employer's obligation to ensure that the CDM co-ordinator carries out his or her duties under the CDM Regulations 2007 and, if the contractor unusually is not the principal contractor under the regulations, to ensure that the principal contractor carries out its duties also is onerous. It should be noted that this ground encompasses both compliance and non-compliance so that the proper carrying out of duties could also attract an extension of time if a delay was caused as a result. The problem for the employer is that the CDM co-ordinator has duties under the regulations that may have to be carried out after the issue of any architect's instruction. Therefore, each instruction could attract an extension of time under this ground even if it did not qualify under another clause. Under SBC, the question for the contractor will be simply whether the employer has complied and, if not, has any delay to progress of the Works resulted.

Grounds that are the fault of neither party

2.29.8   ### *Statutory undertaker's work*

This ground deals with delay caused by the carrying out by a statutory under-taker of work under its statutory obligations in relation to the Works, or its failure to do so. Statutory authorities are organisations such as water, gas and electricity suppliers that are authorised by statute to construct and operate pub-lic utilities.

Statutory undertakers often carry out work other than under statutory obli-gation. Where that occurs, if they have been directly engaged by the employer and delay occurs, any extension of time would be made under the relevant

*2.29.7; **141*** event dealing with impediment, prevention or default of the employer. Obviously, no extension of time would be applicable if the statutory undertak-ers had been engaged directly by the contractor other than in pursuance of their statutory obligations. Therefore, whether or not or under which particu-lar clause an extension of time should be given for delays caused by statutory undertakers depends on the nature of the work being done and the surround-ing circumstances and it is for the contractor to identify the relevant event it thinks is appropriate.

If a statutory undertaker lays gas supply pipes in the road that provides access to the site, not for the purposes of the contract Works but for another site nearby, there would be no grounds for extension of time. It makes no difference that the statutory undertaker concerned might be under a statutory obligation to lay the service, because it would not be carrying out the work in relation to the Works.

2.29.9   ### *Exceptionally adverse weather conditions*

The change in wording in earlier JCT contracts from 'inclement' to 'adverse' was intended to make it clear that the ground was intended to cover any kind of adverse conditions including unusual heat or drought. Notwithstanding that, it is common to hear the ground being referred to as 'inclement weather'. The key words omitted are: 'exceptionally' and 'adverse'. Adverse weather is any kind of weather that impedes the progress of the Works. For example, where wet trades are concerned, excessive heat may seriously damage the work.

A crucial factor is the kind of weather that ought to be expected at the site at the time when the delay occurs. Architects will often request the contractor to provide meteorological reports for the previous ten or fifteen years. Reference to such weather records are normally used to show that the adverse weather was 'exceptional' for that area or for the time of year. In that instance exceptional refers to exceeding what may be reasonably expected based on the evidence of past years.

Even if it can be demonstrated with reference to appropriate historical records that the weather is exceptionally adverse for the time of year it must also be such that it interferes with the Works at the particular stage they have reached. That is so even if the reason why the Works are affected is because the contractor is late though its own fault. For example, the contractor may be unable to proceed with any work, because of torrential rain over a three-day period. If the contractor had not been in culpable delay it would have had the roof on and covered so enabling work to continue inside the building without any delay. However, the architect must consider the situation as it is whatever may be the reason.

142

If despite the weather, work could continue then it cannot be successfully maintained that the Works have been delayed by the exceptionally adverse weather. For example, there may be freezing blizzard conditions, but if all the contractor's work is inside the building and if the building is warm and water-tight, the external conditions will have little or no effect on progress.

The contractor is expected to programme the Works making proper allowance for normal adverse weather, i.e. the sort of weather that is to be expected in the area and at the time of year during the course of the Works. The contractor's programme for those parts of the Works that may be affected by adverse weather, whether in the form of excessive heat, rain, wind or frost should acknowledge the fact that interruptions are likely to occur, and should allow for them. If the contractor is aware at the time of tender that it is tendering for a project that is to be constructed during the winter and if it is constructed in the winter, it is no use in complaining to the architect and requesting an extension of time on the ground of exceptionally adverse weather when the Works are delayed on account of snow. The contractor will be expected to have allowed for snow and ice in winter and higher, occasionally hot, temperatures in the summer.

However, if the contractor can show that the winter weather was more severe than it could have reasonably anticipated or that work that should have been done in the summer had to be done in the winter, an extension of time should be given. That is always assuming that the date for completion was delayed as a result.

Strictly, it is only the 'exceptional' aspect of the adverse weather that will attract an extension of time. Thus, if ten days of snow in January is just on the borderline between usual and exceptional and a project suffers fifteen days adverse weather, the contractor is not entitled to an extension of time for the consequences on the completion date of the whole fifteen days, but only for the extra five days.

The common but unfortunate practice whereby clerks of works keep records of 'wet time' so that every couple of months the architect can give an extension of time covering the total period of wet time is insupportable. A client in that situation may view the architect's actions as negligent.

2.29.10   ### Loss or damage occasioned by one or more of the specified perils

The purpose of this ground is to give the contractor sufficient additional time to fulfil its obligations to repair damage caused by one of the specified perils: fire, lightning, explosion, storm, flood, escape of water from a water tank, apparatus or pipe, earthquake, aircraft or other aerial devices, or articles dropped from them, riot and civil commotion, but excluding what are called the 'Excepted Risks'.

6.8

The contractor is entitled to an extension of time even if the events are caused by the default or negligence of the contractor's own employees.

143

2.29.11   ### Civil commotion or terrorism

'Civil commotion' means, for insurance purposes, 'a stage between a riot and a civil war'. There must be an element of turbulence and the activities of protest-ers in public places may amount to civil commotion. There are three possibili-ties in relation to terrorism. The first is that the Works are delayed because terrorism has been used. For example, part of the Works may be damaged by an explosion.

144
145

The second is that terrorist action has been threatened and, as a result, the area of the site may have to be cleared. The threat of terrorism would probably have to be more substantial than just the fact that other terrorist incidents have occurred in the area. A specific terrorist threat directed at the project or a threat to an area that, if it was to be carried out, would affect the project would qualify. An extension of time would be applicable if the contractor or its operatives received direct threats of injury if work did not cease and the contractor stopped work accordingly.

The third is that terrorist action has been carried out or threatened and the relevant authorities, who may be government, police or army, may cause delay to the Works as a direct result of the way in which the act or threat is dealt with. The activities of the relevant authorities that would qualify under this ground would include such measures as evacuation of premises and the restriction of access. For example, there may be a threat to a particular building and the police may evacuate the surroundings for a period. If the building site is part of the evacuated area, there will be a delay to the Works and, to the extent that the date for completion is affected, an extension of time must be given. This ground is not restricted to the site of the Works and, therefore, it is likely that any threat or action that affected the execution of the Works in any way (such as the forced evacuation or destruction of the contractor's offices) would give entitlement to extension of time.

2.29.12   ### Strikes and similar events

The events include lockouts, and local combination of workmen. So far as strikes are concerned, an extension of time should be given for any delaying circumstance that affects the contractor and its work on the site or persons preparing design for the CDP including a strike affecting any trade involved in preparing or transporting any goods and materials that are required for the Works. It is not immediately obvious how a strike might affect designers employed in the contractor's office or, indeed, an independent firm of archi-tects engaged by the contractor to provide design services. This ground is intended to cover all strikes whether official or unofficial, but it does not cover 'working to rule' or any other obstructive practice that is not actually a strike. An unofficial strike has been described as any strike or other industrial action that is not authorised or endorsed by a trade union. A strike or other similar event must be one in which the trades mentioned in it are directly involved. A strike by workers employed by statutory undertakers that are directly engaged by the employer to execute work that do not form part of the Works is not covered by this ground. The reference to local combination of workmen is an antiquated phrase that may possibly cover activities that fall short of a strike and occur in a specific area. However, it is thought more likely to refer to a small localised strike.

It is probable that a situation where deliveries to site are delayed, not due to a strike, but due to some form of secondary picketing does not fall under this relevant event.

146

147
148

2.29.13   *Government action*

The action must be taken by the government after the Base Date. The 'Base Date' is that date written into the contract particulars. This provision can be relied upon wherever the British Government exercises any statutory power as set out in this ground, e.g. under the Defence of the Realm Regulations. Other circumstances could fall under this head. For example, the closure of some access roads during the foot and mouth epidemic if the roads were an essential means of access to the site of the Works.

A particular significance of this ground is that this relevant event prevents the contract being brought to an end by frustration (see Chapter 23, Section 23.1). The matter is simply dealt with by an extension of time. Since the event is taken out of the realm of *force majeure*, even a long suspension of work on this ground would not entitle the contractor to terminate its own employment.

8.11

2.29.14   *Force majeure*

Force majeure is a term originating in French law. It means more than 'Act of God', which has been described as 'an overwhelming superhuman event'. The event relied upon as *force majeure* must make the performance of the contract wholly impossible. In practice, all the surrounding circumstances must be taken into account. The dislocation of business caused by the general coal strike of 1912 has been held to be covered by the term and it also covered the breakdown of machinery, but not delay caused by bad weather, football matches or a funeral.

The term covers all circumstances that are out of the control of human beings. Therefore, an epidemic is a case of *force majeure*; it has even been decided that a strike of workmen constitutes a case of *force majeure*.

Care must be taken when interpreting *force majeure* in JCT contracts, particularly having regard to the other relevant events. Where the term *force majeure* is used in SBC, its meaning will effectively be restricted, because many

149

150

things that would normally fall under the category of *force majeure* are included under specific headings. Such matters as strikes, fire and exceptional weather are examples.

14.4   Procedure

Schedule 2

The clauses dealing with extension of the contract period are headed 'Adjustment of Completion Date'. That is because 'Variation and Acceleration Quotation Procedures' also includes provisions for fixing a new date for completion. It should be noted that references to extending time and fixing a new date for completion is taken to mean the date for completion of the Works or, if the Works are divided in the contract into sections, of any section. Unless there is a particular reason to do so, reference will not constantly be made here to sections.

The contractor's duty to give notice
2.27.1

General points

The contractor's duty to give notice is much misunderstood or more accurately, it is not read properly, but it is the key duty in the extension of time provisions. There is no requirement for the contractor to actually claim an extension of time although most do so. The contractor must give notice to the architect of every delay. That means that the contractor is to give notice, not only when the progress of the Works is being delayed, but also when it becomes reasonably apparent that it is likely to be delayed in the future. It must be obvious to a contractor, acting in a reasonable manner, whether the progress of the Works is being or is likely to be delayed. Once it becomes reasonably apparent that the progress is actually being delayed or is likely to be delayed, the contractor must notify the architect. The reference to progress must refer to actual progress.

Establishing whether the contractor has been delayed should be a straightforward matter of looking at the facts. It is probably relevant to compare the contractor's actual progress to the progress indicated in the contractor's programme although a failure to comply with the programme would be unlikely, alone, to conclusively demonstrate delay to progress. Strange as it may seem, the contractor has no obligation to comply with its own programme. For example, it may progress the Works faster than shown on the programme or carry out work in a different order.

151

Notice of all delays

It is not sufficiently appreciated that the contractor's duty is not limited to notifying the causes of delay listed as relevant events; it is a duty to give notice of delay, however it is caused. What that means in practice is that the contractor must notify all delays and their causes even if the delay is entirely of the contractor's own making. It must notify breakdowns of machinery, shortage of labour and delays in supplies. The idea is that the architect is in possession of all the information required to monitor the progress of the Works.

2.28.6.1

152

153

154

155

1.7.1

The information must be provided even if it is uncertain whether the current completion date will be affected. Further, if the contractor fails to give notice of a delay that it clearly should have been able to anticipate, the architect can in fact say that the contractor has not used its best endeavours to prevent delay in progress, which it is bound to do. Anecdotal evidence suggests that it is rare, virtually unknown, for a contractor to give notice of delays unless it believes that a relevant event giving rise to an extension of time is involved. The purpose of the notice is simply to warn the architect of the situation, and it is then up to the architect to monitor it. It may be possible for the architect to take some action that may eradicate the delay completely. The contractor is to give the notice 'forthwith'. 'Forthwith' means: 'as soon as it is reasonable to do so' or 'without delay or loss of time'. It appears that the meaning will be adjusted depending on the context. In most building contracts it conveys the fact that the action required must not be delayed. It does not necessarily mean 'immediately'. All notices must be in writing.

Failure to give notice

156

2.28.5

The contractor's notice must specify the cause of delay. Although often overlooked, it is important for the contractor to identify the precise activity (or activities) that is delayed together with its relation to the project's critical path and it is certainly in the contractor's interest to do so. Failure to give a delay notice will not prevent a contractor from getting an extension of time, because the architect has the power and the duty to give an extension in the absence of any written notice once the date for completion has passed. Failure by the contractor to give written notice merely means that the architect does not need to make a decision on extensions until a later date, i.e. on the review of the completion date not later than the expiry of 12 weeks from the date of practical completion whether or not the contractor has notified the relevant event. If the contractor does not give a written notice, it is probable that the architect is not entitled to give an extension of time before the completion date.

Content of notice

The contractor's notice is to state not just the cause or causes of the delay; it must also state the material circumstances. It is important that the notice should go into some detail regarding why the delay is occurring or is likely to occur and the form of such delay. The cause of the delay is all the factors giving rise to the delay. The 'material circumstances' will include, such things as the progress and the proposed order of Works and anything else that might affect progress at the time of the delay. The knock-on effect of the delay, with consequent likely further disruption, would also be a material circumstance.

Summary

In short, the contractor must give prior notice of all delays that it is reasonable for it to expect. The architect then has sufficient time to take appropriate steps to rectify the situation and provide the contractor with the opportunity to bring the contract back on programme. This may be by way of omitting work if it is practicable to do so and if, of course, the employer agrees. If the contractor fails to give notice (even of its own delays), it is in breach of contract and the architect is entitled to take the breach into account when giving a future extension of time. A simple example will make clear how the principle works.

Take the case of an architect who has been given a specific written request for information by the contractor at the right time, neither too early nor too late. The architect has overlooked the request. A week before the information is required, it is reasonably apparent to the contractor that it is not likely to arrive, but it does nothing. On the day it is required, it has still not arrived, but it is not until a week later and the job is seriously delayed that the contractor sends the architect a notice of delay. By the time the architect has diverted staff onto the task and the information is produced, a further two weeks have passed making a total of three weeks delay. The contractor is clearly in breach, because it failed to notify the architect that the work was likely to be delayed a week before the delay occurred. In fixing a new completion date, the architect is entitled to take the contractor's breach into account by asking the question: what would have been the length of delay had notification been received at the correct time? It would still have taken two weeks to produce the information, but the preparation would have been able to start a week before it was required. The contractor would have been delayed one week and that is all the architect need consider in fixing a new completion date. Events are rarely quite as straightforward as that and, in practice, there may be numerous other factors to be considered.

The contractor must identify in its notice of delay any event that it believes is a relevant event. If it does not do so, the architect's duty to consider the notice does not commence. This requirement acknowledges and reinforces the point that the notice of delay may contain causes of delay that are not relevant events. The notice must state the causes of delay that, the contractor believes, entitle it to an extension of time. The relevant events must be identified.

Particulars of effects of delay

The Contractor has a quite onerous obligation under the contract. It must give particulars of the expected effects of each relevant event notified (but not of other delaying factors). Either in its original notice or, where that is not practicable, as soon as possible after the notice, the contractor must write to the architect, giving details of the expected effects on progress. Each relevant event must be assessed by the contractor separately as if no other event had occurred. The contractor must give its own estimate of the expected delay in completion of the Works beyond the completion date. This is a particularly onerous task. The contractor must address each delay separately and its effects even if two or more delays are

3.14

157

2.27.2

acting together. Contractors will commonly, indeed invariably, promote their views of the delay, but rarely split so as to deal with each delay as a separate item. Contractors often simply list things they believe are causing delay, assigning a delay period to each. They then give a view about the combined effect of all the delays as a total delay, but without indicating how it has been calculated. That is not what the contract requires and it does not amount to any evidence of delay.

The contractor must give enough information to enable the architect to form an opinion. So it is not sufficient for the contractor merely to estimate the effect on the completion date, it must also show the effect on every relevant activity between the event and the completion date. It is arguable that a contractor cannot properly comply with this requirement without providing before and after print outs of its computerised programme.

Changes in the submitted particulars

2.27.3   The contractor must inform the architect of any significant change in any of the submitted particulars and estimate of delay and give whatever further information the architect may reasonably require. The contractor must keep the architect up to date with developments on site that are relevant to the notified delay. For example, it may be an ongoing delay for which the contractor must update the architect on a regular basis. The contractor's duty is not dependent upon the architect's request. Failure to update the architect will amount to a breach of contract on the part of the contractor that the architect is entitled to take into account in estimating any extension of time. The architect's time limit for dealing with applications for delay only begins when the required particulars have been received from the contractor. The intention of these provisions is to provide sufficient information to allow the architect to arrive at an informed opinion. Although the architect may not have been on the site at the time of the delay, there is no doubt that an architect must use whatever records are available

158   from any source. The architect cannot avoid dealing with the contractor's delay notices because the contractor has failed to provide information that the architect already has or of which the architect is well aware.

Importantly, it should be noted that it is specifically stated that the architect may require the further information at any time. 'At any time' must be given its

159, 160   plain meaning and there is no restriction in time. The effect of that appears to be that the architect may require further information at any time up to the date on which the architect gives a definitive decision on extensions of time. The architect is required to review the extension of time position up to twelve weeks after

2.28.5   the date of practical completion. Therefore, the architect may require further information up to that time. The architect's requirement must be reasonable.

The architect's opinion

2.28.1   The architect's duty to form an opinion about extension of time does not arise until the contractor has provided both the notice of delay and the particulars including an estimate of expected delay in completion. If the particulars are received before the date for completion, the architect must consider them. The architect has to decide two important things:

- whether any of the causes of delay specified by the contractor in the notice is in fact a relevant event, and
- whether completion of the Works is in fact likely to be delayed by the specified relevant event beyond the completion date.

Obviously, the architect may disagree that the cause specified by the contractor is a relevant event. If that is the case, the architect need not consider the next point. It is remarkable how often contractors fail to refer to any relevant event at all, presumably in the mistaken belief that they are entitled to an extension of time if they are delayed for any reason. Alternatively, contractors often specify relevant events by clause number without specifying any occurrence on site in relation to it. If a contractor fails to identify the correct, or indeed any, relevant event, the architect has no duty to identify it. Rather, the architect's duty seems to be simply to check whether the contractor has named the correct relevant event and whether the notified cause falls under that relevant event.

Importance of the completion date

An architect who concludes that the delay, however long it may be, has no effect on the completion date, must decide that no extension of time is applicable. That situation can occur when a delay occurs to an activity that is not on the critical path and that has a considerable amount of float to absorb the effects of the delay without the non-critical activity becoming critical. It is very easy for an architect to fall into the trap of thinking that a delay of two weeks to an activity equals two weeks extension of time. It is difficult to over-emphasise the importance of the completion date. A delay that does not affect the completion date does not entitle the contractor to an extension of time. Delay to an activity that may or may not have an effect on the completion date must be differentiated from delay to the completion date.

161

Exercise of the architect's opinion

It is entirely a matter for the architect's opinion, whether a delay in the contract completion date is likely to occur or has occurred and also whether the cause of delay falls into the category of a relevant event and therefore something for which the architect should grant an extension. However, the architect does not have completely free rein in the matter and must exercise his or her opinion according to law. As soon as the architect is notified by the contractor of a delay, either occurring or predicted to occur, it is for the architect to carefully monitor the position.

If the contractor feels that the architect has been unreasonable in reaching an opinion, its recourse is to adjudication or arbitration or litigation (depending on which has been included in the contract). On receipt of the contractor's written notice the architect must decide if the cause of delay is a relevant event.

If in the architect's view it is not then, subject to the contractor's right to challenge that opinion by one of the dispute resolution procedures, that is the end of the matter.

Of course, the architect must not arrive at the decision on a whim. The position should be carefully analysed and the effect of individual delays must be considered. However, having reached a decision, that decision has a considerable status under the contract.

162
163

Factors to take into account

The architect must decide whether or not the delay is going to mean a likely failure to complete by the date for completion. The architect must take into account that the contractor shall constantly use its best endeavours to prevent delay. The contractor's duty is to prevent delay, so far as it can reasonably do so, e.g. a delay in progress of the Works at an early stage may be reduced or even eliminated by the contractor using its best endeavours.

In a situation where causes of delay overlap or where they are concurrent (in the broad sense), the architect must consider each cause separately. The cumulative effect on progress must be taken into account: it is delay to progress and the completion date that are the important factors. An architect who decides that one or more causes are relevant events and that the completion date is likely to be delayed as a result must give an extension of time to the contractor.

The architect will have to consider matters of concurrency caused by delays resulting from different relevant events and from the contractor's own culpable delay.

An estimate

The architect is required to grant the extension of time by fixing as a new completion date for the Works a later date that the architect estimates to be fair and reasonable. It should be noted that the architect is only expected to estimate the length of extension and not to ascertain it. Ascertainment would be impossible. 'Fair and reasonable' is not an easy concept to operate in practice. One person's fairness is not necessarily another's. In this instance, it is the architect's concept of fairness that is required.

Informing the contractor

2.28.2 The architect must inform the contractor whether or not an extension is given. That is important. The architect cannot simply sit back and say nothing if there is no extension. For each notification of delay and provision of particulars, the architect must notify the contractor in writing if the decision is not to fix a later completion date as a new completion date. It is important, because the architect's decisions are required before the provisions restricting the level of fluctuations or formula adjustment can be operated if the contractor is in default over completion, which is a point that should not escape those using SBC. The architect is allotted the same time period in which to make the decision whether it is positive or negative.

Time period

The architect must inform the contractor in writing of the decision within a time period that is not delayed, but that takes all the circumstances into account and applies the test of reasonableness. In any event, the architect has a maximum of 12 weeks in which to notify the decision. The 12 weeks runs from receipt by the architect of the required particulars.

The correct operation of these provisions really depends upon both architect and contractor being of one mind as to whether the information supplied by the contractor is sufficient to enable the architect to form an opinion. From the employer's point of view it is important that the architect should decide in good *Schedule 7,* time, because of the fluctuations provisions, the effect of which is that, unless *paragraphs* the architect carries out his or her duties promptly, the right of the employer to *A.9.2.2,* freeze the contractor's fluctuations on the due date for completion is lost.

B.10.2.2 and However, if there are less than 12 weeks left between receipt of the contrac-
C.6.2.2 tor's particulars and the completion date, the architect must try to reach a decision and fix a new date for completion no later than the current completion date. The intention clearly is that the contractor should always have a date for completion towards which it can work. It seems that the architect cannot make the decision after the completion date and if it cannot be made before, the deci-
2.28.5 sion will have to be made as part of the review process. The contractor may be disappointed, but it is the author of its own misfortune.

If it seems that the architect would be able to make a decision if a further week or so was available, the architect may decide to make the best decision practicable (which may well be conservative) before the completion date and then use the additional period thus created to come to a more considered decision. Thus, an architect faced with making a decision just one week before completion date may be able to give two weeks extension of time and the extra two weeks may give the architect the time necessary to give a further one week. However, the architect is not obliged to act in this way.

Some architects have adopted the practice of amending the extension time *2.28* clause so as to do away with the time limits. This is not a wise idea, if only *Schedule 7,* because of the fluctuations provisions. Fluctuations are only to be frozen at *paragraphs* completion date if the printed text of the extension of time clause is not *A.9.2.1,* amended and forms part of the conditions:. If there is no fixed period for mak-
B.10.2.1 and ing a decision, an adjudicator or arbitrator, if called upon, may decide that the *C.6.2.1* architect ought to come to a decision in less than 12 weeks.

What must the decision say?
2.28.3

If the architect's decision is that an extension of time is to be given, the architect, in fixing the new completion date, must state two things. The first thing is the amount of extension of time given for each relevant event and the second thing is the reduction in time attributed to each relevant omission. Previous JCT contracts did not require the architect to state the period of time attributable to each relevant event. That was sensible, because to allocate time periods against relevant events is generally not in the employer's interests. The contractor always, of course, demands these details, because without them it is difficult to challenge the architect's decision unless it is grossly wrong. Moreover, the contractor often mistakenly believes that an extension of time is a pre-requisite to claiming loss and/or expense.

Detailed reasons

It used to be the case that an architect, in giving an extension of time, would set out the reasoning behind it in considerable detail. Of course this merely encouraged the contractor to respond, pointing out where the architect was wrong, in equal detail. The exchange would never come to an end while ever the architect responded. Very few architects now provide the contractor with such details of the reasons for an extension of time (or for its rejection). The contract does not require it and it is doubtful whether it actually assisted the contractor. Obviously, the architect would be obliged to reveal calculations during an adjudication or arbitration if the decision had to be defended, but by that time the contractor must have already made its decision to challenge, based on its own opinion and perhaps that of its expert.

Listing the events

From the new wording, it seems that the architect must list all the relevant events notified by the contractor even if the architect has discounted some of them. Presumably the architect then has to allocate the extension of time among the notified relevant events, allocating 'nil' to relevant events that have been notified but for which the architect has not given any extension of time. Any reductions in time must be allocated to each relevant omission. Note the allocation of reductions is not to relevant events, but to relevant omissions. These are presumably architect's instructions requiring omissions.

Relevant omissions

2.28.4   The architect's powers to reduce time for omissions of work may be exercised only after the first extension of time that the architect gives or after a revision to the completion date stated in a confirmed acceptance of a variation or acceleration quotation (pre-agreed adjustment). The term used in the contract is
2.26.3   'Relevant Omission' that is defined as omissions of work or obligations whether by instruction for variations or for provisional sums for defined work. The architect can only reduce extensions of time on account of omissions of work, etc. instructed since an extension was last given. So each subsequent extension is deemed to take into account all omissions instructed from the date of the previous extension up to the date of the new extension.

Original completion date must be respected

2.28.6.3   The architect cannot fix any earlier date than the original completion date no matter how many omissions have been instructed. The architect's powers to reduce an extension of time are not dependent upon the contractor giving a notice of delay. The architect can simply issue an instruction requiring an omission and then fix a new date for completion earlier than previously fixed, taking the omission instruction into account.

It is suggested that architects wishing to exercise the power to reduce extensions previously granted by taking into account the omission of work or obligations should fix the new date and notify the contractor as soon as possible.

The review

2.28.5   The architect must review the completion date. It is not a matter of choice. The review may be carried out after the completion date has passed, but it must be carried out no later than 12 weeks after practical completion. In doing this the architect must take account of any known relevant events, whether or not specifically notified to the architect by the contractor. It is the architect's final opportunity to consider extensions of time and possibly prevent time becoming at large. Although the contract does not make it absolutely clear, it is likely that the architect can exercise this power only once. Therefore, it is sensible for the architect to wait until after practical completion to carry out the review. Indeed, it is best to issue the conclusions during the last of the 12 weeks so that there is no temptation to review again in response to a last-minute submission by the contractor. When the architect does issue the review conclusions, the details required for an extension of time given before the date for completion (allocation of extensions of time to each relevant event and the reduction in time to each relevant omission) must be given in this case also.

Procedure

In carrying out the review, the architect must do one of three things:

- Fix a completion date later than any date previously fixed. The architect must consider any of the relevant events and it matters not whether any relevant event has been notified by the contractor. Therefore, the architect has a very wide scope to fix a new date for completion.
- Fix a completion date earlier than previously fixed, but may not fix a date earlier than the completion date in the contract. The architect must consider any omission instructions issued since the last extension of time was given.
- Confirm to the contractor the completion date previously fixed.

It is good practice for the architect to write to the contractor soon after practical completion, reminding it of the 12-week period and that the architect has no power to make any extension of time after the expiry of the period.

The contractor should be given a date by which any final submissions should be made. Realistically, the architect should be in possession of everything by the end of week eight at the latest; this is not the time for the submission of large numbers of weighty lever arch files.

If the review is not carried out in time

This clause sets out the extension of time regime after the completion date that is quite separate from what has gone before. It gives the architect the opportunity to make a final decision on extensions of time. What if the contractor provides no information at all to the architect until after the 12 weeks has expired or if the architect forgets about the review? Strictly, the architect has no power to consider the submission and must so inform the contractor. For practical purposes, if the architect has forgotten about the review, it must be carried **164** out as soon as the architect realises the error. There may, of course, be circumstances where the architect believes that, for various reasons after the review has been carried out, a further extension should be given after the deadline. It seems that the only way this can be achieved is if the employer and contractor together agree to waive the contractual time limitation. This is best done in writing. Before the architect advises the employer to follow that route, there must be a clear advantage to the employer in so doing, for example, because there is a danger that time will become at large.

14.5   Important conditions

2.28.6   There are a number of important provisions connected to extending time. The first two apply to the contractor and the second two apply to the architect. The introductory wording strongly suggests that compliance with the first two provisions (the use of best endeavours and the doing of everything reasonably required) is a pre-condition to the issue of valid extensions of time.

Best endeavours

2.28.6.1   The contractor must constantly use its best endeavours to prevent delay to progress and to the completion date. This is a matter that the architect must take into account when deciding upon extension of time. Using best endeavours means taking all the reasonable steps that a prudent and determined person, acting in his or her own best interests and desiring to achieve that result would **165** take. The addition of the word 'constantly' means that it must never cease to use its best endeavours.

166   Clearly, it is not as great an obligation as to 'ensure' or to 'secure', which create an absolute liability to perform the duty set out. A question that often arises is whether 'best endeavours' obliges the contractor to spend additional money preventing delays: for example, taking on additional operatives or plant. If that was the case, there would be little need for an extension of time clause, because the contractor would have to do whatever it took to prevent or reduce delay. It is doubtful whether a contractor has any obligation at all to increase resources on a project over and above the level necessary to complete the work for which the contractor originally tendered. It is clear that the contractor cannot avoid incurring some additional costs in an attempt to maintain the status quo in the face of delays. In practice it is likely that best endeavours means simply that the contractor must continue to work regularly and diligently and nothing more. Provided the contractor is working regularly and diligently and has not contributed to the delay through its fault, the contractor can be said to have used its best endeavours. The contractor's failure to constantly use its best endeavours will disqualify it from any extension of time for the particular relevant event.

167

Everything reasonably required

2.28.6.2

The previous condition always applies to the contractor. The second condition applies only if there is a delay. In the case of a delay the contractor must do everything reasonably required to the satisfaction of the architect in order to proceed with the Works. This is probably the contractor's obligation as part of its duty to proceed regularly and diligently in any event. The architect has no power to order that acceleration measures be taken either under this provision or any other provision in the contract. There is a procedure by which the Works may be accelerated if the contractor's quotation for doing so is acceptable, but that is a long way from giving the architect power to accelerate. The key word in this condition is 'reasonably'. It is thought that it would be completely unreasonable for the architect to require the contractor to expend large additional sums in order to comply with this condition. It covers such things as the architect requesting the contractor to adjust its programme of work or to move operatives from one part of the building to another.

Schedule 2

The completion date in the contract cannot be made earlier

2.28.6.3

The architect cannot fix a completion date earlier than that stated in the contract particulars. What that means is that, no matter how much work is omitted, the contract period as set out by reference to the date of possession and the date for completion in the contract cannot be shortened.

Pre-agreed adjustment

2.28.6.4

A pre-agreed adjustment is a revised completion date fixed by a confirmed acceptance of a variation or acceleration quotation. The architect cannot make a decision about omissions that alters the length of a pre-agreed adjustment. There is an exception to that and it is in the case of a variation quotation in which the variation is the subject of an omission.

Schedule 2

2.28.4 or

2.28.5.2

14.6   Common problems

If the contractor is ahead of its own programme when a delay occurs

168

The architect is required to give an extension of time only if the completion of the Works is likely to be or has been delayed beyond the date for completion or any extended time for completion previously fixed. If a contractor is well ahead with its work and is then delayed by a strike, the architect may reach the conclusion that completion of the Works is not likely to be delayed beyond the date of completion. If a strike occurs when two-thirds of the Works have been completed in half the contract time, the contractor is not then entitled to slow down its work so as to last out the time until the date for completion or beyond, if by doing so it is failing to proceed with the Works regularly and diligently.

The architect must be able to take account of where the contractor actually is in terms of progress when compared with its programme and that if the contractor is ahead of its programme, the architect may take account of that in estimating the appropriate extension of time.

If the contractor does not provide sufficient information to the architect until a few days before the completion date

2.28.2

Contractors sometimes attempt to intimidate architects by waiting until the last moment to provide the required particulars and then maintaining that the architect is obliged to come to a decision before the completion date no matter how little time is left. That kind of contractor is seriously misguided. The contract is clear. It states that the architect must *endeavour* to notify the contractor of the new date for completion before the current completion date. The obligation to endeavour to do something means that the architect must strive or attempt to do it. If there is a very short period left before the completion date, it may not be reasonably practicable for the architect to come to a decision in time no matter how strong the endeavour. After the completion date, the review period begins and continues until 12 weeks after practical completion. The architect will have that period in which to consider and make a final decision about all extensions of time including the contractor's late information.

Must an architect give an extension of time if the contractor has not asked for one?

2.28.5

During the review period the architect must consider everything known including events notified by the contractors and events not notified, but of which the architect is aware. Therefore, the architect must give an extension or a further extension of time if it is clear that it is justified even if the contractor has not requested it. The purpose of this mopping up clause it to make sure that time does not become at large because the architect has not given an extension of time for some delay that is the responsibility of the employer.

The contractor asks for reasons why the architect has not given an extension of time

2.28.3

The contractor is not entitled to have reasons. All it is entitled to is notification of the extension attributed to each relevant event or any reduction in time allocated to a relevant omission. Many architects respond to the contractor's delay notice with long letters explaining in detail how the extension of time has been calculated. This tends to be self-defeating and only serves to provoke the contractor into a further exchange. If the question of extensions goes before an adjudicator or an arbitrator, the architect may well have to explain the reasoning behind an extension, but the contract does not require it and, strictly speaking, the architect need not justify the extension even in adjudication, although it may be prudent to do so.

169

If the architect forgets to carry out a review of the extension of time

The architect has until 12 weeks after the date of practical completion in which to carry out the review and notify the parties. It is not thought that being a week late is any great problem But if the architect forgets to notify employer and contractor until a week after the end of the period it is important that the architect then does so as soon as possible. However, before doing so the parties must be given advance notice of the late issue and of what the review notice is going to contain. That is so that either the employer or the contractor, being forewarned, can start immediate adjudication proceedings if they wish.

170

15 Liquidated damages

15.1 What are liquidated damages?

Liquidated damages are a fixed and agreed sum rather than unliquidated damages that is a sum that is neither fixed nor agreed, but must be proved in court, arbitration or adjudication. A more comprehensive definition of liquidated damages is given below. Previous 1998 and earlier editions of the contract used the words 'liquidated and ascertained damages' but the word 'ascertained' is not significant here. However, it explains (for anyone who was wondering) why liquidated damages is often abbreviated to 'LADs'.

171

Litigation is generally recognised as being expensive and lengthy. In order to recover damages in matters involving breaches of contract it is necessary to prove that the defendant had a contractual obligation to the claimant, that there was a failure to fulfil the obligation wholly or partly and as a result that the claimant suffered loss or damage. Very often it is clear that there is damage, but it is difficult and expensive to prove it. To avoid that situation, the parties may decide, when they enter into a contract, that in the event of a breach of a particular kind the party in default will pay a stipulated sum to the other. This sum is termed liquidated damages.

Penalties

172

In the building industry and elsewhere the terms 'liquidated damages' and 'penalty' are commonly used as though they were interchangeable. In fact, they are totally different in concept. Whereas liquidated damages are intended to be compensatory and should be a genuine attempt to predict the damages likely to flow as a result of a particular breach, a penalty is a sum that is not related to probable damages, but rather stipulated as a threat or even, in some instances, intended as a punishment. The courts will enforce liquidated damages, but not penalties.

The rate

2.32

The contract provides for the contractor to pay the employer liquidated damages at the rate specified in the contract particulars if the contractor fails to complete on time, or the employer may deduct the sum. The amount of

The JCT Standard Building Contract 2011, First Edition. David Chappell.
© 2014 by David Chappell. Published 2014 by John Wiley & Sons, Ltd.

liquidated damages should have been calculated carefully at pre-tender stage. The figure must represent a genuine pre-estimate of the loss likely to be suffered by the employer if the contractor fails to complete on time, or a lesser sum. If the sum arrived at is a genuine re-estimate of the likely loss, then that is the sum that will be recoverable, even if the sum agreed is greater than the actual loss or even if there is no loss. An important point, not always grasped by employers is that liquidated damages are exhaustive of the employer's remedy

173

for the breach of late completion. What that means is that the sum stated as liquidated damages is deemed to cover all the costs and expenses that the employer may suffer as a result of the contractor's late completion. Therefore, the employer cannot separately recover from the contractor extra professional fees, extra rental fees or anything else that was caused by late completion.

15.2   Procedure

Pre-conditions to recovery

Four conditions must be satisfied before the employer is entitled to recover liquidated damages.

- The contractor must have failed to complete the Works by the date for completion in the contract or any extended time.
- The architect must have performed the duty to decide extensions of time.
- The architect must have issued a certificate that the contractor has failed to complete by the completion date (a non-completion certificate).
- The employer must have written to the contractor saying that liquidated damages may be deducted or may be required to be paid.

The architect must consider and make decisions on all the contractor's applications for extensions of time before issuing a non-completion certificate

174

otherwise the certificate will not be valid.

Certificate of non-completion

Contrary to popular belief, the architect may issue the non-completion certificate at any time prior to the issue of the final certificate. In practice, of course, most architects will issue the certificate immediately the completion date has passed in order to allow the employer the maximum possible time and maximum available funds for deduction of liquidated damages. An employer may be able to recover money from an architect who delays the issue of the certificate until just before the issue of the final certificate if, by that time, it is impossible to recover the liquidated damages. However, once the architect has

4.15

1.9

issued the final certificate and if no notice of adjudication, arbitration or legal proceedings has been promptly given by either party, the architect cannot after that issue any valid non-completion certificate nor take any further action

175

under the contract.

Can the architect decide not to issue the non-completion certificate?

2.31.3

The architect cannot avoid issuing the certificate of non-completion if the contractor has failed to complete by the due date. The architect has no discretion in the matter. If the architect fixes a new date for completion after the issue of the certificate, the fixing of a new date cancels the existing certificate and the architect must issue a further certificate. An employer who is then found to have deducted too much by way of liquidated damages, must repay the extra amount. It has been suggested that the contractor would be entitled to interest on the money deducted and repaid. That suggestion is wrong. In recovering liquidated damages in the first instance, the employer was simply complying with the clause in the contract that entitled the deduction. In repaying some or all of them after a further non-completion certificate, the employer is again complying with the contract. In neither instance can the employer be said to be in breach of contract and, therefore, the employer is not liable in damages. Therefore, there is no justification for requiring interest to be paid unless the contract expressly so states. None of the JCT contracts give the contractor any entitlement to interest in such circumstances.

Notice requiring payment

2.32.4

The employer need only serve one notice requiring payment. It remains effective, unless the employer withdraws it, despite the cancellation by the architect of previous non-completion certificates and the issue of further non-completion certificates. Since the decision to deduct liquidated damages rests with the employer, it is unlikely that the notice would ever, in practice, be withdrawn. If the employer decided not to deduct damages, the matter would simply be allowed to rest.

Timing

2.32.1

The timing of the written notice sometimes causes difficulty. The contract seems to suggest that liquidated damages may be deducted provided that the written requirement is served before the date of the final certificate. Following that logic, damages might be deducted from an interim certificate several months before a notice is sent just before the issue of the final certificate. That, of course, would be nonsense and clearly not what the contract intends. The date of the final certificate is the deadline for the written requirement but the requirement must always pre-date the deduction.

The employer should issue the notice as soon as the architect has issued a non-completion certificate and that notice will serve for any future deductions. It is important to remember that failure to serve the written requirement at all before the final certificate will not only prevent deduction from payment due on certificates, it will also preclude recovery of the liquidated damages as a debt.

Form of the notice

Only two things must be specified in the notice and they are:

- whether the employer is claiming a payment or a deduction of the liquidated damages; and
- whether the employer will require the rate of liquidated damages set out in the contract or a lesser rate.

4.12.5

Once the other conditions have been satisfied an employer wishing to deduct the liquidated damages from the amount certified, has until five days before the final date for payment to serve a pay less notice on the contractor. The employer is entitled to deduct liquidated damages at a lesser, but not a greater, rate than the rate in the contract particulars.

15.3 Common problems

Does the contractor's liability for liquidated damages only end with the certificate of practical completion or until the employer retakes possession?

Three things can end the contractor's liability for liquidated damages:

- If the contractor's employment is terminated.
- If the architect issues a certificate of practical completion.
- If the employer takes partial possession.

176

Once the contractor's employment has been terminated, it is impossible for the contractor to have any further influence on the progress of the Works and, therefore, it is no longer responsible for liquidated damages. The obligations of both parties are at an end so far as future performance is concerned.

2.32.2

Once the architect certifies practical completion, liquidated damages stop accumulating. The contract specifically refers to them as being from the completion date in the contract or any extended date to the date of practical completion.

2.37

177

If the employer takes partial possession, liquidated damages cease for the part taken into possession at the date of partial possession. If the employer takes partial possession of the whole of the Works, liquidated damages cease on that date for the whole of the Works.

The employer has not suffered any loss through a delay, but still wants to claim liquidated damages

2.32.1

178

The employer is entitled to claim liquidated damages if the architect has issued a non-completion certificate and if the employer has notified the contractor. It is irrelevant whether the employer has suffered a less than the rate of liquidated damages or even has suffered no loss at all. The key point is simply whether the rate of liquidated damages that was put into the contract was a genuine pre-estimate of the loss expected to be suffered.

The architect has deducted liquidated damages from the calculation of an interim certificate

That is wrong. There is no power in the contract to enable the architect to deduct liquidated damages. Like any other kind of damages, it is a matter for the employer to decide whether or not to deduct them.

16 Financial claims

16.1 Loss and expense claims

Loss and/or expense

The contract refers to the contractor incurring direct loss and/or expense. Consequential losses (more about those later) are not covered by the clause. What the contractor is claiming under this clause is the same as if it was claiming damages through the courts for breach of contract in terms of the way in which damages are worked out and the standard of proof required.

179

Causes of loss and/or expense

4.24

For the contractor to make a claim under the contract, there must be something causing the loss or expense. The causes are set out in the contract (where they are called 'Relevant Matters') and they are not all breaches of contract. There must also be a loss or some expense suffered or incurred by the contractor, otherwise, there is no point in the contractor making an application. This is a relatively simple concept but not fully understood by many contractors or architects.

What is consequential loss?

It is important to understand the difference between direct and indirect (or consequential) loss or damage. Someone in breach of contract is not liable to pay all the losses suffered by the other person. The courts limit the damages to what is reasonable in the circumstances by ruling out all damage that is said to be too remote. It is only the remoteness of, or the entitlement of a person to, damages that is considered here, the amount of damages is a separate issue that will be considered later. The rule has been stated as follows:

There are two parts. The first part refers to damages arising naturally. These damages are often referred to as 'general damages'. They are the kind of damages that anyone would expect to be the result of the breach of contract. For example, the employer may have to pay the cost of putting things right if the contractor, in breach of contract, fails to install a shower fitting correctly.

The JCT Standard Building Contract 2011, First Edition. David Chappell.
© 2014 by David Chappell. Published 2014 by John Wiley & Sons, Ltd.

The second part refers to the kind of damages that were understood as a possibility by both parties at the time they made the contract. These kinds of damages depend upon the knowledge of the parties of special circumstances and they are often referred to as 'special damages'. For example, suppose Ms A buys a car from Acme Used Cars and drives it away intending to use it immediately to drive to Southampton; there to start a pre-booked cruising holiday. Further, suppose the car breaks down on the way to Southampton so that Ms A does not reach the ship in time before its departure. Ms A can certainly claim from Acme the cost of necessary repairs to the car, but she cannot claim the cost of the lost holiday, because Acme knew nothing of the projected holiday or the consequences of a mechanical breakdown. If all those facts had been made known to Acme before or at the time of the sale contract for the car, Ms A might have been able to claim the cost of the holiday also. In practice, it is unlikely that Acme would accept such a liability and there may well be clause in its sale contract to deal with that eventuality, but the principle remains good.

It is enough if the type of loss is within the reasonable contemplation of the parties even though the *extent* of the loss is far greater than they could have

180   contemplated.

In theory, the differences between the types of loss are easy to understand. In practice, there are often difficulties of interpretation.

16.2   Procedure

The contractor's application

Although it is in the employer's interests that the architect gives the contractor an extension of time where the contractor has been delayed by one of the relevant events, the same is plainly not true so far as loss and/or expense is concerned. The architect has no duty to advise the contractor to apply for loss and/or expense and, indeed, an architect giving that kind of advice may be in breach of duty to the employer. Whether or not the contractor decides to make an application for loss and/or expense is entirely its affair. However, the contractor is not entitled to any loss and/or expense whatsoever unless it makes an appli-

4.23   cation. Two aspects of the application deserve careful consideration: its content and timing.

Content

There is no set format for the application, but:

- It must be in writing.
- It should state that the contractor has incurred or is likely to incur direct loss and/or expense as a result of deferment of possession of the site or regular progress being materially affected by one or more of the relevant matters.

Sufficient notice

The application may be sufficient if it refers to the general grounds and identifies the occurrence, stating that loss and/or expense is being or is likely to be incurred.

The first notice that many architects have that there is likely to be a claim is often tagged onto the end of a notification of delay and claim for extension of time. The contractor will often simply include additional words to the effect that it is also seeking loss and/or expense on the same grounds. Although it can be argued that such a casual approach on the part of the contractor is not sufficient to comply with the contract requirements to make application, in practice the question is whether the notice is enough to alert the architect to the fact that the contractor is, or will be, seeking to recover loss and/or expense in respect of particular occurrences.

Sufficient information

The key point is whether the contractor's notice contains enough information to enable the architect to understand what the contractor says were the causes and to decide whether to require records to be taken of the occurrence at an early stage. Notices from the contractor giving no information except that a claim for loss and/or expense is to be expected should be rejected by the architect, because they do not comply with the contract requirements and they do not provide the architect with any useful information.

A simple notice, that a contractor is likely to be claiming loss and/or expense, should be countered by a letter from the architect, pointing out that the letter does not contain sufficient information to constitute a proper application under the contract and asking if the contractor wishes to add anything further. If the contractor opts not to provide further information, the contractor's notice should be ignored when the architect has to consider in the future whether the contractor has made application in at the right time.

Minimum details

The application should clearly specify whether the contractor is relying on deferment of possession or one or more of the relevant matters. The contractor ought to provide as much information as possible about the surrounding circumstances. At the very least, the architect should expect to receive full details of the actual events that are the grounds for the claim and that of the relevant matters the contractor believes apply. Specific written applications must be made in respect of each occurrence. Some contractors make a practice of issuing a standard letter of delay, extension of time and loss and/or expense application every time anything at all happens. If the standard application contains the information required by the contract, it must be considered, even if dozens of standard applications are received. If the standard letter does not satisfy the contract requirements, it must be rejected.

Three requirements

The contract requires compliance with three conditions before the application can even be considered.

Time

181

4.23.1

Application at the right time. This is a pre-condition to the contractor's entitlement to payment. Architects must not forget that they owe a duty to employers to reject claims that do not fulfil this criterion. It is not that they may ignore such claims; rather that they have no power to consider them. The contract requires that the contractor's written application should be made as soon as it has become, or as soon as it should reasonably have become, apparent to the contractor that regular progress of the Works or any part of the Works has been or was likely to be materially affected. Therefore, the application must be made as early as possible and, except in exceptional circumstances, before regular progress of the Works is actually affected.

If the contractor's application is not made at the proper time, then the architect must reject it, whatever its merits may be, and the architect has no power under the terms of the contract to form an opinion about it. Moreover, an architect who proceeds to consider a late application by the contractor may be liable to the employer, particularly if the relevant matters being considered are not such as the contractor could use to formulate a claim at common law for breach of contract. The architect can deal only with the relevant matters that are included in the contractor's application; the architect has no authority to deal with any things affecting regular progress that are not included in a written application from the contractor, although the architect may be fully aware of them.

182

Application may be made after regular progress has been affected and the loss and/or expense has been incurred. The intention that lies behind the condition is that the architect should be kept informed at the earliest possible time of all matters likely to affect the progress of the Works and that the contractor is citing as grounds for claiming loss and/or expense. It is obvious that if the contractor notifies the architect in good time, the architect may be able to take any available action to minimise or completely eradicate the loss and/or expense and the contractor may find it difficult to establish a convincing reason why it could not give earlier notice. If the architect is in doubt whether the contractor's application has been made in due time, a useful test is for the architect to consider whether the alleged lateness of the application prejudices the employer's interests in any way.

Supporting information

4.23.2

Submission at the architect's request of supporting information to reasonably make it possible for the architect to reach an opinion. It is in the contractor's own interest to provide as much relevant information as possible at the time of its written application and not to wait until the architect asks for it.

The information that the architect is entitled to request is that which should reasonably enable him or her to form an opinion. The point is not whether the information is reasonable, but whether whatever is provided will reasonably allow the architect to form an opinion. In many instances it will amount to the same thing so that if the information is not reasonable, the architect cannot reasonably form an opinion. Importantly, an architect is not entitled to delay matters by asking for more information than is reasonably necessary.

It must always be remembered that the contractor is not expected to prove 'beyond a reasonable doubt', but only on the 'balance of probabilities'. In other words, the architect must decide whether it is more likely than not that loss and/or expense has been incurred for one or more of the reasons cited in the contract, i.e. deferment of possession or one of the relevant matters.

4.24

In requesting further information the architect should try to specify the exact information required, for example the labour returns sheets for 5 and 6 March 2012, rather than simply requiring the contractor to 'prove' its claim. The contractor is entitled to know what would satisfy the architect and enable the architect to form a view. This should be the aim of the architect, who otherwise might be accused of delaying tactics.

The contractor is entitled to expect the requests to be properly structured and to relate to the contractor's application. Therefore, it is unreasonable for an architect to ask for further information in a piecemeal fashion. If the architect asks for and receives information, the contractor can expect the architect to make further detailed requests regarding some of the information provided, but not usually for information completely unrelated to what has been produced or about things that the architect already knows. The contractor may get to a point when it sincerely believes that it has provided everything the architect reasonably ought to need and, at that point, the contractor may refuse to provide anything further. There is a danger with that approach that the contractor may omit to provide necessary information and the contractor should be sure of its ground and not simply be tired of digging out old records.

183

Details of loss and/or expense

4.23.3

The contractor at the request of the architect or the quantity surveyor must submit loss and/or expense details reasonably necessary for ascertainment. This does not necessarily mean the submission of an elaborately formulated and priced claim, although it may well be in the contractor's interest to provide it, particularly if it is expected that the matter may end in adjudication or arbitration. Most contractors will submit a fairly detailed claim even if the detail is not what is required.

It is the duty of the architect or the quantity surveyor to ascertain the amount of the direct loss and/or expense and it is necessary for them to look to the contractor to provide the relevant factual information. The contractor's obligation to supply the information does not start until a request is made to the contractor. The details requested might include comparative programme/progress charts in network form pin-pointing the effect upon progress, together with the relevant extracts from wage sheets, invoices for plant hire, etc.

Contractors should think carefully before rejecting requests for further information from the architect or the quantity surveyor. When it receives the request, the contractor should be able to understand exactly what it is being asked to provide. That may seem obvious, but many architects and quantity surveyors are fairly general in their requests. It is not really good enough if the architect or the quantity surveyor simply asks for 'proof' or says that the contractor must provide 'more details'. Although it should be obvious, it bears repeating that neither the architect nor the quantity surveyor should ask the contractor for information that they already possess. As a basic rule, the contractor should be requested to provide no more than is strictly necessary. On receipt of the request the contractor should know that when it is provided, ascertainment of the whole claim will be completed without delay.

184

16.3   Effect on regular progress

The whole basis of the loss and/or expense clause is that the employer deferring (i.e. postponing) possession has given rise to loss and/or expense or that the regular progress of the Works or any part has been or is likely to be materially affected by any one or more of the relevant matters. In other words, it is the effect of the stated matter or cause upon the regular progress of the Works, i.e. any delay or disruption to the regular progress of the contract that is important.

Materially

185

Regular progress must have been, or be likely to be *materially* affected. 'Materially' has been defined as, among other things, 'significant or important', and it is suggested that this definition is applicable here. Trivial disruptions such as are bound to occur on even the best-run contract are clearly excluded. The circumstances must be such as to affect regular progress of the Works to a significant or important degree. A more serviceable word is 'substantially', although perhaps less precise. The particular point at which disruption becomes significant or important is impossible to define in general terms. It must depend upon the circumstances of the particular case.

The cause

This is not the same as saying that merely because the work has proved to cost more or to take longer to complete than was anticipated entitles the contractor to additional payment. It must be possible for the contractor to demonstrate that the cause of the delay or disruption is directly attributable to one or more of the relevant matters and what the effect is upon regular progress of the Works. The words 'regular progress' are obviously related to the contractor's obligation to proceed with the Works regularly and diligently. Whether or not the contractor has progressed regularly and diligently and whether or not the progress has been, or is likely to be, substantially affected is a matter for the opinion of the architect in each case. In carrying out this duty, the architect will be greatly assisted by the contractor's programme provided that it was submitted at the beginning of the project and that it is comprehensive. It is not enough to simply request a programme. If it is to be of maximum assistance, the programme should be in the form of, or at least demonstrate, a critical path network, showing all activities, logic links and the associated resources.

Points on progress

The contractor's progress may already not be regular, due to factors that are within its control or that do not give it any entitlement to claim. That is not fatal to its overall claim under this clause, but it will make it quite difficult to prove entitlement. Among other things, the contractor will have to demonstrate what regular progress should have been and further prove that, irrespective of its failures in this respect, regular progress would have been affected by the relevant matter specified.

It must not be forgotten that there is a distinction between the extension of time and loss and/or expense clauses. Extensions of time must relate to delay in completion of the contract as a whole or, where sections are used, to any defined section. The contractor's application for loss and/or expense may relate to circumstances affecting any part of the Works, even down to individual operations.

186

16.4   The architect's opinion

If the contractor's application is correctly made, the architect must form an opinion. If the architect's opinion is that the contractor has suffered or is likely to suffer direct loss and/or expense due to deferment of possession or, because regular progress has been substantially affected by the relevant matters as stated in the contractor's application, then as soon as that is done, the architect must start the next stage: the ascertainment of the resulting direct loss and/or expense.

The architect's opinion is the important thing. The making of an application by the contractor does not entitle it to money if, in the architect's opinion no money is due. The process of ascertainment, whether by architect or quantity surveyor, cannot begin unless the architect has formed the opinion that deferment of possession has resulted in direct loss and/or expense or that one or more of the relevant matters have materially affected regular progress.

Contractor must play its part

It is often said that the contractor is not obliged to make a claim under this clause, but merely to provide information to the architect that will substantiate a claim. If what is being suggested is that the contractor is entitled simply to provide the architect with large bundles of documents and expect the architect to produce the claim and then consider its merits, that suggestion is quite wrong. The contractor must identify the things causing the problem and also the relevant matters concerned. That is the basis of the claim. Without that, the architect can do nothing.

187

The basic purpose of the application is to enable the architect to know what case the contractor is making in sufficient detail to enable the architect to form an opinion.

16.5   Ascertainment

188

The word 'ascertainment' is defined as meaning 'find out (for certain), get to know'. Ascertainment is not simply something that can be left to the judgement of the architect or the quantity surveyor. They have a duty to find out the amount of the direct loss and/or expense for certain, not to estimate or best guess it. Many applications for loss and/or expense are settled by the quantity surveyor on the basis of figures included in the contract bills. Those figures have no relationship to actual costs and they should only be used as a last resort.

What if ascertainment is not possible?

Obviously, there may be instances where the contractor has poor records and an assessment is the best that can be done. The architect cannot refuse to certify anything at all to the contractor on the ground that proper information is not available if it is clear that the contractor has incurred loss and/or expense, but the precise evidence is not available. In these circumstances, the architect should be careful but remember that the question is whether it is probable that the contractor is entitled to the money it claims or to some other amount.

If the quantity surveyor ascertains

The architect may carry out the ascertainment or may instruct the quantity surveyor to ascertain the direct loss and/or expense. Once the architect has instructed the quantity surveyor, it will be difficult for the architect to certify anything other than the amount ascertained by the quantity surveyor. However, responsibility for certification of the amount lies with the architect who could be negligent if certifying without taking reasonable steps to be satisfied of the

189

correctness of the amount. The architect should, at least, go through the basis of ascertainment with the quantity surveyor to be satisfied that the correct principles have been put into effect. The architect need not accept the quantity

190

surveyor's opinion or valuation when exercising a certifying function.

It is essential that the architect's instruction to the quantity surveyor is clearly set out in writing. The quantity surveyor's agreement to assist must also be in writing so as to establish the quantity surveyor's responsibility to the employer if the ascertainment is carried out negligently. In any event, the employer must be informed of this arrangement, since fees will be involved and, although the contract speaks of the architect instructing the quantity surveyor, the reality is that it can only be done with the agreement of the employer. It is not unknown for an employer, anxious to avoid paying the quantity surveyor the fees for carrying out the ascertainment, to refuse to sanction the instruction and to demand that the architect carries out the ascertainment without assistance. The architect's response to that will depend on the architect's terms of engagement. Usually, an architect's terms of engagement expressly exclude the ascertainment of the contractor's claims. Therefore, the architect might well point out that ascertainment of the claim is not included in the list of architectural services and that dealing with complex cost calculations of that kind is something outside the average architect's expertise.

16.6   Reimbursement under other contract provisions

The loss and/or expense applied for under the contract must be something for which the contractor would not be reimbursed by a payment under any other provision of the contract. The purpose of that is to prevent double payment as might arise, for instance, where increased costs of labour and materials during a period of delay to completion are already being recovered under the fluctuations provisions of the contract.

Where the claims arise as a result of architect's instructions requiring a variation, care must be taken to distinguish between the costs that are included in the quantity surveyor's valuation of the work and those for which reimbursement may be obtained as loss and/or expense. There is, however, another aspect that is often overlooked. Contractors often claim on a 'this or that' basis, hopeful that what they miss under one clause they will recover under the other. This strategy may be successful, but the way the contract is worded means that if the contractor is entitled to be reimbursed under any other provision, it is not *4.23* entitled to be reimbursed as loss and/or expense under the 'claims' clause; even if it has actually received reimbursement under any other provision. It seems that if the contractor is entitled to recover the money as part of the valuation of a variation, it must persevere in its attempts for it cannot recover as loss and/or expense what amounts to a shortfall in the valuation.

The contractors duties are set out in the flowchart Figure 16.1. The architect's duties are set out in the flowchart Figure 16.2.

16.7   Relevant matters forming the basis of a claim

There are now seven broad categories that set out grounds for entitlement to loss and/or expense. The description of impediment, prevention or default includes many causes that used to be listed separately. They are as follows:

- Suspension of work by the contractor due to the employer failing to pay money certified.
- Late instructions drawings, details or levels.

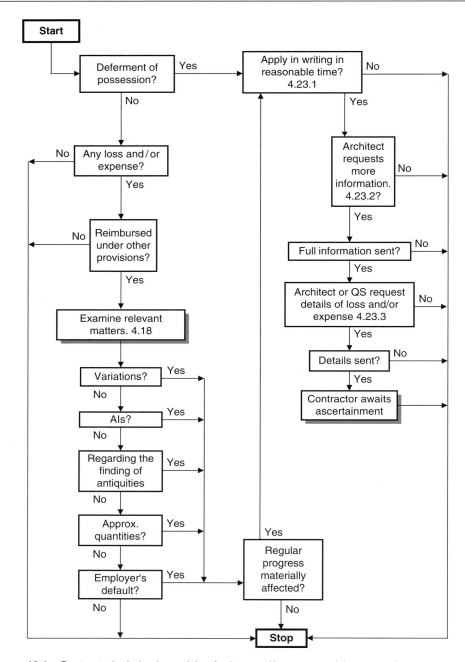

Figure 16.1   Contractor's duties in applying for loss and/or expense (clause 4.23).

- Work not forming part of the contract.
- Failure to give ingress to or egress from the site.
- Compliance or non-compliance with duties in relation to the CDM Regulations.

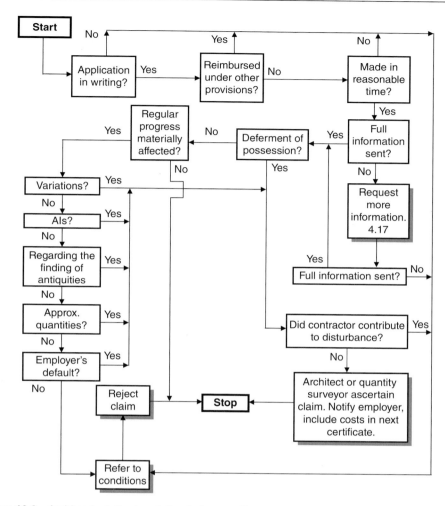

Figure 16.2 Architect's duties in relation to loss and/or expense application (clause 4.23).

Starting with deferment and then in the order in which the relevant matters appear in the contract, the seven categories are as follows:

Deferment of possession of site

4.23

The employer is entitled to defer giving the contractor possession of the site for a period of up to six weeks unless a shorter period was stipulated in the Contract Particulars. This ground can only apply where the employer has actually exercised the right to defer. Obviously, deferment will have an immediate effect on regular progress. But the contractor will have to work hard to found a successful claim for loss and/or expense resulting from deferment of possession. That is because deferment does not extend the contract period; it simply moves it along in time with dates for possession and completion continuing to bear the same relationship to each other. Issues to be considered are the possibility of using operatives elsewhere, delivery dates and important dates for attendance on site of sub-contractors and whether moving the contract period will result in increased costs for labour and/or materials and interest charges.

Variation

4.24.1

This includes all variations, including architect's instructions and anything else that the contract says is to be treated as requiring a variation. Obviously, architect's *3.14* instructions requiring a variation are included and also departures from the stipulated method of preparation of the contract bills, errors or omissions in the bills, *2.14.3* inadequacies in design in the Employer's Requirements (if used) and the correc- *2.16.2* tion of discrepancies in the Employer's Requirements. Variations that are the sub-*Schedule 2,* ject of a confirmation acceptance of a variation quotation are not included because *paragraph 4* any applicable loss and/or expense is to be included in the quotation.

Architect's instructions

4.24.2

These are specific instructions as follows:

2.15
- *Discrepancies in drawings, contract bills, etc.*   These are the ones that occur in or between the contract drawings and/or the contract bills and/or architect's instructions and/or any of the further information issued by the architect. Discrepancies in the printed form or between the printed form and any other document are not grounds for recovery of loss and/or expense,
1.3 because the contract makes clear that the printed form takes precedence over the other documents.

3.15
- *Postponement of any work to be executed under the contract.*   This refers to the architect's power to issue instructions for the postponement of any work to be executed under the provisions of the contract. The cost to the contractor of postponing relatively small items of work may be small if the instruction is issued early so that the contractor can re-plan its work using its best endeavours to prevent delay.

3.16
- *Expenditure of provisional sums (except defined work).*   The contract treats this as an instruction for additional work and it is dealt with accordingly. Compliance with an architect's instruction for the expenditure of a provisional sum for defined work is expressly excluded. That is because, in the case of defined work, the contractor has been given sufficient information to enable it to make appropriate allowance in planning its work at tender stage.

3.17
- *Inspections and tests.*   The architect may require work to be opened up for inspection and to instruct the contractor to arrange for the testing of materials and work to ensure that they comply with the contract. The cost of the opening up and testing must be added to the Contract Sum unless the inspection or tests show that the materials or work are not in accordance with the contract or the bills of quantities have special provision for opening up and the associated cost. The architect has the job of proving that materials or work are not in accordance with the contract. This emphasises

the need to have representatives of both contractor and architect on site when the opening up takes place to avoid work being opened up and quickly corrected before the architect sees it.

Antiquities

4.24.3

3.22.1, 3.22.2

3.22

This concerns the action to be taken in regard to the discovery of antiquities on the site and the architect's instructions about dealing with antiquities.

The position if antiquities are found on or under the site is that the contractor must use its best endeavours not to disturb the object and to cease work as far as is necessary and to take all necessary measures to preserve the object in its position and condition. The contractor must inform the architect or the clerk of works. The architect must then issue instructions and the contractor may be required to allow a third party, such as an expert archaeologist, to examine, excavate and remove the object. There is little doubt that the contractor will be involved in direct loss and/or expense as a result.

Approximate quantity not a reasonably accurate forecast of the quantity of work

4.24.4

This relevant matter is intended to cover the situation where an approximate quantity has been included in the bills of quantities, but the quantity of work actually carried out under that item is different; either greater or less. As long as the approximate quantity is reasonably accurate, the contractor has no claim. What is 'reasonably accurate' will depend upon all the circumstances, but as a rule of thumb an approximate quantity that was within 10% of the actual quantity probably would be difficult to demonstrate as unreasonable. The contractor's entitlement will usually be based on the extra time it requires over and above the time it has allowed for doing the quantity of work in the bills.

The approximate quantity may be an unreasonable estimate, because the actual quantity is substantially less than in the bills. Theoretically, the contractor will also have grounds for a claim under this head, but it will take considerable ingenuity to put together.

Impediment, prevention or default by the employer

4.24.5, 2.29.6

This is identical to equivalent relevant event and the remarks there are generally applicable here. This ground is very broadly written to include breaches of contract on the part of the employer.

16.8   Certification of direct loss and/or expense

The architect is not entitled to wait until the whole of the contractor's application has been dealt with before certifying anything. As parts of the total application are ascertained, the architect or the quantity surveyor must add

4.25
4.4

191
4.16.2.2

them to the Contract Sum. As soon as any amount is ascertained in whole or part, it must be taken into account in the next interim certificate. Not only is this something the contractor will welcome, it also acts as a means of reducing the employer's possible liability for interest charges. Loss and/or expense amounts are not subject to retention.

16.9 Contractor's other rights and remedies

4.26

The contractor's common law and other rights are still available. This is in addition to the rights expressly given by the loss and/or expense provision in the contract that provides remedies for deferment and relevant matters. In particular, the contractor's right to claim damages for breach of contract on the same grounds are preserved.

192

One might reasonably ask why common law rights are necessary if there is a specific way of claiming additional money under the contract? The answer is that the contract remedies are only available if the contractor complies strictly with the provisions set out. On the other hand, the right to claim reimbursement for direct loss and/or expense under the terms of the contract is not connected to any rights or remedies that the contractor may possess in law. If it were not for the loss and/or expense provision, there would be many instances when the contractor would certainly suffer loss and expense but be unable to recover it. But occasionally it may be that because of the limitations imposed by the contract machinery the contractor will be advised to pursue remedies outside the contract.

For example, a contractor who makes its claim under the terms of the contract too late to be considered may still be able to claim on the same grounds at common law, especially if a breach of contract is concerned. It should be noted that the contract does not give the architect power to consider common law claims.

16.10 Common problems

The contractor continues to submit information regarding loss and/or expense right up to the issue of the final certificate

4.23.1

Is there any time limit on the provision of information by the contractor? Can the contractor expect it to be considered by the architect and the quantity surveyor no matter when it is submitted? There is a restriction in the contract on the provision of information. There is a restriction on the making of the initial application by the contractor: it must be as soon as it has become or should reasonably have become apparent to the contractor that regular progress is being affected.

The contract terms do not prohibit the provision and receipt of further information, documentation or details about direct loss and expense after the six month period following practical completion during which the contractor

4.5.1

193

must provide information for the calculation of the final account. The wording of the contract suggests that the contractual provisions simply provide a time table to which the parties are expected to adhere, but the architect or quantity surveyor is not entitled to reject information provided late.

This suggests that, although the provisions generally requiring information to be submitted no later than six months after practical completion are not to be strictly enforced if important new information is submitted, a commonsense view must be taken. That would include considering whether the contractor has already had adequate notice and opportunity to submit more information, whether the information is truly fresh or simply a rehash of information already submitted and whether it is new information that is being submitted or simply a new argument based on existing information. If the architect was obliged to wait until the contractor acknowledged that it had submitted all its arguments, it would be unlikely that the final certificate would ever be issued.

The contractor is claiming for the fees of a claims consultant to help prepare the contractor's claim

194

The traditional approach is that a contractor is not entitled to claim those fees. However, a recent case suggests that claim preparation costs were in principle a valid head of loss and/or expense claim, but appeared to consider it as akin to additional management staff and in that case apparently made a very small allowance. The contract envisages that the contractor will simply submit its application to the architect who will form a conclusion and then the contractor will submit all the cost information required by the quantity surveyor in order to ascertain the sum due. The application is expected to be a straightforward setting out of the grounds for the application and should not usually require the contractor to obtain assistance.

If, however, the matter proceeds to arbitration or litigation, the contractor may be able to claim the employment of someone to present his application as part of its costs.

The architect tells the contractor that a claim for loss and/or expense cannot be considered until the architect has given an extension of time

195

4.23

That attitude is totally wrong. There is no connection between extensions of time and loss and/or expense. Obviously, some of the grounds for extension of time (but not all) are replicated in the grounds for loss and/or expense. However, there is no link between the clauses. The contractor may be entitled to loss and/or expense whether or not it finishes before, after or on, the date for completion. For example, the contractor may be delayed or disrupted in carrying out an activity that is not on the critical path and, therefore, does not give rise to an extension of time. It may still claim loss and/or expense.

17 Architect's instructions

17.1 Purpose

The purpose of instructions is to enable the architect to require the contractor to do various things that are not specifically included in the contract. The most important of these things is the issue of instructions requiring variations. It is not often realised that, if there was not something in the contract giving the architect power to issue instructions, no instructions could be issued. If the architect attempted to issue an instruction, the contractor could lawfully refuse and insist on carrying out just the work included in the contract. Therefore, the kinds of instructions that may be required are in the contract. It must be said that, unlike some other contracts, SBC does not gather all the different kinds of instructions in one place so that the architect and the contractor can both easily see what is covered. Instead, they are scattered all over the document. To rectify that, a list of the instructions in SBC are given in Table 17.1.

17.2 Scope

It can be seen from Table 17.1 that the instructions that the architect may issue are many and varied. The most important instructions are described below. It must be remembered that where an instruction must be issued, the contract uses the word 'shall' (must). Instructions that the architect has power to issue but need not do so say that the architect 'may' issue:

Integration of the CDP with the rest of the Works

2.2.2

The contract refers to the architect giving 'directions' for integration rather than 'instructions'. However, it is conveniently grouped here with instructions, because it is difficult to see the difference between the architect instructing the contractor how to integrate the design of the CPD with the rest of the design and the architect directing the contractor on the point. In any event, the architect is only called upon to issue this kind of direction (instruction) after the architect has issued another instruction amending

---

The JCT Standard Building Contract 2011, First Edition. David Chappell.
© 2014 by David Chappell. Published 2014 by John Wiley & Sons, Ltd.

Table 17.1 Architect's instructions empowered by the SBC 11 contract.

Clause	Instruction
2.2.2	Directing the integration of the CDP with the rest of the Works.
2.10	That setting out errors are not to be amended.
2.12	Necessary to enable the contractor to carry out and complete the Works in accordance with the contract.
2.15	After being notified in writing of a discrepancy in documents.
2.16.1	After receiving a statement from the contractor setting out its proposed amendment.
2.16.2	If the Contractor's Proposals do not deal with a discrepancy in the Employer's Requirements.
2.17.2	After becoming aware of a divergence between the documents or within 14 days of receipt of the contractor's amendment (where applicable).
2.23	That the contractor is to use patented articles, processes or inventions.
2.38	Specifying a schedule of defects not later than 14 days after the end of the rectification period.
	The making good of defects whenever the architect considers it necessary during the rectification period.
	Not to make good defects if the employer consents.
3.4	Confirming the clerk of Works direction.
3.14.1	Requiring a variation.
3.15	Postponing work.
3.16	About the expenditure of provisional sums in the bills of quantities and in Employer's Requirements.
3.17	For the opening up or testing of work or materials.
3.18.1	Regarding the removal from site of work not in accordance with the contract.
3.18.3	Requiring reasonably necessary variations resulting from defective work.
3.18.4	To open up or test as is reasonable in all the circumstances after having had regard to the code of practice to the contract to establish the likelihood of similar non-compliance following defective work.
3.19	Requiring reasonably necessary variations or otherwise resulting from the contractor's failure to carrying out the work in a workmanlike manner.
3.21	Requiring the exclusion from site of any person there employed.
3.22.2	Regarding antiquities reported by the contractor.
4.5.1	To provide the quantity surveyor with all documents necessary for the adjustment of the Contract Sum.
4.5.2.1	Requiring the quantity surveyor to ascertain loss and/or expense.
4.23	Requiring the quantity surveyor to ascertain loss and/or expense.
5.3.1	Requiring the contractor to provide a quotation.
5.3.2	That the variation is to be carried out and valued by a valuation.
6.5.1	To take out insurance in joint names in respect of liability for collapse, subsidence, heave, vibration, weakening or removal of support or lowering of ground water.

(continued)

Table 17.1   (*Cont'd*)

Clause	Instruction
6.16.1.2	To enable compliance to the extent that the remedial measures require a variation.
8.7.2.1	Requiring the contractor to remove from the Works temporary buildings, plant, tools, etc.
Schedule 2, paragraph 4	Confirming acceptance by the employer of a variation quotation or of an acceleration quotation.
Schedule 2, paragraph 5.1.1	That the variation is to be carried out and valued under the valuation rules.
Schedule 2, paragraph 5.1.2	That the variation is not to be carried out.

And, where the Named Specialist Update is incorporated:

Schedule 8, paragraph 7.3	If the contractor, acting reasonably, is unable to enter into a sub-contract with the named specialist.
Schedule 8, paragraph 7.4	If the contractor has reasonable grounds for objection and notifies the architect within 7 days of receipt of an instruction for post-named specialist work or for a replacement for a named specialist.
Schedule 8, paragraph 7.6	If the contractor terminates a named specialist's employment or treats it as repudiated.

some part of the design that affects the CPD. In general, the design of the CDP will be based upon the drawings and bills of quantities provided to the contractor at tender stage and it is the contractor's responsibility to see that its CDP integrates properly at that stage.

Setting out errors not to be amended and an appropriate deduction to be made from the Contract Sum

2.10

The architect is responsible for giving the contractor accurately dimensioned drawings and for determining any levels required. The contractor is responsible for setting out the Works correctly, i.e. in accordance with the information given by the architect. If the contractor sets out incorrectly, it must amend any errors arising and stand the cost itself. In some circumstances, it may be sensible for the contractor's errors to stand without amendment. That may be because the error is trifling or because the project has reached a stage in construction before the error was discovered that means correction would involve substantial demolition and rebuilding and consequent delay. Each situation will be considered on its merits in consultation with the employer and even substantial rebuilding might be the only answer if the error is significant. The architect has the power to instruct the contractor not to amend errors arising from inaccurate setting out, but the employer's consent must first be obtained before issuing the instruction.

An appropriate deduction from the Contract Sum must be made for the errors. That may prove to be a very difficult calculation. It is certainly not equivalent to the cost of demolition and rebuilding. Bad setting out could result in several rooms becoming shorter than intended. It is probable that the deduction can cover, not only the value of work and materials omitted but also, the reduction in value of the rooms to the employer – however, that is to be ascertained. If the result of bad setting out is to leave the employer with a building substantially larger than required, the contractor would not be entitled to any increase for the additional work and materials, but it might face the possibility of a reduction to represent additional costs to the employer (such as increased rates, cleaning charges and running costs).

To enable the contractor to carry out and complete the Works in accordance with the contract

2.12.1

It is crucial that the architect has the power to issue instructions about the carrying out of the Works. Some of these instructions, the kind generally referred to here, are simply clarifications and details rather than variations. The architect's obligation is to issue the instructions to enable the contractor to carry out and complete the Works in accordance with the contract. An important part of the contract is the date for completion. Therefore, the architect must issue the necessary instructions so as to enable the contractor to complete by the complete date in the contract. If the architect fails to do that, the contractor may be entitled to an extension of time, depending on the circumstances.

Discrepancies

2.15

This relates to discrepancies in or between the contract drawings, the bills of quantities, drawings or instructions issued by the architect and, if used, CDP documents.

There are five important points to note:

1. The architect has an obligation to issue instructions under this clause.
2. The architect's obligation to instruct depends on receiving notification from the contractor, although obviously an architect who becomes aware of a discrepancy in some other way should issue an instruction.

4.1
3. If the architect's instruction changes the quality or quantity of the work deemed included in the Contract Sum, or changes employer's obligations or restrictions, a variation results.

4. However, if the discrepancy is in the CDP documents (excepting the Employer's Requirements), the contractor must submit its proposals to remove the discrepancy when the notice is given or as soon as it reasonably can afterwards. So long as the architect's instruction simply deals with removing the discrepancy, there is no addition to the Contract Sum. In other words it is at the contractor's own cost. If the architect strays beyond what is strictly necessary, the extra will be treated as a variation. The wise architect will confine the instruction to confirming the contractor's solu-

2.16.1
tion if it is at all acceptable.

5. If the discrepancy is contained in the Employer's Requirements and the Contractor's Proposals do not deal with it, the contractor must submit its proposals to remove the discrepancy. The architect may either accept it or

2.16.2
decide on something else, but either way it will be treated as a variation.

Not to make good defects

2.38

The important point to remember here is that the employer's consent must be obtained before the architect issues the instruction; the contractor has no right of objection.

Requiring a variation

3.14

This is a most important power, giving the architect the right to require the contractor to carry out variations or to sanction in writing any variation carried out by the contractor without an instruction. The contract states that no such

3.14.5
instruction or sanction will vitiate (i.e. make ineffective) the contract. That is superfluous, because no exercise of a right conferred by the contract can make that same contract ineffective. The statement was probably inserted, because there is no doubt that without a statement in the contract empowering the architect to issue instructions, there would be no power to do so.

By reference to various other parts of the contract, there is some detail regarding what a variation means (see Chapter 18, Section 18.1). In general, it means what one would assume that it means, namely the alteration or modification of the design or quality or quantity of the work shown on the drawings and described in the bills of quantities. Variation is also said to mean the imposition by the employer of any obligations or restrictions or the addition, alteration, or omission of any obligations imposed by the employer in the bills of quantities. The obligations or restrictions relate to access to, or use of, any particular parts of the site or the whole site; limitations of working space; limitations of working hours; the order of execution or completion of work. The architect's right to exercise this power under this clause is dependent on whether or not the contractor raises a reasonable objection.

Expenditure of provisional sums

3.16

The architect must instruct the contractor how any provisional sums are to be treated. Without an architect's instruction, a provisional sum is merely an indication (if it is a defined provisional sum it is a detailed indication) that some work is to be done. If the architect never issued an instruction about a provisional sum, no work relating to it will be done.

Postponement of work

3.15

2.29.2.1

4.24.2.1

8.9.2.1

196

The architect is entitled to issue an instruction to postpone any of the work required by the contract. There is a price to pay and the employer has to pay it, so the architect must take care. If work is postponed, the contractor can claim an extension of time and loss and/or expense. Moreover, the contractor may terminate its employment if the whole or substantially the whole of the Works are suspended for a continuous period of 2 months, or whatever period is in the contract particulars, due to postponement, among other things. In certain circumstances, an instruction given on another matter may imply postponement with all its consequences. The situation should not arise if the architect is careful to word instructions correctly, unambiguously and to quote the correct empowering clause in each case.

Opening up or testing

3.17

The architect is empowered to instruct the contractor to open up for inspection any work that has been covered up, or to arrange for any testing of materials whether or not they are already built in. An architect who suspects that concealed work or materials are defective must decide whether to instruct the contractor to open up or carry out testing. The architect may have no real alternative, but the position is that, if the work or materials are found to be in accordance with the contract (i.e. not defective), the cost (including the cost of making good) must be added to the Contract Sum, unless provision is made for opening up or testing in the bills of quantities. If the work or materials are found to be defective, all the costs must be borne by the contractor.

Removal from site of work not in accordance with the contract

3.18.1

The architect may instruct the contractor to remove defective work from site. Most architects do not comply with this strictly. They simply instruct the contractor to rectify specific defects. It is always sensible to confirm in writing any instructions that the architect gives the contractor on site; indeed the architect must do so. In the case of defective work, the importance is that an instruction given orally may be ignored and, if the defect is subsequently covered up, the architect does not know whether or not it has been corrected. A strict regime of inspections of all the key elements, the recording and the issuing of instructions and the following up of noted defects is an essential part of administering a contract.

Opening up or testing at contractor's cost to show the likelihood of similar defects

3.18.4　This gives the architect a useful power to check for possible defective work. The exercise of that power will give rise to further responsibilities. The architect may only issue an instruction if work or materials already have been found to be defective. However, the check is only for similar defects to the defects already discovered. The whole process is at the contractor's own cost, whether or not the opening up or testing discovers further defects. But if there are no defects found, the contractor may be entitled to an extension of time. Before issuing the instruction, the architect must have read the code of practice that is at the

Schedule 4　back of the contract. The code is very broadly worded and it does not significantly limit the architect's power here.

Exclusion from site of any person there employed

3.21　The architect has the power to order the exclusion from site of any person. The contract says that the power must not be exercised unreasonably or vexatiously. This power seems to be intended for the architect to use if the contractor insists on using incompetent operatives or people who, for one reason or another, are disruptive. For example, an architect who came across an operative who was clearly intoxicated would have good reason to exclude that person from site. The key thing to bear in mind is whether the presence of the person is having an adverse effect upon the quality, standard or progress of the Works.

Remove of temporary buildings, etc. after termination

8.7.2.1　Although not prefaced by the mandatory shall, this is an instruction that the architect is obliged to issue at some time after the employer has terminated the contractor's employment. Usually after the employer has finished using the contractor's plant, etc. to complete the building Works with another contractor.

17.3　Common problems

The architect issues an instruction postponing the date in the contract particulars of possession of the site

　The architect's power to postpone is sometimes misinterpreted. It refers to
3.15　postponement of work, nothing else. It does not allow the architect to postpone the date of possession. If the architect postpones the whole of the Works before the contractor has taken possession, the contractor is still entitled to take possession, but not to carry out any of the Works. The contractor may wish to deal with other things, such as delivery of cabins to site and possibly fencing the site. It is entitled to do so even after an instruction postponing the whole of the Works.

The materials and goods appeared to be in accordance with the contract and were built into the construction. Subsequently they were found to be defective and required replacement causing delay and additional expense.

197

A difficult problem could arise. Much would depend upon the cost of replacement and the effect of leaving the materials in place in the Works. In principle, the cost of replacement and the consequences of any delay would fall onto the contractor. The contractor would be responsible even though neither it nor the architect were able to see the problem before building in. However, if the costs to the contractor of replacing the materials were excessive and if the benefits of the replacement were not comparable to the costs, a court might find that the contractor need not replace the materials, but must simply pay a small compensation. For example, if a contractor used a type of brick that was not specified and looked similar to the one specified, it is unlikely that an arbitrator or judge would order the contractor to demolish the building in order to replace the bricks with a different brick unless, the bricks were substantially inferior in performance from what was specified.

If the specification or bills of quantities state that work must not be covered up until after inspection by the architect

*3.17 and
4.24.2.2*

Failure to observe that provision will place the contractor in breach of contract. The architect may instruct that the work is to be opened up. However, the contractor will still be entitled to payment if the work is found to be in accordance with the contract. The solution to this problem lies in the employer's entitlement to damages for the contractor's breach of obligation not to cover up the work until after it has been inspected. The damages are the money that the employer has to pay out if the work is in accordance with the contract because, if the contractor had complied with the requirement to cover up work only after the architect had inspected, there would have been no need for the architect to issue the opening up instruction. Although there is no machinery in the contract specifically designed to enable the employer to recover that money, there seems to be no reason why the employer cannot do so, after giving the relevant pay less notice, by deducting the amount from the amount payable under the certificate. In practice, a contractor that failed to comply with a requirement to allow inspection before covering up would be unlikely to try to claim payment for opening up.

The employer is assaulted on site by the contractor's person-in-charge

3.21

Occasionally, it has been known for a contractor's person to assault the employer. This appears more likely to occur if the employer regularly visits site without the architect and if relations between employer and the person-in-charge are poor. In these cases, the employer may ask the architect to use the contract power to exclude the person-in-charge from site.

It seems very doubtful that the architect has the power to exclude the person-in-charge in those circumstances. The contract certainly gives the architect power to exclude from the Works any person. However, there is a condition attached. The architect must not act vexatiously or unreasonably. If the architect was not present when the assault took place, the circumstances and indeed the fact of the assault would only be known to the architect from what the employer reported. It is not the architect's job to investigate this kind of allegation. Assault is always a criminal offence and the architect must make a few things clear to the employer:

- The employer must never visit the site without the architect.
- The employer must never communicate directly with the contractor.
- The employer should report any assault to the police.

It is to be hoped that the architect has emphasised the first two things before work on site commenced.

The provision for excluding persons from the Works has to be read in the context of other terms of the contract. It is aimed at excluding from the Works, persons who are hindering the progress of the Works such as an incompetent plasterer who is incapable of producing a satisfactory finish. In most cases, the contractor would itself remove such persons. Although an assault on the employer is obviously wrong, it is not affecting the progress on site and, provided the employer follows the architect's instructions, it is unlikely to be repeated. Therefore, to exclude the person-in-charge would probably be considered unreasonable.

An assault on the architect is a different matter and, to the extent that it might inhibit the architect from carrying out inspections on site, it clearly affects the Works. In that case, the architect is entitled to issue the exclusion from site instruction.

18 Variations

18.1 What is a variation?

5.1
A variation is the alteration or modification of the design, the quality or the quantity of the Works; for example, a change in the width of a parish hall to make it a metre wider. That would be an alteration in design and in quantity. A change in the specification of the doors from softwood to hardwood would be a variation of the quality. It should be noted that removal from the site of any work already carried out or any materials on site also ranks as a variation unless of course it has been instructed to be removed because it is defective.

It is important not to confuse variation of the Works with a variation of the contract, i.e. the terms of the contract; for example a change to the date for possession stated in the contract particulars. Variation of the terms of the contract can only take place if both employer and contractor agree.

Special kind of variation

5.2
Another kind of variation is if the employer imposes or changes obligations or restrictions. The obligations or restrictions must concern one or more of the following:

- access or use of any part of the site;
- limitation of working space or hours;
- carrying out the work in a particular order.

This part is more like varying the contract terms than varying the work content. It clearly does not vary the Works in any way, but only the way in which they are executed. Perhaps that is why the contract refers to the employer imposing or changing rather than the architect although there is no doubt that the architect has the power to issue instructions varying these things. It should be noted that although the order of the work may be changed, or indeed created if there is no order stated in the bills of quantities, there is no provision to insert any specific dates against the parts of the work. Therefore, although the order may be stipulated, the contractor is under no obligation anywhere in the contract to complete the parts by any particular dates. The

The JCT Standard Building Contract 2011, First Edition. David Chappell.
© 2014 by David Chappell. Published 2014 by John Wiley & Sons, Ltd.

architect has no power to require completion of the parts by any dates other than the date for completion of the whole of the Works as stated in the contract particulars. The only way to ensure that the contractor has an obligation to complete individual parts of the Works by specific dates is to use the section completion provisions in the contract.

There are some curious features about this clause. At first sight it appears to be the only variation that the contract expressly authorises the employer to make. The conclusion to be drawn from this is that if the employer imposes obligations or restrictions or changes them, it ranks as a variation under the terms of the contract and is to be valued accordingly. In giving an instruction requiring a variation under this clause, the architect should always refer to the imposition of obligations or restrictions by the employer.

It is doubtful whether, in practice, employers often, if ever, avail themselves of the powers apparently given to them under this clause; which is fortunate in view of the confusion that could result. What follows assumes that it will be the architect acting.

The architect's powers are limited to only those specific obligations and restrictions, and there is no equivalent power in respect of obligations or restrictions of any other kind. It is clear that the architect's power is not confined to varying obligations and restrictions already imposed through the medium of the contract bills but extends to imposing fresh obligations or restrictions – but only of the kinds listed and depending on whether or not the contractor raises a reasonable objection.

These five matters appear to attract little attention in practice. Imposing any of them will inevitably give rise to additional costs to the contractor; some of the restrictions may be far-reaching and it is surprising that more claims have not been founded on them. The reason is possibly because employers have adopted a sensible approach and declined to impose obligations in any of these categories unless absolutely unavoidable. Restricting access to the site or the times of such access could be quite catastrophic and where there is a need for that kind of restriction, it should be included in the contract documents. It is more likely that architect's instructions issued under this head will be concerned with the relaxation of previously imposed restrictions.

Much the same comment can be made for the other categories. Where the architect issues instructions about the use to be made of various parts of the site, it must not be confused with failure to give possession of the whole of the site on the date of possession in the contract. Possession must be given on that date, but the architect can restrict the use. It is doubtful that this allows the architect to

3.15   postpone work, because the architect already has that power. The architect may wish to restrict the contractor from storing certain materials, erecting cranes, siting cabins and the like. Limiting working space probably falls into the same category, while limiting hours might be necessary in response to complaints and visits from local authority inspectors when the project is in progress.

The final matter gives rise to the most difficulty. The correct method for conveying the employer's wishes in regard to sequence of work and completion is for the Works to be divided into sections. Therefore, this power must be exercised with great care where the employer has also opted to divide the Works into sections and to set out individual dates for possession and completion in the contract particulars. The sections must take precedence and things could get very complicated. The architect cannot alter the content of any of the sections, because to do so might invalidate the liquidated damages clause. There is no mechanism in the contract to amend liquidated damages and it may be argued that a substantial change in work content would invalidate the clause. It is thought that an instruction to carry out the work in any particular order may relate to any work if the Works as a whole are not divided into sections. Where the Works are divided into sections, the instruction can only relate to the work within any particular section and, for the reasons noted above, the work content of the sections cannot be restructured.

Reasonable objection

3.10.1   The contractor can refuse to comply if it has a reasonable objection. By what criteria is 'reasonable objection' to be measured? It is thought that an objection would only be considered reasonable to the extent that compliance would make the Works much more difficult to achieve. If the restriction actually made the Works impossible to complete, the contractor would be relieved of its obligations. Therefore, the clause must envisage a lesser consequence, but nevertheless a consequence that caused significant difficulties. For example, a neighbour may threaten to seek an injunction against the employer to prevent work outside certain hours, resulting in an average two hours lost every day. The architect may issue an instruction restricting the hours accordingly. Obviously, no contractor could lodge a reasonable objection to compliance with such an instruction, because although it would inevitably cause a delay, the contractor would receive payment for the variation and also an appropriate extension of the contract period. Therefore the contractor would be suitably protected and the alternative would be that the neighbour may get an injunction in any event and the contractor would be faced with the same restriction to which no objection could be termed 'reasonable'. On the other hand, if an architect had instructed that a contractor could not make full use of the site and that a certain area should not be used a contractor could make reasonable objection if the result was that the contractor had insufficient working space to store essential goods and erect suitable site accommodation. In practice there appear to be few disputes based on this clause, because common sense prevails.

18.2   Does extra work always involve payment?

Extra work in a broad sense must mean work that is extra or additional to the Works that the contractor is required to execute in accordance with the contract. Extra work can arise by a straightforward addition to the contract Works, for example, an architect's instruction to the contractor to lay an additional area of paving to that already specified and for which a rate is included in the bills of quantities. Alternatively, extra work may arise, because the architect has instructed the omission of something and the substitution of something else. For example, the architect may omit a window and instruct a glazed door to be installed instead. The net result may be an increase in the cost of the Works. There are detailed provisions in the con-

5.2 – 5.10   tract for valuation of variations.

SBC contains detailed requirements that must be satisfied before the Contract Sum can be adjusted. The fact that the contractor has carried out work that is additional to what the contract requires does not automatically entitle it to additional payment. On the contrary, if the contractor carried out work that is not instructed, the contractor is probably in breach of its obligations. This is a fundamental principle. If the situation was different, there would be nothing to prevent the contractor, in need of extra profit, to unexpectedly do some work not included in the contract and claim payment simply on the ground that the contractor had done it. There would be nothing to prevent a contractor supplying gold bath taps instead of the specified chrome taps and claiming the difference in cost. However, identifying whether or not extra work attracts payment may not always be so easy.

The contractor will never be entitled to extra payment if it has to carry out work included in the contract, but that it overlooked or misunderstood when pricing. Whether an item of work was included in the contract Works can be a source of dispute.

18.3   Valuation

The procedure for valuing variations is set out in a flowchart in Figure 18.1. All variations instructed by the architect, anything that the contract states is to be treated as a variation, work carried out in compliance with an architect's instruction to expend a provisional sum in the contract bills or in the Employer's Requirements and any work for which an approximate quantity has been included in the contract bills or in the Employer's Requirements must be valued by agreement between the employer and the contractor. That comes as a surprise to many people, architects included. It is only if they cannot agree that the option, which most construction professionals think of as the norm, valuation by the quantity surveyor, comes into play. Note that it is the employer and not the architect or even the quantity surveyor who must agree. Of course, in practice, such agreement between the two parties to the contract is very rare, certainly where valuation is concerned, if for no other reason than that the employer seldom has the necessary expertise to understand all the implications. If the parties do not agree on a valuation figure, they are still free under the contract to decide on a system of valuation. It is only if they neither agree a value nor a system of valuation that the value is to

5.2.1   be calculated by the quantity surveyor in accordance with the valuation rules.

5.3 and   It is only variations that are the subject of variation quotations that are not

Schedule 2   subject to the measurement rules.

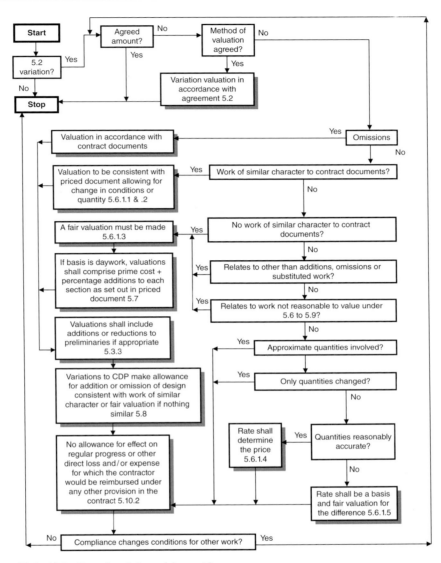

Figure 18.1   Valuation of variations (clause 5).

The rules

5.6

The rules for valuing measured work are relatively simple, at least in principle. There are three criteria that must be taken into account in relation to the work that is measured in the contract bills: whether the work is of similar character to the work that is measured, whether it is carried out under similar conditions and whether it significantly changes the quantity of work.

The rules say that:

■ If all three criteria are the same as those related to an item of work already set out in the contract bills – i.e. if the character and conditions are similar and the quantity is not significantly changed by the variation – the rate or price set out in the contract bills against that item must be used for the valuation of the variation. That is very straightforward.

- If the character is similar to that of an item of work set out in the contract bills, but the conditions are not similar and/or the quantity is significantly changed from the contract bills, the rate or price in the contract bills against that item must still be used as the basis of the valuation of the item but must be adapted so as to make a 'fair allowance' (more or less money), to allow for the changed conditions and/or quantity.
- If the work is not of similar character, it must be valued by the quantity surveyor at fair rates and prices and the rates and prices in the contract bills are no longer relevant. 'What are fair rates and prices?' is itself a fair question. The answer is that they are what the quantity surveyor decides after looking at the contractor's general pricing strategy and comparing the prices with the general level of prices in the area.

From that it is clear that, if the character of the work to be measured is similar to that of an item that is already in the contract bills and to which a rate or price is fixed, the quantity surveyor must use the rates set out in the bills in order to carry out the valuation. A change to those rates can be made only if there is a change in the conditions in which the work is carried out or if there is a significant change in its quantity. The quantity surveyor's discretion only comes into play if the character of the measured work is not similar to anything in the bills. Then the quantity surveyor may make a fair valuation of the work. Therefore, the key word in these rules is 'similar' and it is important that the meaning of the phrase 'similar character' should be properly understood. The JCT has not seen fit to formally define it, presumably relying on its ordinary English meaning.

Similar

Some people have suggested that 'similar' means 'the same' or even 'identical'. That cannot be correct. The words 'similar character' when applied to an individual measured item of work probably mean that the item is almost identical to an item in the contract bills. If the item is of 'similar character' the only grounds upon which the quantity surveyor can vary the price for the item from that which is set out in the bills is that the conditions are not similar or the quantity has significantly changed, otherwise the quantity surveyor must use the price in the bills as it stands.

The word 'similar' is also used to qualify 'conditions'. Again, it is thought that the word does not mean identical or the same. However, there are different considerations. It is possible to precisely define the 'character' of an item by its description in the contract bills. It is not possible to closely define the conditions under which it is to be carried out. Therefore, whether the conditions are 'similar' must be decided by considering what conditions the contractor ought to have reasonably anticipated in light of the available information when the contract was carried out. Therefore, the 'conditions' referred to in the valuation rules are the conditions to be deduced from the provisions of the contract bills, the drawings and other documents.

Quantity

The word 'similar' is not used to qualify 'quantity', the criterion used here being whether or not the quantity had been 'significantly changed' by the variation. A small change in quantity may be significant for some items (especially if the original quantity was small) but a very large change may not be significant in other circumstances. There are no precise rules and it is a matter for the quantity surveyor's experience and judgment in each particular case. It is normal to assume that large increases in quantity require reductions in the rate and *vice versa*. However, that may not always follow.

Rates

It is not always appreciated that the rate or price in the contract bills must be used as the basis of calculation of price and it can be adjusted only to take account of changed conditions and/or significantly changed quantity. Where a contractor puts in a rate that is obviously far too low or far too high, there is no means of altering it. The Contract Sum can be adjusted only in accordance with the express provisions of the contract. Therefore, if the contractor has made a mistake and no one notices until the contract is carried out, the contractor is left with the consequences.

It is sometimes thought that, if a rate is clearly wrong, the quantity surveyor, when valuing variations, is entitled to correct the rate and change it to a reasonable rate before using it as a basis for the valuation. That is incorrect. The contractor has agreed under the terms of the contract to carry out variations to the Works, and the employer has agreed to pay for them according to the rules set out in the contract. The valuation rules do not say that the rates and prices shall form the basis of valuation after the quantity surveyor has accepted that they are reasonable rates. The quantity surveyor is entitled only to work with the rates and prices in the bills and has no power to change them. Neither employer nor contractor can avoid the consequences of bill rates being too high or too low.

A contractor will sometimes take a gamble by putting a high rate on an item of which there is a small quantity or a low rate on an item of which there is a large quantity in the expectation that the quantities of the items will be considerably increased or decreased, respectively. If the contractor's gamble succeeds, it will make a nice profit. Quantity surveyors checking priced bills at tender stage will be alert to such pricing, but there is little to be done about it. It is not unlawful, but rather part of a contractor's commercial strategy.

Fair rates and prices

So far as the quantity surveyor's duty to determine 'fair rates and prices' is concerned, it is likely that the word 'fair' is to be read in the context of the contract as a whole. It is arguable that a 'fair' price for varied work in a contract where

4.2

198

199

200

the contractor has inserted keen prices in the bills of quantities should be a similarly keen price. In general, the quantity surveyor will be expected to determine 'fair rates and prices' following a reasonable analysis of the contractor's pricing of the items set out in the bills, including its allowances for head-office overheads and profit.

Omissions

5.6.2

2.38

5.9

The rule for the valuation of omissions from the contract Works could scarcely be simpler. They are to be valued at the rates set out in the contract bills. There are certain circumstances where this may not appear to be a fair way of valuing omissions. This is particularly the case where the architect, with the consent of the employer, has instructed the contractor not to make good defects that appear during the rectification period. That is presumably why the contract makes provision for an 'appropriate deduction' to be made from the Contract Sum rather than leaving it to the quantity surveyor to simply omit the rate against the item in the contract bills. However, if the omissions substantially change the conditions under which other work is executed, it must be valued accordingly.

Lump sum adjustments

5.6.3

5.6.2

In carrying out valuation, the quantity surveyor must take into account several factors other than the prices in the contract bills for individual items or valuation at fair rates and prices. When considering the valuation of additional or substituted work or the omission of any work or an instruction for the expenditure of a provisional sum for undefined work, the quantity surveyor must make allowance for any percentage or lump sum adjustments in the contract bills. The sums referred to are the percentages or lump sums that are usually to be found in the general summary at the end of the bills. They must be applied *pro rata* to all prices for measured work and, therefore, to all variations.

Preliminary items

5.6.3 ; **201**

The quantity surveyor is also required to make allowance, when valuing and where appropriate for any addition to or reduction of certain preliminary items. The clause does not actually oblige the quantity surveyor to use the rates and prices set out in the bills against such items, but simply to make allowance for any addition to or reduction of such items. However, the quantity surveyor must be able to justify the method of calculating the allowance and, in practice, most quantity surveyors will use the rates and prices in the contract bills.

No effect on regular progress

It must not be assumed that the contract gives the quantity surveyor a broad power to value variations. The quantity surveyor's power is carefully controlled and the prudent quantity surveyor will carefully read the whole of the valuation

5

clause before proceeding to value. There is a particular restriction that no allowance must be made under the valuation rules for any effect upon the regular progress of the Works or for any other direct loss and/or expense for which the Contractor would be reimbursed by payment under any other provision in

4.23, 5.10.2

the contract. The reference here is to the so-called 'claims clause'. That is the only system in the contract under which the contractor can recover loss and/or expense. Therefore, it is sufficient to block the addition of loss and/or expense if the contractor would be (i.e. is entitled to be) reimbursed even if no reimbursement has been made. It follows that, in making any allowances in respect of preliminary items, the quantity surveyor must not make allowance for the significant effect of the particular variation on the regular progress of the Works. This permits the quantity surveyor to make allowance for effects that are less than significant or, as the contract calls them 'material', upon regular progress.

Fair valuation

The quantity surveyor must make a fair valuation of any liabilities directly associated with a variation, if the valuation cannot reasonably be carried out by the other rules. There is no other restriction and the clause appears to oblige the

5.10.1

quantity surveyor to make a fair valuation in such cases. Such liabilities might include the loss to the contractor where a variation to the work results in materials already properly ordered for the Works, as included in the contract, becoming redundant. It will also include the valuation of the effect of any instruction that does not require the addition, omission or substitution of work, i.e. obligations or restrictions.

18.4   Treatment of approximate quantities, defined and undefined provisional sums

Provisional sums

A provisional sum is a sum of money included, usually in the bills of quantities, to cover the cost of something that cannot be entirely foreseen or detailed with complete accuracy at the time that bills of quantities are being prepared. It is to be expended as the architect instructs. When bills of quantities are used, there are two kind of provisional sums that are defined in the SMM:

■ Provisional sum for defined work.
■ Provisional sum for undefined work.

Provisional sums for defined work must state the nature and construction of the work, how and where it is to be included in the building and any specific limitations. Provisional sums for defined work are treated as though they have been taken into account in the contractor's programming and pricing preliminaries. There will be no adjustment unless measured work in the same circumstances would be adjusted.

Undefined provisional sums do not have to state anything other than a means of identifying to what it relates. If the provisional sum is undefined, everything proceeds on the basis that the contractor has not made any allowance for it in programming and pricing preliminaries. This addresses a difficulty that contractors have and that is often misunderstood. The fact is that a contractor will be unable to make any sensible attempt to programme or price preliminaries to deal with a provisional sum that may be little more than a title and a figure. For example, 'mechanical installation = £10,000' tells the contractor nothing except that the architect may or may not issue an instruction for the contractor to carry out or engage others to carry out mechanical installation work. It used to be common, however, for architects to demand that the contractor made some allowance in its programme for provisional sums of this kind. Setting aside the impossibility of complying with such a request, the request itself demonstrates a lack of understanding that the 'bar' on the bar chart is, or should be, simply the result of a series of complicated calculations taking into account the way in which the work will be integrated into other work and the way in

202   which it will be priced.

Approximate quantities

Where work can be described in items in accordance with SMM, but accurate quantities cannot be given, an estimate, called an 'approximate quantity' must be given. The valuation of work for which an approximate quantity is included in the contract bills is covered by the valuation rules. Where the approximate quantity is a reasonably accurate forecast, the valuation must be in accordance with the rates for the approximate quantity. If it is not a reasonably accu-

5.6.1.4 and   rate forecast, the rate forms the basis for the valuation, but the quantity
5.6.1.5   surveyor is to make a fair allowance for the difference in quantity. No allowance for either addition to or reduction of preliminaries can be made if the valuation relates to an architect's instruction to expend a provisional sum for
5.6.3   defined work.

18.5   If the conditions for carrying out other work are altered

The quantity surveyor must take account of the fact that a variation to part of the work can have an effect on the way in which other work, including the contractor's designed portion, must be carried out. Where the introduction of a variation changes the conditions under which other work, which is not varied, is carried out, the quantity surveyor must value that other work as if it had been
5.9   varied. For example, the architect might give an instruction omitting all plastering and substituting a different kind of brick, to be left fair faced. This variation although directly affecting only the plastering and brickwork would obviously have implications for electrical wiring and the fixing of door casings, window frames and skirting.

Other situations that must be treated as though they were the subject of an architect's instruction if there is a substantial change in the way work is carried out are:

- An architect's instruction to expend a provisional sum for undefined work.
- An architect's instruction to expend a provisional sum for defined work, to the extent that the instruction is different from the description in the contract bills.
- Carrying out work for which an inaccurate approximate quantity is included in the contract bills, to the extent that the quantity is more or less than the quantity in the contract bills.

5.9

This simply brings this kind of item under the same rules as variations to measured work. The differences highlight the extent of the contractor's knowledge about the kind of work and the amount at the time the contract was made.

18.6   Valuation of obligations and restrictions

5.10.1

A fair valuation of variations to obligations or restrictions imposed by the employer or variations to obligations or restrictions already imposed in the contract bills and to liabilities directly associated with a variation must be made. There can be no allowance for the effect on the regular progress of the Works or for any loss and/or expense for which reimbursement would be obtained under any other clause. It seems likely that limiting working space or hours will have an effect on regular progress and possibly an instruction to vary the sequence of work will have a similar effect. It is less easy to see that variations to access will effect regular progress, but all the variations to restrictions will have cost implications.

18.7   Schedule 2 quotations

5.3

The methods of valuation by the quantity surveyor can be bypassed if a quotation is requested from the contractor. In order to trigger a quotation, the architect must state in an instruction that the contractor is to provide a quotation in accordance with Schedule 2. The valuation provisions will not apply to a varia-

Schedule 2, paragraph 1

tion for which the contractor has submitted a quotation and, importantly, the architect has issued a confirmed acceptance.

The contractor can indicate disagreement within 7 days or such other period as agreed and the instruction is not then to be carried out unless the architect issues a further instruction to that effect. In such a case the instruction will be

5.6

valued as usual. Provided that the contractor has received sufficient information with the instruction, it must provide a 'Variation Quotation' not later than 21 days from the date of receipt of the instruction.

Quotation

The quotation must contain:

- The value of the adjustment to the Contract Sum that must include the effect on any other work. Calculations must be provided and must refer to the contract bill's rates and prices as relevant.
- Adjustment to the contract period including fixing a new, possibly earlier, completion date.
- The amount of loss and/or expense.
- The cost of preparation of the quotation.

If the architect specifically requests, the contractor must also include:

- details of additional resources required;
- a method statement;
- a base date for fluctuation purposes.

The employer has an important role to play in this process, probably because the circumstances when the contractor will be asked to quote is probably where it is likely that the instruction will have some significant effect on the contract in terms of additional expenditure or time.

Acceptance procedure

Although the instruction is to be issued by the architect, the quotation may be sent to the architect or the quantity surveyor where it is open for acceptance by the employer for at least 7 days. Unusually, the contractor cannot withdraw the quotation before acceptance as it could in the course of ordinary negotiations, because in this instance, the contractor is bound by the contract terms to keep its offer open.

It is for the employer to accept the quotation or otherwise and, if the employer accepts, the architect must confirm the acceptance in writing to the contractor. The purpose of this acceptance is so that the architect can formally confirm that the contractor is to proceed, that the adjustment to the Contract Sum can be made, that a new date for completion (if applicable) can be fixed and the base date is confirmed. The adjustment to the completion date is acknowledged in the extension of time provisions and the architect should not issue a separate extension of time for the same instruction. The adjustment to the completion date noted in the confirmed acceptance is simply to be taken into account by the architect in the normal way when considering further extensions of the contract period.

The provision, that if the employer does not accept the architect must either instruct that the variation is to be carried out and valued under the normal valuation rules or instruct that the variation is not to be carried out, is remarkable for one thing in particular. There is no provision for the employer or the quantity surveyor on behalf of the employer to negotiate on the quoted price. It is either to be accepted or rejected. If it is not accepted, a fair and reasonable amount must be added to the Contract Sum to represent the cost of preparation. Although the description of a 'fair and reasonable amount' is identical to what the contractor is to include in the quotation to represent its costs of preparation, it is not specifically stated that the quantity surveyor must add that same amount and it seems that the quantity surveyor has discretion to add less (but probably not more) than that amount if that appears to be fair and reasonable. However, it is thought that if the quantity surveyor did include a lesser sum, the grounds for doing so would have to be clearly stated and could be challenged by one of the dispute-resolution procedures. The power of the quantity surveyor to value the cost of preparation is subject to the quotation having been prepared on a fair and reasonable basis. Demonstrating an understanding of human nature, the contract makes clear that the mere fact that the

Schedule 2 employer has decided not to accept the quotation is not evidence that it has not
paragraph 5.2 been prepared on a fair and reasonable basis.

5.3 If the employer does not accept the quotation, the quotation cannot be used for any purpose at all. It must be treated as though it had never been submitted. This is to avoid the situation that could arise where the quantity surveyor uses the submitted quotation to assist in valuing another instruction issued by the architect.

Variations to Schedule 2 quotation work

5.3.3 If work carried out under a confirmed acceptance is subsequently varied by the architect, it must be valued by the quantity surveyor on a fair and reasonable basis, but having regard to the figures in the quotation. That means that the quantity surveyor must take the figures into account, not that they must necessarily be followed. There is a requirement that the quantity surveyor must include in the valuation any direct loss and/or expense resulting from compliance with the instruction.

18.8   Acceleration

The architect has no power to order the contractor to accelerate the Work. That is to say the contractor cannot be made to finish earlier than the date for completion in the contract. If progress is delayed, the contractor cannot be made to complete by the completion date if otherwise it would be entitled to an extension of time. However, the contract does allow the architect to invite the

Schedule 2, contractor to quote for finishing earlier than would otherwise be the case if that
paragraph 2 is what the employer wants.

When he gets the architect's invitation (which must be in writing), the contractor can either:

- give the architect a quotation stating the amount of time it can save, the amount of money required and any other conditions the contractor wants to impose; or

■ explain to the architect why it is not practicable to finish earlier than the completion date.

From the receipt of the quotation by either the architect or the quantity surveyor, the procedure is the same as for acceptance of a Schedule 2 quotation (see Section 18.7 above).

18.9 Daywork

5.7

If additional or substituted work cannot be valued under the normal rules or as CDP work, it must be valued as 'daywork', that is to say on the basis of prime cost plus percentages. This is likely to be an acceptable method of valuation to the contractor since it ensures that it will, at least, recover its costs of the work subject only to the limitations set out by the relevant 'Definition of Prime Cost' defined in the contract plus percentages to cover supervision, overheads and profit. However, the employer is unlikely to be happy with it, because there is no incentive for the contractor to work efficiently. Therefore, it is very much a tool of last resort only to be used if measurement in other ways is impossible.

1.1

The machinery set out in the contract for the submission of daywork sheets (the contract refers to 'vouchers') and the associated timescale is not ideal. The daywork sheets must be delivered to the architect or authorised representative for verification not later than seven business days after the work has been executed. A business day is defined in the contract as excluding Saturdays, Sundays and public holidays. Therefore, if the work is carried out on a Monday, the last date for submitting the daywork sheet will be Wednesday of the following week. It is not really workable. If the architect or representative is required to verify what is set out on the daywork sheet, in other words to vouch for its truth, it is difficult to see how the architect can do that two days later let alone in the following week. Realistically, a person can only verify something was done by actually seeing it. The presence of an operative working on a particular part of the Works can only be verified if the person verifying stays with the operative throughout the whole period. No completely satisfactory solution has been proposed for this problem.

3.4

It is usually assumed that, if there is a clerk of works, the clerk of works will be the architect's authorised representative for this purpose. That is probably because there is no other reference in the contract to the architect having a representative. However, despite the fact that the clerk of works is often referred to as 'the eyes and ears of the architect on the site', the contract states that the clerk of works, far from being a representative of the architect, is an inspector on behalf of the employer. Therefore, it is clear that the clerk of works has no authority to verify daywork sheets unless the architect specifically gives that authority. It is of course open to the architect to give that authority to anyone. In giving the authority, the architect should make quite clear in writing to the contractor and any other affected party the extent of the authority being given.

The straightforward and sensible way of dealing with the verification of daywork sheets, is for the contractor to give notice to the architect of its intention to keep daywork records of a particular item of work, for the architect or authorised representative to attend the site and to take records of the time spent and materials used and for the daywork sheets to be submitted for verification at the end of each day. In that way, at least, the quantity surveyor can be reasonably certain that the sheets or vouchers do represent an accurate record of time and materials. In order for this system to work properly, the quantity surveyor must notify the contractor in advance of any intention to value using daywork. It must not be forgotten that the quantity surveyor need not value using daywork; the work can be measured using one of the other methods. Verification is normally carried out by signing the sheets. Often the magic formula 'For record purposes only' is added. However, where daywork is to be the method of valuation in any particular case, the addition of those words has little practical value and certainly does not prevent the contents of the sheets being used for

203   calculation of payment. In these circumstances it appears that the quantity surveyor has no right to substitute his or her own opinion for the hours and other

204   resources on the sheets. Where the employer has set out a system of verification by signing, but has neglected to do so, the sheets will stand without further

205   proof as evidence of the work done unless they can be shown to be inaccurate.

18.10   Valuation of contractor's designed portion

There is an overall stipulation that the rules for percentage or lump sum adjustments, adjustment of preliminary items, daywork and change in conditions for

5.6.3.2, 5.6.3.3,   other work will apply to CDP work if relevant. However, the nature of this work
5.7 and 5.9   makes necessary the inclusion of specific provisions. Therefore an allowance
5.8.1   must be made for the addition or omission of design work. A prudent contractor will include an hourly rate for design work in its CDP analysis. In addition, the valuation of any variations to the CDP work must be consistent with similar character of work in the CDP analysis. Allowance in the valuation is to be made for any change in conditions or significant change in quantity. The comments already made with regard to 'similar' and significant change in quantity also apply here. If there is no work of a similar character, the quantity surveyor is to make a fair valuation. The valuation of omissions is to use the values in the CDP analysis.

18.11   Common problems

If the contractor refuses to carry out a variation until a price has been agreed

The contract is quite clear that the contractor must comply with architect's instructions forthwith (as soon as it reasonably can do so). The only proviso is that the instruction must be one that is empowered under the contract.

3.14.1
5.3

It is clear that the architect can issue instructions for variations. The architect can invite quotations, in which case, the contractor need not comply until after the quotation has been accepted. However, there is nothing in the contract that allows the contractor, in response to a variation instruction, to refuse to comply until the price has been agreed. The architect can issue a 7-day notice requiring the contractor to comply and, if it fails to do so, the employer is entitled to get another contractor to carry out the work.

If the architect refuses to sign the contractor's daywork sheets

5.7
1.1

The contract is states that the architect or the architect's authorised representative should verify daywork sheets (the contract refers to them as 'vouchers') if the work cannot be valued in any other way and the contractor submits the sheets to the architect no later than 7 business days after the work has been done. A business day is defined as any day that is not Saturday, Sunday or a public holiday. The architect must either verify the sheets or say why they are not being verified. If the architect remains silent on the topic, the contractor would be wise to confirm the situation in writing and to refer it to the quantity surveyor for valuation. If the work is not valued the contractor's confirmation will be valuable evidence (because it is the only evidence) in any adjudication.

If the contractor argues that the whole scope and character of the Works has changed

3.14.5

A contractor will sometimes say that the whole scope and character of the Works has changed in order to demand the opportunity to amend its rates. If the whole scope and character of the Works had changed, the contractor would probably be correct and it might be necessary to re-rate the project. In practice that very rarely happens. It would mean that a succession of variations had altered the work and materials to such an extent that they bore little resemblance to what was originally included in the contract documents. The contract expressly states that no variation will render the contract ineffective. Therefore, the contract will accommodate quite substantial variations before it can be said that the whole scope and character has changed.

19 Payment

19.1 The Contract Sum

article 2

4.1

206

4.2

Contracts such as SBC are known as 'lump sum' contracts. The Contract Sum stated in the contract is the amount for which the contractor has agreed to carry out the whole of the Works. The actual amount of work included in the Contract Sum is the work measured in the bills of quantities plus whatever is in the CPD documents (if any).

The Contract Sum is very important. The contractor is entitled to payment of the Contract Sum provided it substantially completes the whole of the Works. The idea of interim payments is simply to provide sufficient money to allow the contractor to carry out the Works. In other words: to provide cash flow.

Some people find it difficult to understand that the Contract Sum is the amount stated in the contract and it never changes. It is certainly true that the contract allows for additions to, and omissions from, the Contract Sum and it may be adjusted only in accordance with the provisions of the contract (see Table 19.1). But when it is adjusted it becomes the adjusted Contract Sum. The new amount is not the Contract Sum, which never changes. Errors or omissions of any kind in the calculation of the Contract Sum are treated as having been accepted by the employer and contractor. The only exceptions are those instances specifically allowed for in the contract. They are discrepancies in or between documents; errors or omissions in description or quantity; and departures from the Standard Method of Measurement (see Chapter 3, Section 3.5).

Contractor's errors

The contractor may make all kinds of errors in pricing the contract documents. It may under- or over-price items, overlook items, or simply make a mistake in adding up totals. Once is price is accepted, however, it may not be altered. The quantity surveyor will have checked the contractor's calculations before the tender was accepted, but may not have noticed the error. It is always bad, from the point of view of both contractor and employer, if the contractor finds, after entering into the contract, that it has made an error that will result in loss of money. The contractor will naturally attempt to recoup its losses by taking

The JCT Standard Building Contract 2011, First Edition. David Chappell.
© 2014 by David Chappell. Published 2014 by John Wiley & Sons, Ltd.

Table 19.1 Contractual provisions regarding adjustment of the Contract Sum.

Clause	Cause of adjustment
2.6	Additional premium for early use by employer
2.10	Deductions for setting out errors not to be amended
2.14.3	Correction, alteration or modification to bills of quantities or CDP documents
2.16.1	Architect's instructions regarding discrepancies in the CDP documents other than Employer's Requirements other than instructions relating to the removal of the discrepancies.
2.16.2	If a discrepancy in the Employer's Requirements not dealt with in the Contractor's Proposals
2.17.2	Architect's instructions in regard to divergence between contract documents and statutory requirements
2.18.3	Emergency work due to divergence between contract documents and statutory requirements
2.21	Statutory fees and charges
2.23	Patent rights and damages
2.38	Architect's instruction not to make good defects
3.11	Non-compliance with instructions and engagement of others by employer
3.14	Architect's instructions requiring variations
3.16	Architect's instructions regarding expenditure of provisional sums
3.17	If architect's instructions for opening up and testing show work in accordance with the contract
3.18.2	Architect's instructions to allow defective work to remain
4.2	General provisions about adjustment
4.5	Final adjustment of the Contract Sum
4.14.2	Contractor's suspension after employer's failure to pay
4.21	Fluctuations
4.23	Loss and/or expense
6.5.3	Premium for insurance of employer's liability
6.10.2	Pool Re cover by contractor
6.10.3	Terrorism cover other than Pool Re cover
6.16.1.2	Architect's instructions or emergency work for Joint Fire Cod remedial measures
6.17	Revisions to the Joint Fire Code
Schedule 3 para B.2.1.2	Employer defaults on insurance
Schedule 3 para C.3.1.2	Employer defaults on insurance

every opportunity to submit claims. So particular care must be exercised, before a tender is recommended for acceptance, that the checks made by the architect or the quantity surveyor have been thorough and that the final figure does not appear suspiciously low in comparison with other tenders.

19.2 Valuation

4.10.2

The quantity surveyor must carry out interim valuations whenever the architect feels that it is necessary to do so. This step will be taken whenever the architect feels unable to know with reasonable accuracy without the aid of the quantity surveyor. Because the process of valuation is specialised, there will be few instances, in practice, when the wise architect will not require the quantity surveyor's assistance. Where fluctuations option C (formula adjustment) has been chosen, a valuation must be prepared by the quantity surveyor before every interim certificate is issued.

4.16

The amount to be included in the architect's certificate is the gross valuation as set out briefly in Table 19.2. From this amount the certificate must show deducted:

- The retention.
- The total of advance payment reimbursement;
- The sums stated as due in previous certificates (note, not any amounts previously paid, but any amounts previously certified. Therefore, the architect need not be concerned, when certifying, about whether the employer has paid or paid in full).
- Any sums paid for an interim payment notice given after the issue of the interim certificate (more of this later).

207

It is important that the architect does not over-certify in case the contractor becomes insolvent before the over-certification can be corrected in the next certificate. Certification is the architect's responsibility whether or not a valuation has been provided by the quantity surveyor. An architect who disagrees with the quantity surveyor's valuation, has a duty to change it. The architect must ensure that the quantity surveyor puts no value on defective work. The quantity surveyor cannot be expected to know what the architect considers to be defective unless the architect gives proper notice; this should be done in writing every month before the valuation is carried out.

Advance payment

4.8

The contract makes provision for advance payment to the contractor if that is what the employer agrees to do. The employer must decide before the contract is signed, because the details of the advance payment and how the contractor is to repay the amount must be shown in the contract particulars. If a bond is required this must also be stated. The contract particulars state that advance payment does not apply if the employer is a local authority. The advance payment is normally made before the issue of the first certificate for payment. No doubt the employer will pay it to the contractor immediately the contract is executed.

Bond

If the employer requires a bond, and it is difficult to see why a bond would not be required, the terms must be those agreed between the British Bankers' Association and the Joint Contracts Tribunal. The text of this bond and of the

Table 19.2 What is included in the gross valuation.

Amounts on which the employer is allowed a retention:

5.2.1
Schedule 3,
paragraphs
B.3.5, C.4.5.2
or 6.11.5.2

■ The total value of work properly executed by the contractor including valuations agreed or that have been valued in accordance with the valuation rules or for which there is a confirmed acceptance of a variation quotation, plus any adjustment by fluctuation option C or by confirmed acceptance of an acceleration quotation excluding amounts for restoration, replacement or repair of loss or damage or removal of debris.

2.24, 3.9.2.1

■ The total value of materials that have been reasonably and not prematurely delivered to, or adjacent to, the Works for incorporation, provided that they are adequately protected against weather and damage. The certificate need not include any materials that the contractor has clearly delivered to site for the express purpose of obtaining payment. The contract has provisions intended to ensure that materials paid for in this way by the employer become the property of the employer. Whether they are successful will very much depend on whether the materials are the subcontractor's property in the first instance.

4.12

■ The value of any off-site materials on the employer's list.

Amounts on which the employer is allowed no retention:

2.6.2, 2.21
2.23
3.17, 6.5
6.10.2
6.10.3
Schedule 3
paragraphs
B.2.1.2 or C.3.1
4.14.2

■ If the contractor has paid or incurred costs for additional premium for the employer's use or occupation, statutory fees or charges, patent rights, opening up or testing if the work is found to be in accordance with the contract, the contractor is entitled to be paid the cost of the opening up and the cost of making good, premium for employer's liability insurance, variation in the rate of Pool Re cover that the contractor is required to renew and the contractor is insuring under option A, insurance other than Pool Re cover is required and the contractor is insuring under option A and premiums for insurance on the employer's default.

4.23
Schedule 3,
paragraphs
B.3.5 or C.4.5.2
or 6.11.5.2

■ If the contractor has correctly suspended as a result of the employer's failure to pay and is due costs and expenses.

■ If the contractor is entitled to payment of direct loss and/or expense due to disturbance of regular progress.

Schedule 7,
Options A or B

■ If the contractor has restored loss or damage and the employer has insured.

■ Fluctuation payments.

Deductions are to be made as follows:

2.10
2.38
3.11
3.18.2
6.10.2

■ If the architect has instructed that errors in setting out should not be amended and an appropriate deduction should be made, if the architect instructs the contractor not to make good and an appropriate deduction is made to the Contract Sum, if the contractor has not complied with an instruction and the employer has had to engage others and if the architect instructs that defective work may remain and an appropriate deduction is made to the Contract Sum.

Schedule 7,
Options A or B

■ If there is a variation in the rate of Pool Re cover that the contractor is required to renew and the contractor is insuring under option A or fluctuations appropriate notice of demand is included at the end of the contract. Most contractors will welcome money 'up front' to assist in setting up the site and funding the start of work and receipt of materials.

Repayment

If the repayment schedule is carefully worked out, the repayments should be more than covered by the monthly certificates. For example, the employer may agree to make an advance payment of £50,000. In the contract particulars, it may say that the contractor is to reimburse the employer at the rate of £5,000 per month, starting with certificate number 2. If the contract period is one year, it will mean that the employer will be totally reimbursed before the contract is due for completion. Obviously, the employer will expect a price advantage when opting to effectively fund the contractor in this way. The bond makes provision for repayment of the money to the employer on demand if the contractor defaults in the repayment.

19.3   Method and timing

The contract sets out specific intervals between payments, but alternatively the parties may make whatever arrangements they wish for interim payments. Where the contract is of relatively high value, it is customary to pay at monthly intervals, but if the value is low or the priced documents make it convenient, it may suit both parties to agree that payment will be made on the completion of certain defined stages. The parties may have the agreement set out in the contract itself before entering into the contract, or they may agree the mode of payment before commencing work. If a particular system of payment is desired, it is best to have it set out in the contract documents at tender stage because:

- The method and regularity of payment will significantly influence the contractor's tender; and
- If no agreement to the contrary is concluded after the parties have entered into a contract, the normal payment provisions will apply; and
- Amendment of the contract to allow for stage payments is not straightforward and sufficient time must be allowed for the necessary re-drafting of the clauses.

208

The contractual payment provisions were amended following changes in legislation. They now contain some pitfalls, for architect and employer that may not immediately be obvious.

The certificate must state to what the payment relates and the basis of calculation.

19.4   Payment procedure

Purpose

The purpose of the payments provisions is to set out the way in which the money that is due to the contractor is paid. There is a series of interim payment in order to provide the contractor with cash flow, culminating in the final payment when all the Works in the contract have been completed and any defects rectified.

The procedure has been carefully worked out so that, if the architect observes them carefully, it will be the architect's certificate that determines the amount of money to which the contractor is due. However, if the architect fails to observe the procedure, the amount due will be determined by applications or notices given by the contractor. This is particularly important if, as often happens, there is a dispute between architect and contractor about the amount that should be paid. The procedure determines whether the employer or the contractor sits on the disputed amount while the actual amount payable is ironed out.

Summary

The payment provisions in the contract are shown in the flowchart in Figure 19.1 In brief, they amount to this: There is a due date every month. The architect must issue an interim certificate within 5 days of the due date and that is what the employer must pay. If not and the contractor has submitted a interim application no later than 7 days before the due date, the application becomes what is called an interim payment notice and that is the amount the employer must pay. If there is neither certification nor application, the contractor may submit an interim payment notice at any time and that is what the employer must pay. In the case of an interim certificate or an interim application that becomes an interim payment notice, the final date for payment is 14 days after the due date. If an interim payment notice is submitted after 5 days from the due date, the final date for payment is postponed by the same number of days as the notice was issued after the 5-day period. Whether the amount payable is decided by certificate or notice, the employer may issue a pay less notice (that replaces and that is somewhat different from the former withholding notice) not later than 5 days before the date for payment.

Overview

The way in which the contractor is paid is similar to, but significantly different from, the payment provisions in the 2005 edition of SBC. The procedure is complicated and what follows is as simple a version as can be managed without doing violence to what the contract says.

The due date

The contract (following what is laid down in the legislation) refers to something called the 'due date'. This expression is not defined in the contract. One might be excused for assuming from the expression that it means the date on

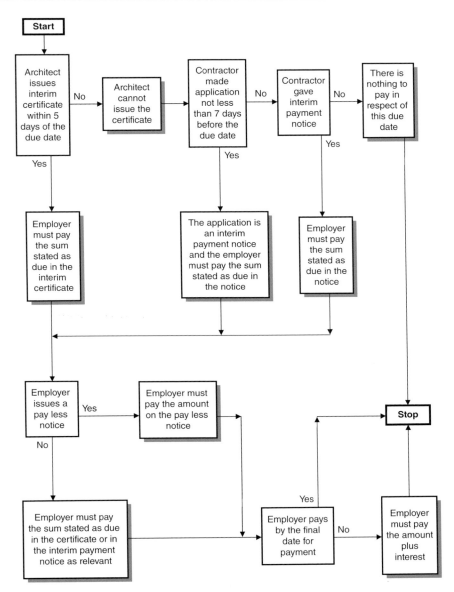

Figure 19.1 Flowchart showing interim payment provisions under SBC11.

4.12.1

which payment is due and payable. That may well be so, but the contract also refers to the 'final date for payment' that is usually (but not invariably) 14 days after the due date. Therefore, it is clear that the due date is important because it marks the date from which the final date for payment and other things are to be calculated. The due dates for interim payments are to be set out in the con-

4.9.1

tract particulars. They are to be monthly until practical completion and, after that, two monthly until the expiry of the rectification period or the issue of the certificate of making good, whichever is the later.

Interim certificates

4.10.1

The Architect must issue each interim certificate no later than 5 days after each due date. That is really important and cannot be stressed too much. If the architect fails to issue a particular certificate within the 5-day period, it cannot be issued at all. A certificate issued after the 5-day period is quite simply invalid, because the architect has no authority under the contract to issue it. The consequence might well be that the employer has to pay the contractor more than the architect's or quantity surveyor's valuation.

4.9.2

The certificate must state the amount due at the due date to the contractor, calculated as already noted. It must specify also the basis on which the amount was calculated. The architect might do this by attaching a copy of the valuation by the quantity surveyor. If the quantity surveyor has already issued a valuation and the architect is certifying that same amount, the architect may simply refer to the valuation. The standard position is that the amount certified is the amount that the employer must pay.

Interim applications

4.11.1

The contractor may make what the contract refers to as an 'Interim Application' to the quantity surveyor no later than 7 days before the due date. The application should state the sum the contractor considers will become due on the due date and showing the basis on which it has been calculated. This application is important, because if the architect fails to issue an interim certificate within the 5-day period and the contractor has made an interim application, that application becomes what the contract calls an 'Interim Payment Notice'. In that case, the amount stated in the interim payment notice is the amount that the employer must pay.

4.12.3

Interim payment notice

4.11.2.2
4.12.3

A contractor that has not made an interim application may give an interim payment notice to the quantity surveyor (note: not to the architect or to the employer) at any time after the 5-day period during which the architect should have issued, but failed to issue, an interim certificate, stating the sum the Contractor considers became due on the due date and showing the basis on which it has been calculated. Then that is the amount that the employer must pay. It is obviously very important that the Architect issues the Interim Certificate on time.

Final date for payment

4.12.4

It has already been stated that the final date for payment of an interim payment is 14 days after its due date. But if the interim payment notice has been given by the contractor after the architect failed to issue an interim certificate within the stipulated 5 days after the due date, the final date for payment is postponed by the number of days after the expiry of the 5-day period that the interim payment notice was given.

Pay less notice

One may envisage a situation where an architect issues a certificate for a sum of, say, £30,000, but issues it after the 5-day period so it is invalid. The contractor may then issue an interim payment notice in the sum of £35,000. At that point, as can be seen from the foregoing paragraphs, the contract says that the employer must pay £35,000. However, all is not lost so far as the employer is concerned. An employer who wishes to pay less than the amount stated as due in the interim certificate or in the interim payment notice, may give what the contract refers to as a 'Pay Less Notice' to the contractor, but this must be done

4.12.5   no later than 5 days before the final date for payment.

The pay less notice must state the amount the employer considers to be due and the basis of its calculation. A pay less notice may be given on the employer's behalf by the architect, the quantity surveyor or any other person whom the employer has notified to the contractor as authorised to do so. The contract makes clear that a pay less notice may not be given until

4.13.1.3   an interim certificate or an interim payment notice has been issued. Even if the contract did not specifically say so, it would not be logical to issue a pay less notice before anyone was aware what it was that the employer was going to pay less. It is likely that the architect has a duty to advise the employer about all the kinds of notice that the employer may or must issue

209   under the contract.

Interest

Interest will become payable to the contractor if the employer fails to pay amounts properly due, either under a certificate or an interim payment notice as applicable after taking into account any valid pay less notice,

4.12.6   within the prescribed period. The interest rate chargeable is 5% over the Bank of England Base Rate that was current at the date when the payment became overdue. Simple interest is payable and it is stated in the contract to be a debt from the employer to the contractor. That means that the employer can claim the debt by any of the dispute resolution procedures agreed in the contract.

19.5   Retention

The rules

The contract states that the amount that the employer may deduct (in practice the architect actually shows the deduction on the interim certificates) from payments as retention is 3%, but a different amount may be inserted in the contract particulars. That percentage may be deducted from work that has not reached practical completion. Once practical completion has been certified or it has been deemed to have occurred following partial possession, the percentage that may be deducted is halved. The Employer may continue to deduct half

4.20

4.18.2

the percentage until the certificate of making good is issued. A separate statement must be issued by the architect or, more usually, by the quantity surveyor with each interim certificate stating the amount of retention deducted.

Protection for the contractor

4.18.1

The employer is a trustee for the contractor. That means that the employer must look after the retention money for the contractor. It is recognised as being the contractor's money. There is no obligation on the employer to invest – that is, no obligation to make the best use of the money on behalf of the contractor and to obtain some interest for the contractor on it.

Separate bank account

4.18.3

210

Because it is held in trust, the contractor has the right to insist that the retention fund be kept in a separate bank account clearly designated as held in trust for the contractor. Indeed it is likely that the employer is under an obligation to place the money in a separate bank account whether or not the contractor requests it. This safeguards the money if the employer becomes insolvent. This provision does not apply to local authorities, presumably on the basis that a local authority will not become insolvent. The object is to safeguard the contractor's interest in the retention. However, the contract is clear that any monetary interest on the contractor's money in the separate bank account belongs to the employer. This seems to be unfair and possibly contrary to the various legislation concerning trust funds. However, that is not something that should concern the architect although, depending on the amount of retention, the contractor may wish to take some legal advice on the matter.

Retention bond

4.19

Schedule 6
Part 3

As an alternative to having a sum deducted from the certified amount on each certificate, the contractor may provide a retention bond before the date of possession. It must be agreed before the contract is signed and the details must be entered in the contract particulars (see the explanation of bonds in Chapter 4, Section 4.8). The terms of the bond are included in the contract and it must be obtained from a surety approved by the employer. An important figure is what is referred to as the 'maximum aggregate sum'. This amount must be entered in the contract particulars and in the bond. It must be the same as the maximum amount of retention that would have been deducted throughout the contract period.

The way the system works is that, if the contractor has provided a bond, no retention is deducted. However, before the issue of each certificate either the architect must prepare or may instruct the quantity surveyor to prepare a statement setting out the amount of retention that would have been deducted. That is important, because:

- If the contractor fails to provide or maintain the bond, the architect must deduct the appropriate amount of retention from the next and subsequent certificates.

- If the contractor eventually provides or reinstates the bond, the employer must pay back the retention withheld.
- If at any time the amount of retention that would be deducted exceeds the maximum aggregate sum, for example because additional work has been instructed, the contractor must arrange with the surety for the maximum aggregate sum to be increased. Failing that, the architect may deduct the extra retention from the next certificate.

If the contractor has also provided a performance bond (quite common but not included in the standard bonds at the back of the contract) and if the employer becomes entitled to make a demand for payment, the contract stipulates that the employer must first make the demand on the retention bond.

A list of the contract provisions allowing deduction from amounts due or to become due to the contractor is given in Table 19.2.

19.6   Final payment

4.5.1

The contract lays down a strict time sequence for the events leading up to, and the issue of, the final certificate (see Figure 19.2). The contractor must provide the architect or the quantity surveyor, if the architect instructs, with all the documents that are reasonably required for the final adjustment of the Contract Sum. The contractor may send them either before practical completion or the last section completion certificate, but no later than six months afterwards. In practice it is usually the quantity surveyor who deals with this and indeed although the quantity surveyor is only to ascertain the loss and/or expense if the architects instructs, it is usually the quantity surveyor who actually does it. The idea of this provision is that the contractor can make sure that the quantity surveyor has everything needed. Most contractors will submit their version of the final account. There is nothing particularly wrong with that provided that the contractor includes all the necessary evidence of expenditure. The contract assumes that the quantity surveyor will have kept a running total for the final account as the project goes forward so that at the end of the project all that is needed is the clarification of anything that may be outstanding. The submission by the contractor of its version of the final account does not remove the quantity surveyor's obligation to calculate it.

211

Armed with the information, the quantity surveyor must prepare a statement of all the adjustments that must be made to the Contract Sum together with a ascertainment of loss and/or expense if relevant. The architect must send a copy to the contractor within three months of receipt of the information from the contractor. In theory, the whole process should take 9 months from practical completion. But if the contractor is unreasonably late in sending its documents, it cannot expect the architect to adhere to this timetable.

Contractor's agreement?

The contract does not state that the contractor must agree the finally adjusted Contract Sum before the final certificate is issued. In practice it is customary to try to obtain agreement, and the contractor is usually sent two copies of the

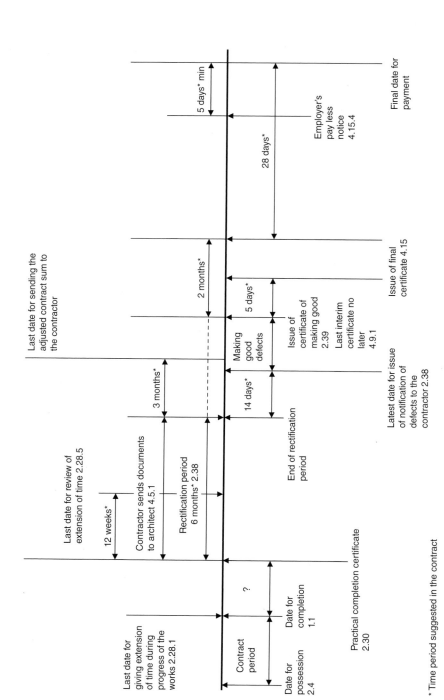

* Time period suggested in the contract

Figure 19.2 SBC11 time chart.

computations, one for it to sign as agreed and to return. Whether or not the contractor agrees the figure, the architect's final certificate is the document that states the amount payable to the contractor. Therefore, if the contractor fails to agree, there is nothing to stop the architect from certifying, indeed the architect must certify, the amount that in the architect's professional opinion is due to the contractor or to the employer, as the case may be.

Issue of the final certificate

The final certificate must be issued no later than 2 months after the latest of the following events:

- The end of the rectification period of the Works or the end of the last section rectification period.
- The issue of the certificate of making good for the Works or for the last section.
- The date the architect sends the contractor a statement of all the adjustments to the Contract Sum and the calculation of the loss and/or expense (if relevant).

4.15.1

In practice, the end of the rectification period is rarely the trigger for the start of the 2-month period, because there are usually defects to be reported to the contractor.

Content of the final certificate

If the architect is using the standard final certificate form prepared by the RIBA, the headings are all there to be completed. Essentially, the architect, usually after receiving the quantity surveyor's final account statement, sets out the Contract Sum as adjusted in accordance with the contract; then the total of all the amounts previously certified, any amounts paid by the employer after an interim payment notice and any amount paid as an advance payment. Then the final certificate shows the difference between the two amounts and whether the balance is payable by the employer or by the contractor.

4.3

4.8, 4.9.2.4,

The due date

In the case of the final certificate, the due date for payment is the date of issue of the final certificate. Importantly, if the certificate is not issued during the 2-month period referred to above, the due date is the end of that period. The final date for payment of the final certificate is 28 days from the due date, whenever that is.

4.15.3

Pay less notice

If the final certificate is properly issued, and if the party who is to pay (it will usually be the employer but it could be the contractor) wishes to pay less than the amount certified, that party must give the other a pay less notice as referred to in Section 19.4 above. The notice must be given no later than 5 days before

4.15.4

4.15.5

the final date for payment. This notice provision serves a similar purpose to the notice provision for interim certificates and the paying party must pay the amount stated in the notice.

Failure to issue the final certificate

4.15.6.1

212

The architect who fails to issue the final certificate by the end of the 2-month period loses the power to issue it at all. That may have serious consequences for the employer (see Section 19.7 below) and the architect may well face an action for professional negligence. If the architect fails to issue the final certificate by the end of the 2-month period, the contractor may, at any time after that, give the employer something that the contract calls a 'Final Payment Notice'. This is a notice that must be copied to the architect and that sets out the amount the contractor considers is due to it together with the basis of calculation. Unless the employer gives a pay less notice, the amount in the final payment notice is the amount the employer must pay. It is notable that the contract assumes that the contractor will only give a final payment notice if there is money due to it but not if the contractor is to pay money to the employer. Therefore, an interesting situation would arise if the architect decided that there was money due to the employer, but failed to issue the final certificate in time. There is no obligation on the contractor to issue a final payment notice. Indeed, as already stated, it has no power to do so. Therefore, there is no mechanism in the contract by which the employer can recover the money due.

4.15.6.2

Once a final payment notice has been given the final date for payment is postponed by the number of days after the end of the 2-month period that the final payment notice is given.

4.15.6.3

The employer may give a pay less notice after the contractor has given a final payment notice provided that the notice is given no later than 5 days before the final date for payment. The notice must show the basis of calculation of the sum the employer considers to be due and that is the sum that the employer must pay.

Interest on the final payment

4.15.7

4.15.9

Interest will become payable to the party to whom payment is to be made (usually the contractor) if the other party (usually the employer) fails to pay the amount properly due, either under the final certificate or the final payment notice as applicable after taking into account any valid pay less notice, within the prescribed period. The interest rate chargeable is 5% over the Bank of England Base Rate that was current at the date when the payment became overdue. Simple interest is payable and it is stated to be a debt.

19.7 The effect of certificates

1.10

No certificate, except the final certificate, is conclusive evidence that any work, materials or goods to which it relates are in accordance with the contract. All certificates, except the final certificate, are included, whether financial or not.

For example, the issue of the certificate of practical completion is not evidence that the architect has approved all the work that has been carried out up to that point and it does not prevent the architect from requiring the contractor to make good work not in accordance with the contract (i.e. defective work). The issue of an interim certificate is not evidence that all the work included is in accordance with the contract. The architect is entitled to omit defective work from a subsequent certificate if it has been inadvertently included in a previous certificate.

The final certificate has a conclusive effect in four respects:

1. Where, and to the extent that, the quality of materials or of the standards of workmanship is specifically described in a contract document or an architect's instruction as something for the architect's approval, the final certificate is conclusive that the quality and standards are to the architect's reasonable satisfaction. But importantly, there is a restriction that the final certificate is not to be conclusive that materials, goods or workmanship comply with any other term of the contract. In other words, the final certificate, sometimes may be conclusive about the architect's satisfaction, but no more than that. Under this contract it is likely that the employer could contend that the contractor would still be liable even though the architect was satisfied, because the contractor has an overall responsibility to construct in accordance with the contract and if the architect's approval is required that is almost certainly in addition to the contractor's overall duty.

2. That the terms of the contract that require additions, deductions or adjustments to the Contract Sum have been correctly operated.

3. That all extensions of time to which the contractor is entitled have been given.

4. Reimbursement of loss and/or expense is in final settlement of all the contractor's claims in respect of the relevant matters whether claims are for breach of contract, breach of a duty of care or breach of a statutory duty or any other claim.

There are exceptions to the conclusivity of the final certificate:

- If there have been any accidental inclusions or exclusions of any items, or any arithmetical errors in any computation, they may be corrected.
- If anything is the subject of legal proceedings or adjudication or arbitration commenced before the final certificate has been issued the certificate will be conclusive when either the proceedings are concluded or if 12 months elapses without either employer or contractor taking any step in the proceedings. whichever is the earlier.
- If either party has referred a matter to adjudication, arbitration or legal proceedings within 28 days after the date of issue of the final certificate, the certificate will not be conclusive about that matter.
- Because of the temporarily binding nature of an adjudication decision, if it is given after the issue of the final certificate, either party has 28 days from the date of the decision in which to refer the matter to arbitration or legal proceedings.

213

■ If the matter is not one about which the certificate is stated to be conclusive, the parties have the normal limitation periods of either six or twelve years (usually from practical completion) in which to bring an action, depending on whether the contract is under hand or a deed respectively.

19.8   Off-site materials

4.17

At one time, it was left to the architect to decide whether or not to include in a certificate the value of materials or goods stored by the contractor off-site. Usually, the off-site storage takes place in the contractor's yard or storage facility. Under this contract, the position is different. If the employer agrees to pay for certain materials or goods that will be stored off-site until required, a list of the items concerned must be given to the contractor and attached to the bills of quantities from which the contractor prepares its price. An appropriate note must be made in the contract particulars. It is relatively rare for such a list to be prepared. If there is no list, the architect has no power to certify off-site materials or goods.

Unique and not unique

Where a list has been prepared, it must differentiate between what the contract calls uniquely identified items and items that are not uniquely identified. The contract does not say what it means by these descriptions, therefore, they mean exactly what they say. One list is for things that can be described so that there is no doubt what they are because they are *uniquely* identified. That might include such things as kitchen and bathroom fittings, ironmongery and suchlike. The list of things that are not uniquely identified contains all the remainder of the off-site materials. Examples of things that are not uniquely identified would be sand, cement, plaster, screws, nails and so forth.

Problems

2.25

The inclusion of off-site materials in a certificate may raise serious problems. The contract states that, once the employer has paid for them, the materials become the employer's property. The contractor is not permitted to remove the materials, nor to allow anyone else to do so, except for use on the Works. All the while, the contractor is to remain responsible to the employer for any loss or damage. There are two dangers. First, that the supplier may have incorporated what is called a 'retention-of-title' clause in the contract of sale to the contractor. That means that, despite anything that might be written into this contract, the materials remain the property of the supplier until payment is received from the contractor: the supplier retains title or ownership. The second danger is that it is difficult to be sure that the materials inspected at the contractor's yard are not really intended for some other project. It has been known for a contractor to label and set aside, say, sink units for a particular contract until after inspection by the architect, then re-label them for the benefit of another architect and a different contract. This is sharp practice but, if the contractor goes into liquidation, that is no consolation for the employer.

Safeguards

In an attempt to safeguard the employer against the danger of paying for goods or materials to which the employer cannot subsequently prove ownership, the contract sets up a system of checks:

4.17.1
- The listed items must be in accordance with the contract. That is to say that they must be as specified and not be defective.

4.17.2.1
- The contractor must have provided reasonable proof of ownership of the listed items. This is not an easy thing to do. The best that can be done is to be as sure as possible that there is nothing that suggests that the contractor does not own the items. For example, the contractor may provide a copy of the subcontract with the subcontractor together with a statement from the subcontractor that the contractor has complied with any preconditions that need to be fulfilled before ownership is transferred. Whether the subcontractor has secured ownership from its supplier is another question.

4.17.2.2
- The contractor must provide the employer with reasonable proof that the items are insured for full value under a policy that protects employer and contractor in respect of specified perils. The policy must be effective to cover the whole period from the commencement of the contractor's ownership to delivery to or adjacent to the Works.

4.17.3
- Wherever the items are situated off-site, they must be set apart from other goods or materials or they must be clearly marked with a reference and identity the employer as the name of the person who ordered them and the destination as being the Works.

Schedule 6, Part 2

4.17.4 and 4.17.5
- In the case of items that are not uniquely identified, the contractor must have provided a bond in terms set out in the contract. Where the items are uniquely identified, the matter of the bond is left to the employer's discretion. In either case, the contract particulars must state the amount for which the bond is required. It is difficult to envisage why the employer would not require a bond in all circumstances.

19.9   Fluctuations

4.21
'Fluctuations' is one of those words that is used a lot but not always properly understood, at least by architects. It refers to changes in price, usually in an upwards direction. If the contract did not allow for fluctuations, all the prices would be fixed. That is to say that they would not be subject to any changes. The best way to understand that is to examine what the contract does say about fluctuations. It assumes that the employer will choose one of three available options and insert the details in the contract particulars before seeking tenders.

It is possible to delete all the options so that no fluctuations of any kind are allowed. The three options are each quite complicated, but essentially they are as follows:

Schedule 7,
Option A

■ A: contribution, levy and tax fluctuations. This is a minimum fluctuation provision. It allows for fluctuations in the amounts payable by the contractor as an employer of workers. It assumes that the Contract Sum is based on the types and rates of contribution, levy and taxes that were payable at the base rate (see Chapter 2, Section 2.9). If any of these payments increase or decrease or if new types are introduced or existing types are changed or cease to operate, the Contract Sum will be adjusted accordingly.

■ B: This includes contributions, levies and taxes, but also rates of wages, materials, goods, electricity and fuels and landfill tax. This is what is known as a full fluctuations clause that gives the contractor the opportunity to recover increases in all of these items. Theoretically, the contractor would recover less money if, for example, the rates of wages dropped.

■ C: This is used where full fluctuations are to be calculated by use of the Formula Rules issued by the JCT. As with option B, the option results in the contractor getting the benefit of all fluctuations albeit on a formula basis.

19.10   Common problems

The architect refuses to issue the final certificate

214

The architect cannot refuse to issue the final certificate simply because the contractor has not provided the information for the final account to be calculated. Neither that nor even the quantity surveyor's calculation of the final account is a pre-requisite to the issue of the final certificate. That would place the architect's necessary duty at the whim of the contractor. If the quantity surveyor will not calculate the final account because the contractor has not provided all the information required, the architect must instruct the quantity surveyor to do the best he or she can with the information available. If the quantity surveyor still refuses, the architect must issue the final certificate in the sum that the architect believes is correct.

At one time, architects were nervous about issuing final certificates because it was thought that the final certificate was conclusive in any proceedings that the contractor's work was in accordance with the contract documents. That meant that the employer could not recover the cost of rectifying defects after the final certificate was issued unless the employer challenged it within 28 days. The final certificate has not been conclusive in that way for some years now and the architect should not be overly concerned about issuing it. Indeed, the contract requires its issue and failure to issue the certificate at the correct time would be a serious breach of contract by the architect and render the architect
4.15   unable to issue the final certificate at all.

Contractor refusing to agree the final account

4.5.2

Many quantity surveyors are in the habit of sending the final account to the contractor (as required by the contract) and asking them to sign the account to show that it agrees with it. The contract does not require the contractor's agreement. The quantity surveyor's intention is to remove the possibility that the contractor will challenge the final account when the final certificate is issued. It is not clear what effect the contractor's signature has. It seems unlikely that the mere fact that the contractor has signed the final account has any great significance when the contract clearly allows the contractor to challenge the final certificate in adjudication or arbitration or legal proceedings (whichever of the two is chosen in the contract). Therefore, quantity surveyors should not require the contractor to sign the final account. If the quantity surveyor does so and the contractor refuses to sign, it makes no difference to the architect's duty to issue the final certificate. Usually the architect will use the quantity surveyor's valuation of the final account; signed or unsigned.

1.9.2 to 1.9.4

Dealing with defective work that was not apparent when the last interim certificate was issued

Each interim certificate is cumulative. That is to say that each certificate is calculated on the basis of all the work carried out and materials supplied since the date of possession. If defective work comes to light after the architect has issued an interim certificate so that it is effectively over-certified, the employer could issue a pay less notice taking the defective work into account. If it is too late for that, the architect can take it into account in the next certificate. The defective work is simply omitted from the valuation by the quantity surveyor. In the case of a really serious defect, that may mean that the architect issues a negative certificate.

What the architect cannot do is to issue a replacement certificate for a lower sum. The only reason for issuing a replacement certificate would be if there was a clear arithmetical error or other obvious error on the face of the certificate. Unwittingly certifying defective work does not fall into this category.

20 Contractor's design

20.1 Contractor's Designed Portion (CDP)

It has long been the law that the overall responsibility for design rests with the architect and the architect can only avoid this responsibility by obtaining the employer's consent to assigning the design responsibility to another (see Chapter 10, Section 10.1). A sub-contractor may be given design responsibility, but the contractor is not responsible for the sub-contractor's design failure and the architect is still ultimately liable unless the employer has expressly consented to the transfer of liability to the sub-contractor.

SBC 11 incorporates extensive provisions to enable the contractor to be given design responsibility for specific items. This must not be confused with any design responsibility of a sub-contractor.

In essence, the CDP provisions are a design and build contract in miniature and share many of the features of the DB contract, although in briefer terms.

20.2 Documents

Details of the CDP are to be inserted in the ninth recital. A footnote, somewhat superfluously, advises that a separate sheet may be used if the space is not sufficient to include all the items. If indeed a separate sheet is required, the employer ought to seriously consider whether the DB contract would not be more suited to the project.

The tenth and eleventh recitals indicate the process by which the employer provides a set of Employer's Requirements with the other documents included in the invitation to tender and, in response, the contractor provides a set of Contractor's Proposals showing the design and construction together with an analysis of the portion of the Contract Sum that relates to the CDP. Details of these documents are to be inserted in the contract particulars for identification purposes. When the contract is executed and these documents are signed by the employer and the contractor, they become part of the contract documents.

A question that continually arises in regard to the DB contract and to the CDP portion of SBC 11 is whether, in case of conflict, the Employer's

The JCT Standard Building Contract 2011, First Edition. David Chappell.
© 2014 by David Chappell. Published 2014 by John Wiley & Sons, Ltd.

215

2.3.1, 2.3.2,
3.14.3
and 5.2.3

Requirements or the Contractor's Proposals take precedence. A careful reading of the contract makes clear that the Employer's Requirements take precedence. The whole philosophy of the CDP is that the contractor is required to provide what the employer has set out in the Employer's Requirements, not that the employer is obliged to accept what the contractor offers in the Contractor's Proposals.

2.9.4

Schedule 1

The contractor is obliged to provide the architect with copies of design documents reasonably necessary to explain or amplify the Contractor's Proposals. The architect is entitled to request any related calculations or information. The contractor must also provide copies of any levels or other setting out information used for the CDP. The procedures for submission of design information from the contractor are set out in the contract and the contractor must submit the information as necessary in accordance with those procedures or with any other procedure set out in the contract documents. No work must be done until the contractor has complied with the relevant procedure.

20.3   The contractor's obligations

2.2

The contractor's obligations in regard to the CDP are set out as follows:

- Complete the design for the CDP including the selection of specifications for materials goods and workmanship to the extent that they are not stated in the Employer's Requirements or the Contractor's Proposals. Compliance with the Employer's Requirements is the primary objective.

3.8.2

- Comply with the architect's directions about the integration of the CDP work with the rest of the Works, subject to the contractor's right to object.
- Comply with the relevant parts of the CDM Regulations, particularly as they affect the designer.

Completing the design

216

2.13.2

The contractor's obligation to complete the design of the CDP can give rise to misunderstandings. It may be thought that it is the contractor's job to check the Employer's Requirements to make sure that everything works properly before carrying on with the design. However, in this contract, it expressly states that the contractor is not responsible for what is in the Employer's Requirements, nor for verifying whether any design is adequate. Therefore, if there is any defective design included in the Employer's Requirements that causes the contractor's completion of the design to be defective, the contractor will not usually be responsible.

2.14.2

2.17

If any inadequacy is found in the Employer's Requirements and if the Contractor's Proposals have not corrected it, the Employer's Requirements must be corrected and the correction is to be treated as a variation. This clearly includes any defective design. If the inadequacy consists of a divergence from statutory requirements, It must be dealt with under that provision.

2.3.3

Where materials, goods and workmanship are neither stated to be to the architect's satisfaction nor described in the contract documents, they are to be of a standard appropriate to the CDP.

Discrepancies in CPD documents

2.16.2

Where there is a discrepancy in the Employer's Requirements, what is in the Contractor's Proposals will take precedence if it is consistent with statutory requirements. The Contract Sum is not to be adjusted. If the Contractor's Proposals do not deal with the situation, the contractor must make proposals for amendments. The architect may agree the amendment or decide how to deal with the discrepancy. Either case is treated as a variation.

2.16.1

If the discrepancy is not in the Employer's Requirements but in other CPD documents, the contractor must notify the architect in writing and, as soon as it can, it must send a statement setting out how the discrepancy is to be removed. The architect is not obliged to issue any instructions about the discrepancy, even though notified, until the contractor sends its statement showing its proposals. The architect must then issue instructions with which the contractor must comply. The instructions can simply tell the contractor to proceed with its proposal in its statement or the architect may give other instructions. There will be no addition to the Contract Sum for the instructions if they simply relate to removing the discrepancy, but there will be an addition (i.e. a variation) for any part of the instructions that stray beyond that purpose.

To take a simple example: if the Contractor's Proposals show window frames as painted softwood in one place and UPVC in another, the contractor might propose that they are all painted softwood. The architect may instruct painted softwood or UPVC without any addition to the Contract Sum because either instruction is simply removing the discrepancy. However, if the architect instructs the contractor to provide the windows in high-quality hardwood with superior fittings, it would be going beyond what was necessary to remove the discrepancy. In that situation, there would be an addition to the Contract Sum. The addition would be the difference between the cost of the hardwood windows and the cost of whichever is the most expensive of the softwood or UPVC options. That makes perfect sense.

2.17.1

2.17.2.1

If there is a divergence between statutory requirements and one or more of the CDP documents, either the architect or the contractor must notify the other, depending on which one becomes aware of it first. The contractor must submit its proposals for amending the documents so as to remove the divergence. The architect must issue instructions about the divergence within 14 days of receipt of the contractor's proposals. The contractor must comply with the instruction at no cost to the employer. Obviously, the contract assumes that if the contractor's proposal is adequate to remove the divergence, that is what the architect will instruct unless there is a very serious reason to instruct something else. If the architect does instruct something else, it must be reasonable in proportion to the divergence.

However, if the divergence is a result of a change in statutory requirements after the base date, the instruction to amend the CDP is to be treated as a variation.

2.21.2

The contractor is not to be reimbursed any fees or charges that it pays solely relating to the CDP work.

2.40

3.23

Before practical completion, the contractor must provide the employer with whatever design drawings and other information are specified in the contract documents or, even if not specified, the information that the employer may reasonably require showing the CDP as built including the maintenance and operation of the CDP and any included installations. This does not affect the contractor's obligations to provide information for the health and safety file.

Integration

3.11

Integration with the rest of the Works is a fruitful area for claims. The contract refers to the architect giving 'directions' for integration rather than 'instructions'. Although the difference may be difficult to discern, it does mean that the architect cannot issue a 7-day compliance notice if the contractor fails to comply with the direction. The contractor may say that the architect's directions for integration unavoidably result in additional work and, therefore, cost. It is easy to confuse the situation. The principles, however, are straightforward although application to particular circumstances may need some thought. There are four basic situations:

3.14.3

- If the invitation to tender is supported by clear documents showing the rest of the design and especially any likely interfaces with CDP work, the contractor must allow in the Contractor's Proposals for the proper integration of the CDP with the rest of the design. If the rest of the design, so far as it affects the CDP, remains unchanged and if the architect does not instruct a variation requiring an alteration in the Employer's Requirements, the contractor can have no claim for any additional cost.

- If the invitation to tender is not supported by sufficient information to enable the contractor to properly design the interface between the CDP and other work and the contract documents are executed without the ambiguity being clarified, the contractor, in principle, has a claim for any additional cost resulting from the architect's directions on integration.

- If, after the contract is signed, the architect subsequently issues instructions about either the rest of the work that affects the CDP or about the CDP through the Employer's Requirements, the architect must issue directions on integration and the contractor has a claim for additional cost.

- If the contractor is obliged to alter the CDP in order to correct its own error, the contractor must bear those costs itself even though the architect will probably have to issue some directions about the integration of the corrected CDP.

20.4   Liability

Copyright

2.41.1

The contractor retains the copyright in all the contractor's design documents. Any drawings, designs or other documents provided to the contractor by the employer are, of course, excluded.

2.41.2

The contract states that the employer has an irrevocable, royalty-free and non-exclusive licence to use the CDP documents in various ways, but excluding the right to reproduce the designs for an extension to the Works.

Irrevocable

'Irrevocable' means exactly that. Once the contract is executed by the parties, the licence cannot be revoked for any reason. However, the clause is subject to the overriding proviso that all monies due and payable to the contractor have been paid. That will normally mean that the monies shown due on all certificates have been paid unless the employer has issued a pay less notice. That means in practice that, although the employer can use the designs so long as payment is properly made to the contractor, the licence will cease to be effective if proper payment stops. It seems that the employer could be in a serious situation if payment is stopped without good reason, because the reproduction of the design that, until then, was lawful, will suddenly become unlawful because it is an infringement of the contractor's copyright.

Royalty-free and non-exclusive

'Royalty-free', as the words suggest, simply means that the employer will not have to pay the contractor any royalty for the use of its copyright documents. The words 'non-exclusive' are to prevent the employer acquiring an exclusive licence. An exclusive licence would not only prevent the contractor from granting a licence to someone else to use the documents in the future, but it may prevent the contractor itself using the documents for another purpose.

Misuse

The contractor is not liable if any other person misuses its design documents. Anyone called upon to produce a design for another person according to a specific brief, will know that the finished design is seldom used precisely as the original intention. That is because ideas change. There is nothing wrong with that, quite the contrary, but the contractor cannot be held liable for any change of use. The clause is probably superfluous, because the contractor could not be held liable in any event for the result of employer misuse, unless the likelihood of misuse is so common that it is easy to foresee.

Fitness for purpose

218

2.19.1

The contractor would normally have a fitness for purpose liability for what it designed and constructed, but that is modified in this contract so that the liability is to the same standard as that of an architect. That is: reasonable skill and care. Therefore, like an architect, the contractor does not guarantee the result of the design, but only that reasonable skill and care was taken in its production.

Dwellings and restriction of liability

2.19.2

219

The contractor is also liable under the Defective Premises Act 1972 (in Northern Ireland the Defective Premises (Northern Ireland) Order 1975) if the CDP involves dwellings. If dwellings are not involved the parties may, if they wish, restrict the contractor's liability for loss of use, loss of profit and other consequential loss by inserting an appropriate sum in the contract particulars. It is not clear why the employer would want to agree to this other than perhaps to reduce the contractor's tender. The contractor would probably not be liable for these kind of losses in any event unless their likelihood was specifically made known to the contractor before the contract was signed.

Sub-letting

3.7.2

The contractor, without the architect's written consent, may not sub-let the design of the CDP. In practice, of course, most contractors called upon to carry out some portion of the design will need to sub-let it to the relevant consultant. Therefore, the architect's consent must not be unreasonably delayed or withheld. A reasonable reason for withholding consent might be if the contractor is suggesting a consultant or, perhaps in the case of a heating design, a sub-contractor whom the architect knows and can demonstrate to be unsatisfactory.

20.5   Variations

Employer's Requirements

3.14.3

3.16, 5.1.2.3
and 5.1.2.4

It is made clear that an instruction requiring a variation to the CDP can only be issued in respect of the Employer's Requirements. Neither the employer nor the architect can issue an instruction directly about the design in the Contractor's Proposals. Therefore, it is for the architect to instruct a change to the Employer's Requirements to which the contractor responds by altering its design. Instructions about the expenditure of provisional sums and work as approximate quantities must refer to sums or quantities in the Employer's Requirements. There is no provision to instruct the expenditure of provisional sums or work as approximate quantities if they are in the Contractor's Proposals. The Employer's Requirements take precedence over the Contractor's Proposals.

Objections

3.10.3

There is a very important qualification to the contractor's obligation to comply with the architect's directions or instructions. If the contractor's opinion is that compliance will badly affect the design of the CDP, the contractor must specify how the design will be affected by a written notice to the architect within 7 days of receipt of the direction or the instruction. Unless and until confirmed by the architect, the contractor need not comply. The architect should carefully check the reasons for the contractor's objection before proceeding.

Valuation

5.8.4

5.8

Valuation of variations in CDP work is not to be carried out in accordance with the usual rules for valuation although they apply so far as they are relevant. Whether and to what extent they are relevant must be decided by the architect or the quantity surveyor, as the case may be, doing the valuation. The contract contains some slightly different rules. The reference document is the CDP analysis.

In general, the valuation of varied work is to be consistent with the value of work of similar character in the CDP analysis, but appropriate allowance must be made for change in the conditions under which the work is carried out. If there is significant change in quantity, allowance must be made for that also. What is significant, ideally will be a matter for the quantity surveyor to decide based on experience of when economies of scale begin to take effect. If there is no work of a similar character to the variation in the CDP analysis a fair valuation is to be made in the usual way. Where CDP work is omitted, it is to be valued in accordance with the values in the CDP analysis.

5.8.1

Allowance must be made in the valuation of CDP work for addition or omission of design work. How this is to be done is not stated. It is important that the contractor includes among its prices in the CDP analysis something for design. The easiest way to do that is probably as an hourly rate or rates. Of course, the contractor must be scrupulous in keeping detailed time sheets for the design work to substantiate any claim for payment. Where no separate price is indicated for design, it is suggested that the quantity surveyor will have to make a reasonable estimate.

20.6   Insurance

Period

6.12.1

The contractor must take out professional indemnity insurance of the type and amount stated in the contract particulars. The details must be very carefully completed, because failure to do so may result in the insurance not being required or in inappropriate terms. The architect should advise the employer to take advice from an experienced broker before this part is completed. The period for insurance expires either 6 or 12 years from the date of practical completion. 12 years should be chosen to match the limitation period if the contract is executed as a deed. The insurance must be taken out without delay after the contract is entered into unless it has already been taken out. Often, the design will be done by others and they will have ongoing professional indemnity insurance. The contractor will probably try to put forward its sub-contractors' insurances to satisfy this clause. Strictly, sub-contract insurance would not be acceptable. The contractor should be the insured. The employer or the architect is entitled to ask the contractor to produce documentary *6.12.3* evidence that the insurance has been taken out or is being maintained. The evidence will usually be in the form of a broker's certificate.

Availability

The contractor must maintain the insurance until the expiry of the period stated in the contract particulars. That is if the insurance remains available at *6.12.2* commercially reasonable rates. This is a fairly common proviso with which most architects will be familiar. What is commercially reasonable will depend on several factors, not least the contractor's own financial circumstances. In order to decide whether the rate is commercially reasonable it is probably simply necessary for the contractor to ask itself whether it makes commercial sense to maintain the insurance at the particular rate quoted. Unless the contractor is carrying out CDP work on a regular basis, it is doubtful whether it would make commercial sense except at a fairly nominal amount.

A difficult situation may arise if the insurance ceases to be available at commercially reasonable rates. Although the situation is stated in the contract as if it was a factual occurrence, it is clear that it will depend on the subjective judgment of the contractor. It is not obvious how an employer could argue that a rate was commercially reasonable if the contractor argued to the contrary. In the event that the insurance ceases to be available, the contractor must immediately give notice to the employer so that the employer and the contractor can discuss how best to protect their respective positions. The employer is obviously in a very exposed position. One answer might be for the employer to undertake payment of the amount by which the premium exceeds a commercially reasonable rate. That is not an answer that will find much favour with the employer.

20.7   Common problems

An instruction is withdrawn and the contractor is paid nothing for abortive design costs

If no method of calculating the cost of design is included in the CDP analysis, the contractor may well be deprived of substantial additional costs where extra CDP work is instructed. This is particularly the case where the design work is aborted so that the contractor has produced a design in answer to an instruction to vary some CDP work and the instruction is then withdrawn. If design is priced separately, the contractor will be entitled to payment at that rate for the design work done, but not used. If there is no way of separating the design work, the contractor may be paid nothing at all, on the basis that if the rate for design is part of the rate for carrying out the work, there can be no payment for design if the work is not carried out. At best, the contractor may be looking at a nominal payment.

Contractor arguing that it can refuse to allow the use of its designs unless paid in full

2.41.2

The contract is worded so that the contractor's design work (CDP) is carried out and integrated into the Works. The design will be the copyright of the contractor and the contract states that the employer has an irrevocable licence to copy and use the contractor's design documents and reproduce them for any purpose relating to the Works. 'Irrevocable' means exactly that: the licence cannot be revoked. However, all that is made subject to the contractor having been paid in full 'all sums due and payable'. The sums that are due and payable will be stated in the architect's interim certificates, the contractor's interim payment notices or the employer's pay less notice depending on circumstances. Therefore, if the employer fails to pay any sum that becomes due and payable under the contract, the contractor is entitled to revoke the employer's licence or, more precisely, the employer's licence will automatically cease in those instances, to resume when the employer pays the amount owing.

If the contractor fails to maintain professional indemnity insurance for CDP work

6.12 and 6.13

It may happen that the contractor stops the professional indemnity insurance without notifying the employer. This is a breach of the contract provisions that require the contractor to continue the insurance for the period of either 6 or 12 years as stated in the contract particulars and to notify the employer if the insurance ceases to be available at commercially reasonable rates. If this occurs after the final certificate is issued, it is not a matter for the architect for whom the final certificate marks the end of power and duty under the contract. If it happens before the issue of the final certificate, the architect must advise the employer to seek immediate legal advice.

The problem is that, until grounds for a claim arise, the employer will have suffered no loss as a result of the lack of insurance. Once the claim arises, it will be too late if there is no insurance. The contractor, if a limited company, may simply liquidate. This is a real difficulty to which there is no easy answer. The employer's solicitors may be able to obtain a mandatory injunction requiring the contractor to take out insurance, but the part of the contract allowing the contractor to notify the employer, at which the employer and contractor are supposed to sit to discuss the best way forward seems to suggest that the obligation to insure is not absolute. The employer may have to take out the insurance and, if the final certificate has not been issued, recover the cost by means of a pay less notice.

Part IV   Closing Stages

21   Practical completion

21.1   Definition

220

The meaning of 'practical completion' has been the source of much dispute. It is not really clear why this should be the case, because the courts have defined practical completion under the JCT contracts. It is not the same as 'substantial completion', nor does it mean 'almost complete'. The point that emerges is that the architect is not to certify practical completion if any defects are apparent or if anything other than very trifling items remains outstanding (the courts refer to *de minimis* items). Within these guidelines, the architect is free to exercise discretion. There will be differences of opinion on the question of what are 'trifling' items. Probably, what constitutes trifling items can fluctuate considerably depending on circumstances. A practical test to apply is whether the employer would be seriously inconvenienced while the trifling items are being finished. If the employer would be seriously inconvenienced, the architect is probably justified in withholding the certificate.

21.2   What the contract says

2.30

The contract states that the architect must issue a certificate 'forthwith' when, in his or her opinion, practical completion of the Works or a section is achieved and the contractor has complied sufficiently with the requirements to provide and to ensure that any subcontractor provides certain information for the health and safety file and to provide as-built drawings. The subcontractor, of course, is to provide the information through the contractor to the CDM

The JCT Standard Building Contract 2011, First Edition. David Chappell.
© 2014 by David Chappell. Published 2014 by John Wiley & Sons, Ltd.

221

Co-ordinator. 'Forthwith' in this context means 'without undue delay' or in ordinary language: as soon as it can reasonably be done.

It should be noted that the architect must issue one certificate to cover three things:

- practical completion in a physical sense; and
- the supply of health and safety information; and
- provision of as-built drawings for the CDP work.

The consequences of the certificate are considerable.

Pre-practical completion lists

There is no obligation on the architect to tell the contractor what items remain to be completed before the issue of the practical completion certificate. The temptation to issue lists of outstanding items should be resisted. The contractor knows what is required by the contract. The issue of lists at this stage is confusing and often leads to disputes. This is particularly the case, because such lists are often referred to as 'snagging lists' as though the items on such lists are something other than defects and breaches of contract. The onus of inspecting the work and preparing work lists for the contractor lies with the person-in-charge.

Handover meetings

The contractor is not bound to notify the architect when practical completion has been achieved, but it is wise to do so, probably some weeks in advance. Some architects are in the habit of arranging so-called 'handover meetings' at which representatives of the employer and sometimes the employer's maintenance organisation are present. This can be a prudent move by the architect on the principle that many eyes are better than two. There will also be consultants on hand to inspect their own particular portions of the Works. However, the decision to issue a certificate is solely a matter for the architect. The responsibility cannot be passed to the employer simply because the employer is present.

The exception to that is if the employer insists that the building is ready, even though the architect's view that the building has not achieved practical completion is made clear to the employer. The employer may agree with the contractor to take possession of the building despite the architect's protests. This often happens if an employer is anxious to get into a building. However, the architect must not issue a certificate until the contractual requirements have been satisfied.

If the architect issues a practical completion certificate simply because the employer or the employer's solicitor has instructed it, the architect will be negligent. In issuing a certificate, the architect is giving formal expression to the architect's professional opinion. To issue a certificate at the behest of someone else is clearly wrong.

Occupation

2.6

222

Occupation by the employer is not the same as practical completion and, in the absence of a certificate of practical completion, it is probable that the employer may still recover or deduct liquidated damages (but see Section 21.4 below on partial possession). The architect should write to the employer and make the position clear. If the employer later discovers that outstanding items cause trouble, or if the contractor does not complete as quickly and efficiently as it promised, the architect's duties will have been carried out properly with due regard for the employer's interests. The architect's duty to issue a certificate of practical completion will remain, but not until, in the architect's opinion, the works have achieved that state.

21.3   Consequences

Once practical completion of the Works or the Section has been certified, there are several very important consequences. All of them are to the contractor's benefit:

Schedule 3,
Option A
2.32

4.20

4.5.1
2.28.5
2.38

- The contractor's liability for insurance of the Works or of a section ends.
- Liability for liquidated damages ends.
- The employer's right to deduct full retention ends and half the retention percentage becomes due for release within 14 days.
- The six months period begins during which the contractor must send all documents to the architect necessary for adjustment of the Contract Sum.
- The period of final 12 weeks review of extensions of time begins.
- The rectification period begins.

21.4   Partial possession and sectional completion

2.33–2.37
2.30.2

There is often confusion between partial possession and sectional completion. Sections used to be dealt with in the form of a supplement involving a great many detailed changes to the contract. Sensibly, SBC uses wording that also applies to sections if the relevant parts of the contract particulars have been completed.

Difference

The crucial difference between partial possession and section completion is that partial possession may only be exercised if the contractor consents, even though that consent must not be unreasonably withheld or delayed. The employer having entered into the contract with one completion date, the decision to take partial possession is very much an afterthought. Sections, on the other hand, establishes the employer's right to have the building completed in sections on specific dates and the contractor's consent is not required. Each section is treated (almost) like a separate contract with distinct dates for possession and completion, separate amounts for liquidated damages, individual consideration for extensions of time and practical completion. Obviously, the sections are not actually separate contracts. The sections will have been established at tender stage or, at the very latest, when the contract was executed.

Matters can become quite complicated if the project is divided into sections and the employer subsequently decides to take possession of part of one or more sections.

No certificate

It should be noted that the architect does not certify partial possession, but merely records it with a written statement that simply states which part or parts has been taken into possession by the employer and the date when it occurred. This nicely separates the architect from any responsibility for the decision. In practice, it is useful for the architect to incorporate a plan (and perhaps sections) suitably marked up to illustrate the part taken into possession clearly.

Although partial possession is not the same as practical completion, the contract says that practical completion is to be deemed to have occurred for two specific purposes:

2.38
4.20.2

- The start of the rectification period for that part and the subsequent issue of a certificate of making good.
- The issue of a certificate releasing half the retention.

223

When a contract refers to something being *deemed*, the parties to the contract agree to act as though the thing deemed is true although they know it to be false. Although that may appear very strange, it is really simply done for convenience – sometimes it saves a great deal of tedious verbiage in the contract.

Insurance

2.36

If insurance options A or B apply, the obligations of the contractor or of the employer come to an end so far as the part taken into possession is concerned. Where the employer is insuring under option C, the obligation under paragraph C.1 to insure the existing structure must include the part taken into possession.

Liquidated damages

2.37

Liquidated damages reduce proportionately to the value of the amount taken into possession. Therefore, if the total value of the Works is £900,000 and the liquidated damages amount is £900 per week and if £600,000 worth of the

Works is taken into partial possession by the employer, the liquidated damages for the remainder of the Works will be £300.

Partial possession of the whole Works

224

A court has said that if partial possession is taken of the whole of the Works under the partial possession clause, it actually amounts to practical completion of the whole of the Works. The judgment is hardly surprising. What is perhaps surprising is that possession of a whole can be termed *partial*.

21.5   Common problems

If the employer takes partial possession of half the building so that practical completion is deemed to have occurred and the architect certifies practical completion of that part

2.34

When the employer takes partial possession of half the building and the architect issues a statement to the contractor confirming the possession, practical completion is deemed to have occurred for that half. Therefore, there is no need for the architect to issue a practical completion certificate. Indeed, the architect may be unable to issue the certificate because the contractor may not have complied with the requirement to provide information for the health and safety file or as-built drawings.

The employer and the contractor have agreed together that the contractor can have another two weeks extension of time

For the employer to reach an agreement with the contractor in this way, suggests a lack of confidence in the architect that the architect should be at pains to address.

If the employer and the contractor have done this properly and exchanged letters or signed an agreement to that effect, the position is that they have agreed to vary the contract. In that case, they have agreed that the completion date will be two weeks later than the current date. The agreement should be attached to the original contract documents and, if it becomes necessary for the architect to give a further extension, it will be given from the new date.

What the architect must not do is to give an extension of time confirming what the employer and the contractor have agreed. That is because their agreement is not the same as the architect's decision. If the architect issues an extension to confirm their agreement, it amounts to the architect's decision for which he or she will have to take responsibility. If the parties have not put anything in writing, the architect cannot confirm the agreement by means of an architect's instruction (which is often done). The architect must advise the employer that either it must be put into a written agreement or the architect cannot take it into account in any future extensions of time.

After the contractor's insolvency, the employer completed the Works using another contractor and the liquidator of the original contractor is demanding a practical completion certificate for the original contractor

After termination due to contractor insolvency, the employer entered into a new contract with another contractor to complete the Works. A certificate of practical completion cannot be issued to the original contractor, because the original contract was never complete. It is the second (completion) contract that is complete and for which the architect must issue a certificate of practical completion. No further certificates of any kind are to be issued in respect of the first contract.

22 Defects liability

22.1 During construction

The contract sets out a whole series of procedures aimed at assisting the architect to deal with defective work. This is work that the contract refers to as 'work not in accordance with the Contract'. In other words, work that does not comply with the contract documents (for example, the drawings, specifications or bills of quantities) or subsequent instructions. It is obvious that 'defects' may not all be because work is not in accordance with the contract. It may be because the architect has made an error in the information given to the contractor. That is why the contract uses its rather long-winded phrase. For simplicity 'defective work' or 'defects' will be used here to mean defects that are the contractor's responsibility.

Removal from site

3.18.1

225

It is curious that the contract does not refer to rectifying or making good defective work discovered while the project is in progress. It refers to removing it from site. Strangely, the architect has no power to simply order defective work or materials to be rectified. To be effective, the instruction must actually order removal from site. Hopefully, the contractor will usually correct defective work or materials without the necessity of an instruction. In practice most architects, if an instruction is necessary, simply tell the contractor to rectify the defect. Although not strictly correct, most contractors do not seem to query the format of the instruction, but rather whether the defect is actually a defect at all.

Accepting the defect

3.18.2

If the employer agrees, an option is for the architect to issue an instruction to the contractor allowing the defect to remain. Obviously, that will very much depend on the nature of the defect and the employer's attitude. For example, if there is a fault in the finish of some hardwood doors, it is not difficult to remove the doors and attend to the finish. If, however, there is a fault in part of the floor finish, it may be difficult to perform an invisible correction on that part of the

The JCT Standard Building Contract 2011, First Edition. David Chappell.
© 2014 by David Chappell. Published 2014 by John Wiley & Sons, Ltd.

floor, possibly making the repair more obvious than the fault. If the area is large, it may be justified to require the contractor to replace the whole floor, but not usually if the fault is small within a very large floor area. The contractor must be consulted. In other words, its opinion must be sought. But there is nothing that says that the architect must get the contractor's agreement. Obviously, the prudent architect will always give proper consideration to anything the contractor has to say. The architect's instruction is not a variation, but what the contract calls 'an appropriate deduction' must be made from the Contract Sum. The contract is purposely vague, because calculating the right amount of money to deduct will be difficult. It represents compensation to the employer for the difference between what the contractor should have provided and what actually was provided.

Necessary instructions

It may be that, even after the contractor has corrected a defect and certainly after the employer has allowed a defect to remain uncorrected, it is necessary to issue instructions requiring a variation. To the extent that the variation is reasonably necessary as a result of the defect, there will be no addition to the Contract Sum and no extension of time due to the contractor. Again, the contractor must be consulted first but its opinion need not be accepted. Presumably, the purpose of the consultation is because the contractor may be able to suggest
3.18.3   an acceptable alternative.

Other defects

It may be that the architect is concerned that there are similar defects elsewhere in the building. The contract permits the architect to issue instructions to the contractor to open up parts of the Works for inspection or to subject parts to
3.18.4   testing. The instructions must be reasonable taking everything into account. One of the things that the architect must take into account (the contract says that the architect must 'have due regard') is the 'Code of Practice' at the back of
Schedule 4   the contract. There are fifteen points listed in the code ranging from the need to show the employer that the defect is a one off to anything else that may be relevant. The points in the code must be read through and considered in the light of the particular defect concerned. If it is reasonable to issue the instruction and further similar defects are discovered, there is no addition to the Contract Sum or any extension of time due to the contractor for any delay caused by the opening up or testing. If no similar defects are found, the contractor may be entitled to an extension of time, but not to any money. One may envisage a situation where the architect discovers that the foundation to a concrete floor is not properly compacted and the floor develops cracks. This is a serious fault and the architect could use this clause to order cores to be taken in a proportion of other ground-floor floors on the site. The discovery of further lack of compaction under other floors would probably be enough to justify taking a core out of every floor.

22.2   Rectification period

2.38

The contract refers to the rectification period formerly known as the 'defects liability period'. It starts when practical completion is certified or is deemed to have occurred. The length of the period is to be stated in the contract particulars. The change in name appears to be aimed at removing a misconception that was implied by the former name. It was commonly thought, by contractors and architects alike, that at the end of the defects liability period the contractor's liability for any defects in the Works ceased. That was obviously wrong. What does end is the contractor's right to correct the defects (and even that right is limited, as will be seen). Afterwards, the employer is free to take legal action for damages if further defects appear, although in practice the employer will normally be satisfied if the defects are corrected.

22.3   Definition

The period is for the benefit of all parties but principally for that of the contractor. The idea is to allow a specific period of time for defects to appear, list the defects, and give the contractor the opportunity to remedy them. Any defect is a breach of contract on the part of the contractor, who has agreed to carry out the work in accordance with the contract documents. If there was no rectification period, the employer's only remedy for defects would be to take action at common law. So the insertion of the period provides a valuable method of identifying defective work and having it corrected. Without it, the contractor would have no right or duty to return. This is a sensible provision aimed at keeping the costs of making good to a minimum.

Contractors commonly refer to the rectification period as the 'maintenance period'. This is misleading and wrong. Maintenance implies a far greater responsibility than simply making good defects, for example, touching up scuffed paintwork and attention to general wear and tear. Even in other standard form contracts where the term is used (i.e. ACA 3 and GC/Works/1 (1998)), the actual wording of the clause usually restricts the obligation to making good defects.

22.4   Defects, shrinkages or other faults

The contractor is required to make good 'defects, shrinkages, or other faults'. At first sight, this might appear to be all-embracing. In fact the law says that the phrase 'other faults' is to be interpreted as being things of the same kind as what has already been listed. That is to say that they must be faults that are similar to defects or shrinkages. So the list is more restrictive that might at first sight appear. A defect occurs when something is not in accordance with the contract. If an item is in accordance with the contract, it is not defective for the purposes of this clause. It might be less than adequate in some way, but that could be due to a fault in design, and, therefore, the architect's responsibility. Shrinkages are a source of dispute on many contracts. As noted in Section 22.1 above, they become the contractor's liability only if they are due to material or workmanship not in accordance with the contract.

For example, shrinkage most commonly occurs in timber; caused by a reduction in moisture content after the building is heated. It is the architect's job to specify a suitable moisture content for the situation. If shrinkage occurs during the rectification period, it can only be because the timber was supplied with too high a moisture content, or because the architect's assumption about the appropriate moisture content was incorrect. Only the first explanation is the contractor's liability. In practice, it is often very difficult to decide which explanation applies.

22.5 Frost

There is no longer an express reference to frost damage in the contract. There never was the necessity, because the contractor's liability for frost damage follows naturally from its general obligations under the contract.

The contractor is liable to make good frost damage caused by frost that occurred before practical completion – in other words, when the contractor was in control of the building works and could have taken appropriate measures to prevent the damage by introducing heating or stopping vulnerable work. Any damage caused by frost after practical completion is at the employer's own expense. The difference is usually easy to spot on site. Frost damage occurring after practical completion is often due to faulty detailing or maintenance.

22.6 Procedure

The rectification period starts on the date given in the certificate of practical completion as that on which practical completion was achieved or in the case of partial possession, when the statement records that possession of the part took place. The architect is to fill in the length of period required in the contract particulars. If no period is inserted, the length will be six months. The period should be agreed before tender stage with the employer, who will ask for the architect's advice.

Length of period

Although six months is a common rectification period, there are really no good reasons why the period should not be extended to nine or, better, 12 months. Specialist work such as heating often needs a 12-month period to fully test the system through all the seasons of the year. It is possible that a contractor asked to tender for a contract including a 12-month general rectification period would increase its tender figure slightly because it is being kept out of half the retention fund for a longer period; but lengthening the period does not increase its actual liability, only the contractor's right to return to make good defects.

Defects included

2.38

226

The contract simply refers to defects, etc. 'which appear'. Although the time limit is the end of the period, the wording of the clause gives the architect the power to notify the contractor of all the defects that appear, including those that are present at the date of practical completion. Any other interpretation would make nonsense of the contractor's obligations.

Notification

2.38.1

2.38.2

The architect is to notify defects to the contractor not later than 14 days after the expiry of the period. This is normally done as soon as possible after the end of the period. The architect should have inspected just before the period expired. The architect must send the contractor an instruction enclosing a schedule of defects. The architect's power to require defects to be made good is not confined to the issue of the schedule. Notification can be made to the contractor of defects at any time within the period that the architect considers it necessary to do so, but not after the issue of the schedule. Therefore, the architect can issue instructions for making good defects throughout the rectification period if necessary.

Making good

The requirement is for the contractor to make good the defects that are notified. No particular time limit is set, but it must carry out its obligation within a reasonable time. What is a reasonable time will depend on the circumstances, including the number of defects, their type, and any special arrangement to be made with the employer for access.

Ideally, the contractor should return to site within a week or so after receiving the architect's list and bring sufficient labour to make good the defects within, say, a month. If the architect decides to exercise the right to require defects to be made good during the currency of the period, it is good practice to confine such requests to urgent matters in order to be fair to all parties. Obviously, the contractor will find it easier to organise making good of all the defects together rather than visiting the site especially to deal with defects at irregular intervals.

Instructing not to make good

All defects that are the fault of the contractor are to be made good at the contractor's own cost. However, if the employer agrees, the architect may instruct the contractor not to make good some or all of the defects. The architect should obtain a letter from the employer authorising the instruction of the contractor that making good is not required. In that case an appropriate deduction must be made from the Contract Sum.

An appropriate deduction

The contract gives no guidance on the method of arriving at an appropriate deduction. The job is best left to the quantity surveyor. Although no provision is made for the contractor to agree the amount of any such reduction, obviously it must be based on the cost of making the defects good by the contractor itself.

227

Although the architect does not have to give the contractor a reason for not requiring it to make good, instructions will probably be issued for one or three principal reasons:

- if the employer prefers to live with the defects rather than suffer the inconvenience of the contractor returning; or
- if the contractor's work record is so bad during the carrying out of the contract that the architect has no confidence that it will make a satisfactory job of making good; or
- if the contractor has refused or failed to carry out the making good within a reasonable time despite reminders.

In the second and third instances, the architect would probably be justified in obtaining competitive quotations for the rectification work and deducting the amount from the Contract Sum. However, where it is simply for the convenience of the client that the contractor is instructed not to make good, the amount that can be deducted from the Contract Sum would be what it would have cost the contractor to make good.

228

Certificate of making good

When the architect is satisfied that the contractor has properly completed all making good of defects that have been notified, a certificate to that effect must be issued. The certificate is important because it marks one of the dates starting the 2-month period within which the final certificate must be issued.

2.39
4.15.1.2

The certificate of making good is something else that is much misunderstood. It is specifically stated to refer to the defects, shrinkages or other faults that the architect has instructed the contractor to make good. The architect cannot lawfully withhold the issue of the certificate because further defects have come to light after the end of the rectification period. There is no doubt that the contractor is liable for any later defects, but they are not defects to which the certificate is intended to relate. Ultimately, later defects may have to be dealt with by means of a deduction by the employer from the amount certified in the final certificate subject to the issue of the relevant pay less notices. Moreover, if the architect with the employer's consent has instructed the contractor that some of the defects previously notified must not be made good, the certificate of making good can be issued provided that the rest of the defects notified have been made good.

2.38

4.15.4

22.7   Common problems

The contractor is not dealing with defects notified at the end of the rectification period

The contract says that the contractor must deal with defects within a reasonable time after receiving a schedule of defects in an instruction of the architect. What is a reasonable time will depend on the circumstances; the complexity of the defects in particular. If the contractor does not act within a reasonable time,

3.11 the architect should send a letter requiring it to comply within 7 days. If the contractor does not comply, the architect should instruct the contractor not to

2.38 make good the defects and the employer can arrange for another contractor to do the work. In this instance, the whole of the cost including any additional architectural fees may be deducted from the Contract Sum. Therefore, the final account will show that figure deducted.

The contract particulars show six months as the rectification period for the Works generally, but twelve months for electrical and mechanical work

It is quite common, but wrong, to find two separate periods being inserted into the contract particulars. Unless the Works are divided into sections, there can be only one rectification period for the whole of the Works. If two rectification periods are stated, there must be two certificates of making good and two releases of retention. Unless sections are employed, the contract does not allow two certificates of making good or the release of the second half of the retention in two parts. If it is desired to have a longer rectification period for electrical and mechanical work, it is necessary to make the M and E work into a separate section. To operate that in practice of course means separate extensions of time and separate section completion certificates. It is probably easier to simply make the rectification period twelve months for everything.

The architect has deducted the cost of a new carpet from a certificate, because the contractor seriously damaged it when making good a defect in the floor

The architect is not entitled to do that. The carpet is not part of the Works but something that the employer has had fitted following practical completion. The architect can only deal with the Works. The way to deal with this is for the employer to issue a pay less notice when the architect issues the next certificate, probably the final certificate, and the employer can then recover the costs of damage to the carpet in that way. The architect should advise the employer of that approach.

23 Termination

23.1 General points

Although people talk about bringing the contract to an end, what they usually mean is that they are bringing their obligations under the contract to an end, leaving the contract in place, because many contracts have provisions to deal with the consequences of termination. SBC is no exception to that. The termination clauses in SBC refer to termination of the contractor's employment under the contract. It is important to understand that if there were no termination clauses in the contract, the only way to bring the employment of the contractor to an end would be in accordance with one of the ways under the general law of contract. Under the general or common law obligations, and sometimes the contract itself, can be brought to an end in several ways. The fact that there is a termination clause does not prevent either the employer or the contractor from ending obligations under the common law if they decide that it suits them better to do it that way. Under the common law obligations/the contract can be brought to an end by:

- performance; or
- agreement; or
- frustration; or
- breach and its acceptance; or
- operation of law; or
- novation.

We will look at these in order.

Performance

This is obviously the best way of bringing obligations and the contract to an end, because both parties have carried out their obligations under the contract and nothing further remains to be done. The purpose for which the contract was created is satisfied and the contractual relationship ceases.

The JCT Standard Building Contract 2011, First Edition. David Chappell.
© 2014 by David Chappell. Published 2014 by John Wiley & Sons, Ltd.

Agreement

Agreement of all parties is also a good way to bring the contract to an end. The best way to do that is to enter into another contract whose sole purpose is to end the first contract. In most cases, when a contract is ended by mutual agreement it is because each party gains something; which is essential for a valid contract. Sometimes that may not be very clear and it is sensible for the parties to execute the agreement to end the contract as a deed that will avoid that problem.

Frustration

230

Frustration occurs when, without fault on either side, a contract cannot be performed because changed circumstances would alter the performance to something radically different from that which the parties agreed to do. The fact that a contractor experiences greater difficulty in carrying out the contract or that it costs it far more than it could reasonably have expected is not sufficient ground for frustration. A contract will not be frustrated by the something that happens but that has already been taken into account in the contract. If prop-

231

erty in which a contractor was to install a new heating system was totally

232

destroyed by fire, that would be frustration of the heating contract.

Where a contract is discharged by frustration, both parties are excused from further obligations and money already paid under the contract is recoverable, but if the party to whom sums were paid or payable has incurred expenses, or has already acquired some benefit from the contract, that has to be sorted out;

233

usually by a court. In practice, it is very rare for a contract to be frustrated.

Breach

234

Sometimes one of the parties commits a breach of contract that is so serious it entitles the other party to accept it and cease all further obligations under the contract. Such a breach must strike at the very root of the contract. Under a building contract that could occur if the client prevents the architect from issuing extensions of time and financial certificates and engages another architect to complete the work. That would be a very clear repudiation of the architect's terms of engagement by the client. Acts of repudiation are often less clear (see Chapter 1, Section 1.1).

Not every breach of contract by one party will entitle the other to refuse to perform its own obligations; the breach must be such as makes clear an intention to repudiate the whole of the contractual obligations. The innocent party can either accept a repudiation and sue at once for damages; or it can continue to perform its obligations under the contract and hold the other party liable for

235

all the money due under the contract. Of course, that applies only if the innocent party is capable of performing its own obligations under the contract. For example, if contractors are refused possession of the site, they have no option but to accept the repudiation, because they cannot then lawfully enter upon and occupy the site.

Operation of law

This is included for completeness, but it is very unlikely that an architect will encounter this situation. Essentially, it may occur if one of the parties becomes bankrupt or sufficient time passes to stop the contract remaining effective. How much time will depend on all the circumstances.

Novation

Most architects and contractor encounter this when an architect working on the design of a building signs a novation agreement and works for the contractor instead of the employer. Novation is replacement of one contract by another usually with a change in the identity of one of the parties although the terms of the second contract are often very similar to the terms of the first. Invariably, this method of bringing a contract to an end is by agreement of all parties.

23.2   Termination by the employer

Termination is one of those things that is best avoided. If it is impossible to avoid, it must be done properly, or the consequences will be unpleasant for the employer. The whole procedure is surrounded by difficulties and pitfalls for the unwary. Among them are the following.

Some problems

If termination is properly carried out, the employer will be faced with a project to finish with the aid of another contractor. In theory, the employer can recover all the costs from the first contractor, but of course the employer cannot recover the time lost. Even the recovery of costs is likely to be uncertain unless the amount of retention is greater than the amount to be recovered so that a simple deduction can be made. If termination is not properly carried out, the contractor may be able to bring an action for damages for unlawful repudiation of the

236

contract. Many of the grounds for termination may give rise to dispute.

The employer will look to the architect for advice on whether or not to terminate the contractor's employment. Indeed, it will probably be the architect who brings the matter to the attention of the employer. This will often be because the situation on site has deteriorated to such a stage that the architect is pessimistic about the chances of ever achieving completion. Ideally, termination should be set in motion before that stage is reached, but in practice it is difficult to decide just when there is no hope of recovering the situation. These

8.3.1
8
6.11 and
paragraph
C.4.4 of
Schedule 3

provisions are without prejudice to the employer's other rights and remedies.

The procedure for termination is set out in a flowchart in Figure 23.1. The provisions for termination in the contract cover termination by the employer, by the contractor, or by either party. There are provisions for termination under insurance and terrorism situations, confusingly not all in the same place. Notices are very important. A notice is simply a letter setting out whatever the

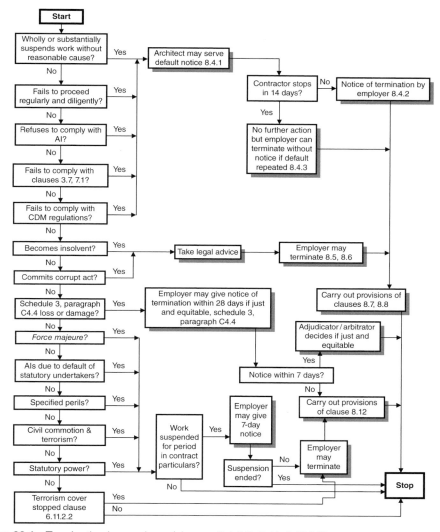

Figure 23.1   Termination by employer (clauses 8.4-8.6, 8.11, 6.11.2.2).

notice is supposed to say. All notices must be given by hand delivery or by special delivery or recorded signed for post. Notice is deemed to have been received on the second business day after the date of posting unless one of the parties can prove to the contrary.

1.7.4 and 8.2.3

23.3   Grounds: contractor's defaults

There are five separate grounds for termination before practical completion has been certified. They are that the contractor:

8.4.1

■   wholly or substantially suspends the carrying out of the Works without reasonable cause; or

- fails to proceed regularly and diligently with the Works; or
- refuses or neglects to comply with a written notice from the architect requiring it to remove defective work or improper materials or goods and, as a result, the Works are materially affected; or
- fails to comply with certain contract provisions about consent to sub-contracting or assignment; or
- fails to comply with the contract requirements about CDM Regulations.

7.1, 3.7

3.23

Procedure

If the architect believes that actions or inactions on the part of the contractor fall into one of these categories, the architect may issue a default notice to the contractor. A prudent architect will advise the employer of the possibility of the architect issuing a default notice followed by termination of the contractor's employment if it does not rectify the default. An architect who fails to issue a default notice or to advise the employer that it should be issued may be guilty of professional negligence. The default notice is a serious step and although the contract does not require the architect to obtain the employer's consent before it is issued, it is always wise to do so. The architect may issue a default notice and it is then open to the employer whether or not to issue a termination notice. The procedure must be followed precisely. The contractor must be served with a notice of default, which must clearly specify the default. It is very important that the architect says precisely what is wrong. The architect must send the letter. It must be sent by special delivery, recorded signed for post or by hand delivery. It is wise to obtain a receipt for hand delivery. If the contractor continues the default for 14 days after receipt of the notice, the employer may terminate the contractor's employment by a further notice by special delivery or recorded signed for post or hand delivery. It is usual for the architect to draft the letter for the employer's signature. The employer has twenty one days from the end of the 14 days in which to serve the termination notice.

237

238

Key points

There are two important points. First, if the contractor stops its default within the 14 days, the employer can take no immediate action. If the employer has the right, but does not give notice of termination within the twenty one day period and if the contractor repeats the same default at any time afterwards, the employer may terminate immediately or within a reasonable time without the necessity for a further 14 days' notice. This is a very powerful remedy in the hands of the employer.

Secondly, the notice of termination must not be given unreasonably or vexatiously. There must be no malice or intention to annoy. This is particularly applicable to the case where the contractor has stopped a default for some weeks or months but commits the same default again. Special care must be taken that a charge of unreasonableness cannot successfully be levelled at the employer.

239

Despite the provisions of the contract that say that the employer may issue a notice of termination without another notice, it would be prudent for the architect to send a warning letter, being careful to state that it is not a notice of default, because a further notice of default would be invalid and could lead to complications. But a simple warning letter lets the contractor know that the employer intends to exercise the right to terminate. Usually, that will be sufficient to stop the default immediately. If it does not, the employer would certainly not be acting unreasonably in then terminating the contractor's employment. Great care must be taken that the latest default is the same as the original default. There is certainly scope for a contractor to challenge a termination on those grounds. If there is any doubt, the termination procedure should be set in train again.

240

Considering the grounds

Before the architect advises the employer to give notice, the five grounds must be carefully considered:

8.4.1.1

Wholly or substantially suspends the carrying out of the Works, etc.:

The contractor need not have completely ceased work. If a contractor, in the middle of a million pound contract, has only one or two men on site doing some work, it would not be regarded as having wholly suspended the Works, but it would certainly have substantially done so. This ground appears to be intended to cover the situation where the contractor has, in effect, abandoned the work or most of it. Note that the suspension must be without reasonable cause. Before the architect sends the initial notice of default, it would be sensible to ask the contractor why it has stopped. The course of action would depend on the reply. For example, the contractor might have suspended work for some reason that entitled it to an extension of time. It might have suspended as a right under the contract because the employer had failed to pay some money due to the contractor.

4.14

8.4.1.2

Fails to proceed regularly and diligently with the Works:

This ground is more than simply failing to keep to a programme. The contractor's programme is not a contract document and, therefore, it is not obliged to comply with it. It may be a good indication of the contractor's intentions. It is sometimes suggested that a contractor will be able to argue its way out of any termination on this ground if any progress at all is being made. That is not correct (see Chapter 6, Section 6.5 for an explanation of 'regularly and diligently').

241

8.4.1.3

Refuses or neglects to comply, etc.:

Refusal to comply with the architect's instructions to remove defective work can be dealt with by the issue of a seven-day compliance notice. If the contractor does not comply within 7 days, the employer may engage others to do the work. Even one-off instances of neglect are covered in appropriate

3.11

circumstances. There would be no question of the instance being used improperly because it would be used in accordance with the contract provisions. However, this ground is probably intended to cover the situation when the contractor ignores instructions to such an extent that the work is in danger of grinding to a halt. It would also refer to the case where so much work is defective work that further work cannot be done without 'building in' the defective work and necessitating any future satisfactory work being taken down to make good the defective parts. The work on site would have to be in a very sorry state before termination should be attempted under this ground.

8.4.1.4   *Fails to comply with certain contractual provisions about consent to sub-contracting and assignment*

3.7

The object of the prohibition on sub-contracting without consent is to prevent the contractor from arranging for another contractor to carry out part of the Works. Because sub-contracting is traditional in the building industry, the contract makes provision for it provided that the architect consents. If the contractor does sub-let without consent, the architect must decide whether the sub-contractor is suitable. If it is, there would seem to be no point, and little chance of success, in trying to terminate the contract. Even if the sub-contractor is clearly unsuitable, a less draconian method of dealing with the situation, probably by a letter, would probably be appropriate. Termination under this ground is best reserved for the occasions when the contractor sub-lets the whole or large portions of the Works without the architect's approval.

7.1

Neither party may assign the contract without the written consent of the other. If the contractor tries to do so, the architect may issue a default notice. Attempting to assign the right to payment is clearly a serious matter.

8.4.1.5   *Fails to comply with contractual requirements regarding the CDM Regulations*

3.23

Essentially, this ground refers to a failure on the part of the contractor to comply with the contractual provision that obliges it to comply with the duties of the principal contractor if the contractor takes that role and, if not, it must comply with all the reasonable requirements of the principal contractor. The contractor must also ensure that each sub-contractor provides information reasonably required for the health and safety file. Termination may seem a severe remedy, but where health and safety is at stake and criminal penalties are heavy, the employer must take decisive action.

23.4   Grounds: insolvency of contractor

8.1

Insolvency is defined in considerable detail. It includes company administration, receivership and winding up, individual bankruptcy, arrangement or composition of debts. Even when a receiver or manager is appointed, it may be in the best interests of the employer to continue the contract. This can be decided only after a thorough discussion between all parties concerned. The employer would also be prudent to obtain legal advice regarding the implications in a particular case. The contractor's employment may be reinstated if agreement can be reached between the employer and the contractor. If the contractor is insolvent, the employer may at any time terminate the contractor's employment by written notice that should be given by special delivery, recorded signed for post or by hand delivery. Termination is effective on the date the notice is received by the contractor. The contractor must immediately inform the employer if insolvency is likely, but often this is not done.

8.5

8.5.2

23.5   Grounds: corruption

The employer may terminate the contractor's employment:

- if the contractor has given or received bribes in connection with this or any other contract with the employer;
- or if the contractor commits any other offence in relation to the contract or any other contract with the employer under the Bribery Act 2010;
- or if the employer is a local authority, under section 117(2) of the Local Government Act 1972.

A most onerous part of the provisions of this clause, so far as the contractor is concerned, is the fact that its employment may be terminated because of the corrupt actions of one of its employees or of some person acting on the contractor's behalf. That is the case even though the contractor may have no knowledge of the affair.

In any case, corruption is a criminal offence for which there are strict penalties, and the employer is entitled at common law to rescind the contract and/or recover any secret commissions.

Legal advice is indicated, followed by a simple notice of termination, if that is the decision.

23.6   Grounds: neutral causes

The employer (or the contractor) may terminate the contractor's employment if the carrying out of the whole or substantially the whole of the uncompleted Works is suspended for two months, or whatever period is entered in the contract particulars, because of *force majeure*; architect's instructions regarding discrepancies, variations or postponement issued as a result of negligence or default of a statutory undertaking; loss or damage to the Works caused by specified perils; civil commotion or terrorist activity; or the exercise by the UK Government of any statutory power directly affecting the Works.

8.11

For either party to operate this clause, the Works must be totally lacking in any significant progress for the entire period as a result of the same cause. One week of frenzied activity on the part of the contractor, in the middle of the period, may be sufficient to prejudice any attempt at termination, even if the site relapses into inactivity thereafter. It is probable, however, that the period must be viewed as a whole. It seems doubtful that a contractor could succeed in delaying termination just by spasmodic bouts of activity at widely spaced intervals.

A seven-day period of notice is required at the end of the specified period during which work has been suspended. The notice, which must be given by special delivery, recorded signed for post or by hand delivery, must state that unless the suspension is ended within seven days after receipt of the notice, the employment of the contractor may be terminated. If the suspension does not end, the employer may, by further written notice by special delivery, recorded signed for post or by hand delivery, terminate the contractor's employment. The notice must not be given unreasonably or vexatiously.

All the causes of suspension are events beyond the control of the parties. They have all been discussed when considering extensions of time (see Chapter 14, Section 14.3). It is likely that both parties will be relieved to bring the contractor's employment to an end in such circumstances.

23.7   Grounds: insurance risks and terrorism cover

Schedule 3
Option C

If the employer has been responsible for taking out insurance for work in or extensions to existing structures, the employer (or the contractor) may terminate the contractor's employment if there is significant loss or damage to those structures caused by any risks covered by the Joint Names Policy. The contractor must give notice in writing to the architect and to the employer as soon as the damage is discovered. The notice must state the extent, nature and location of the damage. Although the 28 days begin to run from the occurrence and not from the notification, in practice if the damage is likely to be such as to form the basis for termination, it will be discovered and notified immediately it occurs.

Option C.4.4

If either the employer or the contractor believes that the damage is significant, one should give notice to the other by special delivery, recorded signed for post or by hand delivery within the same 28-day period. The contract makes clear that termination may only take place 'if it is just and equitable. This goes to the heart of the matter and points to the difference between this ground for termination and termination for neutral causes, which requires a long period of suspension. What is just and equitable depends on the particular circumstances. The sort of situation in which termination would clearly be just and equitable involves such catastrophic damage that it is uncertain not only when work could recommence but whether work could recommence at all. Consider the case of a large shopping complex, worth several million pounds. It may be that a small alteration and extension contract is let, worth £150,000. If, during the course of the work, the whole complex is totally destroyed by fire, it will be just and equitable to terminate the contractor's employment. (In that case, the contract may also be considered to be frustrated under the general law.) Even much less than total destruction in such circumstances would give grounds for termination under this paragraph.

Either party is entitled to seek adjudication or whichever of arbitration or legal proceedings has been chosen in the contract particulars on the question of whether it is just and equitable. The right is limited in two ways:

- The procedures must be invoked within seven days of receipt of a notice of termination.
- The procedure is to decide whether termination will be just and equitable.

It is, at best, doubtful whether this attempted restriction will be effective in the case of the right to adjudicate, which is backed by statute and exercisable at any time.

Terrorism cover

If terrorism cover ceases to become available, the contract provides that on receipt of a notice from the insurers, the employer may give written notice to the contractor stating that the contractor's employment will terminate on a stated date. The date must be after the insurer's notice, but before the date on *6.11.2.2*   which the terrorism cover is to cease.

23.8   Consequences of termination for contractor's default or insolvency

Particular consequences of insolvency

Although the contractor's insolvency will bring on the same consequences as for its default or corruption, there are some particular consequences only applicable to insolvency. It is important to note that it is the contractor's insolvency that triggers these consequences and not a notice of termination. The consequences apply even if no notice of termination is given by the employer. There are three consequences:

- The provisions regarding the cessation of further payment, an account for the Works after completion and making good defects and if the employer does not wish to complete are to apply as if notice of termination has been given, but other contract terms requiring further payment to the contractor or any release of retention, will not apply. Therefore, it seems that even if an interim certificate has already been issued, the employer is not obliged to pay it. It is probable that this extends to the situation where the employer is *8.5.3.1*   actually already in default of payment.
- The contractor's obligation to carry out and complete the Works is said to be suspended, but there is no indication when such suspension might end. It is likely that the suspension is intended to take effect at insolvency and a notice of termination from the employer would make the suspension a permanent cessation. The point of this provision is that, when insolvency occurs, the contractor is not in breach of contract by failing to proceed with *8.5.3.2*   the Works.

■ The employer is entitled to take reasonable measures to ensure that the site, the Works and materials on site are adequately protected and to make sure that the materials are kept on site. This is because, on hearing of the contractor's insolvency, many unpaid suppliers will attempt to recover unfixed materials. Whether or not they are entitled to do so will depend on many factors and the employer must take specialist advice. The contractor is to allow the employer to take these measures and not to hinder or delay them. In practice, if the contractor is insolvent, it is unlikely to take other than a passive role. A receiver or liquidator may potentially cause problems and these provisions should go some way to preventing such problems from developing.

8.5.3.3

General consequences

The general consequences of termination for the contractor's default, insolvency or corruption are as follows:

■ The employer may employ another contractor to complete the Works and any design part of the CDP and the employer and the other contractor may take possession of the site. The completion of a partly finished building by another contractor is always an expensive procedure. In order to avoid a potential dispute, it is wise to take extensive photographic records of the state of the building and have a full inspection carried out to record the work done and what is yet to be done together with any defective work and then have bills of quantities prepared for the completion work and to go out to tender in the normal way. This will prevent the original contractor from saying that the employer has not obtained a reasonable price.

8.7.1

■ The employer may use any temporary buildings, etc. for the benefit of a subsequent contractor. The architect should advise the employer whether use of the contractor's plant is desirable and may constitute a saving. If it is decided not to use it, the architect should instruct the original contractor to remove it from the Works.

8.7.2.1

■ Although not expressly stated, the contractor must give up possession of the site of the Works. If the contractor does not do so within a reasonable time after receiving the notice of termination, it will become a trespasser, and the architect should send it a letter pointing that out. The contractor's liability for insurance ceases, and the employer must take out appropriate insurance cover without delay. This is best done at the time the notice of termination is sent and the architect should remind the employer about this. The contract does not say that the contractor must ensure that the Works are left in a safe condition, but the contractor (like anyone else) has a duty of care to those it can reasonably foresee could suffer injury. The contractor must not, therefore, leave any part of the building in a precarious condition.

■ The contractor must provide the employer with copies of all the CPD documents then prepared.

8.7.2.2

■ Until the Works are complete and defects during the rectification period are made good, no money will become due to the contractor except as a result of the final accounting. Even where money has already become due, the employer is not bound, and would not be wise, to make any further payment to the original contractor if the employer has issued a pay less notice. No money need be paid if the contractor has become insolvent since the last date when a pay less notice could have been given.

8.7.3

8.7.4

■ When the contract is completed and any defects made good and the subsequent contractor paid in full, the employer or the architect must draw up a set of accounts. In most cases, it will be left to the architect, probably with the assistance of the quantity surveyor, to prepare the accounts. If the Employer prepares them, they are referred to as a 'statement' but if the architect prepares them, they are called a 'certificate'. This is not an interim or final certificate under the payment provisions of the contract. It is an entirely different certificate. Indeed, it is simply the account prefaced by words something like: 'I certify that this is an accurate account prepared in accordance with clause 8.7.4 of the contract.' The accounts must show:

— All the expenses and direct loss and/or damage caused to the employer by the termination. It will include the cost of completing the contract, including all professional fees consequent on the termination, the cost of engaging another contractor and if appropriate the cost of securing the site after insolvency.

— The amount paid to the original contractor before termination.

— The amount that would have been payable for the Works.

If the total of the first two amounts is greater or less than what would have been paid had the contract been completed in the normal way, the difference is a debt payable by the original contractor to the employer, or *vice versa*.

Invariably, the contractor owes a debt to the employer. The architect must carefully calculate, with the assistance of the quantity surveyor, the final amounts. It is essential that, on paper at least, the employer has been put in the same position as would have been the case had the contract not been terminated but had continued in an orderly way to its conclusion. Obtaining payment from a contractor who may be insolvent is another matter.

If the employer decides not to complete

8.8 ; 242

The employer has the option to decide not to complete the Works. The employer has six months from the date of termination to decide. If the employer opts not to complete the Works, a written notification must be sent to the contractor. Within a reasonable time afterwards the contractor must be sent a statement (no doubt the architect or quantity surveyor will actually prepare it) that must set out:

■ the total value of work properly carried out at termination or at the date of insolvency and any other amounts due to the contractor under the contract; and

■ the expenses and direct loss and/or damage caused to the employer for which the contractor is liable whether that is due to the termination or some other cause.

The employer must take account of amounts previously paid and calculate the resultant balance due to the contractor or to the employer. The likelihood is that the employer will do rather worse under this system than if the employer opts to complete the Works. That is because under this system latent defects in the Works may not make themselves known until some time after the financial aspects of the termination have been settled. Contrast that to the situation where the employer immediately continues the Works using a new contractor. By the time the Works are complete and all defects are rectified at the end of the rectification period, the employer should be fully aware of all the financial implications and there will be less likelihood of defects remaining latent.

23.9   Consequences of termination for neutral causes or insurance risks

The consequences of termination covered by these clauses are covered in Sections 23.15 and 23.1.

23.10   Termination by the contractor

If the contractor is successful in terminating its employment under the contract, the results for the employer will be catastrophic. Among the consequences are these:

- The employer will be left with the project to complete with another contractor. Completion bills of quantities must be prepared, and a great deal of additional expense will be incurred in the form of increased cost of completion and additional professional fees without being able to claim these costs from the contractor. The employer will be looking around to blame, and possibly take legal action against, someone; possibly one or all of the professional team.
- The completion date will be considerably exceeded.
- Under some of the grounds for termination, the contractor is entitled to receive loss of the profit it expected to make on the whole contract.

243

The procedure for termination by the contractor is set out in a flowchart in Figure 23.2.

23.11   Grounds: employer's defaults

There are five separate grounds for termination and they are as follows:

- The employer does not pay the contractor by the final date for payment the amount properly due under any certificate including VAT.
- The employer interferes with, or obstructs, the issue of any certificates.
- The employer fails to comply with the assignment provisions.
- The employer fails to comply according to the contract with the CDM Regulations.

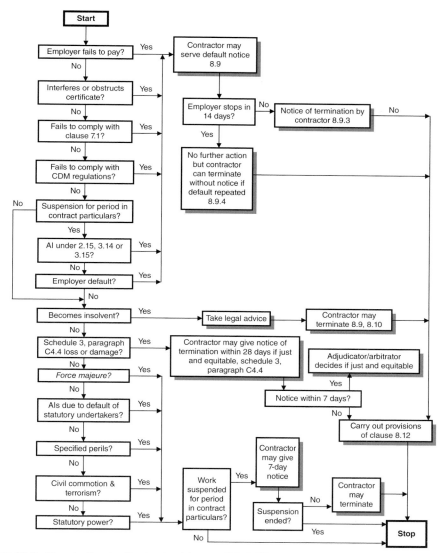

Figure 23.2   Termination by Contractor (clauses 8.9–8.11).

■ The carrying out of the whole or substantially the whole of the Works is suspended for a continuous period of two months or whatever period is stated in the contract particulars due to one of the following reasons:

2.15, 3.14,   — Architect's instructions in regard to discrepancies; or variations; or
3.15   postponement;

            — any impediment or default of the employer, the architect, the quantity surveyor or any of the employer's persons.

Unless, of course, it is caused by the contractor's default or negligence.

If the contractor decides to terminate on any of the above grounds, the procedure must be followed precisely, otherwise the contractor may be simply attempting unlawful repudiation of the contract. The contractor must send a notice to the employer (not to the architect) by special or recorded delivery or by hand delivery, specifying one of the matters referred to in this clause. The contract differentiates

8.9.1,
8.9.2

between the first four grounds that it calls 'specified defaults', and the fourth ground dealing with suspension that it calls 'specified suspension events'. The difference appears to be based on grammatical rather than contractual necessities. They will all be referred to here as 'matters' for convenience. If the employer continues the default in respect of the notified matter for 14 days after receipt of the notice, the contractor may within 21 days serve notice, by special delivery or recorded delivery or hand delivery, to terminate its employment under the contract.

The remarks regarding postage of notices in Section 23.3 above are applicable.

8.9.4

The contractor has the same important power to terminate its employment within a reasonable time if the matter is repeated as is given to the employer. This means in theory that if the employer, having defaulted once and been given notice, defaults a second time in payment by only one day or if a suspension event is repeated even for a relatively short period, and the regular progress of the Works is substantially affected as a result, the contractor can serve notice of termination. In practice, such a step might be held to be unreasonable or vexatious. But there would be nothing unreasonable in the contractor's giving notice of termination if the payment on a second occasion was a week late or almost the whole of the Works were suspended for a second time for a week. Most contractors are reluctant to terminate because it gives them a bad reputation, whatever the reason. So in all likelihood and prudently, the contractor will send a warning letter in the event of a second default. However, as is the case with a letter in the same circumstances sent by the employer, the letter must make clear that it is not another default or suspension notice.

Before taking any steps along the road to terminating its employment the contractor should consider the five grounds carefully.

8.9.1.1

The employer does not pay the contractor by the final date for payment, etc.

This is the employer's responsibility. The architect must make the employer aware, at the beginning of the contract, that prompt payment is vital. The con-

4.9

tractor's entitlement to payment arises on the due dates (see Chapter 19 for a full explanation of the payment provisions). The amount will often be the sum certified in the architect's certificate, but that is not always the case. If the architect fails to issue the certificate within 5 days of the due date, the amount due will be either:

- the amount in any interim application made by the contractor no later than 7 days before the due date; or
- if no such application has been made, it will be the amount on any interim payment notice that may be given to the employer after the expiry of the five-day period from the due date. In that case, the final date for payment will be regarded as postponed by the same number of days from the end of

4.12

the five-day period until the notice is given.

If the architect issues a certificate within five days of the due date, or if no certificate is issued but the contractor has issued an interim application for

4.12.1

payment no less than 7 days before the due date, the final date for payment remains the same as stated in the contract. Let us call the due date Day 7. If no certificate has been issued before the end of Day 12 and if no interim application for payment has been made by the contractor before Day 1, but if an interim payment notice has been issued by the contractor on, say, Day 16, the final date for payment is postponed by the number of days between Day 12 and Day 16 (i.e. 4). Therefore, the final date for payment would be 14 + 4 days after Day 7.

If the architect is acting properly, the amount due will be the amount in the architect's certificate. Therefore, the architect's responsibility is to ensure that the certificate is issued promptly and that the employer receives the certificate promptly. This perhaps needs stressing. There are still both architects and contractors who wrongly think the payment period does not begin to run until the contractor presents its copy of the certificate to the employer. Where possible, financial certificates should always be delivered by hand and a receipt obtained. If that is not practical, they should be sent by 'next day' special delivery.

8.9.1.2

The employer interferes with or obstructs the issue of any certificate

It is important to note that this ground refers to any certificate, not merely financial certificates. There are other certificates (Table 4.3) that the architect is required to issue that the employer conceivably may try to prevent. It will, of course, be difficult for the contractor to prove that the employer is obstructing the issue of a certificate unless the architect or the employer tells the contractor. The architect has a clear duty under the contract to issue certificates. It must be made plain to the employer that the employer who tries to interfere with that duty is in breach of contract. If, despite the warning, the employer absolutely forbids the architect to issue a certificate, the architect is in a difficult position. The architect's duty is then to write and confirm the instructions received, setting out the consequences to the employer. The architect has no duty to deliberately inform the contractor, but if the contractor suspects and terminates anyway, the architect will not be able to deny the facts in any proceedings that may follow.

8.9.1.3

The employer failing to comply with the assignment provisions

7.1

This refers to the prohibition on assignment that states that neither party may assign the contract without the written consent of the other. Assignment of rights and duties can only be done effectively by novation, but if the employer tried to assign the right to the completed building to another person, it would be a serious matter for which the contractor could terminate.

8.9.1.4

The employer failing to comply according to the contract with the CDM Regulations

3.23

This clause refers to a failure on the part of the employer to comply with the contract provisions regarding the CDM Regulations. The employer must ensure that the CDM co-ordinator carries out his or her duties correctly. If, unusually, the contractor is not the principal contractor under the Regulations, the employer must ensure that the principal contractor also carries out its duties properly. If the contractor notifies any amendment to the construction phase plan, the employer must notify the CDM co-ordinator and the architect immediately. If the employer fails to comply, the contractor should not hesitate to threaten termination, because the consequences of failure to comply with the Regulations are serious. Contractors should also remember that an employer may be taking that role once in a lifetime and should be properly advised on the responsibilities by the architect.

8.9.2

The carrying out of the whole or substantially the whole of the Works is suspended for a continuous period of two months or whatever period is stated in the contract particulars

If the carrying out of virtually the whole of the Works is suspended for the specified period for either of the reasons set out, the contractor may terminate as described.

The first reason relates to the architect issuing instructions regarding the correction of discrepancies, instructions requiring a variation, or instructions postponing the carrying out of the Works. If the contractor is delayed for two months as a result, it will be in very serious trouble. For any period up to or exceeding two months, it would be entitled of course to put together a claim for loss and/or

4.23

expense. For any contractor handling this value of work, a two-month delay could be disastrous. This clause quite reasonably gives the contractor the option of termination if it foresees no quick end to the suspension and it feels unable to afford to keep the site open. The clause emphasises that the delay must not be due to the contractor's own negligence or default, but that is pretty obvious.

The second reason is any impediment or default of the employer, the architect, the quantity surveyor or and of the employer's persons. The very broad, catch-all clause replaces a series of clauses in earlier editions that included a failure of the architect to provide information on time, work or materials that the employer was going to supply and the employer's failure to provide access. The new clause renders them all redundant, because they are all examples of default by the employer or persons engaged or authorised by the employer.

23.12   Grounds: insolvency of employer

8.5

The grounds for termination under this clause are the same as for the contractor's insolvency (see Section 23.4 above). Termination is not automatic, and notice must be served by special or recorded or hand delivery. It takes effect on

8.2.2

receipt by the employer. It is highly unlikely that the contractor would wish to continue and take its chance of being paid. After the employer becomes insolvent and before the notice of termination takes effect, the contractor's

8.10.3

obligation to proceed and complete the Works is suspended. This is to avoid the silly situation that would otherwise exist during this, probably brief, period when the contractor would be legally obliged to continue until it could terminate its employment. The contractor must be given notice in writing if the employer makes a proposal, calls a meeting or becomes subject to proceedings or appointment in regard to any of the insolvency matters listed in the contract.

23.13   Grounds: neutral causes

8.11.2

The grounds for termination under this clause have already been covered in Section 23.6 above. If the contractor wishes to terminate, however, there is a condition to the effect that it is not entitled to give notice if the loss or damage due to specified perils is caused by the contractor's own negligence or default or of its servants or agents or anyone employed on the Works other than the employer or a person engaged by the employer or by a local authority or statutory undertaking carrying out work solely in accordance with statutory obligations. This proviso is only expressly stating what must be implied – that the contractor must not be able to profit as a consequence of its own default.

244

23.14   Grounds: insurance risks and terrorism cover

The grounds and procedure for termination under this clause are exactly the same as for the employer (see Section 23.7 above).

23.15   Consequences of termination for employer's default, neutral causes or insolvency of the employer, etc.

6.10.2.2, 8.9,
8.10, 8.11 and
paragraph
C.4.4 of
Schedule 3

The contract lays down the procedure to be followed after termination resulting from the employer's default, employer's insolvency, neutral causes, the non-availability of terrorism cover or loss or damage to existing structures etc. The following should be noted:

8.12.3

- Any terms of the contract that require further payment will cease to apply except as a result of the submission of the contractor's account.
- The contractor must remove from site all its temporary buildings, plant, equipment etc., but no doubt a contractor in this position would not need any encouragement to do so.
- The contractor must provide the employer with copies of as-built drawings.
- There is no express provision for the contractor to give up possession of the site, which is a pity, but if the contractor has removed all its plant, etc. already, it can hardly claim to be in possession.
- The contractor's liability to insure the Works ends at termination, and the architect must immediately remind the employer to insure.
- Without wasting any time the contractor must prepare an account setting out the following:
  - The total value of the work done at the date of termination together with any other amounts due under the terms of the contract (e.g., reimbursement of premiums, fees, etc.).

— Direct loss and/or expense.
— Costs of removal from site.
— The cost of materials properly ordered for the Works and for which the contractor has paid or is legally obliged to pay (i.e. because a contract has been entered into). Materials properly ordered are those that it is reasonable that the contractor has ordered at the time of termination. In deciding whether something has been properly ordered the suitability of the materials and the delivery period must be taken into account. Obviously, materials paid for become the property of the employer.
— Any direct loss and/or damage caused to the contractor by the termination. This is potentially the most damaging clause to the employer, depending on the value of the contract remaining incomplete. Quite rightly, and in accordance with normal contract principles, the contractor is to be paid the profit it would have expected to have made if the contract had run its course. Loss and/or expense is only to be included if the termination is as a result of the employer's default, the employer's insolvency or where the loss or damage to the Works due to specified perils resulted from the negligence or default of the employer or persons authorised or acting as agents of the employer.
— Any sums previously paid to the contractor to be deducted.

8.12.4

The employer must pay the amount properly due within 28 days of its submission by the contractor and without deducting any retention. The employer will clearly require the architect and the quantity surveyor (if appointed) to check the account, and the employer's obligation is merely to pay the amount properly due. If it is intended to pay less than the balance shown on the contractor's account, the employer should issue a written notice to the contractor to that effect within 5 days of receiving the account. The notice should demonstrate

245

how the lesser amount has been calculated. If no such notice is served, it appears that the employer is still entitled to serve a set-off notice showing the basis of calculation of the lesser amount no later than 5 days before the expiry of the 28 days. However, it is clear that the account submitted by the contractor is not the 'amount due'. Therefore, even if no notices were served, the employer would not be obliged to pay the amount in the contractor's submission, if it could be demonstrated that a different amount was, in fact, due.

23.16   Consequences of termination for insurance risks

paragraph C.4.4 of Schedule 3

6.11.2.2

After either party has terminated the employment of the contractor due to loss or damage having occurred to existing structures, etc. or because terrorism cover has become unavailable, all the provisions noted in Section 23.15 above apply, except that the contractor is not entitled to any direct loss and/or damage caused by the termination. This is to reflect the fact that these consequences refer to termination for causes beyond the control of the parties.

23.17   Suspension of the Works by the contractor

4.14 ; 246   The contract allows the contractor to suspend if the employer fails to pay.

The employer's failure that triggers the contractor's right to suspend is a failure to pay in full by the final date for payment and if the failure continues seven days after receipt of a written notice from the contractor with a copy to the architect that states that it intends to suspend performance of its obligations and states the reasons (failure to pay) for doing so. Although the clause does not expressly mention it, it is obviously good practice for the contractor to refer to the 7 days that the employer has in which to pay. The contractor may suspend its obligations until such time as payment is made in full. The amount expressly includes VAT. Therefore, the contractor has a right to suspend if the employer pays the whole of the amount certified, but only half the amount of applicable VAT. The contractor's right to suspend cannot be exercised about any amount for which the employer has issued a pay less notice. For example, if the architect issues a certificate that £10,000 is due to the contractor but the employer properly issues a pay less notice stating that only £6,000 should be paid, the contractor cannot suspend when the employer fails to pay the £4,000 difference. A contractor who suspends is entitled to an appropriate extension of

2.29.5, 4.14.2   time and to a reasonable sum for costs and expenses reasonably incurred.

It is worth noting that suspension of obligations is rather wider than just suspension of the Works. For example, the contractor can suspend all its obligations under the contract including the obligation to keep the Works insured. Of course, the contractor would retain its ordinary obligations under the general law and under statute to ensure that the site was left in a safe condition. However, it would not remain liable for maintaining it in that condition. If a contractor does suspend, it is prudent for it to send the appropriate notices to all regulatory bodies.

If the contractor merely gives notice to the employer, he will comply with the statutory requirements for suspension, but not with the contract. The contract requires a copy to be given to the architect. However, the remedies under statute are similar to those under the contract. Therefore, failure to copy the architect with the notice is unlikely to affect the contractor's entitlements. In practice, it seems unlikely that the contractor will forget to copy the architect. It is much more likely that a contractor may give the notice only to the architect, forgetting the employer completely, thus neither complying with the Act nor the contract and rendering any subsequent suspension an extremely dubious action.

23.18   Common problems

The date on which the architect's default notice was received and thus from which the 14 days begin to run

The contract allows an assumption to be made about the date on which the notice would arrive in the ordinary course of the post. It is deemed received on the second business day after posting. The assumption will stand even if the contractor never

247

248

1.7.4

actually received it. However, that is subject to proof to the contrary and if the assumption is wrong and the contractor can prove that the notice of termination was premature, the consequences may be serious. The wise course is for the architect to arrange for Royal Mail to confirm the delivery date. Although the contract allows only three methods of giving the default notice (by hand, by recorded signed for or by special delivery), many architects send the notice by e-mail, particularly if e-mail has become the standard method of communication for a particular project. Giving the notice by e-mail is not valid if, as in this case, the acceptable methods of giving notice have been clearly set out. It is common for the default notice to be sent by special delivery post and by e-mail at the same time. If the contractor refuses to accept the special delivery letter, it is likely that the e-mail would then be acceptable if the contractor could prove non-delivery of the letter.

If termination is disputed

If, following termination of the contractor's appointment by the employer, the contractor invokes dispute resolution procedures, the employer is faced with a dilemma. Should the employer proceed in accordance with the contract and engage another contractor to complete the Works or simply wait to see the outcome of the proceedings. The employer may think it prudent to await the outcome, because if the adjudicator or arbitrator decides that the termination was invalid and it is not possible to reinstate the original contractor, it will be entitled to substantial damages (including loss of profit).

The employer wants to terminate the contractor's employment, because the workmanship is very poor

3.18.1
3.11

8.1.4.3

An employer may be concerned that the contractor is incapable of producing good work as there are so many instances of poor workmanship. The employer may decide that the only way forward is to get rid of the contractor and employ another. The problem for the employer is that there is nothing in the contract that straightforwardly permits termination on the ground of poor workmanship. If there are defects in the Works, the architect should instruct the contractor to remove the defective work from site. If the contractor fails to comply the architect can issue a 7-day compliance notice. If the contractor fails to carry out the instruction within the 7 days, the employer can engage another contractor to carry out the instruction and the additional costs will be deducted from the Contract Sum. If the contractor's failure to comply with these instructions becomes persistent so that it begins to seriously affect the Works as a whole, the architect is entitled to issue a default notice. If the contractor does not rectify the default within 14 days, the employer may terminate the contractor's employment.

Part V   Intractable Problems

24   Dispute resolution procedures

24.1   General

Neither the contractor, nor the employer, nor any of the construction professionals actually need to know very much about the detail of dispute resolution procedures. If any of the procedures are employed, the employer or the contractor will almost certainly engage specialists in the particular procedures to advise them. Indeed, it is most unwise for construction professionals to attempt to give anything other than basic advice in these areas. What follows goes slightly beyond the basics, because it is often useful to be able to understand more than one is actually called upon to advise upon.

Four systems

The contract provides for four systems of dispute resolution. The first system is mediation. It cannot be used unless the parties agree. It is briefly considered at the end of this chapter. The other systems are adjudication, arbitration and legal proceedings. People understandably get very confused about when each system may be used. The way it works is this:

- Every construction contract that does not involve a residential occupier must have an adjudication clause and either employer or contractor can refer a dispute to adjudication at any time. Adjudication is intended to be a quick process. The decision is binding, but only until the dispute is dealt with by one of the other two systems. If the dispute is never referred to one of the other systems, the adjudication decision is effectively permanently binding. The parties can of course agree that the adjudicator's decision will be finally binding.
- The parties must chose that of the other two systems (arbitration or legal proceedings) they wish to have as their main dispute resolution system.

The JCT Standard Building Contract 2011, First Edition. David Chappell.
© 2014 by David Chappell. Published 2014 by John Wiley & Sons, Ltd.

They can refer a dispute straight to this system without going through adjudication if they wish.

- Therefore, a party with a dispute may refer it for a decision by adjudication and, if dissatisfied (or if the other party is dissatisfied) may then refer the same dispute to either arbitration or legal proceedings (whichever is in the contract).
- Alternatively, the party with a dispute may ignore adjudication and refer the dispute immediately to either arbitration or legal proceedings (whichever is in the contract).

There are advantages and disadvantages with all these systems and the rest of this chapter attempts to highlight the pros and cons and give a general indication of the processes involved in each system. However, it cannot be emphasised too strongly that for each of these systems, the parties need to be properly represented by specialists in the particular field. It may be tempting to think that all the employer or client need to do in each case is to telephone their solicitor. It must be understood that solicitors, like other professions, specialise. Many solicitors carry out litigation (legal proceedings), but there are all kinds of litigation and a solicitor is required who has a good knowledge of construction law. So far as adjudication and arbitration are concerned, some solicitors seem to be uncomfortable with these processes and a party may get better representation from an architect or quantity surveyor who has specialist knowledge and experience in the field. There are a good many independent consultants practising in these areas.

The Construction Act 1996

In 1996 the Housing Grants, Construction and Regeneration Act (commonly called the Construction Act) (the Act) was enacted (in Northern Ireland Part II of the Act is virtually identical to the Construction Contracts (Northern Ireland) Order 1997). The Act was amended by the Local Democracy, Economic Development and Construction Act 2009 (the Act to the same effect in Northern Ireland is the Construction Contracts (Amendment) Act (Northern Ireland) 2011). S.108 of the Act expressly introduces a contractual system of adjudication to construction contracts. Excluded from the operation of the Act are contracts relating to work on dwellings occupied or intended to be occupied by one of the parties to the contract. SBC, in common with other standard *article 7* forms, incorporates the requirements of the Act. Therefore, all construction *and 9.2* Works carried out under these forms are subject to adjudication even if they comprise work to a dwelling house. In essence s.108 of the Act provides that:

- A party to a construction contract has the right to refer a dispute under the contract to adjudication.
- Under the contract:
  - A party can give notice of intention to refer to adjudication at any time.
  - An adjudicator should be appointed and the dispute referred within 7 days of the notice of intention.

- The adjudicator must make a decision in 28 days or whatever period the parties agree.
- The period for decision can be extended by 14 days if the referring party agrees.
- The adjudicator must act impartially.
- The adjudicator may use his or her initiative in finding facts or law.
- The adjudicator's decision is binding until the dispute is settled by legal proceedings, arbitration or agreement.
- The adjudicator is not liable for anything done or omitted in carrying out the functions unless in bad faith.

■ If the contract does not comply with the Act, the Scheme for Construction Contracts (England and Wales) Regulations 1998 as amended (the Scheme) will apply (in Northern Ireland it is the Scheme for Construction Contracts in Northern Ireland Regulations (Northern Ireland) 1999 as amended).

Adjudication at any time

249

250

The right to refer to adjudication 'at any time' means that adjudication can be commenced even if legal proceedings (and arbitration) are in progress about the same dispute. Adjudication can be sought even if repudiation of the contract has taken place. A dispute may be referred to adjudication and the adjudicator may give a decision even after the expiry of the contractual limitation period. Of course the referring party runs the risk that the respondent will use the limitation period defence. In which case the claim will normally fail.

Adjudication decision

251

In the vast majority of cases, anecdotal evidence suggests that the parties accept the adjudicator's decision and do not take the matter further. Even where there are challenges through the courts against the enforcement of an adjudicator's decision, the challenge is concerned with matters such as the adjudicator's jurisdiction or whether the adjudicator complied with the requirements of natural justice, not whether the adjudicator's decision was correct. The courts cannot interfere with the adjudicator's decision, no matter how obviously wrong, provided that the adjudicator has the jurisdiction (i.e. properly appointed and carrying out the duties correctly) to answer the questions posed by the referring party.

252

The parties must comply with the adjudicator's decision following which, if they are not satisfied, either party may instigate proceedings through the stipulated system of obtaining a final decision. It is important to remember that, in doing so, the parties are not appealing against the decision of the adjudicator and the arbitrator or court will ignore the adjudicator's previous decision in arriving at an award or judgment, respectively. However, the same dispute cannot be referred to adjudication twice. Once decided by adjudication, a disgruntled party must go to arbitration or legal proceedings (whichever is in the contract). The whole idea behind adjudication is that it is a quick cheap method of resolving disputes. That is why, unless the parties agree, there is no provision for the winner to recover legal costs from the other side. Parties are encouraged to seek modest representation. Indeed, the original idea was probably that employer and contractor could simply argue their own cases. However, the rate at which the courts have been called upon to make decisions about various aspects of adjudication means that a party is very unwise if they do not seek representation for all but perhaps the very simplest and financially modest disputes.

article 8
9.3 to 9.8
article 9

If the parties wish to have a final and binding decision rather than submit a dispute to adjudication, they have a choice between arbitration and legal proceedings. It should be noted that legal proceedings will apply unless the contractor particulars are completed to show that arbitration is to be the procedure.

The advantages of arbitration

- *Speed* – A good arbitrator should dispose of most cases in months, not years.
- *Privacy* – Only the parties and the arbitrator know the details of the dispute and the award.
- *The parties decide* – The parties can decide the timescales, the procedure and the location of any hearing.
- *Expense* – Theoretically, it should be more expensive than litigation, because the parties (usually the losing party) have to pay for the arbitrator and the hire of a room, but in practice the speed and technical expertise of the arbitrator usually keep costs down.
- *Technical expertise of the arbitrator* – The fact that the arbitrator understands construction should shorten the time schedule and possibly avoid the need for expert witnesses if the parties agree.
- Appeal – The award is final, because the courts are loath to consider any appeal.

Disadvantages of arbitration

- In theory, it is more expensive because the parties (usually the losing party) pay the cost of the arbitrator and the hire of a room for the hearing.
- If the arbitrator is not very good, the process may be slow and expensive.
- The arbitrator may not be an expert on the law, which may be a major part of the dispute.
- Parties who are in dispute may find it difficult to agree about anything. Therefore, the arbitrator may be appointed by the appointing body and the procedure, the timing and the location of the hearing room may be decided by the arbitrator with the result that neither party is satisfied.

Advantages of legal proceedings

- The judge should be an expert on the law.
- The Civil Procedure Rules require judges to manage their caseloads and encourage pre-action settlement through use of the Pre-Action Protocol.

- Cases can reach trial quickly.
- The claimant can join several defendants into the proceedings to allow interlocking matters to be decided.
- Costs of judge and courtroom are minimal.
- A dissatisfied party can appeal to a higher court.

Disadvantages of legal proceedings

- Even specialist judges know relatively little about the details of construction work.
- Parties cannot choose the judge, who may not be experienced in construction cases.
- Costs will be added because expert witnesses or a court appointed expert witness will be needed to assist the judge.
- Cases can take years to resolve.
- Lengthy timescale and complex processes may result in high costs.
- Appeals may result in an unacceptable level of costs.

Arbitration

253

Arbitration is probably still the most satisfactory procedure for the resolution of construction disputes and employers would be advised to complete the contract particulars accordingly. Where the parties have agreed that the method of binding dispute resolution will be arbitration, a partly who attempts to use legal proceedings instead will fail in a costly way if the other party asks the court to grant a stay (postponement) of legal proceedings until the arbitration is concluded. The court has no discretion about the matter and the successful party will claim its costs. The result is not only that the party intent on legal proceedings will have to revert to arbitration, but it will have to pay the other party's legal costs incurred in opposing the legal proceedings.

The remainder of this chapter sets out the procedures in more detail for the benefit of the reader who wishes to know a little more about dispute resolution. However, it must be borne in mind that reading what follows is not sufficient, in itself, to qualify anyone to attempt to represent a party in adjudication or arbitration.

24.2   Adjudication

The contract provisions

Although in most instances it will be the contractor that initiates adjudication, there is nothing to stop the employer from doing so. For example, the employer may seek adjudication if the architect over-certifies or makes an extension of time that seems excessive.

The architect is not a party to the contract and, therefore, cannot be the respondent to an adjudication under SBC (the architect can be a party to an adjudication with the employer under the architect's appointment document). Architects can obviously act as witnesses, but they have no duty to run an adjudication on behalf of the employer. Representing someone in an adjudication usually calls for some degree of skill and experience that most construction professionals, acting in the normal course of their professions, will not readily acquire. Where the dispute is other than very straightforward or where one party has retained the services of a legal representative, the other party is well advised to do likewise.

It should be noted that only disputes arising 'under' the contract may be referred. Thus, for example, an adjudicator has no power to consider formal settlement agreements about various matters made by the parties in connection with the contract of which the adjudication clause forms part.

254

Adjudication is rapidly replacing arbitration as the standard dispute resolution process albeit that it is rather rough and ready. The reason is probably because it is a very quick process. Unfortunately, it is sometimes used for complex disputes involving large amounts of money and copious documents for which it is not suited. Adjudications involving a £1 million or more with time extended by agreement to three or four months are a travesty of what the Act intended.

Use of the Scheme is made subject to certain provisos:

9.2.1
- The adjudicator and nominating body are to be those stated in the contract particulars.
- If the dispute concerns whether an instruction (issued after a defect has been found and the architect is seeking to have parts of the work opened up or tested) is reasonable, the adjudicator, if practicable, must be someone with appropriate expertise and experience. If not, the adjudicator must appoint an independent expert with appropriate expertise and experience to give advice and to report in writing whether the instruction is reasonable

9.2.2
in all the circumstances.

It is unclear why this particular instruction should have been singled out, because it is perfectly sensible to argue that the adjudicator must always have relevant expertise and experience or seek expert assistance.

The scheme: notice of adjudication

To start an adjudication, any party to a construction contract may give to all the other parties (there is usually only one other party) a written notice of an intention to refer a dispute to adjudication. The notice must describe the dispute and who are the parties involved, It must give details of the time and location, the redress sought and the names and addresses of the parties to the contract.

The notice is the trigger for the adjudication process and it is also one of the most important documents. Great care must be taken in its preparation because the dispute that the adjudicator is entitled to consider is the dispute identified

255
256
in the notice of adjudication. The dispute cannot be changed later by the referring party, although it can be elaborated and more detail provided.

257

For example, if the notice of adjudication states the dispute as being the amount due in an architect's certificate and if the redress sought is simply the adjudicator to decide the amount due, the adjudicator will have no power to order payment of that amount although, doubtless, that would be what the referring party wishes. The adjudicator can only answer the question posed in the notice of adjudication.

However, the adjudicator may take into account any other matters that both parties agree should be within the adjudication's scope. Moreover, the adjudicator is expressly empowered to take into account matters that the adjudicator considers are necessarily connected with the dispute. To take a simple example, it is probably essential for an adjudicator to decide the extent of extension of time allowable, even if not asked, before deciding about the amount of liquidated damages properly recoverable. The express empower-

258

ment merely puts into words what would be the legal position in any event,

The scheme: appointment of the adjudicator

The procedure for selecting an adjudicator in the Scheme is relatively complex (see flowchart Figure 24.1) that reflects the general nature of the Scheme.

Parties may agree

The overriding point is that the parties are entitled to agree the name of an adjudicator after the notice of adjudication has been served. If the parties can agree, they have the best chance of an adjudicator who has the confidence of both parties. Sadly, parties in dispute find it difficult to agree on anything at all.

Named adjudicator

If there is a person named in the contract, that person must first be asked to act as adjudicator. There are difficulties with having a named person: the person may be away or ill or even dead when called upon to act; the person's expertise may be unsuitable for the particular dispute or pressure of work may force that person to decline. If an adjudicator is named in the contract, but for some reason cannot act or does not respond, the referring party has three options.

- The first is to ask any other person specified in the contract to act.
- The second is to ask the adjudicator nominating body in the contract to nominate.
- The third is to ask any other nominating body to nominate.

It will readily be seen that this procedure is simply a clarification of existing options.

The nominated adjudicator has 2 days in which to accept from receiving the request. The adjudicator must be a single person and not a body corporate. Therefore, a firm of quantity surveyors cannot be nominated although one of

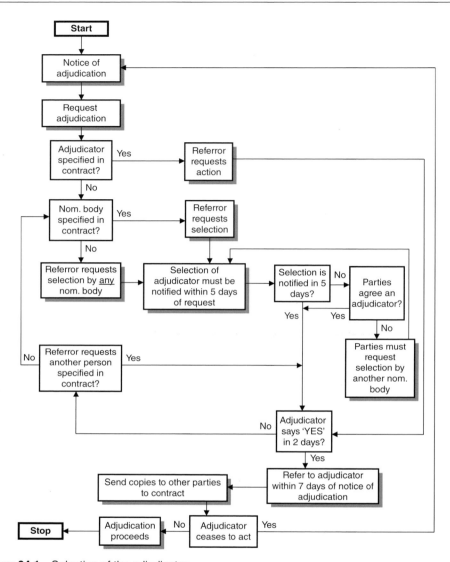

Figure 24.1   Selection of the adjudicator.

the directors or partners can be nominated. The nominating body has 5 days from receipt of the request to communicate the nomination to the referring party. Invariably, a nominating body will also notify the respondent, but surprisingly the Scheme does not expressly require that notification.

Nominating body

If there is no named person or if that person will not or cannot act, the referring party must ask the nominating body indicated in the contract particulars to nominate an adjudicator. There are problems with this approach also. Not all adjudicators are of equal capability. Indeed, some of them are quite poor. Some have a tenuous grasp of the law, while many others wrongly believe that adjudicator's job is to make decisions according to their own gut feeling notions of right and wrong without reference to law. If the referring party asks for a nomination, both parties are stuck with the result unless they agree to revoke the appointment. However, for the reason already stated, such an agreement is unlikely.

The nominating body is to be stated in the contract particulars. The bodies listed are:

- Royal Institute of British Architects.
- The Royal Institution of Chartered Surveyors.
- constructionadjudicators.com.
- Association of Independent Construction Adjudicators.
- Chartered Institute of Arbitrators.

Four of the bodies should be deleted. If there is no adjudicator named and no body is selected, the referring party may choose any one of the bodies to make the appointment. If there is no list of appointing bodies, perhaps because all of them have inadvertently been deleted, the referring party is free to choose any nominating body to make the appointment.

A nominating body is fairly broadly defined in the Scheme as a body that holds itself out publicly as a body that will select an adjudicator on request. The body may not be what is referred to as a 'natural person', i.e. a human being, nor one of the parties.

In the event that the nominating body fails to nominate within 5 days, the parties may either agree on the name of an adjudicator or the referring party may request another nominating body to nominate. In either case the adjudicator has two days to respond as before.

Objections

The fact that either party objects to the adjudicator will not invalidate the appointment nor any decision reached by the adjudicator. There is a misconception among the uninitiated that a party has only to register an objection to the adjudicator in order to bring the process to an end or at least suspend it. Nothing could be further from the truth. It is entirely a matter for each party the extent to which it wishes to participate in the adjudication. If a party objects, it should make quite clear that any participation is without prejudice to that position and to the party's right to refer the objection to the courts in due course. It may be catastrophic for a party knowing of grounds for objection to continue the adjudication without further comment. In such cases, the party may well be deemed to have accepted the adjudicator,

259

Adjudicator ceasing to act

The Scheme makes elaborate provision if the adjudicator resigns or the parties revoke the appointment. The provisions are sensible. The adjudicator may resign at any time on giving notice in writing to the parties. It should be noted that the notice need not be a reasonable length and, therefore, immediate resignation is possible. The referring party may serve a new notice of adjudication and seek the appointment of a new adjudicator as noted above. If the new adjudicator requests and if reasonably practicable, the parties must make all the documents available that have been previously submitted.

An adjudicator, who finds that the dispute is essentially the same as a dispute that has already been the subject of an adjudication decision, must resign. Although, oddly, not given as a reason for resignation, the significant variation of a dispute from what was referred in the referral notice, so that the adjudicator is not competent to decide it, is a trigger for entitlement to payment of the adjudicator's fees.

Revocation of the appointment by the parties does not seem to be a common occurrence. When it occurs, the adjudicator is entitled to determine a reasonable amount of fees and expenses. The parties, as before, are jointly and severally liable for any balance. Parties will find it difficult to challenge the amount of fees determined by an adjudicator unless the adjudicator can be shown to have acted in bad faith,

260

The scheme: procedure

The procedure is indicated by the flowchart in Figure 24.2. A request for the appointment of an adjudicator must include a copy of the notice of adjudication. This is to assist those making the nomination and the prospective adjudicator so that a suitable person is nominated. There is little time available because the referring party must submit the dispute in writing to the adjudicator, with copies to each party to the dispute, no later than 7 days after the notice of adjudication. This submission is known as the 'referral notice'. Looking at the procedure for appointment of the adjudicator, it is clear that the timetable is tight.

Referral

The referral notice, which is the referring party's claim, must be accompanied by relevant parts of the contract and whatever other evidence the referring party relies upon in support of the claim.

The Scheme does not indicate that the respondent may reply to the referral notice, but the adjudicator is obliged to allow a reasonable period for the reply. The length of time is a matter for the adjudicator to decide, but in view of the restricted overall period for the decision, it is likely that somewhere between 7 and 14 days is the most that any respondent can expect. The adjudicator must reach a decision twenty-eight days after the date of receipt by the adjudicator of the referral notice. The period may be extended by 14 days if the referring party consents or, if both parties agree, for any longer period.

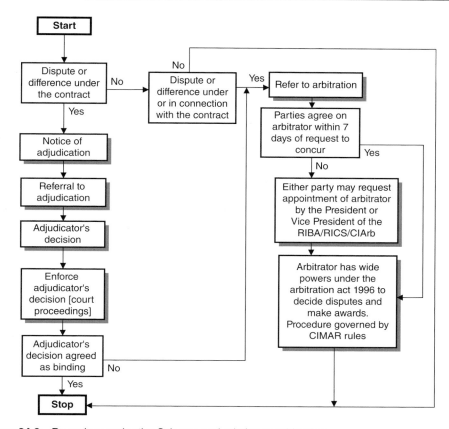

Figure 24.2 Procedure under the Scheme and relation to arbitration.

The adjudicator must deliver a copy of the decision to the parties as soon as possible after the decision has been reached.

If the adjudicator does not comply with this timetable in reaching the decision, either party may serve a new notice of adjudication and request a new adjudicator to act.

Enforcement of the decision

If one of the parties fails to comply with the adjudicator's decision, the other may seek enforcement of the decision through the courts. The courts will normally enforce the decision unless there is a jurisdictional or procedural problem. In enforcement proceedings, the court is not being asked to comment on the adjudicator's decision or reasoning although a court will quite often do so. Where a court is asked to enforce an adjudicator's decision, the important part of the judgment is simply the reasons why the judge decided to enforce or not. Any comments the judge may make on the adjudicator's decision itself may be interesting, but do not affective whether or not the decision is enforced.

The scheme: adjudicator's powers and duties

Several disputes

Unless the parties agree, the adjudicator may only adjudicate at the same time on one dispute between the parties. If the parties agree, the adjudicator may adjudicate on more than one dispute under the same contract. The adjudicator may deal with related disputes on several contracts even if not all the parties are parties to all the disputes, provided they all consent. Moreover, the parties may agree to extend the period for decision on all or some of the disputes. It is clear that multiple dispute procedures bring their own complications for which the Scheme, wisely, does not try to legislate. For example, it is not clear whether multiple disputes, certainly under different contracts, must be adjudicated on during one big adjudication. Where there are different contracts and the parties vary from one contract to another, it will be a matter of discussion and agreement whether the adjudicator should conduct separate adjudications, albeit at the same time.

Acting according to law

The adjudicator's duties are to act impartially in accordance with the relevant contract terms, to reach a decision 'in accordance with the applicable law in relation to the contract' and to avoid unnecessary expense. Sadly, some adjudicators seem to be unaware of their obligations to apply the law to their decisions and decisions are made on the basis of the adjudicators' idea of fairness, moral rights or justice. Fortunately, there are also some very good adjudicators with a clear understanding of their roles.

Summary of powers

The adjudicator is given some very broad and some very precise powers.

- To take the initiative in ascertaining the facts and the law.
- To decide the procedure in the adjudication.
- To request any party to supply documents and statements.
- To decide the language of the adjudication and order translations.
- To meet and question the parties.
- To make site visits, subject to any third party consents.
- To carry out any tests, subject to any third party consents.
- To obtain any representations or submissions.
- To appoint experts or legal advisers, subject to giving prior notice.
- To decide the timetable, deadlines and limits to length of documents or oral statements.
- To issue directions about the conduct of the adjudication.

Failure to comply

The parties must comply with the adjudicator's directions. If a party does not comply, the adjudicator has power:

- To continue the adjudication notwithstanding the failure.
- To draw whatever inferences the adjudicator believes are justified in the circumstances.
- To make a decision on the basis of the information provided and to attach whatever weight to evidence submitted late the adjudicator thinks fit.

A party may have assistance or representation as deemed appropriate with the proviso that when considering oral evidence or representations, representation of each party is restricted to no more than one person unless the adjudicator decides otherwise.

Final certificate

Sometimes, a contract may provide that a decision or certificate is final and conclusive in certain circumstances. Unless that is the case, the adjudicator is given power to open up, revise and review any decision or certificate given by a person named in the contract. It is worth noting that to be exempt from revision by the adjudicator the decision or certificate must be stated to be both final and conclusive. A contract that simply states that a certificate is conclusive is open to review. On that basis, the final certificate under SBC is exempt because it is called 'final' and stated to be conclusive. Obviously it is reviewable if the reference is made before the expiry of 28 days from the date of issue.

1.10.2

Power to order payment

The adjudicator is also given power to order any party to the dispute to make a payment, its due date and the final date for payment and to decide the rates of interest, the periods for which it must be paid and whether it must be simple or compound interest. In deciding what, if any interest must be paid, the adjudicator must have regard to any relevant contractual term. To 'have regard' to a contractual term is a rather loose phrase that probably means little more than to give attention to it. It falls short of the need to actually comply with it,

261

Confidential information

The adjudicator must consider relevant information submitted by the parties and if the adjudicator believes that other information or case law should be taken into account, it must be provided to the parties and they must have the opportunity to comment, Neither the adjudicator nor any party to an adjudication may disclose information, noted by the supplier as confidential, to third parties unless the disclosure is necessary for the adjudication.

262

The scheme: The adjudicator's decision

263

The adjudicator must reach the decision within 28 days (or within any validly extended period) after receipt of the referral. The decision must be delivered to each party as soon as possible after the decision is reached.

In the absence of any directions about the time to comply, compliance must be immediate on delivery of the decision to the parties.

The decision is to be binding and must be complied with until the dispute is finally determined by arbitration, legal proceedings or agreement.

If either party requests, then the adjudicator must give reasons for the decision. If an adjudicator gives any reasons, they are to be read with the decision and may be used as a means of interpreting and understanding the decision and the reasons for that decision. Comments about the decision

264

given by the adjudicator after delivering the decision are irrelevant.

The adjudicator is entitled to reasonable fees that the adjudicator may determine. The parties are jointly and severally liable for payment if the adjudicator makes no apportionment or if there is an outstanding balance. However, an adjudicator who does not produce a decision that is enforceable may not be entitled to a fee. Much depends on what it says in the adjudicator's terms of

265

engagement.

The adjudicator will not be liable for anything done or omitted in carrying out the functions of an adjudicator unless the act or omission is in bad faith. Similar protection is also given to any employee or agent of the adjudicator. It is perhaps worth noting that, as an incorporated term of the contract, this paragraph is not binding on persons who are not parties to the contract.

The scheme: Costs

Nothing in the Scheme allows the adjudicator to award the parties costs. This is in harmony with the philosophy of the Act, which does not encourage the parties to incur large amounts of costs in pursuing claims. In arbitration and litigation, by contrast, where costs are normally awarded against the losing party, the dispute can deteriorate into a fight about costs rather than the point at issue. That is because of the huge costs that can be incurred by each side. The adjudicator could be given power to award costs, either expressly by the parties or by implied agreement.

24.3   Arbitration

General

266 ; article 8

SBC arbitration procedures are very brief. Arbitration can take place on any matter at any time. Arbitrators appointed under the JCT Agreement are given extremely wide express powers. Their jurisdiction is to decide any dispute or difference of any kind whatsoever arising under the contract or connected with it. The scope could scarcely be broader. The arbitrator's powers extend to:

- Rectification of the contract to reflect the true agreement between the parties.
- Directing the taking of measurements or the undertaking of such valuations as the arbitrator thinks desirable to determine the respective rights.
- To ascertain and make an award of any sum that should have been included in a certificate.
- Opening up, reviewing and revising any certificate, opinion, decision, requirement or notice issued, given or made and to determine all matters in dispute as if no such certificate, opinion, decision, requirement or notice had been given.

9.5

Governing rules

9.3
9.8

1.11

The JCT 2011 edition of the Construction Industry Model Arbitration Rules (CIMAR) current at the contractual base date, are to govern the proceedings,. The provisions of the Arbitration Act 1996 are expressly stated to apply to any arbitration under this agreement. That is to be the case no matter where the arbitration is conducted. Therefore, even if the project and the arbitration takes place in a foreign jurisdiction, the UK Act will apply provided that the parties contracted on SBC and the contract provision that the law of England applies is not amended.

The following matters are specifically excluded from arbitration:

- Disputes about Value Added Tax, where legislation provides some other method of resolving the dispute.
- Disputes under the Construction Industry Scheme, where legislation provides some other method of resolving the dispute.
- The enforcement of any decision of an adjudicator.

Questions of law

267 ; 9.7

268

The contract records that the employer and contractor agree, in accordance with the relevant sections of the Act, that either party may by proper notice to the other and to the arbitrator apply to the courts to decide any question of law arising in the course of the reference and appeal to the courts on any question of law arising out of an award. Clauses like this have been held by the courts to be effective.

Think first

Arbitration, like litigation, is almost always costly in terms of both money and time. No matter how powerful and convincing the case may be, there is no guarantee of success. Even the successful party will often look back at the cost, the time spent and the mental stress involved and conclude that it was not worth the effort.

Some people will threaten arbitration over trivial matters in an attempt to gain an advantage. Unfortunately, even with the recent review of dispute resolution procedures and introduction of the adjudication process that approach will not disappear. It will not always be possible to avoid arbitration and, therefore, employers and contractors must ensure that they appreciate how the process operates. Only then can they recognize the possible consequences.

A formal process

A common misconception is that the arbitration process is an informal get together to enable the parties and the arbitrator to have a chat about the dispute before the arbitrator draws all the views together in order to arrive at a consensus decision about who should be successful. That is more like a description of a conciliation meeting. The majority of arbitrations are conducted quite formally, like private legal proceedings – which is what they are. The arbitration begins by inviting the parties to the 'preliminary meeting', but that does not mean a friendly discussion. It is a formal meeting to establish all the important criteria that need to be decided before the arbitration can proceed. The arbitrator normally works from an agenda. Sometimes parties attempt to gain an advantage by springing a surprise request on the arbitrator at that meeting. Experienced arbitrators have no difficulty in dealing with such requests, but there is a limit to the degree to which the arbitrator can ensure that one party is not disadvantaged by such tactics. A party should not go to a preliminary meeting without taking a fully briefed legal adviser experienced in arbitration.

The employer and contractor are free to agree who should be appointed, or should appoint, the arbitrator and they have freedom to agree important matters such as the form and timetable of the proceedings. This raises the possibility of a quicker procedure than would otherwise be the case in litigation and even matters such as the venue for any future hearing might be arranged to suit the convenience of the parties and their witnesses.

Hearings

If oral evidence and cross-examination is to be carried out, it is usually done at a hearing. Hearings, which are the private equivalent of a trial, are conducted in private, not in an open court. Parties are free to choose whether to represent themselves or whether to be represented and by whom. They need not, in the traditional courtroom way, be represented by solicitor and counsel. It is not usually advisable for the parties to represent themselves, because difficult legal points can arise in apparently the simplest of arbitrations. Some arbitrations are won by clever tactics. Therefore, experienced help is essential.

Procedure

Arbitrations begun under the contract must be conducted subject to and in accordance with the JCT 2011 edition of CIMAR, current at the base date of the contract. If any amendments have been issued by JCT since that date, the parties may jointly agree to give written notice the arbitrator to conduct the

9.3 reference according to the amended rules. CIMAR is a comprehensive body of rules, generally of admirable clarity. The whole document, at the time of writing, is available on www.jctcontracts.com. As might be expected JCT/CIMAR is very detailed. Among other things, they offer the parties a choice of three broad categories of procedure by which the proceedings will be conducted, as follows:

rule 7 ### Short hearing procedure

This procedure is not very common. It limits the time available to the parties within which to orally address the matters in dispute before the arbitrator. Before the hearing, either by simultaneous exchange or by consecutive submissions, each party will provide to the arbitrator and to each other a written statement of their claim, defence and counterclaim (if any). Each statement must be accompanied by all relevant documents and any witness statements on which it is proposed to rely. The JCT procedures usefully insert some time scales for certain of the steps.

If it is appropriate to do so, either before or after the short hearing, the arbitrator may inspect the subject matter of the dispute if desired. This procedure is particularly suited to issues that fairly easily can be decided by such an inspection of work, materials, plant and/or equipment or the like. The arbitrator must decide the issues and make an award within a month after concluding hearing the parties.

It is possible to present expert evidence. However, it is costly and often unnecessary; particularly if the arbitrator has been chosen specifically on the grounds of specialist knowledge and expertise. Parties can sometimes agree to allow the arbitrator to use that specialist expertise when reaching the decision and so the use of independent expert evidence under the short hearing procedure is all but actively discouraged.

This procedure with a hearing is ideally suited to many common disputes that are relatively simple and provides for a quick award with minimum delay and associated cost.

rule 8 ### Documents only procedure

This will rarely be a viable option. It is not viable unless all the evidence is contained in the form of documents. Nevertheless, if the criteria are satisfied, it can offer real economies of time and cost. It is best suited to disputes that are capable of being dealt with in the absence of oral evidence and where the sums in issue are relatively modest and do not warrant the time and associated additional expense, of a hearing. Parties, in accordance with a timetable devised by the arbitrator, will serve on each other and on the arbitrator a written statement of case that, as a minimum, will include;

- An account of the relevant facts and opinions upon which reliance is placed.
- A statement of the precise relief or remedy sought.

If either party is relying on evidence of witnesses of fact, the relevant witness statements (called 'proofs'), signed by the witnesses concerned, will be included with the statement of case. If the opinions of an expert or experts are required, they must similarly be given in writing and signed. There is a right of reply and if there is a counterclaim, the other party may reply to it.

Despite the title of this procedure, the arbitrator may set aside up to a day during which to question the parties and/or their witnesses if it is considered desirable. The arbitrator must make a decision within a month or so of final exchanges and questioning, but there is provision for the arbitrator to notify the parties that more time for the decision will be required. The JCT procedures again set out a useful timetable.

rule 9

Full procedure

If neither of the other options is considered satisfactory, CIMAR makes provision for the parties to conduct their respective cases in a manner similar to conventional High Court proceedings, offering the opportunity to hear and cross-examine factual and expert witnesses.

This is the most complex procedure and the JCT procedure that sets out a detailed timetable for various activities within the procedure is of real assistance to the parties and to the arbitrator.

The rules lay down that parties will exchange formal statements. In difficult or complex cases, multiple statements may be exchanged. Each submission must be sufficiently detailed to enable the other party to answer each allegation made.

The arbitrator should give detailed directions concerning everything necessary for the proper conduct of the arbitration. Directions may also be given requiring the disclosure of any documents or other relevant material that is or has been in each party's possession. Probably, the parties will be required to exchange written statements setting out any evidence that may be relied upon from witnesses of fact in advance of the hearing. There will also be directions given regarding any expert witnesses, the length of the hearing or hearings and the time available for each party to present it case.

The appointment of an arbitrator

9.4.1

It is at the option of either party to begin arbitration proceedings. As a first step, one party must write to the other requesting them to concur in the appointment of an arbitrator. Whoever does so, proceedings are formally commenced when the written notice is received. The notice must identify the dispute and require agreement to the appointment of an arbitrator. It is good practice for the party seeking arbitration to insert the names of three prospective arbitrators. This saves time and often both parties can agree on one of the names. The arbitrator must have no relationship to either of the parties nor should they have connections with any matter associated with the dispute.

9.4.1 and rule 2.3

It is important for the parties to make a sincere effort to agree on a suitable candidate rather than having one appointed whose skills and experience may be entirely unknown. If the parties cannot agree upon a suitable appointment within 14 days of a notice to concur or any agreed extension to that period, either party can apply to a third party to appoint an arbitrator. There is a list of appointors in the contract particulars. All but one should be deleted. The default provision is the President or a Vice-President of the Royal Institute of British Architects. Of course it is always open to the parties to the contract to insert the name of a different appointor of their choice at the time the contract was executed. It will be necessary to complete special forms and to pay the relevant fee. Although the system of appointing an arbitrator varies, the aim is the same. The object is to appoint a person of integrity who is independent, having no existing relationships with either party or their professional advisers and who is impartial. It should go without saying that the arbitrator should have the necessary and appropriate technical and legal expertise. Claimants who have a dispute to refer and respondents receiving a notice to concur should waste no time in taking proper expert advice on how best to proceed.

rule 2.5

If the arbitrator's appointment is made by agreement, it will not take effect until the appointed person has confirmed willingness to act, irrespective of whether terms have been agreed. If the appointment is the result of an application to the appointing body, it becomes effective, whether or not terms have been agreed, when the appointment is made by the relevant body. There is no fixed scale of charges for arbitrator's services and fees ought to depend on their experience, expertise and often on the complexity of the dispute. Arbitrators usually require an initial deposit from the parties and, if there is to be a hearing, there will be a cancellation charge graded in accordance with the proximity of the cancellation to the start of the hearing. A cancellation means that it is difficult for the arbitrator to secure work at short notice to fill the void. In cases where the cancellation fee is substantial, due to proximity to the hearing date, it might be sensible to ask the arbitrator to account to the parties for activities during the hearing period with a view to deducting the fee from the cancellation charge.

After appointment, the arbitrator will consider which of the procedures summarised above appears to be most appropriate as a forum for the parties to put their cases. The arbitrator must choose the format that will best avoid undue cost and delay and that is often a most difficult balancing act. Therefore, parties must within 14 days after acceptance of the appointment is notified to the parties, provide the arbitrator with an outline of their disputes and of the sums in issue along with an indication of which procedure they consider best suited to them. After due consideration of all parties views and unless a meeting is considered unnecessary, the arbitrator must, within 21 days of the date of acceptance, arrange a meeting (the preliminary meeting) that the parties or their representatives will attend to agree (if possible) or receive the arbitrator's decision upon everything necessary to enable the arbitration to proceed. It is obviously preferable for the parties to agree which procedure is to apply. If they cannot agree, the documents-only procedure will apply unless the arbitrator, after having considered all representations, decides that the full procedure will apply.

The parties are always free to conduct their own cases, but if disputes have reached the stage of formal proceedings it is usually better to engage experienced professionals to act for them.

Powers of the arbitrator

The 1996 Arbitration Act significantly broadened the arbitrator's powers beyond what was previously the case. For example, an arbitrator may:

- Order which documents or classes of documents should be disclosed between and produced by the parties.
- Order whether the strict rules of evidence shall apply.
- Decide the extent to which the arbitrator should take the initiative in ascertaining the facts and the law.
- Take legal or technical assistance or advice.
- Order security for costs.
- Give directions in relation to any property owned by or in the possession of any party to the proceedings that is the subject of the proceedings.
- Make more than one award at different times on different aspects of the matters to be determined.
- Award interest.
- Make an award on costs of the arbitration between the parties.
- Direct that the recoverable costs of the arbitration, or any part of the arbitral proceedings, are to be limited to a specified amount.

Figure 24.2 shows the outline of adjudication and arbitration in simple flow-chart form.

Third party procedure

One of the perceived advantages of litigation over arbitration is that claimants can take action against several defendants at the same time and any defendant can seek to join into the proceedings another party who may have liability. This facility is not readily available in arbitration that usually takes place only between the parties to the contract.

However, where there are two or more related sets of proceedings on the same topic, but under different arbitration agreements, anyone who is charged with appointing an arbitrator must consider whether the same arbitrator should be appointed for both. In the absence of relevant grounds to do otherwise, the *rules 2.6 and* same arbitrator is to be appointed. If different appointors are involved they *2.7* must consult one another. If one arbitrator is already appointed, that arbitrator must be considered for appointment to the other arbitrations.

This situation commonly occurs when there is an arbitration under the main contract and also between the contractor and a sub-contractor about the same issue, perhaps one of valuation or extension of time. It is also possible that there are two contracts between the same two parties and an issue arises in both that is essentially the same point. Usually, the same arbitrator ought to be appointed for that situation.

24.4   Legal proceedings (litigation)

article 9

article 8

The legal proceedings option simply provides that the English courts will have jurisdiction over any dispute or difference arising out of or in connection with the contract and will be determined by legal proceedings. Obviously, if the work is to be done in Northern Ireland or Scotland, the relevant courts will be substituted for the English courts. Parties wishing to adopt this procedure will delete the arbitration option. It should be remembered that the default position has changed under this contract. If neither option is deleted, legal proceedings is the default position.

24.5   Mediation

9.1

The contract states that, by agreement, the parties may choose to resolve any dispute or difference arising under the contract through the medium of mediation. It is unclear why this clause has been included in the contract at all. The key to the redundant nature of this clause is in the phrase 'The Parties may by agreement…'. The parties, of course, may do virtually anything by agreement. They can agree to scrap the whole contract and sign a different one if they are both of one mind on the matter. One assumes that this clause was inserted purely to remind the less sophisticated users of the form that mediation is a possibility. Why the draftsman of the contract did not also refer to the possibility of conciliation or negotiation is not clear. In general, there is little point in including as terms of a contract anything to be agreed. The whole point of a written contract is that it is evidence of what the parties have already agreed. To have a clause that effectively states: 'we may agree to do something else', is a waste of space.

In practice, mediation seems to be effective if the mediator is competent and if the parties really do want to compromise. Mediation can take whatever form the parties agree. The principle of mediation is usually that the mediator meets with the parties individually and frankly discusses their cases, pointing out any drawbacks but not revealing the drawbacks of one party to the other. When the mediator believes that the parties have reached a realistic understand of their respective cases, the parties meet together under the guidance of the mediator. If an agreement can be reached, it is immediately put on paper and signed by the parties.

24.6   Common problems

The adjudicator is clearly incompetent and one party refuses to be bound by the adjudication

Undoubtedly there are some adjudicators who produce bad decisions. Sometimes the decision is so bad as to make even the winner surprised. Unfortunately, the adjudicator's decision is binding on the parties even if it is

269   demonstrably wrong. Provided the adjudicator has answered the question asked by the dispute, the decision is binding. The decision cannot be challenged on the basis of the adjudicator's competence, but only on the grounds that he or she was lacking in jurisdiction or had failed to give consideration to the cases advanced by both parties. Therefore, a party cannot refuse to be bound and the other party can apply to the court to enforce the decision.

The contractor is now asking the adjudicator to pay back its £6,000 fee, because the court refused to enforce the adjudicator's decision

Unless the adjudicator has something written into his terms of engagement that says that he is entitled to be paid whether or not the decision is enforceable, an adjudicator who produces a decision that the court will not enforce is not

270   entitled to the fee and, if already paid, it must be repaid.

The architect has informed the adjudicator that she is representing the employer, but the contractor says that is unfair

The contractor cannot successfully object to representation of the employer by the architect in adjudication. The architect is already engaged and paid by the employer. It is only at certain times during the progress of the Works that the architect must act fairly between the parties, for example, when the architect is deciding whether the contractor is entitled to an extension of time or when the architect is certifying payment.

On a practical note, the architect is not usually well equipped to represent the employer. Although adjudication started its life as a simple way of dealing with disputes that did not require detailed legal knowledge, the number of judicial decisions that have been made in relation to adjudication strongly suggests that the employer should engage a specialist in the adjudication field. This would be particularly the case if the dispute centred on some certificate or other action by the architect. In that kind of adjudication, the architect may have to give a witness statement and, if there is a hearing, may be asked to appear.

Notes and references

Chapter 1

1 *Crowshaw v Pritchard and Renwick* (1899) 16 TLR 45.
2 Parris J, Standard Form of Building Contract: JCT 1980 (1985) Collins Professional and Technical Books.
3 *Hudson's Building Cases* (3rd edition) Vol 2 at page 632.
4 The Local Democracy, Economic Development and Construction Act 2009.

Chapter 2

5 David Chappell, Michael Cowlin, Michael Dunn; Building Law Encyclopaedia, (2009) Wiley-Blackwell, Oxford, p.172–3.
6 The Copyright, Designs and Patents Act 1988 as amended.
7 *Bowmer & Kirkland Ltd v Wilson Bowden Properties Ltd* (1996) 80 BLR 131.
8 *Convent Hospital v Eberlin & Partners* (1988) 14 Con LR 1.
9 *Patman and Fotheringham Ltd v Pilditch* (1904) HBC 4th edition vol 2, 368.
10 *Tweddle v Atkinson* (1861) 1 B & S 393.
11 *McGruther v Pitcher* [1904] 2 Ch 306; *Adler v Dickson* [1954] 3 All ER 788; *Scruttons Ltd v Midland Silicones Ltd* [1962] 1 All ER 1.
12 *Hedley Byrne & Co Ltd v Heller & Partners Ltd* [1963] 2 All ER 575.
13 *Murphy v Brentwood District Council* (1990) 50 BLR 1.
14 *Rotherham Metropolitan Borough Council v Frank Haslam Milan and Co Ltd* (1996) 59 Con LR 33.
15 *Adcock's Trustees v Bridge RDC* (1911) 75 JP 241.
16 *Gilbert Ash (Northern) v Modern Engineering (Bristol)* [1973] 3 All ER 195.

Chapter 3

17 *Rutter v Charles Sharp & Co Ltd* [1979] 1 WLR 1429.
18 Architects Act 1997.
19 S. 59 of the Finance Act 2004.
20 *Temloc Ltd v Errill Properties Ltd* (1987) 39 BLR 30.
21 *Pozzolanic Lytag Ltd v Bryan Hobson Associates* [1999] BLR 267.

The JCT Standard Building Contract 2011, First Edition. David Chappell.
© 2014 by David Chappell. Published 2014 by John Wiley & Sons, Ltd.

22 *Brodie v Cardiff Corporation* [1919] AC 337.

23 This provision was added following the decision in *Co-operative Insurance Society v Henry Boot Scotland Ltd* [2003] EWHC 1270 (TCC).

24 See *Equitable Debenture Assets Corporation Ltd v William Moss* (1984) 2 Con LR 1; *Victoria University of Manchester v Hugh Wilson and Lewis Womersley and Pochin (Contractors) Ltd* (1984) 2 Con LR 43; *University Court of the University of Glasgow v William Whitfield & John Laing (Construction) Ltd* (1988) 42 BLR 66; *Edward Lindenberg v Joe Canning & Jerome Contracting Ltd* (1992) 29 Con LR 71; *Plant Construction plc v Clive Adams Associates and JMH Construction Services Ltd* [2000] BLR 137.

25 *Re Cosslett (Contractors) Ltd, Clark, Administrator of Cosslett (Contractors) Ltd in Administration v Mid Glamorgan County Council* [1996] 4 All ER 46.

26 *London Borough of Merton v. Stanley Hugh Leach Ltd* (1985) 32 BLR 51.

27 *Construction Partnership UK Ltd v Leek Developments* [2006] EWHC B8 (TCC), *Bernuth Lines Ltd v High Seas Shipping Ltd* [2006] 1 Lloyd's Rep 537; *Golden Ocean Group Ltd v Salgaocar Mining Industries PVT Ltd and Another* [2012] 3 All ER 842.

28 *London Borough of Merton v Stanley Hugh Leach Ltd* (1985) 32 BLR 51.

29 Architects Act 1997.

30 *Scheldebouw BV v St James Homes (Grosvnenor Dock) Ltd* (2006) 105 Con LR 90.

31 *Balfour Beatty Civil Engineering Ltd v Docklands Light Railway Ltd* (1996) 45 Con LR 1.

32 *J F Finnegan Ltd v Ford Sellar Morris Developments Ltd (No.1)* (1991) 25 Con LR 89.

Chapter 4

33 In Northern Ireland, legislation to the same effect is the Construction Contracts (Northern Ireland) Order 1997 that was amended in line with the 2009 Act by the Construction Contracts (Amendment) Act (Northern Ireland) 2011 that came into force on 14 November 2012.

34 *Cutter v Powell* (1795) 6 Term Rep 320.

35 *Ibmac Ltd v Marshall Ltd* (1968) 208 EG 851.

36 *Sumpter v Hedges* [1898] 1 QB 673.

37 *Hoenig v Isaacs* [1952] 2 All ER 176.

38 *H Dakin & Co Ltd v Lee* [1916] 1 KB 566.

39 *Forman & Co Proprietary Ltd v The ship 'Liddlesdale' LR* (1900) AC 190.

40 *Hancock v B W Brazier (Anerley) Ltd* [1966] 2 All ER 901; *Young and Marten Ltd v McManus Childs Ltd* (1969) 9 BLR 77; *Test Valley Borough Council v Greater London Council* (1979) 13 BLR 63; *IBA v EMI and BICC* (1980) 14 BLR 1.

41 *Tameside Metropolitan Borough Council v Barlows Securities Group Services Ltd* [2001] BLR 113.

42 Section 32 of the Act.

43 *Gray and Others v T P Bennett & Son and Others* (1987) 43 BLR 63; *Sheldon and Others v R H M Outhwaite (Underwriting Agencies) Ltd* [1995] 2 All ER 558; *Cave v Robinson Jarvis and Rolf* [2003] 1 AC 384.

44 *British Steel Corporation v Cleveland Bridge Company* [1984] 1 All ER 504.

45   *Laserbore v Morrison Biggs Wall* (1993) CILL 896.

46   *I E Contractors Ltd v Lloyds Bank plc and Rafidain Bank* [1990] 2 Lloyd's Rep 496.

47   *Try Build Ltd v Blue Star Garages* (1998) 66 Con LR 90.

48   *Marubeni Hong Kong and South China Ltd v Government of Mongolia* [2005] EWCA Civ 395, *Wuhan Guoyu Logistics Group Co Ltd & Others v Emporiki Bank of Greece SA* [2012] EWCA Civ 1629.

49   *Vossloh Aktiengesellschaft v Alpha Trains (UK) Ltd* [2010] EWHC 2443 (Ch).

50   *Sweet (UK) Ltd (formerly Cyril Sweett Ltd) v Michael Wight Homes Ltd* [2012] EW Misc 3 (CC).

Chapter 5

51   *Partington & Son (Builders) Ltd v Tameside Metropolitan Borough Council* (1985) 5 Con LR 99.

52   *Lanphier v Phipps* (1838) 8 C & P 475.

53   *Samuels v Davis* [1934] 2 All ER 3.

54   *Bolam v Friern Hospital Management Committee* [1957] 2 All ER 118.

55   *Sidaway v Governors of the Bethlem Royal Hospital and the Maudsley Hospital* [1985] 1 All ER 643.

56   *J D Williams & Co Ltd v Michael Hyde & Assoc* [2001] BLR 99.

57   *Wimpey Construction UK Ltd v D V Poole* [1984] 2 Lloyd's Rep 499.

58   *London Borough of Merton v Lowe & Pickford* (1981) 18 BLR 130.

59   *T E Eckersley & Others v Binnie & Partners & Others* (1988) 18 Con LR 1.

60   *Introvigne v Commonwealth of Australia* (1980) 32 ALR 251.

61   *Victoria University of Manchester v Hugh Wilson & Lewis Womersley and Pochin (Contractors) Ltd* (1984) 2 Con LR 43.

62   *Brickfield Properties Ltd v Newton* [1971] 1 WLR 862.

63   *Young & Marten Ltd v McManus Childs* [1968] 2 All ER 1169.

64   *Viking Grain Storage Ltd v T H White Installations Ltd* (1985) 3 Con LR 52.

65   *John Mowlem & Co Ltd v British Insulated Callenders Pension Trust Ltd* (1977) 3 Con LR 64.

66   *Century Insurance Co Ltd v Northern Ireland Road Transport Board* [1942] 1 All ER 491.

67   *Moresk Cleaners v Hicks* (1966) 4 BLR 50.

68   *Sealand of the Pacific v Robert C McHaffie Ltd* (1975) 32 BLR 76.

69   *Shanklin Pier v Detel Products* [1951] 2 All ER 471.

70   *Queensland Government Railways and Electric Power Transmission Pty Ltd v Manufacturers Mutual Insurance Ltd* [1969] 1 Lloyd's Rep 214; *Kier Construction Ltd v Royal Insurance Co (UK) Ltd and Others* (No.1) (1992) 30 Con LR 45.

71   *Investors in Industry Commercial Properties Ltd v South Bedfordshire District Council and Others* (1985) 5 Con LR 1.

72   *Sutcliffe v Thackrah* (1974) 1 All ER 859.

73   *Rees and Kirby Ltd v Swansea Corporation* (1985) 5 Con LR 34.

74   *Clayton v Woodman & Sons (Builders) Ltd* [1962] 2 All ER 33.

75   *Greater London Council v Cleveland Bridge* (1984) 8 Con LR 30.

76   *Oldschool v Gleeson (Construction) Ltd* (1976) 4 BLR 103.

77   *AMF International Ltd v Magnet Bowling Ltd* [1968] 2 All ER 789; *Sutcliffe v Chippendale and Edmondson* (1971) 18 BLR 149.

78   *Token Construction Co Ltd v Charlton Estates Ltd* (1973) 1 BLR 48.

79   *Westminster Corporation v J Jarvis & Sons Ltd* (1970) 7 BLR 64.

80   *R B Burden Ltd v Swansea Corporation* [1957] 3 All ER 243.

81   See the government contract (GC/Works/1(1998)) or the Association of Consultant Architects contract (ACA 3).

82   *Bowmer & Kirkland Ltd v Wilson Bowden Properties Ltd* (1996) 80 BLR 131; *Redheugh Construction Ltd v Coyne Contracting Ltd and British Columbia Building Corporation* (1997) 29 CLR (2d) 39–46.

83   *Bath and North East Somerset District Council v Mowlem* (2004) 100 Con LR 1.

84   *New Islington and Hackney Housing Association Ltd v Pollard Thomas and Edwards* [2001] BLR 74.

85   *Balfour Beatty Ltd v Chestermount Properties Ltd* (1993) 62 BLR 1.

86   *Hydraulic Engineering Co Ltd v McHaffie, Goslet & Co* (1878) 4 QBD 670.

87   *Wells v Army & Navy Co-operative Society Ltd* (1902) 86 LT 764; *Greater London Council v Cleveland Bridge & Engineering Co Ltd* (1986) 8 Con LR 30.

88   This is in line with the decision in *Glenlion Construction Ltd v The Guinness Trust* (1987) 39 BLR 89.

89   *Oldschool v Gleeson (Construction) Ltd* (1976) 4 BLR 103; *Bowmer & Kirkland Ltd v Wilson Bowden Properties Ltd* (1996) 80 BLR 131.

90   *Crown Estates Commissioners v John Mowlem & Co Ltd* (1994) 70 BLR 1.

91   It is suggested that clause 3.20 should always be deleted.

92   The existence of a duty on the part of the architect is discussed in more depth in David Chappell, *Building Contract Claims*' 5th edition (2011) Wiley-Blackwell, Oxford.

93   *Argyropoulos & Pappa v Chain Compania Naviera SA* (1990) 7-CLD-05-01.

94   For example see *Temloc Ltd v Errill Properties Ltd* (1987) 39 BLR 30 at page 39: '… that means that the certificate by the architect fixing the later completion date …'.

Chapter 6

95   *Greater Nottingham Co-operative Society v Cementation Piling and Foundations Ltd* (1988) 41 BLR 43.

96   *West Faulkner Associates v London Borough of Newham* (1995) 11 Const LJ 157.

97   *London Borough of Merton v Stanley Hugh Leach Ltd* (1985) 32 BLR 51.

98   *Robinson v Harman* (1848) 1 Ex 850.

99   *Ruxley Electronics and Construction Ltd v Forsyth* (1995) 73 BLR 1.

100   *John Barker Construction Ltd v London Portman Hotels Ltd* (1996) 50 Con LR 43.

101   *Hampshire County Council v Stanley Hugh Leach Ltd* (1991) 8-CLD-07-12.

102   *Yorkshire Water Authority v Sir Alfred McAlpine and Son (Northern) Ltd* (1985) 32 BLR 114.

103   *Glenlion Construction Ltd v The Guinness Trust Ltd* (1987) 39 BLR 89.

104   Section 7 of the Unfair Contract Terms Act 1977.

105   *Wells v Army & Navy Co-operative Society Ltd* (1902) 86 LT 764.

106   *Neodox Ltd v. Borough of Swinton and Pendlebury* (1958) 5 BLR 34.

107   *Ashville Investments Ltd v Elmer Contractors Ltd* (1987) 37 BLR 55.

108   S. 112 of The Housing Grants, Construction and Regeneration Act 1996 (as amended).

109 *Brunswick Construction v Nolan* (1975) 21 BLR 27; *Equitable Debenture Assets Corporation Ltd v William Moss* (1984) 2 Con LR 1; *Victoria University of Manchester v Wilson and Womersley* (1984) 2 Con LR 43; *University Court of the University of Glasgow v William Whitfield & John Laing (Construction)* (1988) 42 BLR 66; Edward *Lindenberg v Joe Canning* & Jerome Contracting Ltd (1992) 9-CLD-05-21; *Plant Construction plc v Clive Adams Associates and JMH Construction Services Ltd* [2000] BLR 137.

Chapter 7

110 *Luxor (Eastbourne) Ltd v. Cooper* [1941] 1 All ER 33.
111 *Cory Ltd v. City of London Corporation* [1951] 2 All ER 85.
112 *Argyropoulos & Pappa v. Chain Compania Naviera SA* (1990) 7-CLD-05-01.
113 *Rapid Building Group Ltd v. Ealing Family Housing Association Ltd* (1984) 1 Con LR 1.
114 *Whittal Builders v Chester-Le-Street District Council* (1987) 42 BLR 82 (the second case).
115 *Temloc Ltd v. Errill Properties Ltd* (1987) 39 BLR 30.
116 *Abbey Developments Ltd v PP Brickwork Ltd* [2003] EWHC 1987 (TCC).
117 *D.R. Bradley (Cable Jointing) Ltd v. Jefco Mechanical Services* (1988) 6-CLD-07-21; *C J Elvin Building Services Ltd v Noble* [2003] EWHC 837 (TCC).
118 *Wates Construction (London) Ltd v. Franthom Property Ltd* (1991) 53 BLR 23.
119 *London Borough of Lewisham v Shepherd Hill Civil Engineering* 30 July 2001 unreported.

Chapter 8

120 *R B Burden v Swansea Corporation* [1957] 3 All ER 243.

Chapter 9

121 *Kensington and Chelsea and Westminster Area Health Authority v Wettern Composites* (1984) 1 Con LR 114.

Chapter 10

122 *St Martins Property Corporation Ltd and St Martins Property Investments Ltd v Sir Robert McAlpine & Sons Ltd and Linden Gardens Trust Ltd v Lenesta Sludge Disposals Ltd, McLaughlin & Harvey PLC, and Ashwell Construction Company Ltd* (1992) 57 BLR 57.
123 *Murphy v Brentwood District Council* (1990) 50 BLR 1.
124 SCWa/E, SCWa/P&T, SCWa/F.
125 SBCSub or SBCSub/D.
126 *Edwards v National Coal Board* [1949] 1 KB 704.
127 *Hampshire County Council v Stanley Hugh leach ltd* (1991) 8-CLD-07-12.
128 *Reynolds v Ashby* [1904] AC 466.

Chapter 11

129 *Vonlynn Holdings Ltd v Patrick Flaherty Contracts Ltd* (1988) 26 January 1988 unreported; *AMEC Building Contracts Ltd v Cadmus Investment Co Ltd* (1997) 13 Const LJ 50; *Abbey Developments Ltd v PP Brickwork Ltd* [2003] EWHC 1987 (TCC).

130 *Milnes v Huddersfield Corporation* (1886) 11 App Cas 511; *Clegg Parkinson and Co v Earby Gas Co* [1896] 1 QB 56; *Read v Croydon Corporation* [1938] 4 All ER 631; *Willmore v South Eastern Electricity Board* [1957] 2 Lloyds Rep 375.

131 *Street v Sibbabridge Ltd* (1980) unreported.

Chapter 12

132 *Pozzolanic Lytag Ltd v Brian Hobson Associates* [1999] BLR 267.

133 A full definition is to be found in clause 6.8.

134 *Kruger Tissue (Industrial) Ltd v. Frank Galliers Ltd and DMC Industrial Roofing & Cladding Services (A Firm) and H.H. Construction (A Firm)* (1998) 57 Con LR 1; *Horbury Building Systems Ltd v Hampden Insurance N.V.* [2004] EWCA Civ 418.

Chapter 13

135 *Whittal Builders v. Chester-Le-Street District Council* (1987) 40 BLR 82 (the second case).

136 *Wells v Army & Navy Co-operative Stociety Ltd* (1902) 86 LT 764.

Chapter 14

137 *Wells v Army & Navy Co-operative Society Ltd* (1902) 86 LT 764.

138 *Percy Bilton Ltd v. Greater London Council* (1982) 20 BLR 1.

139 *Methodist Homes Housing Association Ltd v Messrs Scott & McIntosh* 2 May 1997, unreported; *H Fairweather & Co Ltd v London Borough of Wandsworth* (1987) 39 BLR 106; *City Inn Ltd v Shepherd Construction Ltd* [2007] CSOH 190 upheld on appeal [2010] Scot CS CSIH 68.

140 s.112(4) of the Housing Grants, Construction and Regeneration Act 1996 as amended.

141 *Henry Boot Construction Ltd v Central Lancashire Development Corporation* (1980) 15 BLR 8.

142 *Walter Lawrence v Commercial Union Properties* (1984) 4 Con LR 37.

143 *Norwich City Council v Harvey* (1989) 45 BLR 14.

144 *Levy v Assicurazioni Generali* [1940] 3 All ER 427 at 431 per Luxmore LJ, approving an extract from Welford and Otterbarry's *Fire Insurance*, 3rd edition, at p. 64.

145 It used to be referred to as one of the excluded risks if the contract was to be carried out in Northern Ireland. That is no longer the case and Northern Ireland has its own Adaptation Schedule to deal with the matter.

146 S.237(2) of The Trade Union and Labour Relations (Consolidation) Act 1992.

147 *Boskalis Westminster Construction Ltd v Liverpool City Council* (1983) 24 BLR 83.

148 Probably derived from the Combination Laws: a series of statutes from 1799 to 1825 that banned combinations of workers against their masters. The phrase has been continued in subsequent legislation.

149 *Oakley v Portsmouth & Ryde Steam Packet Co* (1856) T1 Exchequer Reports 6 1F.

150 *Lebeaupin v Crispin* [1920] 2 KB 714.

151 *Glenlion Construction Ltd v The Guiness Trust* (1987) 39 BLR 89.

152 *London Borough of Merton v Stanley Hugh Leach Ltd* (1985) 32 BLR 51.

153 *London Borough of Hillingdon v Cutler* [1967] 2 All ER 361.

154 *Roberts v Brett* (1865) 11 HLC 337.

155 'Immediately' normally means that an action must be performed with all reasonable speed: *Alexiadi v Robinson* (1861) 2 F & F 679.

156 *London Borough of Merton v Stanley Hugh Leach Ltd* (1985) 32 BLR 51.

157 *London Borough of Merton v Stanley Hugh Leach Ltd* (1985) 32 BLR 51.

158 *London Borough of Merton v Stanley Hugh Leach Ltd* (1985) 32 BLR 51.

159 *Herschel Engineering Ltd v Breen Properties Ltd* (2000) 16 Const LJ 366.

160 *A & D Maintenance and Construction Ltd v Pagehurst Construction Services Ltd* (2000) 17 Const LJ 199.

161 *The Royal Brompton Hospital National Health Service Trust v Frederick Alexander Hammond and Others (No 7)* (2001) 76 Con LR 148.

162 *John Barker Construction Ltd v London Portman Hotels Ltd* (1996) 50 Con LR 43.

163 *Balfour Beatty Construction Ltd v London Borough of Lambeth* [2002] BLR 288.

164 *Cantrell & Another v Wright & Fuller Ltd* (2003) 91 Con LR 97.

165 *IBM (UK) Ltd v Rockware Glass Ltd* [1980] FSR 335.

166 *John Mowlem & Co v Eagle Star Insurance Co Ltd* (1995) 62 BLR 126.

167 *Jet2.com Ltd v Blackpool Airport Ltd* (2012) 142 Con LR 1.

168 *London Borough of Hounslow v Twickenham Garden Developments Ltd* (1970) 7 BLR 81.

169 *Balfour Beatty Construction Ltd v London Borough of Lambeth* [2002] BLR 288.

170 *Cantrell & Another v Wright & Fuller Ltd* (2003) 91 Con LR 97.

Chapter 15

171 *Clydebank Engineering Co v Don Jose Yzquierdo y Castenada* [1905] AC 6.

172 *Cellulose Acetate Silk Co Ltd v Widnes Foundry* [1933] AC 20.

173 *Temloc Ltd v. Errill Properties Ltd* (1987) 39 BLR 30.

174 *Token Construction Co Ltd v Charlton Estates Ltd* (1973) 1 BLR 48.

175 *H Fairweather Ltd v Asden Securities Ltd* (1979) 12 BLR 40.

176 *Suisse Atlantique Société d'Armement SA v N V Rotterdamsche Kolen Centrale* [1966] 2 All ER 61.

177 *Skanska Construction (Regions) Ltd v Anglo-Amsterdam Corporation Ltd* (2002) 84 Con LR 100.

178 *Clydebank Engineering Co v Don Jose Yzquierdo y Castenada* [1905] AC 6.

Chapter 16

179   See *F G Minter Ltd v Welsh Health Technical Services Organisation* (1980) 13 BLR 7 CA.

180   *Parsons (Livestock) Ltd v Utley Ingham & Co Ltd* [1977] 2 Lloyds Rep 522.

181   *Hersent Offshore SA and Amsterdamse Ballast Beton-en-Waterbouw BV v Burmah Oil Tankers Ltd* (1979) 10 BLR 1; *Diploma Constructions Pty Ltd v Rhodgkin Pty Ltd* [1995] 11 BCL 242; *Wormald Engineering Pty Ltd v Resource Conservation Co International* [1992] 8 BCL 158; *Opat Decorating Service (Aust) Pty v Hansen Yuncken (SA) Pty* [1995] BCL vol 11, 360, *City Inn Ltd v Shepherd Construction Ltd* [2001] Scot HC 54; decision upheld on appeal: [2003] BLR 468.

182   *Walter Lilley & Co Ltd v Mackay & Another* (2012) 143 Con LR 79.

183   *London Borough of Merton v Stanley Hugh Leach Ltd* (1985) 32 BLR 51.

184   *Walter Lilley & Co Ltd v Mackay and Another (No.2)*(2012) 143 Con LR 79.

185   *The Concise Oxford Dictionary.*

186   *Methodist Homes Housing Association Ltd v Messrs Scott & McIntosh* 2 May 1997, unreported.

187   *British Airways Pension Trustees Ltd v Sir Robert McAlpine & Sons Ltd and Others* (1994) 72 BLR 26.

188   *The Concise Oxford Dictionary.*

189   *Sutcliffe v Thackrah* [1974] 1 All ER 859.

190   *R B Burden Ltd v Swansea Corporation* [1957] 3 All ER 243.

191   *F G Minter Ltd v Welsh Health Technical Services Organisation* (1980) 13 BLR 7.

192   *London Borough of Merton v Stanley Hugh Leach Ltd* (1985) 32 BLR 51.

193   *Skanska Construction UK Ltd v The ERDC Group Ltd* [2003] SCLR 296.

194   *Walter Lilley & Co Ltd v Mackay & Another (No 2)* (2012) 143 Con LR 79.

195   *Methodist Homes Housing Association Ltd v Messrs Scott and McIntosh* 2 May 1997, unreported.

Chapter 17

196   *M. Harrison & Co Ltd v. Leeds City Council* (1980) 14 BLR 118.

197   *Young and Marten Ltd v McManus Childs Ltd* (1969) 9 BLR 77.

Chapter 18

198   *Dudley Corporation v Parsons & Morrin Ltd*, 8 April 1959 CA, unreported; *Henry Boot Ltd v Alstom Combined Cycles Ltd* [1999] BLR 123.

199   *Convent Hospital v Eberlin & Partners* (1988) 14 Con LR 1. The case went to appeal, (1989) 23 Con LR 112, but not on this point.

200   Support for this view may be seen in the judgments in *Cotton v Wallis* [1955] 3 All ER 373 and *Phoenix Components v Stanley Krett* (1989) 6-CLD-03-25.

201   The items are the type referred to in the Standard Method of Measurement, 7th edition, Section A (Preliminaries General Conditions).

202   General Rules 10.1–10.6 of SMM 7 usefully set out the minimum information that the contractor must know before it can plan and price the effects of the item in question.

203 *Inserco v Honeywell* 19 April 1996, unreported.

204 *Clusky (t/a Damian Construction) v Chamberlain, Building Law Monthly,* April 1995, p.6.

205 *JDM Accord Ltd v Secretary of State for the Environment, Food and Rural Affairs* (2004) 93 Con LR 133.

Chapter 19

206 *Hoenig v. Isaacs* [1952] 2 All ER 176.

207 *Sutcliffe v. Thackrah* [1974] 1 All ER 319.

208 The Housing Grants, Construction and Regeneration Act 1996 was amended by the Local Democracy Economic Development and Construction Act 2009 that came into effect on the 1 October 2011.

209 *Rupert Morgan Building Services (LLC) Ltd v Jervis* [2004] BLR 18.

210 *Wates Construction (London) Ltd v. Franthom Property Ltd* (1991) 53 BLR 23.

211 *Penwith District Council v V P Developments* [1999] EWHC Technology 231.

212 There is some doubt whether this is in accordance with the Housing Grants, Construction and Regeneration Act 1996 (as amended).

213 *National Coal Board v Neill* [1984] 1 All ER 555.

214 *Penwith District Council v V P Developments Ltd* [1999] EWHC Technology 231.

Chapter 20

215 *Moresk Cleaners Ltd v Hicks* (1966) 4 BLR 50.

216 That was the conclusion of the court in *Co-operative Insurance Society Ltd v Henry Boot (Scotland) Ltd* [2002] EWHC 1270 (TCC).

217 *Introvigne v Commonwealth of Australia* (1980) 32 ALR 251.

218 *Viking Grain Storage Ltd v T H White Installations Ltd* (1985) 3 Con LR 52.

219 *Hadley v Baxendale* (1854) 9 Ex 341.

Chapter 21

220 *Westminster Corporation v. J. Jarvis & Sons Ltd* (1970) 7 BLR 64; *H.W. Nevill (Sunblest) Ltd v. Wm Press & Son Ltd* (1981) 20 BLR 78.

221 *Roberts v Brett* (1865) 11 HLC 337.

222 *BFI Group of Companies Ltd v. DCB Integrated Systems Ltd* (1987) CILL 348; *Impresa Castelli SpA v Cola Holdings Ltd* (2002) 87 Con LR 123.

223 *Re Coslett (Contractors) Ltd, Clark, Administrator of Coslett (Contractors) Ltd in Administration v Mid Glamorgan County Council* [1997] 4 All ER 115.

224 *Skanska Construction (Regions) Ltd v Anglo-Amsterdam Corp Ltd* (2002) 84 Con LR 100.

Chapter 22

225 *Holland Hannen and Cubitts (Northern) v. Welsh Health Technical Services Organisation* (1981) 18 BLR 80.

226   *William Tomkinson & Sons Ltd v The Parochial Church Council of St Michael* (1990) 6 Const LJ 319.

227   *William Tomkinson & Sons Ltd v. Parochial Church Council of St Michael* (1990) 6 Const LJ 319.

228   *Pearce & High v John P Baxter and Mrs Baxter* [1999] BLR 101.

Chapter 23

229   *Photo Production Ltd v Securicor Transport Ltd* [1980] AC 827.

230   *Davis Contractors Ltd v Fareham Urban District Council* [1956] 2 All ER 148.

231   *Wates v Greater London Council* (1983) 25 BLR 7.

232   *Appleby v Myers* (1867) 16 LT 669.

233   Law Reform (Frustrated Contracts) Act 1943.

234   *Photo Production v Securicor Transport Ltd* [1980] 1 All ER 556.

235   *White & Carter (Councils) Ltd v McGregor* [1961] 3 All ER 1178.

236   It has been held that it is not repudiation where a party has honestly relied on a contract provision, even though mistaken: *Woodar Investment Development Ltd v. Wimpey Construction UK Ltd* [1980] 1 All ER 571.

237   *West Faulkner v London Borough of Newham* (1994) 71 BLR 1.

238   *Wiltshier Construction (South) Ltd v. Parkers Developments Ltd* (1997) 13 Const LJ 129.

239   *John Jarvis v. Rockdale Housing Association Ltd* (1986) 10 Con LR 51.

240   *Robin Ellis Ltd v Vinexsa International Ltd* (2003).

241   *West Faulkner v. London Borough of Newham* (1994) 71 BLR 1.

242   *Tern Construction Group (in administrative receivership) v. RBS Garages* (1993) 34 Con LR 137.

243   *Wraight Ltd v. P.H. & T. (Holdings) Ltd* (1968) 8 BLR 22.

244   *Alghussein Establishment v Eton College* [1988] 1 WLR 587.

245   Clause 8.12.5 makes no express reference to this, but the requirements of the Housing Grants, Construction and Regeneration Act 1996 (as amended) appear to apply.

246   The right is included in accordance with s. 112 of the Housing Grants, Construction and Regeneration Act 1996 (as amended).

247   *Ener-G Holdings plc v Hormell* (2012) 144 Con LR 43.

248   *Ener-G Holdings plc v Hormell* (2012) 144 Con LR 43.

Chapter 24

249   *Herschel Engineering Ltd v Breen Property Ltd* (2000) 16 Const LJ 366.

250   *Connex South Eastern Ltd v M J Building Services plc* [2005] 2 All ER 871.

251   *Bouygues United Kingdom Ltd v Dahl-Jensen United Kingdom Ltd* [2000] BLR 522.

252   *City Inn Ltd v Shepherd Construction Ltd* [2002] SLT 781.

253   s.9 of the Arbitration Act 1996.

254   *Shepherd Construction v Mecright Ltd* [2000] BLR 489.

255   *McAlpine PPS Pipeline Systems Joint Venture v Transco plc* [2004] All ER (D) 145.

256   *Ken Griffin and John Tomlinson v Midas Homes Ltd* (2002) 18 Const LJ 67.

257   *F W Cook Ltd v Shimizu (UK) Ltd* [2000] BLR 199.

258   *Karl Construction (Scotland) Ltd v Sweeney Civil Engineering (Scotland) Ltd* (2002) 18 Const LJ 55; *Sindall Ltd v Solland* (2001) 80 Con LR 152.

259   *R Durtnell & Sons Ltd v Kaduna Ltd* [2003] BLR 225.

260   *Linnett v Halliwells LLP* (2009) 123 Con LR 104

261   *R v Greater Birmingham Appeal Tribunal ex parte Simper* [1973] 2 All ER 461.

262   *Balfour Beatty Construction Ltd v London Borough of Lambeth* [2002] BLR 288.

263   *Ritchie Brothers (PWC) Ltd v David Philip (Commercials) Ltd* [2005] CSIH 32; *Hart Investments Ltd v Fidler and Another* (2006) 109 Con LR 67; *Mott MacDonald Ltd v London & Regional Properties Ltd* 2007) 113 Con LR 33.

264   *Joinery Plus Ltd (in administration) v Laing Ltd* (2003) 19 Const LJ T47.

265   *Systech International Ltd v P C Harrington Contractors Ltd* (2012) 145 Con LR 1.

266   *Ashville Investments Ltd v Elmer Contractors Ltd* (1987) 37 BLR 55.

267   Sections 45(2)(a) and 69(2)(a).

268   *Vascroft (Contractors) Ltd v Seeboard plc* (1996) 52 Con LR 1.

269   For example, see *Bouygues United Kingdom Ltd v Dahl-Jensen United Kingdom Ltd* [2000] BLR 522.

270   *Systech International Ltd v P C Harrington Contractors Ltd* (2012) 145 Con LR 1.

Table of cases

The JCT Standard Building Contract 2011, First Edition. David Chappell.
© 2014 by David Chappell. Published 2014 by John Wiley & Sons, Ltd.

Subject index

The JCT Standard Building Contract 2011, First Edition. David Chappell.
© 2014 by David Chappell. Published 2014 by John Wiley & Sons, Ltd.

Clause number index to text

The JCT Standard Building Contract 2011, First Edition. David Chappell.
© 2014 by David Chappell. Published 2014 by John Wiley & Sons, Ltd.